Advance Praise for
Courageous Compassion

"In the sixth installment of their extraordinary *Library of Wisdom and Compassion* series, H. H. the Dalai Lama and Ven. Thubten Chodron transport us through the higher reaches of the Buddhist path, as envisioned by the Theravāda, Sūtrayāna, and Mahāyāna traditions. Led by two expert guides, we come to appreciate the perfections we must practice, the stages of spiritual ascent we must traverse, and the sublime awakened states awaiting at journey's end. At once informative and deeply inspiring, *Courageous Compassion* should have a place on the bookshelf of every Buddhist, along with the other volumes in this masterful collection."
—Roger Jackson, author of *Mind Seeing Mind: Mahāmudrā and the Geluk Tradition of Tibetan Buddhism*

"In this volume H. H. the Dalai Lama and Ven. Thubten Chodron address how to develop and sustain compassion in the ordinary life we have today all the way up to the completion of our spiritual path. The turn to applying compassion requires not only profound knowledge of the Buddhist textual tradition but also great sensitivity to the circumstances of people's ordinary lives and to twenty-first-century societies. This book brings both to bear as it asks, What would our lives look like if we lived and acted purely out of compassion?"
—Damchö Diana Finnegan, PhD

"In this sixth volume of their extraordinary series mapping the Buddhist path to awakening, H. H. the Dalai Lama and the Ven. Thubten Chodron, in conversation both with the Pāli and the Indo-Tibetan Mahāyāna traditions, show how to build on the insight, the understanding, and the cultivation achieved through study and practice in order to become a powerful agent for the welfare of oneself and others, and to ascend to the advanced stages of the path to awakening. Their account is rich in scholarship, deeply humane, and powerfully inspirational."
—Jay L. Garfield, Doris Silbert Professor in the Humanities, Smith College and the Harvard Divinity School

THE LIBRARY OF WISDOM AND COMPASSION

The Library of Wisdom and Compassion is a special multivolume series in which His Holiness the Dalai Lama shares the Buddha's teachings on the complete path to full awakening that he himself has practiced his entire life. The topics are arranged especially for people not born in Buddhist cultures and are peppered with the Dalai Lama's unique outlook. Assisted by his long-term disciple, the American nun Thubten Chodron, the Dalai Lama sets the context for practicing the Buddha's teachings in modern times and then unveils the path of wisdom and compassion that leads to a meaningful life, a sense of personal fulfillment, and full awakening. This series is an important bridge from introductory to profound topics for those seeking an in-depth explanation from a contemporary perspective.

Volumes:

1. *Approaching the Buddhist Path*
2. *The Foundation of Buddhist Practice*
3. *Saṃsāra, Nirvāṇa, and Buddha Nature*
4. *Following in the Buddha's Footsteps*
5. *In Praise of Great Compassion*
6. *Courageous Compassion*

More volumes to come!

THE LIBRARY OF WISDOM AND COMPASSION • VOLUME 6

Courageous Compassion

Bhikṣu Tenzin Gyatso,
the Fourteenth Dalai Lama

and

Bhikṣunī Thubten Chodron

Wisdom

Wisdom Publications
199 Elm Street
Somerville, MA 02144 USA
wisdomexperience.org

Library of Congress Cataloging-in-Publication Data
Names: Bstan-'dzin-rgya-mtsho, Dalai Lama XIV, 1935– author. | Thubten Chodron, 1950– author.
Title: Courageous compassion / Bhikṣu Tenzin Gyatso, the Fourteenth Dalai Lama, and Bhikṣuni Thubten Chodron.
Description: Somerville, MA: Wisdom Publications, [2021] | Series: Library of wisdom and compassion; volume 6 | Includes bibliographical references and index.
Identifiers: LCCN 2020040731 (print) | LCCN 2020040732 (ebook) | ISBN 9781614297475 | ISBN 9781614297628 (ebook)
Subjects: LCSH: Bodhicitta (Buddhism)
Classification: LCC BQ4398.5 .B75 2021 (print) | LCC BQ4398.5 (ebook) | DDC 294.3/422—dc23
LC record available at https://lccn.loc.gov/2020040731
LC ebook record available at https://lccn.loc.gov/2020040732

ISBN 978-1-61429-747-5 ebook ISBN 978-1-61429-762-8

25 24 23 22 21
5 4 3 2 1

Photo credits: cover, Gen Heywood; p. xii, Ānandajoti Bhikkhu / PhotoDharma.net; p. xxii, Tenzin Choejor/OHHDL; p. 4, Stephen Ching; p. 6, Ānandajoti Bhikkhu / PhotoDharma.net; p. 26, REUTERS/AsiaNewsPhoto; p. 110, Nuns' Media Team at Dolma Ling, courtesy of Tibetan Nuns Project | TNP.org; p. 196, Stephen Ching; p. 266, Kenryuu Ong; p. 286, Andrey Kartiev; p. 374, Olivier Adam; p. 400, Flickr/storebukkebruse
Cover and interior design by Gopa & Ted 2. Typeset by Tony Lulek.

Printed on acid-free paper that meets the guidelines for permanence and durability of the Production Guidelines for Book Longevity of the Council on Library Resources.

Printed in the United States of America.

Publisher's Acknowledgment

The publisher gratefully acknowledges the generous help of the Hershey Foundation in sponsoring the production of this book.

Contents

Preface

His Holiness and I are pleased to offer you *Courageous Compassion*, the sixth volume of *The Library of Wisdom and Compassion*. The present volume details the activities of bodhisattvas, compassionate beings who seek full awakening in order to benefit others most effectively. This volume follows volume 5, *In Praise of Great Compassion*, which explains the methods to develop great compassion and the altruistic intention of bodhicitta. Both of these practical and inspiring volumes present us with another vision of how to live besides the habitual patterns that many people fall into these days—patterns that lead to boredom, anxiety, and a sense of meaninglessness on the one hand, or being too busy trying to fulfill our own or others' unrealistic notions of success on the other.

As we saw in volume 5, generating bodhicitta depends on taking refuge in reliable spiritual guides—the Three Jewels of the Buddha, Dharma, and Saṅgha. This, as well as the core Buddhist practices of the higher trainings in ethical conduct, concentration, and wisdom, are explained in volume 4, *Following in the Buddha's Footsteps*.

To follow in the Buddha's footsteps we must be familiar with our current situation in saṃsāra—the unsatisfactory cycle of existence fueled by ignorance, afflictions, and polluted karma—as well as its alternatives, liberation and full awakening. This centers on understanding the four truths of the *āryas* as presented in volume 3, *Saṃsāra, Nirvāṇa, and Buddha Nature*. Awareness of our buddha nature, the fundamental purity of our minds, enhances our confidence in being able to attain the spiritual freedom of nirvāṇa.

An essential element in comprehending duḥkha—our unsatisfactory experiences in saṃsāra—and its causes is understanding the law of karma and its effects, how our actions have an ethical dimension that influences the conditions of our birth and what we experience while alive. This, in turn, is based on valuing the preciousness of a human life that has the opportunity to encounter, learn, and practice the Buddha's liberating teachings. However, this opportunity is short-lived; we are mortal beings, so it is essential to set our priorities wisely and make our lives meaningful. As beginners or advanced students of the path, knowing how to select excellent spiritual mentors to guide us on the path is important, as is knowing how to develop healthy relationships with them that enable us to be receptive to their teachings. These topics are elaborated in volume 2, *The Foundation of Buddhist Practice*, which also explains the importance of relying on reasoning to examine the teachings and how to establish a daily meditation practice and structure meditation sessions.

Since the *Library of Wisdom and Compassion* is designed for people who have not necessarily grown up knowing Buddhism, volume 1, *Approaching the Buddhist Path*, explores the Buddhist view of life, mind, and emotions, provides historical background to the origins and spread of the Buddha's teachings, and introduces us to a systematic approach to the spiritual path. Tools on the path, how to evaluate our progress, working with emotions, and the way to apply Buddhist ideas to contemporary issues are also discussed in this volume.

More volumes are to come. They will go in depth concerning the nature of reality, the emptiness of inherent existence, and the profound practice of tantra. Now let's turn to the present volume, *Courageous Compassion.*

Overview of Courageous Compassion

The story of how the *Library of Wisdom and Compassion* came to be written is found in the prefaces to previous volumes. Here, I'd like to share a little about preparing the present volume, which depended in part on conferring with His Holiness regarding particular topics. It is said that highly realized yogīs see our world as a pure land. My asking about this during one interview sparked a long, very dynamic discussion in Tibetan, with His Holiness conferring with the four geshés and rinpochés who were present. After a while they broke out into laughter. Smiling and chuckling, His Holiness turned to me and said, "We don't know. Maybe this, maybe that." Later, I brought up the topic of what buddhas perceive, and again there was a long, animated debate in Tibetan that ended with laughter and the conclusion that all of us must become buddhas in order to know this. Out of compassion, His Holiness and Samdhong Rinpoche then explained what some of the great treatises say about what the Buddha perceived. As you'll see in chapter 11, His Holiness's treasured teacher Gen Nyima-la agreed that only buddhas can answer this question!

When he came up with the idea for the *Library of Wisdom and Compassion*, His Holiness emphasized that it must be unique and not focus only on Buddhism as practiced in Tibetan communities. He wants people, especially his students, to have broad knowledge and educated appreciation of the Buddha's teachings by being familiar with both the Pāli and Sanskrit traditions, and within the Sanskrit tradition, Buddhism as practiced in both Tibetan and Chinese communities. He aims for increased cooperation among Buddhists of all traditions based on knowledge of one another's tenets and practices. In reading this series, you'll see the fundamental premises that are shared in all Buddhist traditions, as well as interpretations unique to each one.

The present volume contains two parts: the first concerns the bodhisattva practices and activities, the second concerns the three vehicles—the paths of śrāvakas, solitary realizers, and bodhisattvas—and their resulting fruits of arhatship and supreme awakening. Part I begins with an introduction to the practices of the bodhisattvas, compassionate beings who have bodhicitta and practice the bodhisattva deeds. Although we may not yet be bodhisattvas, we can still practice as they do and in that way gain familiarity with compassionate and wise actions. Bodhisattvas' activities are spoken of in terms of six perfections: the perfections of generosity, ethical conduct, fortitude, joyous effort, meditative stability, and wisdom. These six practices in turn can be spoken of as ten, with the last four subsumed in the sixth, the perfection of wisdom. The additional four perfections are skillful means, unshakable resolve, power, and pristine wisdom. The Sanskrit tradition's explanation of the ten bodhisattva perfections is found in chapters 2 and 3.

Chapter 4 encourages us to share the Dharma with others with skill and compassion. The contents of this chapter come predominantly from a conference with His Holiness and a group of Western Buddhist teachers in Dharamsala in 1993. Western Buddhist teachers shared with His Holiness their activities in Western Dharma centers and the way that Dharma was spreading in the West. Since Buddhism is new to Western countries, challenges and problems naturally arise, as well as confusion about how to teach, the role of rituals, Western students' relationships with Asian teachers, and Western teachers' relationships with Dharma students. During this conference, as well as in other venues and in the interviews for this series, His Holiness shared his thoughts, making it clear that he was not establishing policies. The position of the Dalai Lama is not like that of the Pope, and he does not have institutional control over Tibetan Buddhist organizations or teachers. Rather, he was sharing thoughts and suggestions that people were free to accept or reject. Some of his advice relating to spiritual mentors' behavior was explained in chapters 4 and 5 of *The Foundation of Buddhist Practice*.

Many people are unaware that the Pāli tradition describes a bodhisattva path. Bodhicitta and bodhisattvas in the Pāli tradition were explained in chapter 8 of *In Praise of Great Compassion*, and chapter 5 in the present volume explains the bodhisattva practices as presented in the Pāli sage Dhammapāla's *Treatise on the Pāramīs*, written in the sixth century. His treatise complements the Sanskrit tradition's explanation, and both open our minds to a new way of being in the world.

Part II delves into the topic of the three vehicles and their fruits and describes the stages of the paths and grounds that Fundamental Vehicle and Mahāyāna practitioners accomplish as they progress toward their respective spiritual aims of arhatship and buddhahood. The paths and grounds of the Fundamental Vehicle practitioners—śrāvakas and solitary realizers—as set forth in the Pāli tradition is found in chapter 6, and as set forth in the Sanskrit tradition in chapter 7. The remaining chapters are from the perspective of the Sanskrit tradition. Chapter 8 speaks of the five bodhisattva paths, and chapter 9 and 10 explain the bodhisattva grounds that occur during the bodhisattva paths of seeing and meditation. The attainments of these practitioners are truly magnificent and admirable. Chapters 11 and 12 speak of the final goal: supreme awakening, buddhahood.

The paths and grounds are not usually included in the stages of the path (T. *lam rim*) material but are taught separately. However, His Holiness wants students to learn important aspects of the philosophical studies found in the monastic curriculum, and for that reason the paths and grounds as well as many other topics have been included in the *Library of Wisdom and Compassion*. His Holiness often reminds us that we should meditate on everything we study, and not think that some texts are for study and smaller manuals are for meditation.

Each chapter contains reflections that you are encouraged to contemplate. The reflections not only review some of the major points but also provide the opportunity to put these teachings into practice and transform your mind.

Please Note

Although this series is coauthored, the vast majority of the material is His Holiness's teachings. I researched and wrote the parts about the Pāli tradition, wrote some other passages, and composed the reflections. For ease of reading, most honorifics have been omitted, but that does not diminish the great respect we have for the most excellent sages, learned adepts, scholars, and practitioners. Foreign terms are given in italics parenthetically at their first usage. Unless otherwise noted with "P" or "T," indicating Pāli or Tibetan, respectively, italicized terms are Sanskrit. When two italicized terms are listed, the first is Sanskrit, the second Pāli. For consistency, Sanskrit spelling is given for Sanskrit and Pāli terms in common usage (nirvāṇa, Dharma, arhat, ārya, and so forth), except in citations from Pāli scriptures. To maintain the flow of a passage, it is not always possible to gloss all new terms on their first usage, so a glossary is provided at the end of the book. "Sūtra" often refers to Sūtrayāna, and "Tantra" to Tantrayāna—the Sūtra Vehicle and Tantra Vehicle, respectively. When these two words are not capitalized, they refer to two types of scriptures: sūtras and tantras. "Mahāyāna" here refers principally to the bodhisattva path as explained in the Sanskrit tradition. In general, the meaning of all philosophical terms accords with the presentation of the Prāsaṅgika Madhyamaka tenet system. Unless otherwise noted, the personal pronoun "I" refers to His Holiness.

Appreciation

My deepest respect goes to Śākyamuni Buddha and all the buddhas, bodhisattvas, and arhats who embody the Dharma and with compassion teach us unawakened beings. I also bow to all the realized lineage masters of all Buddhist traditions through whose kindness the Dharma still exists in our world.

This series appears in many volumes, so I will express appreciation to those involved in each individual volume. This volume, the sixth in the *Library of Wisdom and Compassion*, has depended on the abilities and efforts of His Holiness's translators—Geshe Lhakdor, Geshe Dorji Damdul, and Mr. Tenzin Tsepak. I am grateful to Geshe Dorji Damdul, Geshe Dadul Namgyal, and Bhikṣuṇī Sangye Khadro for checking the manuscript, and to Samdhong Rinpoche for clarifying important points and his encouraging presence. I also thank Bhikkhu Bodhi for his clear teachings on the Pāli tradition and for generously answering my many questions. He also kindly looked over the sections of the book on the Pāli tradition before publication. The staff at the Private Office of His Holiness kindly facilitated the interviews, and Sravasti Abbey supported me while I worked on this volume. Mary Petrusewicz skillfully edited the manuscript. I thank everyone at Wisdom Publications who contributed to the successful production of this series. All errors are my own.

Bhikṣuṇī Thubten Chodron
Sravasti Abbey

Abbreviations

AN Aṅguttara Nikāya. Translated by Bhikkhu Bodhi in *The Numerical Discourses of the Buddha: A Translation of the Aṅguttara Nikāya* (Boston: Wisdom Publications, 2012).

BCA *Engaging in the Bodhisattvas' Deeds* (*Bodhicaryāvatāra*) by Śāntideva. Translated by Stephen Batchelor in *A Guide to the Bodhisattva's Way of Life* (Dharamsala, India: Library of Tibetan Works and Archives, 2007).

CP *Basket of Conduct* (*Cariyāpiṭaka*). Translated by I. B. Horner in *The Minor Anthologies of the Pāli Canon*, vol. 3 (London: Pāli Text Society, 2007 [1975]).

C Chinese

CTB *Compassion in Tibetan Buddhism* by Tsong-ka-pa. Translated and edited by Jeffrey Hopkins (Ithaca, NY: Snow Lion Publications, 1980).

DBS *The Ten Grounds Sūtra* (*Daśabhūmika Sūtra*). Translated by Bhikṣu Dharmamitra (Seattle: Kalavinka Press, 2019).

DN Dīgha Nikāya. Translated by Maurice Walshe in *The Long Discourses of the Buddha* (Boston: Wisdom Publications, 1995).

EOM Jetsun Losang Dadrin (Tayang). *A Brief Presentation of the Grounds and Paths of the Perfection Vehicle, Essence of the Ocean of Profound Meaning*. Translated by Jules Levinson. Unpublished MA thesis, University of Virginia, 1983.

Iti *The Udāna and the Itivuttaka*. Translated by John Ireland (Kandy, Sri Lanka: Buddhist Publication Society, 2007).

IU *A Few Good Men: The Bodhisattva Path according to the Inquiry of Ugra* (*Ugraparipṛcchā*). A Study and translation by Jan Nattier (Honolulu: University of Hawai'i Press, 2005).

LC *The Great Treatise on the Stages of the Path* (T. *Lam rim chen mo*) by Tsongkhapa, 3 vols. Translated by Joshua Cutler et al. (Ithaca, NY: Snow Lion Publications, 2000–2004).

LP *Lamp of the Path* by Atiśa Dīpaṃkaraśrījñāna.

MMA *Supplement to "Treatise on the Middle Way"* by Candrakīrti. Translated by Jeffrey Hopkins in *Compassion in Tibetan Buddhism* by Tsong-ka-pa (Ithaca, NY: Snow Lion Publications, 1980).

MMK *Treatise on the Middle Way* (*Mūlamadhyamakakārikā*) by Nāgārjuna.

MN Majjhima Nikāya. Translated by Bhikkhu Ñāṇamoli and Bhikkhu Bodhi in *The Middle-Length Discourses of the Buddha* (Boston: Wisdom Publications, 1995).

MPU *Exegesis of the Great Perfection of Wisdom Sūtra* (*Mahāprajñāpāramitā Upadeśa*). Translated by Bhikṣu Dharmamitra in *Nāgārjuna on the Six Perfections* (Seattle: Kalavinka Press, 2009).[1]

P Pāli

R *Heap of Jewels Sūtra* (*Ratnakūṭa*): *A Treasury of Mahāyāna Sūtras*. Edited by Garma C. C. Chang (University Park: The Pennsylvania State University Press, 1983).

RA *Precious Garland* (*Ratnāvalī*) by Nāgārjuna. Translated by John Dunne and Sara McClintock in *The Precious Garland: An Epistle to a King* (Boston: Wisdom Publications, 1997).

RGV *Sublime Continuum* (*Ratnagotravibhāga*, *Uttaratantra*) by Maitreya.

Sn *Suttanipāta*. Translated by Bhikkhu Bodhi in *The Suttanipāta* (Somerville, MA: Wisdom Publications, 2017).

SN Saṃyutta Nikāya. Translated by Bhikkhu Bodhi in *The Connected Discourses of the Buddha* (Boston: Wisdom Publications, 2000).

SR *King of Concentration Sūtra* (*Samādhirāja Sūtra*).

T Tibetan

TP *A Treatise on the Pāramīs* by Acariya Dhammapāla. Translated by Bhikkhu Bodhi (Kandy: Buddhist Publication Society, 1978). Also at https://www.accesstoinsight.org/lib/authors/bodhi/wheel409.html.

Vism *Path of Purification* (*Visuddhimagga*) by Buddhaghosa. Translated by Bhikkhu Ñāṇamoli (Kandy: Buddhist Publication Society, 1991).

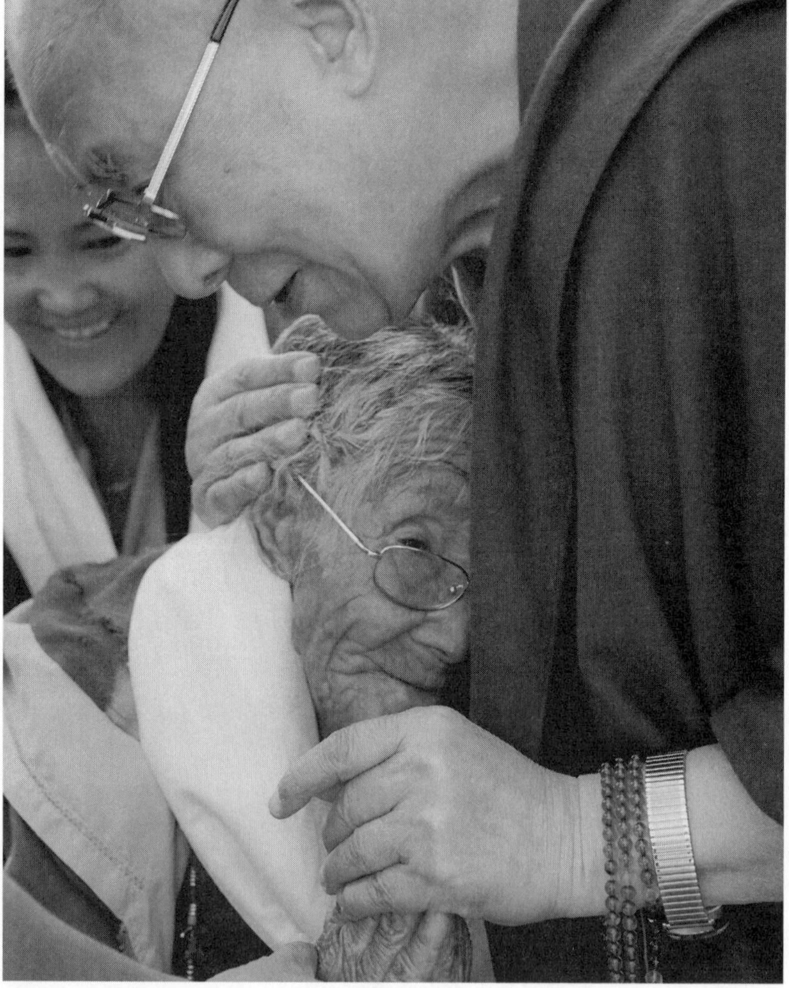

Introduction

DEAR READERS, it's a privilege for me to share the Buddha's teachings as well as a few of my ideas and experiences with you. Wherever I go I emphasize that all seven billion human beings on our planet are physically, mentally, and emotionally the same. Everybody wants to live a happy life free of problems. Even insects, birds, and other animals want to be happy and not suffer. What distinguishes us human beings is our intelligence, although there are occasions when we use it improperly—for example, when we design weapons to kill one another. Animals like lions and tigers that stay alive by attacking and eating other animals have sharp teeth and claws, but human beings' nails and teeth are more like those of deer. We use our intelligence to fulfill our desires, but compared to other animals our desires seem to have no limit. We have one thing and want two; we have something good and we want something better. Satisfaction eludes us.

Right here and now I'm sitting in a peaceful place and imagine that you are too. But at this very moment, in other parts of the world people are killing each other. Devising ever better military strategies and ever more lethal arms is a poor use of human intelligence. Developing new nuclear weapons that are more effective in destroying people is the worst. I've been to both Hiroshima and Nagasaki. On my first visit to Hiroshima I met a woman who had been there when the nuclear bomb was dropped; somehow she survived. In the museum I saw a watch that had stopped at the exact instant of the explosion; it was half melted by the heat of the blast. Instead of using our human intelligence to create joy, the result has sometimes been fear and misery.

Now in the twenty-first century we must make an effort not to repeat the errors of the last century with its endless series of wars. Historians estimate that 200 million people died by violent means during that century. It's time to say, enough. Let's make the twenty-first century a time of peace and compassion by recognizing the sameness of all eight billion human beings alive today. Strongly emphasizing differences in nationality, religion, ethnicity, or race culminates in feelings of us and them; we feel divided and we act divided. It is important to remind ourselves that at a deeper level all human beings are the same. We all want to live a happy life. Being happy is our right. To create a peaceful society we must heed the ways to achieve inner peace. This involves creating the circumstances for freedom, being concerned with human rights, and protecting the environment.

There are no natural boundaries between human beings on this earth; we are one family. At a time of increasing natural disasters, climate change and global warming affect all of us. We must learn to live together, to work together, and to share what we have together. Making problems for one another is senseless. We will achieve genuine peace in the world if we pursue demilitarization, but before countries can demilitarize, as individuals we must disarm ourselves internally. To begin, we must reduce our hostility and anger toward one another. That entails each of us looking inside ourselves and releasing our self-centered attitude and painful feelings rather than blaming others for things we don't like. As long as we don't accept responsibility for our own actions and thoughts, we will experience the same results as before. But when we realize that our actions affect others and care about their experience, we will stop harming them. When we change our behavior, others will also change theirs. Then real change is possible.

A mother gave birth to each of us and cared for us with love. I am sad that our educational system fails to nurture this sense of loving-kindness and aims instead to fulfill material goals. We need to reintroduce such inner values as warm-heartedness to our educational system. If we could be kinder, we'd be happier as individuals, and this would contribute to happier families and more harmonious communities. Human beings are social animals. What brings us together is love and affection—anger drives us apart. Just as we employ physical hygiene to protect our health, we must use "emotional hygiene" to tackle our destructive emotions and achieve peace of mind.

I belong to the twentieth century, an era that is past. I want to share with those of you who are young: if you start to collect the causes now, you'll live to see a happier, more peaceful world. Don't be content with the present circumstances; take a more far-sighted view. When the heart is closed, it leads to fear, stress, and anger. Nurturing the idea of the oneness of humanity has the effect of opening the heart. When you think of all other human beings as your brothers and sisters it's easy to communicate with them all. It makes it easier to smile, to be warm and friendly. This is what I try to do. Beggars or leaders—all human beings are the same. If I think "I am a Buddhist, I am Tibetan, I am the Dalai Lama," it just increases my sense of isolation. If I think of myself as a human being who is like everyone else, I feel at ease: I belong, I can contribute to others' well-being, I can communicate and share with others. We have to take the initiative to connect with one another.

All religions convey a message of love, compassion, and self-discipline. Their philosophical differences arose to suit people of different dispositions, at different times, and in different places and conditions. The fundamental message of love remains the same. Buddhism, especially the Nālandā tradition, with its emphasis on reasoned investigation, takes a realistic stance that accords with the scientific method. To become a twenty-first century Buddhist, simply having faith and reciting the sūtras is not enough; far more important is understanding and implementing what the Buddha taught.

Bhikṣu Tenzin Gyatso, the Fourteenth Dalai Lama

Thekchen Chöling

Part I. How to Live with Compassion: The Bodhisattva Perfections

All of us appreciate others' kindness and compassion. Even before we came out of our mother's womb, we have been the recipients of others' kindness. Although being on the receiving end of compassion mollifies our anxiety and suffering, being compassionate toward others brings even more joy and feelings of well-being. This is what the eighth-century Indian sage Śāntideva meant when he said (BCA 8:129–30):

> Whatever joy there is in this world
> all comes from desiring others to be happy,
> and whatever suffering there is in this world
> all comes from desiring myself to be happy.
>
> What need is there to say much more?
> The childish work for their own benefit,
> the buddhas work for the benefit of others.
> Just look at the difference between them!

We need to learn methods to release our self-centeredness and cultivate genuine love and compassion for others. This does not entail feeling guilty when we are happy or sacrificing our own well-being, but simply recognizing that our self-centeredness is the cause of our suffering and cherishing others is the cause of the happiness of both self and others. *In Praise of Great Compassion* explains the two methods for doing so: the seven cause-and-effect instructions and equalizing and exchanging self and others. Now we'll look at the activities that bodhisattvas engage in with compassion and wisdom to benefit the world.

1 | Introduction to the Bodhisattva Perfections

We may not yet be bodhisattvas, but we can certainly engage in the same activities they do. In the process, we can continually expand and boost the intensity of our love and compassion.

Bodhisattvas train in bodhicitta for eons, so do not think that having one intense feeling of bodhicitta or reciting the words of aspiring bodhicitta is all there is to it. In *Engaging in the Bodhisattvas' Deeds*, the first two chapters lead us in cultivating bodhicitta, and the third chapter contains the method for taking the bodhisattva vow. The other seven chapters describe the practices of bodhisattvas, training in the six perfections. Although these bear the names of familiar activities—generosity, ethical conduct, and so forth—now they are called "perfections" because they are done with the motivation of bodhicitta that aims at buddhahood, the state of complete and perfect wisdom and compassion.

As you progress through the bodhisattva paths and grounds, you will deepen and expand your bodhicitta continuously, as indicated in the twenty-two types of bodhicitta mentioned in the *Ornament of Clear Realizations*.[2] With joy make effort to understand bodhicitta and the bodhisattva path, and endeavor to transform your mind into these. Avoid conceit and cutting corners; in spiritual practice there is no way to ignore important points and still gain realizations. Cultivate fortitude, courage, and the determination to be willing to fulfill the two collections of merit and wisdom over many years, lifetimes, and eons. The result of buddhahood will be more than you can conceive of at this moment.

The Two Collections of Merit and Wisdom

Bodhicitta is a primary mind conjoined with two aspirations. The first is to work for the well-being of all sentient beings, the second is to attain full awakening in order to do so most effectively. Once you have generated bodhicitta and are determined to attain buddhahood, you'll want to accumulate all the appropriate causes and conditions that will bring it about. These are subsumed in the collection of merit (*puṇyasaṃbhāra*) and the collection of wisdom (*jñānasaṃbhāra*). The collection of merit is the method or skillful means aspect of the bodhisattva path that concerns conventional truths such as other living beings; the collection of wisdom is the wisdom aspect of the bodhisattva path that focuses on the ultimate truth, emptiness. When completed, the two collections lead to the form body and truth body of a buddha. In *Sixty Stanzas* (*Yuktiṣaṣṭikā*) Nāgārjuna summarizes these two principal causes:

> Through this virtue, may all beings complete
> the collections of merit and wisdom.
> May they attain the two sublime buddha bodies
> resulting from merit and wisdom.

TWO ASPECTS, TWO COLLECTIONS, TWO TRUTHS, PERFECTIONS, AND RESULTS

ASPECT OF THE PATH	COLLECTION	TRUTH (BASIS)	PERFECTIONS (PATH)	RESULT
Method	Merit	Conventional	Generosity, ethical conduct, fortitude, joyous effort	Form bodies of a buddha
Wisdom	Wisdom	Ultimate	Meditative stability, wisdom, joyous effort	Truth bodies (nature truth body and wisdom truth body)

Note: There are various ways of categorizing the six perfections by way of method and wisdom. In another way, the first five perfections are included in method.

The collection of merit consists of virtuous actions motivated by bodhicitta. The collection of merit includes mental states, mental factors, and karmic seeds related to these virtuous actions. It deals with conventional truths, such as sentient beings, gifts, precepts, and so forth. To fulfill it, bodhisattvas practice the perfections of generosity, ethical conduct, and fortitude, as well as all other virtuous actions such as those done with love and compassion, prostrating, making offerings, and meditating on the defects of saṃsāra.

The collection of wisdom is a Mahāyāna pristine knower that realizes emptiness. It consists of learning, contemplating, and meditating on the ultimate nature of persons and phenomena that is supported by bodhicitta, and includes both inferential reliable cognizers of emptiness that are free from the two extremes of absolutism and nihilism and āryas' meditative equipoise on emptiness. The collection of wisdom is not necessarily a union of serenity and insight, but being a Mahāyāna exalted knower, it must be conjoined with actual bodhicitta and bear the result of buddhahood.

The collection of merit is primarily responsible for bringing about a buddha's form bodies (*rūpakāya*), and the collection of wisdom is primarily responsible for bringing about a buddha's truth bodies (*dharmakāya*). The word "primarily" is significant because each collection alone cannot bring about either of the buddha bodies. Both collections are necessary to attain both the form bodies and the truth bodies. (Here "body" means a corpus of qualities, not a physical body.) Bodhisattvas fulfill their own purpose by gaining the buddhas' truth bodies and omniscient minds. They fulfill others' purpose by manifesting in buddhas' countless form bodies through which they benefit, teach, and guide sentient beings.

With bodhicitta as their motivation, bodhisattvas delight in creating the cause for buddhahood by practicing the perfections. Practices and activities that comprise the collections of merit and wisdom become perfections because they are conjoined with actual bodhicitta, which differentiates them from the practices of merit and wisdom cultivated by śrāvakas and solitary realizers. Although śrāvakas and solitary realizers collect merit and wisdom, they are not the fully qualified collections of merit and wisdom and are thus considered secondary collections. Because solitary realizers' progress in merit and wisdom is superior to that of śrāvakas, some solitary realizers are able to become arhats without depending on hearing a master's teaching during their last lifetime in saṃsāra.

Likewise, bodhisattva-aspirants who have not yet generated actual bodhicitta and entered the Mahāyāna path of accumulation create merit and enhance their wisdom, but their practices are called "similitudes" of the two collections and are not fully qualified collections. However, people who aspire to enter the bodhisattva path plant the seeds to be able to do the actual collections later.

Our virtuous actions accompanied by a strong wish for a good rebirth act as a cause for the places, bodies, and possessions associated with fortunate rebirths. Those accompanied by the determination to be free from cyclic existence are similitudes of the collections and lead to liberation. Only when our virtuous actions are accompanied by bodhicitta do they constitute the actual collections. Practitioners of the Perfection Vehicle build up the actual collections over three countless great eons on the bodhisattva path. The first eon of collecting merit and wisdom is done on the path of accumulation and the path of preparation; the second eon is fulfilled on the first seven of the ten bodhisattva grounds that span the path of seeing and part of the path of meditation; the third eon is done on the last three of the ten bodhisattva grounds called the "three pure bodhisattva grounds"—the eighth, ninth, and tenth. Bodhisattvas who follow the Vajrayāna fulfill the two collections more quickly due to the special practice of deity yoga that combines method and wisdom into one consciousness.

The method side entails cultivating an aspiring attitude—that is, we enhance our intentions to give, to not harm others, to remain calm in the face of suffering, and so on. With the practice of wisdom, we learn and contemplate the teachings on emptiness, bringing conviction and ascertainment that all persons and phenomena lack inherent existence. This wisdom complements and completes the practices on the method side of the path. Similarly, our virtuous actions of the method aspect of the path enhance wisdom by purifying the mind and enriching it with merit, which increases the power of wisdom. Method practices help the understanding of emptiness to arise when it hasn't occurred, and when it has, merit enables wisdom to increase, deepen, and become a more powerful antidote to the afflictive and cognitive obscurations. Ultimately, however, it is wisdom that determines progress on the path because advancing from one bodhisattva ground to the next occurs during meditative equipoise on emptiness.

The Six Perfections

Cultivating contrived bodhicitta through effort is virtuous and auspicious; it paves the way to generate uncontrived bodhicitta, which entails engaging in the bodhisattvas' deeds. These deeds can be subsumed in the six perfections—generosity (*dāna*, *dāna*), ethical conduct (*śīla*, *sīla*), fortitude (*kṣānti*, *khanti*), joyous effort (*vīrya*, *viriya*), concentration (*dhyāna*, *jhāna*), and wisdom (*prajñā*, *paññā*). The sixth perfection, wisdom, can be further expanded into four, making ten perfections—the first six, plus skillful means (*upāya*), unshakable resolve (*praṇidhāna*, *panidhāna*), power (*bala*), and pristine wisdom (*jñāna*, *ñāṇa*). To ripen others' minds, we train in the four ways of gathering disciples—generosity, teaching the Dharma according to the capacity of the disciples, encouraging them to practice, and embodying the Dharma in our life. These four can be included in the six perfections, so the six are said to be the main bodhisattva practices to ripen both our own mind and the minds of others.

You may wonder: From the beginning, the lamrim teachings encourage us to be generous and ethical, to have fortitude and practice with joyous effort, and to develop meditative stability and wisdom. Why, then, are these six practices explained only now? Also, practitioners of all three vehicles cultivate these qualities. Why are they explained now as unique Mahāyāna practices?

Let's use generosity as an example. It is practiced not only in all Buddhist traditions but also in all religions. People who are not interested in any religion but value kindness and compassion also practice generosity. A difference exists, however, between the mere practice of generosity and the perfection of generosity. The perfection of generosity is not simply an absence of miserliness when giving or a casual wish to share things. Nor is it being generous with the motivation to be rich in future lives. Rather, it is giving done with the aspiration to become a buddha in order to benefit all beings most effectively.

In addition to being motivated by bodhicitta, the perfection of generosity is sealed by the wisdom of emptiness. That is, when giving, we reflect on the ultimate nature of the giver, the gift, the recipient, and the action of giving. All of them are empty of inherent existence but exist dependent on one another. Through this reflection, any attachment or misconceptions that could arise from generosity are purified. Based on bodhicitta and assisted by the wisdom of emptiness, the perfection of generosity encompasses both the method and wisdom sides of the path and is enriched by them.

The term perfection—*pāramitā* in Sanskrit and *pāramī* in Pāli—has the meaning of going beyond the end and reaching perfection or fulfillment. The Tibetan term *pha rol tu phyin pa* means to go beyond to the other shore. These practices take us beyond saṃsāra to the freedom of full awakening where both obscurations have been eliminated and all good qualities have been developed limitlessly. "Go beyond" connotes the goal—full awakening, or the Mahāyāna path of no-more-learning—as well as the method for arriving at that goal—the six perfections done by those on the learning paths. Motivated by bodhicitta and refined with meditation on emptiness, these practices take us beyond both saṃsāra and the pacification of saṃsāra that is an arhat's nirvāṇa. For example, bodhisattvas who conjoin their actions of giving with unpolluted wisdom see the giver, the object given, the recipient, and the action of giving as empty of inherent existence. Because their wisdom is supramundane, the generous actions conjoined with it lead them beyond saṃsāra. Ārya bodhisattvas, who have achieved an extraordinary level of training in the six perfections, are objects of veneration and respect, for they both perceive ultimate truth directly and seek to benefit all beings.

Generosity and other perfections that are not conjoined with such wisdom are considered mundane because the agent, object, and action are seen as truly existent. To integrate the wisdoms of emptiness and dependent arising into your practice of generosity, reflect that you as the giver (agent), the gift that is given (object), the recipient, and the action of giving do not exist from their own side; they exist dependent on one another. A person does not become a giver unless there is a gift, recipient, and action of giving. Flowers do not become a gift unless there is a person giving them and one receiving them. Seeing all the elements of generosity as appearing but empty makes our generosity extremely powerful, transforming it into the supramundane practice of the perfection of generosity.

Similarly, when purifying nonvirtue during your practice of ethical conduct, contemplate that prostrations and mantra recitation, for example, do not have inherent power to purify destructive karma. Their ability to do so arises dependent on the strength of your regret, your motivation, the depth of your concentration, and faith in the Three Jewels. Both prostrations and the seeds of destructive karma they destroy are dependent arisings; they exist nominally, by being merely imputed by term and concept.

How can purification occur if both the seeds of destructive actions and the purification practices lack inherent nature and exist like illusions? It is analogous to soldiers in a hologram destroying an arsenal in a hologram. The scene and its figures appear, but none of them exists in the way they appear. If seeds of destructive karmas had their own intrinsic nature, independent of all other things, nothing could affect them and they would be unchangeable. But because they do not exist under their own power, they can be altered and removed by purification practices that alter the factors upon which they depend. This contemplation differentiates the perfection of generosity and so forth from the same actions done by others. The presence of the bodhicitta motivation differentiates the perfection of generosity from the giving done by śrāvakas and solitary realizers.

Each of the perfections is a state of mind, not a set of external behaviors. When certain mental qualities are cultivated, they undoubtedly affect a person's behavior. However, external behavior may or may not be indicative of particular mental qualities. For example, a person may outwardly appear generous while her internal motivation is to manipulate the recipient. Likewise, we shouldn't think that bodhisattvas always give extravagantly. A practitioner may have deep bodhicitta and a strong aspiration to give but, due to lack of resources, only give a small amount. Practitioners of the six perfections are extremely humble. They hide their realizations and do not seek fame or recognition.

REFLECTION

1. Activities such as generosity, ethical conduct, and so forth are valued by all religions and by people who have no religion as well. What makes them perfections?
2. In addition, what makes them become supramundane practices of the perfections?

3. Examine the dependent nature of each perfection. For example, someone can't be a giver without there being a gift and the action of giving; the action of fortitude can't exist without a person who practices it and a person who is problematic or harmful.

4. Contemplate how engaging in the practice of the perfections with the awareness of emptiness entails seeing the agent who does the action, the action itself, and the object acted upon as empty of inherent existence but existing dependently.

The Basis, Nature, Necessity, and Function of the Six Perfections

Maitreya's *Ornament of the Mahāyāna Sūtras* (*Mahāyānasūtrālaṃkāra*) describes the six perfections in detail. The following explanation is taken predominantly from that text.

The Basis: Who Engages in the Perfections?

Those who are a suitable basis for these practices have awakened their Mahāyāna disposition—that is, they have great compassion, deep appreciation, and fortitude for the Mahāyāna Dharma. They rely on a qualified Mahāyāna spiritual mentor and receive extensive teachings on the Mahāyāna texts that teach the six perfections. In that way, they learn what the bodhisattva practices are and how to do them correctly. These practitioners are not satisfied with intellectual knowledge: they reflect and meditate on these teachings to collect both merit and wisdom and they engage in the practice of the perfections at every opportunity. The Mahāyāna disposition is awakened before a practitioner generates bodhicitta. When this disposition is nourished and developed, it will lead a practitioner to generate uncontrived bodhicitta and enter the bodhisattva path.

Nature: What Constitutes Each Practice?

Knowing what constitutes each perfection gives us the ability to practice it more carefully.

- Generosity is physical, verbal, and mental actions based on a kind thought and the willingness to give.
- Ethical conduct is restraining from nonvirtue, such as the seven nonvirtues of body and speech and the three nonvirtues of mind that motivate them, as well as other negativities.[3]
- Fortitude is the ability to remain calm and undisturbed in the face of harm from others, physical or mental suffering, and difficulties in developing certitude about the Dharma.
- Joyous effort is delight in virtues such as accomplishing the purposes of self and others by creating the causes to attain the truth bodies and form bodies of a buddha.
- Meditative stability is the ability to remain fixed on a constructive focal object without distraction.
- Wisdom is the ability to distinguish conventional and ultimate truths as well as to discern what to practice and what to abandon on the path.

In the *Precious Garland*, Nāgārjuna speaks of the six perfections and their corresponding results. He adds a seventh factor, compassion, because it underlies the motivation to engage in the six perfections (RA 435–37).

> In short, the good qualities
> that a bodhisattva should develop are
> generosity, ethical conduct, fortitude, joyous effort,
> meditative stability, wisdom, compassion, and so on.
>
> Giving is to give away one's wealth;
> ethical conduct is to endeavor to help others;
> fortitude is the abandonment of anger;
> joyous effort is enthusiasm for virtue.
>
> Meditative stability is unafflicted one-pointedness;
> wisdom is ascertainment of the meaning of the truths;
> compassion is a state of mind that savors
> only loving-kindness for all sentient beings.

REFLECTION

Read the above verses again while contemplating their meaning.

1. How can you generate these various practices and apply them in your life?
2. What emotions or attitudes make you hesitate to engage in these practices even though you hold them in high regard?
3. How can you remove these mental impediments so that you can joyfully enrich your life and the lives of others through engaging in these practices?

The Necessity and Function of the Perfections

The six perfections are necessary (1) to accomplish the welfare of other sentient beings, (2) to fulfill the aims of ourselves and others, and (3) to receive a precious human life in future rebirths so that we can continue to practice. These are explained below.

Accomplishing the Welfare of Other Sentient Beings

Our practice of each perfection functions to benefit sentient beings:

- By giving generously, we alleviate poverty and provide others with the basic necessities of life and other practical items as well as with things they enjoy.
- By living ethically, we refrain from harming them, thus easing their fear and pain.
- By being patient with others' inconsiderate or harmful behavior, we avoid causing them either physical pain or the mental pain of guilt, remorse, and humiliation.
- With joyous effort, we continue to help others without laziness, resentment, or fatigue.
- With meditative stability, we gain the superknowledges, such as clairvoyance (the divine eye), and use them to benefit sentient beings.
- With wisdom, we are able to teach others so that they can actualize the wisdoms understanding conventional truths, ultimate truths, and

how to benefit others. Through this we eliminate their doubts and lead them to awakening.

Fulfilling Our Own Aims

The last three perfections—joyous effort, meditative stability, and wisdom—are cultivated primarily to fulfill our own aims—that is, to spur us on the path to buddhahood. Wisdom realizing the ultimate truth directly eliminates our ignorance, afflictions, and polluted karma so that our mind can be transformed into a buddha's omniscient mind. To develop this wisdom that is a union of serenity and insight, we need deep meditative stability that makes the mind pliant and able to meditate on a virtuous object for as long as desired. To develop meditative stability, joyous effort is important to overcome laziness and resistance to Dharma practice.

Fulfilling the Aims of Others

The first three perfections primarily help to fulfill others' aims. These center around ethical conduct. If we are attached to our possessions, body, and friends and relatives, we will harm others to procure and protect them. By cultivating generosity, our attachment will decrease and we will not harm others to get what we want. If our anger is strong, it will move us to cause others pain and misery. By cultivating fortitude, we will abandon harming others. Not only will they not feel pain from our harm but they will also not create more destructive karma by retaliating. Furthermore, they could be inspired by our fortitude and become more interested in learning how to subdue their own anger.

The first three perfections benefit others in another way as well. Through our being generous, they receive what they need and desire. Generosity also attracts others to us, so that we can teach them the Dharma and guide them on the path to awakening.

Even though we may practice generosity, harming others will damage our virtuous actions and diminish any benefit we could provide others. By living ethically, we stop injuring others physically and mentally. In addition, our ethical conduct draws others to us because they know we are trustworthy. This enables us to benefit them even more.

To practice generosity and ethical conduct well, fortitude is indispensable. If others are not grateful after we give them something, we might become angry and retaliate. That would harm them and violate our own ethical conduct. By practicing the fortitude of not retaliating, our ethical conduct will be stable and we will not become discouraged by others' lack of gratitude when we are generous and kind to them. Fortitude with students, benefactors, and others we encounter in society is necessary because if we are irascible, they will avoid us—depriving us of the opportunity to benefit them.

Ensuring a Precious Human Life in the Future

Fulfilling the collections of merit and wisdom will take a long time. Thus it is essential to ensure that we obtain fortunate rebirths in which all the conducive circumstances for Dharma practice are present. If we are careless and fall to an unfortunate birth, we will not be able to help ourselves or practice the Dharma, let alone benefit others. To fulfill the purposes of self and others, a precious human life with excellent conditions is needed. Practicing the six perfections creates the causes to obtain this.

- Poverty creates difficulties in practicing the Dharma. Thus we need resources in future lives, and generosity creates the cause to obtain them.
- To make use of the resources, a human life is essential; ethical conduct is the principal cause of attaining an upper rebirth.
- Someone who ruminates with anger or loses their temper is not pleasant to be with and will lack good friends in the Dharma. Practicing fortitude creates the cause to have a pleasing appearance, good personality, and kind companions who encourage our Dharma practice and practice together with us.
- Being unable to follow through and complete projects is a hindrance to benefiting others. To be able to complete our virtuous projects in future lives and to be successful in all constructive activities we undertake, practicing joyous effort in this life is important. It creates the cause to have these abilities and to attract others to practice together with us in future lives.
- If our mind is filled with many afflictions in future lives, we will create great destructive karma. Having a stable and peaceful mind is important to maintain focus on what is important and not be distracted by

uncontrolled thoughts and emotions. Practicing meditative stability in this life creates the cause for this.

- The ability to clearly discriminate between misleading teachers and those imparting the correct path is essential, as is the ability to discern what to practice and what to abandon on the path. Cultivating the wisdom that correctly understands the law of karma and its effects creates the cause to have such wisdom in future lives.

Engaging in all six perfections and reaping their results facilitates our Dharma practice in future lives. If the practice of even one perfection is weak or absent, our opportunity to progress on the bodhisattva path in future lives will be limited. For example, without the meditative stability that subdues the gross afflictions, our meditations on bodhicitta and emptiness will be weak; without wisdom, even if we have a good rebirth in the next life, we won't have one after that because our ignorance will prevent us from creating the causes.

In short, Nāgārjuna sums up the temporal results of engaging in the six perfections that will facilitate our Dharma practice in future lives (RA 438–39):

> From generosity comes wealth; from ethics happiness;
> from fortitude comes a good appearance; from [effort in] virtue
> brilliance;
> from meditative stability peace; from wisdom liberation;
> compassion accomplishes all aims.
>
> From the simultaneous
> perfection of all seven,
> one attains the sphere of inconceivable wisdom—
> protector of the world.

Thinking about these teachings in relationship to our own lives will deepen our understanding and invigorate our Dharma practice. It is easy to be blasé about having the conditions to continue Dharma practice in future lives. However, imagining being born in circumstances that lack all the conducive conditions wakes us up to the need to create the causes to have them in future lives. Since those causes must be created now, our mind returns to the present with renewed vigor and interest in practice.

How the Six Perfections Relate to Other Practices

Although monastics and lay followers alike practice all six perfections, the first three—generosity, ethical conduct, and fortitude—are said to be easier for lay practitioners. In that context, generosity is giving material wealth and protection, ethical conduct is living in the five lay precepts and the bodhisattva precepts, and fortitude is the fortitude of gaining certitude about the Dharma, especially about the teachings on emptiness. The last three perfections—joyous effort, meditative stability, and wisdom—are likewise practiced by everyone but are said to be more pertinent to monastics.

Although we are encouraged to practice all six perfections as best as we can from the beginning, it is easier to cultivate and perfect them in their given order. Generosity precedes ethical conduct because attachment to possessions and greed to have more and better are obstacles to abandoning nonvirtuous actions. Ethical conduct is needed for fortitude because by practicing ethical conduct, it is easier to control afflictions and remain calm in the face of harm or suffering. Fortitude is needed to gain joyous effort because the internal calm that fortitude brings sustains joyous effort. Joyous effort is needed to develop meditative stability because meditative concentration does not come quickly and requires continuous effort over time. Meditative stability is essential for developing sharp, clear wisdom that penetrates the meaning of any topic, especially ultimate reality.

The six perfections comprise the two collections, as discussed above. They can also be included in the three higher trainings of bodhisattvas. Here generosity, ethical conduct, and fortitude are included in the higher training of ethical conduct; meditative stability pertains to the higher training of concentration; and wisdom is incorporated in the higher training of wisdom. Joyous effort is needed for all of them.

The Three Higher Trainings and Their Corresponding Perfections

HIGHER TRAINING	PERFECTIONS INCLUDED IN IT
Ethical conduct	Generosity, ethical conduct, fortitude
Concentration	Meditative stability
Wisdom	Wisdom

The six perfections also make up the two purposes of a practitioner: to obtain a higher rebirth and to actualize the highest good—liberation and full awakening. The first four perfections assist in attaining a higher rebirth. Meditative stability and wisdom are the keys to the highest good.

The Causes for Higher Rebirth and the Highest Good

CAUSES FOR HIGHER REBIRTH	CAUSES FOR THE HIGHEST GOOD
Generosity, ethical conduct, fortitude, joyous effort	Meditative stability, wisdom

From another perspective the six perfections can be included in the three types of generosity. The perfection of generosity is the generosity of giving material possessions. Ethical conduct and fortitude are the generosity of fearlessness because by acting ethically we protect others from the fear of our harming them and by having fortitude we do not cause others pain by losing our temper. The perfections of meditative stability and wisdom are the generosity of Dharma because instructions on serenity and insight are the principal teachings to give to sentient beings when they are receptive vessels. Joyous effort is needed to complete all three types of generosity.

The Three Types of Generosity and Their Corresponding Perfections

TYPE OF GENEROSITY	PERFECTIONS INCLUDED IN IT
Generosity of giving material possessions	Generosity
Generosity of fearlessness	Ethical conduct, fortitude
Generosity of Dharma	Meditative stability, wisdom

The six perfections are necessary to keep us on the path and to enable us to accomplish our heartfelt spiritual aims. Two factors inhibit us from embarking on the path: attachment to wealth and attachment to family and home. By sharing our resources, generosity lessens the first. By keeping monastic precepts, ethical conduct alleviates the second.

We may go beyond these two attachments but still abandon the spiritual journey as a result of two hindrances: the first is resentment for others' bad behavior and their lack of appreciation and respect, the second is discouragement regarding the length of time needed and the depth of practice required to accomplish our aims. Fortitude counteracts the first by strengthening our ability to handle hardship. Joyous effort remedies the second by increasing our delight and enthusiasm for creating virtue. These two together soothe the mind and give us great confidence and perseverance to continue on the path no matter what.

We may continue to practice, but our virtue may go to waste and our efforts may bring negligible results due to two causes: distraction and mistaken intelligence. Distraction scatters the mind to sense objects, useless thoughts, and disturbing emotions, diminishing the force of our virtue. Meditative stability remedies this by keeping our attention focused on a virtuous object and enables us to penetrate the Buddha's teachings and integrate their meaning in our mind. Mistaken intelligence inhibits comprehending and practicing the Buddha's teachings correctly and could actively misunderstand the teachings and lead to activities that cause unfortunate rebirths. Wisdom prevents this by correctly ascertaining what is and is not the path, and in this way guides our body, speech, and mind in the right direction.

Factors Inhibiting the Accomplishment of Spiritual Goals and Their Antidotes

INHIBITING FACTORS	HOW THEY INTERFERE	PERFECTIONS THAT ARE THEIR ANTIDOTE
Attachment to wealth	Inhibits embarking on the path	Generosity

INHIBITING FACTORS	HOW THEY INTERFERE	PERFECTIONS THAT ARE THEIR ANTIDOTE
Attachment to family	Inhibits embarking on the path	Ethical conduct
Resenting others' bad behavior and lack of respect	Abandon the spiritual journey	Fortitude
Discouragement	Abandon the spiritual journey	Joyous effort
Distraction that scatters the mind	Virtue going to waste and efforts bringing negligible results	Meditative stability
Mistaken intelligence that inhibits correct understanding of the Buddhadharma	Virtue going to waste and efforts bringing negligible results	Wisdom

All six perfections can be included in the practice of each one. For example, giving even a glass of water—a small act of generosity—can be done with bodhicitta. The mental state is most important, and in this case it is the wish to give in order to accumulate merit to attain awakening for the sake of all sentient beings as well as to directly benefit the recipient.

Not harming others physically or verbally when getting the water and when giving it is ethical conduct. Refraining from a condescending attitude or rude behavior and eschewing harsh speech when offering also constitute ethical conduct. If the recipient harms us physically or verbally in return, remaining calm and not retaliating in response to their ingratitude is the practice of fortitude. Giving the water is done with joyous effort that takes delight in being generous. Stability of mind is necessary so that the mind does not get distracted while giving. Stability also maintains the bodhicitta motivation and prevents the mind from becoming polluted by afflictions while giving.

Prior to giving, wisdom is needed to know what, when, and how to give. While giving, contemplating the emptiness of the giver, gift, recipient, and action of giving cultivates wisdom. An early Mahāyāna sūtra, the *Inquiry of Ugra* (*Ugraparipṛcchā*), describes how this is done (IU 244):

When the householder bodhisattva sees someone in need, he will fulfill the cultivation of the six perfections:

1. If as soon as the householder bodhisattva is asked for any object whatsoever, his mind no longer grasps at the object, in that way his cultivation of the perfection of generosity will be fulfilled.
2. If he gives while relying on bodhicitta, in that way his cultivation of the perfection of ethical conduct will be fulfilled.
3. If he gives while bringing to mind love toward those in need and not producing anger or animosity toward them, in that way his cultivation of the perfection of fortitude will be fulfilled.
4. If he is not depressed due to a wavering mind that thinks "If I give this away, what will become of me?" in that way the perfection of joyous effort will be fulfilled.
5. If one gives to someone in need and, after having given, is free from sorrow and regret, and moreover gives [these things] from the standpoint of bodhicitta and is delighted and joyful, happy, and pleased, in that way his cultivation of the perfection of meditative stability will be fulfilled.
6. And if, when he has given, he does not imagine the phenomena [produced by his generosity] and does not hope for their maturation, and just as the wise do not settle down in [their belief in] any phenomena, just so he does not settle down [in them], and so he transforms them into supreme, full awakening—in that way his cultivation of the perfection of wisdom will be fulfilled.

REFLECTION

1. Review the example above that illustrates how the other perfections are also practiced while engaging in the perfection of generosity.
2. Using ethical conduct as the chief perfection being practiced, reflect on how the other five perfections are practiced in tandem.

3. Do the same for the perfections of fortitude, joyous effort, meditative stability, and wisdom—showing how the other perfections can be practiced together with it. This exercise will expand your awareness of how to make even small actions very worthwhile.

While learning about the perfections, you may become discouraged, thinking that the practices are so difficult and you will never be able to do them. If this happens, instead of expecting yourself to be an expert when you are a beginner, accept your present level of abilities and continue to increase them in the future. The Buddha did not start off fully awakened and there was a time when he too found practicing the bodhisattva deeds very challenging. However, because causes bring their corresponding results, through steady practice you will be able to begin, continue, and complete the bodhisattvas' practices. Ratnadasa said in *Praise of Endless Qualities* (*Guṇapāryantastotra*, CTB 201):

> Those deeds which, when heard of, scare worldly [people],
> and which you could not practice for a long time,
> will in time become spontaneous for all familiar with them.
> Those not so familiar find it hard to increase attainments.

Śāntideva agrees (BCA 6.14ab):

> There is nothing whatsoever
> that is not made easier through acquaintance.

Seeing that this is the case, let's recall our buddha nature and transform our mind!

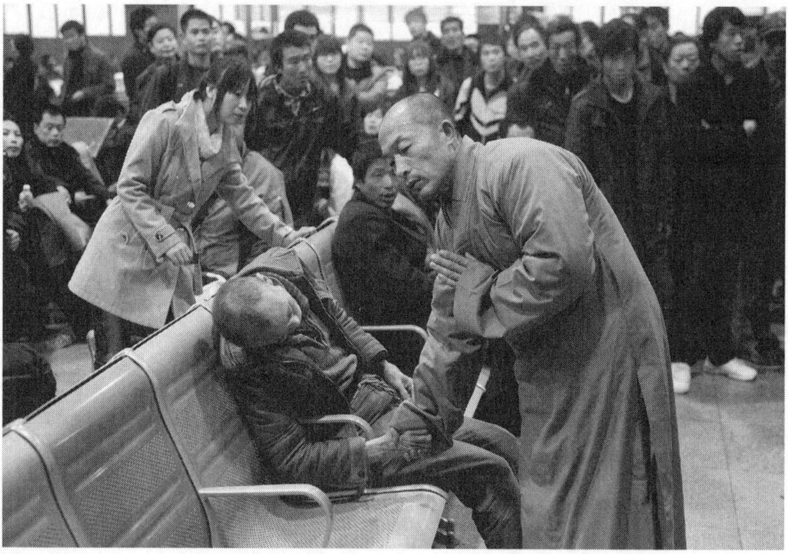

2 | Living as a Bodhisattva: The Perfections of Generosity, Ethical Conduct, and Fortitude

HAVING GENERATED BODHICITTA and taken the bodhisattva precepts, now do your best to live like a bodhisattva, imbuing all your actions with great compassion, wisdom, and bodhicitta. Pay special attention to the foremost bodhisattva actions, the ten perfections: generosity, ethical conduct, fortitude, joyous effort, meditative stability, wisdom, skillful means, unshakable resolve, power, and pristine wisdom. As you do this, be unassuming and don't flaunt your spiritual practice. As my spiritual mentor Tsenshap Serkong Rinpoche once told Chodron, who is also his student, "If I am a good cook, I don't need to advertise it. If I cook a meal, people will know for themselves."

The Perfection of Generosity

Generosity is the mind with a kind thought that wants to give. It not only directly helps others but also releases the pain of miserliness and fills our mind with joy. In the *Heap of Jewels Sūtra*, the Bodhisattva Surata says (R 244–45):

> One who accumulates billions
> and is greedily attached [to this wealth],
> unable to give it away,
> is said by the wise
> to be a person ever poor in the world.

A penniless person
who will readily give whatever he has
is said by the wise
to be the noblest and richest on earth.

Giving is the first perfection because it is the easiest for us to do. Generosity acts as the cause to receive resources—food, shelter, clothing, medicine, and other pleasurable objects—in this and future lives. Candrakīrti in the *Supplement to "Treatise on the Middle Way"* says (MMA 10):

All these beings want happiness,
but human happiness does not occur without resources.
Knowing that resources arise from generosity,
the Subduer first discoursed on that.

Generosity can take many forms, and four types of generosity are commonly discussed: (1) giving material possessions or money, (2) giving protection, (3) giving love, and (4) giving the Dharma.

Giving Material Possessions and Money

Giving material goods is a wonderful opportunity to connect with others, especially when we give with a pleasant expression and use both hands. It's important to give at an appropriate time, without harming or inconveniencing anyone. We can also encourage others to be generous by inviting them to join us in making a gift or an offering.

Once you have decided to give something, give it soon, not letting the gift decay or get damaged. Avoid giving a little at a time when you could make the offering all at once, and definitely don't belittle the recipient or give harmful objects such as weapons, poisons, and so on. Make sure that your gift was obtained with right livelihood.

Some people fear that if they give they will be impoverished because they won't have that object later when they need it. Karmically, the opposite occurs: according to what we give, generosity is the cause to receive wealth, protection, love, and Dharma teachings. Even people who selfishly seek wealth will reap good results in future lives by being generous now. Although they are motivated to receive the karmic "reward" of giving, their generosity will still bring them abundance and the comfort of their material needs being met. Candrakīrti tells us (MMA 11):

> Even for beings with little compassion,
> brutal and intent on their own aims,
> desired resources arise from generosity,
> causing extinguishment of suffering.

In addition, those who are generous will come in contact with holy beings who will guide them on the path in this or future lives. The karmic connection from making offerings to Dharma practitioners, especially to bodhisattvas who are motivated by pure compassion, enables the giver to receive teachings in future lives and thus to progress on the path to liberation.

In the *Inquiry of Ugra Sūtra*, the Buddha encourages us by speaking of the benefits we receive by practicing generosity (IU 240–41):

> The bodhisattva...should reflect as follows: "What I give away is mine; what I keep at home is not mine.[4] What I give away has essence; what I keep at home has no essence. What I give away will bring pleasure at another [i.e., future] time; what I keep at home will [only] bring pleasure right now. What I give away does not need to be protected; what I keep at home must be protected. [My] desire for what I give away will be exhausted; [my] desire for what I keep at home increases. What I give away I do not think of as mine; what I keep at home I think of as mine. What I give away is no longer an object of grasping; what I keep at home is an object of grasping. What I give away is not a source of fear; what I keep at home causes fear. What I give away supports the path to awakening; what I keep at home supports the party of Māra."

REFLECTION

1. Think of something that you hesitate to part with, even though someone else could derive happiness from receiving it.

2. Contemplate as the Buddha said above: "What I give is not mine. I will not

need to protect it anymore and I will be free from the fear of it getting lost, broken, or stolen. My painful mental obsession for it will decrease, and I will feel the pleasure of giving instead. Furthermore, my greed, anger, and confusion about it will diminish and I will create merit that will support my future awakening."

3. Contemplate: "With a miserly attitude, if I keep it, I will fret over it and my mind will be stressed, fearful, and trapped by clinging. I will eventually have to separate from it, and all that will remain then is the destructive karma I created through attachment to it."

4. Compare the happy feeling in your mind when you think of the benefits of giving and the painful mental feelings when you imagine clinging to the object and keeping it for yourself. In this way, encourage yourself to be generous.

Bodhisattvas' generosity differs from that of ordinary beings in many respects. Because ordinary beings do not immediately see the results of their generosity, many of them do not give. Bodhisattvas, on the other hand, are free from miserliness and do not seek their own benefit when they give. Having taken the bodhisattva precepts, they have pledged to lead all sentient beings to awakening and to help them temporarily as much as possible. Whenever bodhisattvas give, they experience the supreme joy that comes from seeing others benefit from their actions. There is not a touch of sadness, fear, or sense of loss after they give, only happiness. In fact, when bodhisattvas hear someone say, "Please give me...," they feel overwhelming joy. Such joy is not experienced by śrāvaka and solitary-realizer arhats who abide in the peace of nirvāṇa, let alone by ordinary beings. Knowing these benefits, let's try to practice generosity as bodhisattvas do.

In *Precious Garland*, Nāgārjuna counsels the king to use his wealth to benefit others and create merit now while he has the chance. The time of death is not certain, and while dying, he will be unable to practice generosity. Meanwhile, his ministers will be planning to divide up the treasury and still leave some for the new ruler (RA 316–17):

> When dying, since you will lose your independence,
> you will be unable to give away [your possessions]
> through ministers who shamelessly cease to value you
> and seek the affection of the new king.
>
> Therefore, while healthy, quickly use all your resources
> to build Dharma sites,
> for you stand in the midst of death's causes
> like a lamp in the midst of a storm.

You may not be a monarch, but Nāgārjuna's advice is still valuable. Give now and give with a bodhicitta motivation. Then while dying, rejoice at your merit and know that your wealth was distributed as you wish.

It may sometimes happen that you know the benefits of giving and the disadvantages of stinginess but still cannot bring yourself to give something to a person who has asked for it. The Buddha advises to humbly explain to the person (IU 258–59):

> At this point my strength is meager and my roots of virtue are immature. I am only a beginner in the Mahāyāna. I am subject to thoughts of not giving. I still have the perspective of grasping, and am stuck in taking things as I and mine. And so, good person, I beg you to forgive me and not to be upset. [In the future] I will act, accomplish, and exert myself in order to fulfill your desires and those of all beings.

In other words, when giving a particular item is too much of a stretch for your present mental capacity, acknowledge your limitation without feeling ashamed or denigrating yourself. At the same time, resolve to put energy into eliminating this hindrance so that you will be able to joyfully give in the future.

Be careful also about going to the other extreme of giving so much away that you leave yourself bereft. Be practical so that you do not become a burden to others by being unable to take care of yourself. Remember, it is the strength of your kind motivation that is the most important factor, not the size of the offering.

Misunderstanding the meaning of generosity, people sometimes think it entails giving whatever another person wants. This is not the case; we must give with wisdom. If a person with a drug or alcohol problem asks for money that we know will be used to feed their substance abuse, giving it to them is not an act of kindness and generosity. In this case, the most helpful action is to not give the money but to help the person enroll in a treatment program. We do this not with anger or stinginess but out of care and concern for the person.

Similarly, giving children whatever they want does not help them grow into responsible adults. In fact, it can impair their ability to function in society later on because they will take possessions for granted and expect all their wishes to be fulfilled. Teaching children how to deal with the frustration of not getting what they want will help them for the rest of their lives. Likewise, teaching them to be generous with their possessions is helping them more than catering to their every desire. Similarly, when children quarrel about a toy or device, teaching them methods to resolve conflicts nonviolently will help them much more than stepping in and fixing the external situation.

Each situation in which we are asked for help needs to be examined individually, in light of our motivation, capability, and the repercussions of our action. Not giving out of miserliness is self-centered, but if we have the wish to give but are unable to, there is no fault. Being generous does not mean that we have to cure all the poverty and need in the world. While sentient beings are still in cyclic existence, a perfect world is impossible. Nevertheless, do what you can with a caring attitude.

People often want to be generous but are confused when they receive requests for donations from a myriad of charities. Is not giving something to each a transgression of the bodhisattva precept to give whenever asked? No, it isn't. The bodhisattva precept refers to giving in situations where the person is in desperate need, directly asks us for help, and has no one else to turn to. If you receive requests for help from too many charities, pick those whose causes touch you the most and contribute to them. In your mind have a supportive and compassionate attitude and make prayers for the welfare of the others.

Learning to be a kind recipient is also practicing generosity and ethical conduct, for we're giving someone the opportunity to take delight in giving. Sometimes we are too proud, afraid of feeling obliged, or immersed in feeling unworthy to accept others' generosity. Rebuffing their gifts—be they material possessions, loving support, or the offer of help—is stinginess on our part. As a result, the giver may feel hurt, rejected, or demoralized. Recalling that our aim is to benefit sentient beings, let's open our hearts and accept their kindness and generosity, neither exploiting it nor rejecting it. Admiring their kind actions and rejoicing in their merit can invigorate us to "pay it forward."

REFLECTION

1. Contemplate your fortune in having the possessions you have—which is the result of being generous in previous lives. Think how wonderful others who are lacking in possessions would feel if they could enjoy such fortune.
2. Clean out a closet or dresser in your home, removing everything you haven't used in the last year.
3. Note if the thought "But if I give it away, I won't have it" arises, and remind yourself of the benefits of generosity.
4. Take those things to a charity, hospital, nursing home, school, and so forth, and with joy in your heart, donate them.

Giving the Body

Bodhisattvas may give their bodies to someone in need only when they have no clinging to their bodies. To such bodhisattvas, giving their body and life is like giving a carrot to someone; they have no attachment, fear, or hesitation. Some bodhisattvas attain the ability to give their body on the path of preparation. Bodhisattvas on the first ground, who excel in the perfection of generosity, do not experience any physical or mental suffering when giving their body or life. Because of their great merit, they do not experience physical pain, and because of their profound wisdom realizing emptiness, they experience no mental suffering. Nāgārjuna says (RA 221–23):

What is called immeasurable merit
and also that called immeasurable wisdom
quickly eradicate the suffering
of both body and mind.

Hunger, thirst, and other such physical suffering
occur in unfortunate rebirths due to one's misdeeds.
[Bodhisattvas] do not engage in misdeeds;
due to merit, they have no such suffering in other rebirths.

From confusion comes the mental suffering
of attachment, anger, fear, lust, and such.
[Bodhisattvas] quickly eliminate this
by realizing that [all phenomena] are foundationless.

Furthermore, being free from the self-centered thought and having deep compassion, their attention is focused on the suffering of others (RA 226):

They have no physical suffering;
how could they have mental suffering?
Through their compassion they feel pain
for the world and so stay in it long.

Ordinary bodhisattvas who have not yet attained the first ground feel physical suffering when giving parts of their body. However, the pain they experience serves only to intensify their compassion for other sentient beings, who experience far greater pain in the hells. It reinforces their commitment and increases their activities to lead sentient beings to awakening until all realms in cyclic existence are emptied of beings. Candrakīrti said (MMA 15):

Through his own suffering in cutting and giving away his body
he sees with knowledge others' pain
in hells and so forth, and strives quickly
to eliminate their suffering.

However, many great masters say that bodhisattvas who have not yet reached the first ground (on the path of seeing) should not give their lives because they are not yet capable of controlling their rebirth. It is better for these bodhisattvas to remain alive in this body and practice the Dharma for the remainder of their life.

Similarly, it is wiser for ordinary beings, who still cling to their bodies, to maintain their precious human lives and use them to purify negativities, create merit, and to study, contemplate, and meditate on the Dharma. Nowadays people can safely donate a kidney or another part of the body, and if they wish they can donate various organs after they die.

Although we are not yet capable of giving away our body, it is helpful to imagine doing so, since one day we will have to relinquish this body. The inner maṇḍala offering, where we imagine the parts of our body becoming the various aspects of the universe in its purified form, is a good way to do this. Our trunk becomes Mount Meru, our hands and feet the four continents, the upper and lower parts of our arms and legs become the eight subcontinents, our intestines the rings of water, our two eyes the sun and moon, our two ears the umbrella and victory banner, and our inner organs transform into gorgeous offerings that fill the entire sky. To offer this to the holy beings, we recite:

> The objects of attachment, aversion, and ignorance—friends, enemies, and strangers, my body, wealth, and enjoyments—I offer these without any sense of loss. Please accept them with pleasure, and inspire me and others to be free from the three poisonous attitudes. *Idam guru ratna maṇḍala kam nirya tayami.*

Visualizations such as those in the practice of Cutting the Ego (Chod) and the Kusali offering in the Vajrayoginī practice are also helpful in this regard.

In short, practice giving your possessions and making offerings as much as you can—for example, by offering water bowls to the Three Jewels each morning, offering your food before eating, and giving to those in need. Doing practices in which you imagine giving your possessions and virtues of the past, present, and future are also beneficial. With each actual or imagined action of giving, remember to contemplate that the agent, action, and object are empty of inherent existence but exist dependent on one another. If miserliness arises, counteract it by recalling that you will have to separate from your resources sooner or later in any case. Therefore it would be better to actually give them or at least to give them in your imagination in order to increase delight in giving and free your mind from the pain of miserliness. Śāntideva tells us (BCA 3.11–12):

> Without any sense of loss,
> I shall give up my body and enjoyments
> as well as all my virtues of the three times
> for the sake of benefiting all.
>
> By giving away all,
> my mind aspires to transcend sorrow (nirvāṇa).
> When I give away everything
> it is best to give to sentient beings [now].

Giving Protection from Danger and Fear

Helping travelers, providing medical services and medicine, teaching Dharma to the incarcerated, providing aid to refugees, and volunteering in a homeless shelter are examples of giving protection from danger and fear. Tutoring and acting as mentors for at-risk youth, helping single mothers apply for social services, running a no-kill animal shelter that facilitates animal adoptions, providing legal services for immigrants, migrants, and refugees—there are many ways to reach out and help living beings experiencing fear and danger in the world today. All actions to protect the environment—be it recycling, researching renewable energy sources, planting trees, helping endangered species, taking injured wild animals to a wildlife shelter or sanctuary, and so forth—are also included in the generosity of protecting others. Rescuing insects drowning in water is another form of giving protection.

All of us have experienced fear and danger in the past; we know the feeling of relief that fills us when someone—a friend, relative, stranger, and sometimes even a former enemy—gives us a helping hand.

Giving Love

Giving love complements giving protection and is done in similar situations. It includes giving love to abused children, orphans, the grieving, the neglected, and all other beings. Many people need emotional support while going through difficult situations such as divorce, losing their job, and family problems. When we are able, let's help them. We must be sensitive to each individual situation, however, not pushing our solutions on others or embarrassing them. Giving love also includes volunteering in social welfare projects, using our education and creativity to help others, and consoling those who are grieving.

Giving the Dharma

Giving the Dharma is said to be the supreme form of generosity because it enables others to create the causes for temporal and ultimate happiness. As with all forms of generosity, our motivation is important; when sharing the Dharma, the purity of motivation is of even greater importance, because sharing the Dharma with a corrupt motivation could cause widespread and long-term harm. For example, with a motivation that wants to use others to obtain fame and wealth, someone gives incorrect teachings. Others believe these fallacious speculations and practice incorrectly, leading them to unfortunate rebirths. Such wrong teachings may remain in circulation even after the person who first spoke them has died. Nāgārjuna said (MPU 81):

> The giving of Dharma consists of constantly employing a pure mind and wholesome thoughts in the offering of instruction to everyone. Just as it is with the giving of material gifts, wherein there is no measure of blessings or virtue associated with it if one fails to maintain a wholesome mind, so too it is with the giving of the Dharma: If one fails to maintain a pure mind and wholesome thoughts, then it is not the case that this actually qualifies as the generosity of Dharma.
>
> But if the speaker of Dharma is able to maintain a pure mind and wholesome thoughts as he praises the Three Jewels, opens the door to understanding offenses and blessings, explains the four truths, and thus goes about teaching and transforming beings so

> that they are caused to enter the buddha path, this does qualify as true and pure Dharma generosity.

As Buddhist practitioners, share whatever knowledge you have of the Dharma when people ask for advice. When sharing the Dharma, do not expect special treatment, respect, or offerings, but simply give Dharma instructions or advice to others as one friend to another. Giving Dharma teachings for payment is doing business—the worst kind of business!

Not everyone wants to teach the Dharma and not everyone is qualified to be a Dharma teacher; but there are many other ways to give the Dharma to others such as chanting mantras to children and teaching them the melodies to chant them too. Doing our recitations out loud so that animals and insects around us hear them, reading texts and prayers to those recovering from an illness or those whose lives are coming to a conclusion, contributing funds to print Dharma books for free distribution, and donating books on Buddhism to college libraries as well as public libraries are also acts of giving the Dharma. Volunteering at a Dharma center, monastery, or temple supports the sharing of the Dharma.

When friends ask for advice on how to deal with problems, describe Dharma methods without using any Buddhist words. This is easy to do because so many of the Buddha's teachings—especially those on working with emotions and building healthy relationships—are common-sense instructions that people of any or no religion can easily apply in their lives.

Bodhisattvas' Practice of Generosity

Nāgārjuna describes bodhisattvas' perfection of generosity (MPU 99–100):

> As for that giving performed by bodhisattvas, it is done with the realization that the act of giving is neither produced nor destroyed. It is conducted in a state that has gone beyond polluting impurities, is unconditioned, and is characterized by being like nirvāṇa. That giving is performed for the sake of all beings. This is what is referred to as the perfection of generosity.
>
> There are those who say that when one gives everything of every sort, giving exhaustively of all inner and outer resources,

> and also gives without seeking any reward as a result, this kind of giving qualifies as the perfection of generosity...
>
> One knows that the thing that is given is ultimately empty [of inherent existence] and characterized as being like nirvāṇa. Because one employs this kind of mind in giving to beings, the result accruing from it is inexhaustible and it is therefore referred to as the perfection of generosity...
>
> [Bodhisattvas] employ a kind of giving that is coated with nirvāṇa-like reality-concordant wisdom through which [that giving] becomes inexhaustible. Moreover, bodhisattvas give for the sake of all beings. Because the number of beings is inexhaustible, that giving too is inexhaustible.
>
> Bodhisattvas give for the sake of the Buddhadharma. The Buddhadharma is immeasurable and boundless. So too is that giving also immeasurable and boundless.

For these reasons, bodhisattvas' generosity surpasses that of śrāvakas. Although we may not yet be capable of practicing generosity in that vast way, we can rejoice in the bodhisattvas' generosity and aspire to practice generosity as they do. This is done by familiarizing ourselves with the above elements of generosity that Nāgārjuna pointed out. In short, by practicing generosity whenever possible with the motivation of bodhicitta and the awareness of emptiness, our minds will be very joyful and we will progress on the path to buddhahood.

REFLECTION

1. Think of examples of how you can practice the generosity of protection.
2. Think of examples of how you can practice the generosity of love.
3. Think of examples of how you can practice the generosity of the Dharma.

Asaṅga in his *Mahāyāna Compendium* recommends practicing generosity with six supremacies: (1) the *supreme basis* is practicing generosity based on bodhicitta; (2) *supreme things* is that you give all that can be given, and when that is limited, maintain the aspiration to give away everything; (3) *supreme aim* is giving to all sentient beings for the sake of their temporal happiness and ultimate benefit; (4) *supreme skillful means* is when generosity is informed by nonconceptual wisdom, or in the case of beginning bodhisattvas, with wisdom that conceptually knows that all phenomena are empty; (5) *supreme dedication* is dedicating the merit from practicing generosity to the full awakening of self and others; and (6) *supreme purity* is stopping both afflictive and cognitive obscurations.

Contemplating these six one by one before, during, and after giving transforms our generosity from an ordinary, mundane act of giving to giving that is deeply meaningful for self and others. Try it!

Maitreya's *Ornament of the Mahāyāna Sūtras* contains a concise verse with deep meaning that explains how the Buddha engages with all six perfections. Here the example of generosity is used; the italicized word changes according to each perfection:

> Buddha's *generosity* is
> not attached, unattached, never attached;
> it is not at all attached,
> not attached, unattached, never attached.

"Attachment" here means stickiness, an attitude that prevents our practice of that perfection from being in accord with the Dharma. Pointing out these seven discordant elements helps us to improve our practice, making it accord with bodhisattvas' deeds.

1. *Not attached*: Attachment indicates the opposite of that perfection, which in the case of generosity is miserliness regarding possessions. Turning away from miserliness is being not attached.
2. *Unattached*: Here attachment appears in the form of procrastination. By being unattached, we will seize the present opportunity.
3. *Never attached*: This attachment is to limits, such as limited objects, recipients, areas, or time. It prevents us from practicing wholeheartedly—for example, being easily satisfied with offering a little when we're capable of offering more. Without attachment, we

will make effort to go beyond self-imposed limits and narrow ways of thinking. In regard to generosity, we will overcome our hesitation to give.

4. *Not at all attached*: Here attachment is to the hope for reward; this is giving with the expectation of receiving something in return in this life. Our generosity is done in the spirit of a transaction. We give in order to receive; the gift isn't free because expectations are attached. Afterward if our expectations are not met, we feel cheated and complain, when in fact our corrupt motivation is the problem. Being not at all attached, our motivation for practicing each perfection is free from seeking reward or acknowledgment here and now.
5. *Not attached*: The attachment is expecting a beneficial karmic return in future lives. This attitude is unbecoming for a bodhisattva who aims for awakening and wastes an opportunity to create virtue. Being not attached, bodhisattvas don't expect good results in future lives, even though these may come naturally as an effect of virtue.
6. *Unattached*: Here attachment is for the self-centered attitude that is a formidable obstacle because it seeks only our own liberation. This is countered by renewing our bodhicitta motivation. Being unattached is giving with the full force of a generous motivation.
7. *Never attached*: This attachment undermines the purity of our practice. It has two aspects. The first is being tinged by the latencies of stinginess that obscure the mind. The second is grasping true existence. When giving, try to be fully aware that the agent, object, and action of generosity are empty of true existence. See them as existing by mere designation.

Although these seven are not explicitly mentioned in the context of each perfection, contemplate them on your own. It will enhance your practice of the other perfections.

Train so that your generosity is like a snake shedding its skin: there is no regret. Be like a deer who doesn't have any sense of ownership. Giving without these seven impediments is a bodhisattva's generosity. Although our generosity may fall short of this, remember that we are *practicing* generosity; the expectation is not that we will be perfectly generous at the beginning. As the old adage goes, "practice makes perfect."

The Perfection of Ethical Conduct

The second perfection, ethical conduct, is a mind that has abandoned all thoughts of harming others. In particular, the ethical conduct of a bodhisattva is a state of mind that has relinquished the self-centered attitude. There are three types of ethical conduct:

1. *Restraining from destructive actions* is to abandon the ten nonvirtues and to abide in whatever precepts and commitments we have taken.
2. *Gathering virtue* involves taking every possible opportunity to enhance the collections of method and wisdom in order to progress on the path.
3. *Benefiting sentient beings* is to enact our love and compassion by helping those in need.

These three occur in a fixed sequence. Restraining from harm establishes the foundation for engaging in virtuous actions, which in turn enables us to work for the welfare of sentient beings.

The Ethical Conduct of Restraining from Destructive Actions

Ethical conduct evolves from generosity, because if we are generous, not attached to possessions, and not greedy for more, then we will not harm others to get things. In the *Supplement*, Candrakīrti emphasizes the first type of ethical conduct, in which we abandon naturally negative actions—that is, actions that when done by ordinary beings are almost always motivated by afflictions. Of particular importance is abandoning the ten nonvirtuous paths of karma, the first seven being destructive actions (killing, stealing, unwise or unkind sexual behavior, lying, divisive speech, harsh speech, and idle talk) and the last three being the afflictions that motivate them (covetousness, malice, and wrong views). Furthermore, keeping whatever precepts we have taken is of crucial importance. These include the prātimokṣa precepts for monastics and lay followers, the bodhisattva precepts, and tantric precepts and commitments. If we have taken lay or monastic precepts, engaging in proscribed actions such that the four branches of the basis, attitude, performance, and completion are complete constitutes a full transgression of the precept.

There are four gates through which ethical misdeeds occur. By learning and remembering these we can avoid misdeeds and transgressions of precepts.

(1) By *not knowing what to abandon and what to practice*, we easily harm others. For example, being ignorant of the ten nonvirtues and not remembering the precepts we have taken set the stage for unethical actions that harm others.

(2) *Lacking respect for the precepts and not thinking that ethical conduct is important* facilitate misdeeds. Someone may know what to abandon and practice but not think that ethical conduct is important. Such a person easily interferes with the well-being of others because they don't care about the effects of their actions on themselves or others.

(3) *Carelessness and heedlessness*. Someone may know the ten nonvirtues and may know the precepts they promised to uphold, but not monitor their behavior. Lacking mindfulness and introspective awareness, they don't recognize when afflictions and harmful intentions arise in their minds and easily act on whatever impulsive thoughts enter their mind.

(4) *Strong afflictions*. When the mind is unsubdued, afflictions can arise strongly and overwhelm someone's ethical restraint. Before they know it, afflictions are in control, forcing them to get involved in harmful actions. Even if they intellectually know the antidote for that affliction, it is weak and they cannot call it up when it is most needed.

The more we are aware of the above four factors and seek to counteract them, the more peaceful our demeanor will be and the purer our ethical conduct will be. The tools to shut the four doors to transgressions are mental factors in our mind. We must learn to identify them in our own experience and then strengthen them through Dharma study and practice. The antidotes to the four gates for transgressions are:

(1) Learn the ten nonvirtues and the four branches for them to be complete.[5] Know the precepts and commitments you have taken and study them well.

(2) Develop faith and respect for the precepts. Understand the disadvantages of unethical behavior and the benefits of ethical conduct. Live near your preceptor, Dharma teachers, and virtuous friends so that you have support in your practice of ethical conduct and good examples to follow. Remembering that the precepts in your mindstream represent the Buddha, you won't be indifferent toward them.

(3) Be careful and conscientious in your actions. Cultivate mindfulness of your precepts and develop introspective awareness to monitor the thoughts and emotions in your mind.

(4) Learn the antidotes to the afflictions and apply them. Contemplate impermanence to counteract attachment, fortitude to subdue anger, and rejoicing to counter jealousy. Meditating on precious human life and buddha nature are excellent antidotes to depression and lack of self-confidence. Breathing meditation calms the mind when doubt, restlessness, or rumination arise. Also cultivate integrity, which abandons negativities because of holding to our own values, and consideration for others, which abandons negativities because of not wanting others to lose faith in us, in the Dharma, or in human beings in general.

As said in the "Eight Verses of Thought Transformation" (3):[6]

> In all actions I will examine my mind,
> and the moment a disturbing attitude arises,
> endangering myself and others,
> I will firmly confront and avert it.

REFLECTION

Contemplate the four gates through which ethical wrongdoings occur, making examples from your life or from the lives of people you see in the news. Then reflect on their antidotes and see how those would prevent the wrongdoing and save so many people from experiencing pain.

1. By not knowing what to abandon and what to practice, you easily harm others.

2. The remedy is to learn the ten nonvirtues and the four branches for them to be complete. Know the precepts and commitments you have taken and study them well.

3. Lacking respect for the precepts and not thinking that ethical conduct is important makes you apathetic toward the effects of your actions on yourself and on others.

4. Counteract this by developing faith and respect for the precepts. Understand the disadvantages of unethical behavior and the benefits of ethical conduct. Live near your preceptor, Dharma teachers, and others who support your good conduct.

5. Carelessness and heedlessness lie behind not monitoring your behavior and not recognizing afflictions and harmful intentions when they arise.

6. The antidote to this is being conscientious in your actions. Cultivate mindfulness of your precepts and develop introspective awareness to monitor your thoughts and emotions.

7. Being overwhelmed by strong afflictions renders you unable to control your physical, verbal, and mental actions.

8. The counterforce is to learn the antidotes to the afflictions and practice them repeatedly in your meditation so that you are familiar with them when an actual situation arises.

Abandoning destructive actions brings coolness to the mind as the fire of guilt and remorse has been reduced. Practicing the ten virtuous pathways of action brings delight and peace to the mind. It is said that a special fragrance called the "scent of pure ethical conduct" naturally surrounds people who have pure ethical conduct.

Ethical conduct is like a dike; it holds us back from involvement in a harmful situation. It is like a lamp that illuminates dark corners of our mind so that we can clean them. It is like our goatee being on fire; we must focus on what is happening inside ourselves, not on others.

Bodhisattvas on the second ground excel in ethical conduct. Whether they are awake or asleep, standing, sitting, walking, or lying down, their body, speech, and mind are free from even subtle ethical misdeeds. Although our ethical conduct may not be of that caliber now, we should direct our intentions to that and cultivate pure ethical conduct as best as we can. Through the force of our sincere intention, gradually all our actions will become wholesome.

Practicing ethical conduct is extremely important for ordinary beings as well as for āryas. We may create much merit by practicing generosity, but if we neglect ethical conduct—which is the primary cause of fortunate rebirths—we will enjoy the wonderful fruits of generosity in an unfortunate realm. For example, instead of having a precious human life with good resources and conducive conditions in which we can practice the Dharma easily, we will be reborn as a pampered dog in a wealthy family. I hear that some people in the West take their dogs to spas, have their claws manicured, and give them the most delicious and expensive dog food available. While the dog may enjoy the food—I'm not sure about the spa and the manicure—the dog's merit of generosity has been exhausted with no long-term benefit having accrued, because it was unable to create merit in a dog rebirth.

On the other hand, if someone practices ethical conduct as well as generosity, both will ripen as the conducive circumstances of a precious human life. On that basis they can continue practicing the Dharma, creating more and more causes for awakening. In the process of doing this, they will also create the causes for good rebirths in the future in which they will have all excellent conditions necessary for Dharma practice. This is like accruing compounded interest; Candrakīrti, on the other hand, likens practicing generosity without ethical conduct to frittering away both principal and interest.

It is extremely difficult to practice ethical conduct when born in an unfortunate realm, making the creation of the causes for another higher rebirth very problematic. Candrakīrti warns (MMA 22):

> If when one has freedom and a favorable rebirth,
> he does not act to hold [himself back from falling],
> he will fall into an abyss and lose control;
> how will he raise himself from there in the future?

While we have a precious human life, it is crucial to engage in ethical conduct not only to prevent suffering in lower rebirths from which it is hard to escape but also to create the causes for fortunate rebirths that can be used to practice the Dharma again. Candrakīrti encourages us (MMA 23):

> Thus the Conqueror, having discoursed on generosity,
> spoke on the following [perfection], ethical conduct.

When virtues are nurtured in the field of ethical conduct,
the enjoyment of effects is unceasing.

Because ethical conduct is the basis of all good qualities, it is called a "field." When the virtues of generosity, fortitude, and so forth are cultivated in this field, the crop of fortunate rebirths and excellent resources ripens. With these conducive circumstances, we can continue to practice until attaining full awakening without being hindered by unfortunate rebirths or lack of resources. Although our long-term aim is buddhahood, a series of excellent rebirths is gained along the way.

For ordinary beings, ethical conduct is the cause for higher rebirths; for those on the śrāvaka, solitary realizer, and bodhisattva paths it is the cause of the highest goodness—liberation and awakening. Although other causes also factor into attaining these two, ethical conduct is the fundamental basis without which the other causes won't ripen in the desired way.

Ethical conduct brings desired results in this life too. Our hearts are lighter and we have less regret and remorse. People trust us; being confident that we will not harm them, they are relaxed around us. Even animals feel the difference between people who have abandoned harming others and those who are angry and fearful.

The Ethical Conduct of Gathering Virtue

Gathering virtue is using all opportunities to engage in virtuous actions. Refraining from nonvirtue is virtuous in itself, and doing the opposite of nonvirtuous actions—for example, saving life instead of killing—is virtuous too. Keeping whatever precepts we have taken creates great merit. The eight Mahāyāna precepts is a special one-day practice that creates great merit because it is done with the bodhicitta motivation. These precepts resemble the eight one-day prātimokṣa precepts to abandon killing; stealing; sexual behavior; lying; intoxicants; sitting on high or luxurious beds or seats; using scents, cosmetics, and jewelry; singing, dancing, and playing music; and eating after midday. Because these precepts are taken motivated by bodhicitta, monastics can also take them.[7] This practice is good to do on special Buddhist holy days, on full and new moon days, or whenever you need a day of mindfulness and spiritual reflection.

We should also take care not to destroy virtue already created by succumbing to anger or wrong views and do our best to enhance virtue in the future. The latter can be done by ensuring our motivation is one of bodhicitta before beginning the action, sealing the action at its conclusion by contemplating the emptiness of the sphere of three, and dedicating the merit to full awakening.

The Ethical Conduct of Benefiting Sentient Beings

The third type of ethical conduct—helping sentient beings—involves guiding others so they will aspire to and engage in constructive attitudes and actions. Benefiting sentient beings does not mean we fix all their problems, for it is far more valuable to teach them how to think, speak, and act clearly so that they are able to remedy their problems themselves. Our job is to give them the confidence and skills to create virtue and to handle situations skillfully without harming others, not to make them dependent on us because we seek to feel needed and valued by others.

There are eleven groups of people to be particularly diligent about benefiting:

1. Aiding *those who are suffering or ill* by giving them assistance—for example, helping someone who cannot walk well, preparing food for someone recovering from an injury or illness, visiting people in the hospital. The wonderful work done by hospice staff and volunteers is included here too.
2. Guiding *people who are obscured or ignorant of means to help themselves* is accomplished, for example, by explaining proper behavior to the reckless, counseling those preparing to be released from prison on what to say in job interviews, and instructing young adults on the way to manage finances.
3. *Those who need help to realize their desires* are aided by helping them to move homes, plan events, and think ahead to what they may need in the future.
4. Helping *sentient beings who are afraid, in danger, or about to be killed or injured* includes, for example, buying an animal that is about to be slaughtered, stepping in to redirect people's attention to prevent a dispute, guiding someone who is lost to their destination, and intervening when one person or group is bullying another.

5. Aiding *people who are grieving* the death of a dear one or the loss of their social position is, for example, consoling them, listening to their concerns, helping them with daily errands, and guiding them to reimagine their future.
6. Helping the *poor and needy* is accomplished by giving them material aid in a respectful and appropriate manner, encouraging them to get in touch with their good qualities, and helping them to see their value as human beings no matter what their outer circumstances may be.
7. Offering assistance to *those who need a place to stay*, such as the poor, Dharma practitioners, travelers, and stray animals involves thinking of appropriate places where they will be comfortable and safe.
8. Benefiting *people who want to be in harmony* is accomplished by teaching them good communication skills, encouraging them to forgive, speaking of the benefits of reconciliation, and so forth.
9. Assisting *those who want to follow the path* includes aiding those who want to make offerings, to study the Dharma, or to go on pilgrimage. It may also entail helping people who want to learn the Dharma to meet qualified spiritual mentors and attend teachings.
10. Helping *sentient beings who are acting negatively or are about to do so* may entail preventing them from doing that action or explaining the drawbacks of such actions. We may offer spiritual counsel to those who are on the verge of following a wrong path by steering them toward a virtuous path. Other times we have to take a firm stand to stop someone who is harming others. Taking special interest in a child who is bullying others can help that child see ways to connect with others—which is what they want to do—in a way that will bring happy results.
11. There are *those who can only be helped by a demonstration of supernormal powers*. If all else fails to stop someone's destructive actions or to prove the validity of the Dharma, supernormal powers can be used if one has them.

These eleven groups coincide with the groups of people in the last category of auxiliary precepts of engaged bodhicitta. The difference is that the precepts specify to abandon not helping them whereas the perfection of ethical conduct emphasizes paying special attention to helping them.

Other sentient beings to help are those who trust and are attracted to you, by showing them the Dharma; those who are praiseworthy, by pointing out their good qualities and actions; and those who want to learn the Dharma, by practicing the four ways of attraction (see chapter 4). As much as possible, try to act in accordance with others' wishes and needs as long as their wishes are not harmful to yourself or others. However, do not use others' wishes—"my friends asked me to go to the movies"—as a means to rationalize being distracted from Dharma practice or acting in detrimental ways.

Bodhisattvas' Practice of Ethical Conduct

Motivation is most crucial when practicing ethical conduct. Seeking a good reputation, praise, power, or offerings corrupts virtuous actions. Even though you may look like the epitome of virtue, if your motivation is not virtuous your actions amount to nothing more than using others to fulfill your worldly desires. Remaining humble is essential. In the *Heap of Jewels*, Bodhisattva Surata advises (R 245):

> The wise persuade others to do good;
> fools are always for evil.
> It is better to be scolded by the wise
> than to be praised by fools.

When practicing ethical conduct, avoid being arrogant because of the purity of your conduct. Some people become proud thinking that they are especially holy or that they are the only ones who purely keep the Vinaya. Such arrogance increases self-grasping, whereas ethical conduct is meant to decrease it. We must be vigilant not to let pride sabotage our efforts to abandon harming others, accumulating virtue, and benefiting others. For this reason, *Ārya Maitreya's King of Unshakable Resolves* (*Āryamaitripraṇidhānarāja*) says:

> By having the flawless ethics of the Dharma law,
> pure ethical conduct,
> and ethical conduct without conceit,
> may I complete the perfection of ethical conduct.

An excellent way to eliminate arrogance and purify our ethical conduct is to abandon all grasping of I and mine by meditating on emptiness. The *Heap of Jewels* states (CTB 195):

> Kāśyapa, some monastics have proper ethics; they abide restrained by the prātimokṣa ethical code. Their rites and spheres of activity are perfect, and they view even coarse and subtle transgressions with concern. They thoroughly assume and train in the precepts and possess pure activities of body, speech, and mind. Hence their livelihood is thoroughly pure, but they propound a self. Kāśyapa, they are the first of those seeming to have proper ethical conduct which in fact is faulty... Furthermore, Kāśyapa, even though some monastics thoroughly assume the twelve qualities of training,[8] they view them with the apprehension [of inherent existence]. Abiding in grasping at I and mine, Kāśyapa, they are the fourth of those whose ethics appear to be proper but are faulty.

As with generosity and the other perfections, the perfection of ethical conduct is of two types: mundane and supramundane. Candrakīrti points out the difference between them (MMA 26):

> If there is any apprehension of the three—
> forsaken by whom, what, and with regard to whom—
> such ethical conduct is described as being a mundane perfection.
> That empty of attachment to the three is supramundane.

The unpolluted wisdom that does not grasp the inherent existence of the sphere of three makes a bodhisattva's practice of ethical conduct supramundane. The sphere of three is (1) *by whom*, the person or agent who abandons the destructive action, (2) *what*, the object that is abandoned—that is, the destructive action, and (3) *with regard to whom*, the person who was not harmed—that is, the field with regard to whom the destructive action is abandoned. This wisdom is sometimes called "objectless" wisdom or wisdom realizing the unapprehendable because it does not apprehend true existence and instead realizes the opposite, the emptiness of true existence of all persons and phenomena.

In conclusion, Nāgārjuna says (MPU 333):

> Bodhisattvas' upholding of ethical precepts is not done on account of fear, nor is it done out of stupidity, or doubt, or confusion, or out of a private quest for their own nirvāṇa. The upholding of ethical precepts is carried out solely for the sake of all beings, for the sake of success in the Buddha's path, and for the sake of gaining all the excellent qualities of buddhahood... This is what is meant by the perfection of ethical conduct... [In addition] if bodhisattvas' practice is based on the unfindability of either misdeed or non-misdeed, it is at this time that it qualifies as the perfection of ethical conduct.

He continues by explaining that because sentient beings are not findable under ultimate analysis, misdeeds and precepts aren't findable either. "Findable under ultimate analysis" means that when we search for exactly what a sentient being, misdeed, precept, or any other phenomenon is, we cannot isolate an inherently existent essence that is it. Everything depends on other factors that compose it. When we scrutinize an action of lying to find out exactly what it is, we see that although it depends on the motivation to deceive, the person who is lying, the false statement, the process of uttering the lie, and the other person understanding what was said, we cannot isolate one of these components and say, "This is the action of lying." However, although the action of lying cannot be found with ultimate analysis, it does exist dependently. We can't say that there was no misdeed on the conventional level.

In addition, Nāgārjuna explains (MPU 333): "It is on account of the existence of the misdeed of killing that the corresponding ethical precept exists. If there were no misdeed of killing, there would be no corresponding ethical precept either." That is, the misdeed and the precept exist in mutual dependence. Because one exists, so does the other. Here, too, we find that things do not exist independently, but exist dependently on the conventional level.

REFLECTION

Contemplate the proper way to live ethically and keep precepts.

1. Living ethically is the right thing to do, so refrain from being conceited; there's nothing to be arrogant about for living this way.
2. Don't cling to the idea of a self, an I who is living in a wholesome way. Such clinging could easily lead to arrogance, which brings complacency, from which your ethical conduct could degenerate.
3. Keep precepts with self-respect and love for sentient beings, not out of fear.
4. Live ethically motivated by the aspiration to attain buddhahood, not a desire for your own nirvāṇa.
5. Rejoice in your merit and wise decisions.

The Perfection of Fortitude

The Sanskrit term *kṣānti*, translated as fortitude, patience, or forbearance, refers to the ability to calmly endure discomfort, suffering, and pain. As the antidote to anger, fortitude is the ability to remain resolute and calm no matter what situation we encounter. Life is full of difficulties: people criticize or even beat us, we lose our job, our reputation suffers, we get sick or are injured, relationships change, those we love die, and we will too. Fortitude enables us to meet all these situations with a calm mind, free of upset and anger.

With fortitude difficulties become milestones in our practice. Rather than retreat, we face the challenge. And challenges there will be—this is saṃsāra. In difficult situations there are always choices. They may not include all the choices we prefer, but we have met the Buddha's teachings and know the methods to subdue the afflictions. As Śāntideva reminds us (BCA 4.28, 29, 36ab):

> Although enemies such as hatred and craving
> have neither arms nor legs,
> and are neither courageous nor wise,
> how have I, like a slave, been used by them?
>
> For while they dwell within my mind
> at their pleasure, they cause me harm.
> I patiently endure them without any anger,
> but this is an inappropriate and shameful time for patience.
>
> Therefore as long as this enemy [the afflictions] is not slain with certainty before my very eyes,
> I shall never give up exerting myself toward that end.

Life presents us with many opportunities to practice fortitude. Worldly people abhor this, but for bodhisattvas who want to practice the perfection of fortitude, it is a cause of delight. Why? To become buddhas, bodhisattvas need to perfect their practice of fortitude, and to do that they need difficult people and problematic situations. Usually others are kind and there aren't many chances to practice fortitude. So when such opportunities come their way, bodhisattvas greet them with delight and meet the challenge they present. In that way, misery has a hard time touching bodhisattvas because they don't allow anger, resentment, vengeance, and belligerence to inhabit their minds.

The Unsuitability and Disadvantages of Anger

Anger, resentment, grudge-holding, spite, and so on are emotions that frequently arise in us when our desires are frustrated or when something interferes with our happiness. Although anger seems like a natural response to these situations, that doesn't mean it is a productive one. In fact, anger has many disadvantages, which Candrakīrti points out in his *Supplement* and Śāntideva notes in *Engaging in the Bodhisattvas' Deeds*. Getting angry at someone who has harmed us does not cure our pain or stop the harm. Anger may give us a false sense of power, but that provides little benefit and could lead to greater harm; if we retaliate, the other party will not lie still but will escalate the conflict.

In addition, anger makes us miserable in this life and motivates us to act in detrimental ways that bring suffering in future lives. It is contradictory to say that we do not want to suffer and then willingly create the causes for suffering. The harm someone does to us now is due to our previous destructive karma. If we react to this harm with violent words or actions, we create the karmic cause for more suffering in the future, which is exactly what we do not want.

While the disadvantages of anger toward an ordinary sentient being are many, those of being angry at a bodhisattva are far harsher: great destructive karma is accumulated, great virtue is destroyed, and one must wear the armor—that is, engage in the six perfections—from the beginning of the bodhisattva path.

Both Candrakīrti and Śāntideva speak of the detrimental effects of one bodhisattva becoming angry at another bodhisattva. This could be a case of projecting either real or imaginary faults; it could also be that the angry bodhisattva does not recognize the other person as a bodhisattva, or even if he does, his mind is overpowered due to being habituated with anger. The angry bodhisattva is one who is on the path of accumulation or preparation—that is, he is still an ordinary being who has not realized emptiness directly. Ārya bodhisattvas no longer manifest anger, so this cannot apply to them.

If a higher bodhisattva becomes angry with a lower bodhisattva, it destroys the merit accumulated over one hundred eons through practicing generosity and ethical conduct, making offerings and paying homage to the buddhas, and so forth. In addition he must train in the six perfections for as many eons as he had moments of hatred, harm, and obstinacy toward the other bodhisattva.

If a lower bodhisattva who has not received a prophecy of her awakening becomes angry at a higher bodhisattva who has received a prophecy,[9] even though she does not express the anger physically or verbally, she must wear the armor from the beginning for as many eons as times she held an angry thought. This means, for example, if a bodhisattva who is almost ready to go from the great path of accumulation to the path of preparation becomes angry at a prophesied bodhisattva, she will not progress to that higher path for as many eons as there were moments of anger and she must train in the path from the beginning of the path of accumulation. In addition, she creates the cause to be born in the hells for as many eons as moments of hatred she felt. The *Compendium of All the Weaving* (*Sarvavaidalya-saṃgraha*) says that confessing these faults three times a day for seven years will prevent the ripening of this negative karma, but still ten eons must pass before the bodhisattva is able to progress to the next path.

If a bodhisattva becomes angry at a bodhisattva of equal spiritual attainment, he creates the cause to be born in the hells for as many eons as moments he held hatred for the other bodhisattva. Furthermore, many eons of virtue are destroyed.

If the results of anger toward a bodhisattva are so severe for bodhisattvas, they are much greater for us ordinary beings. When someone who is not a bodhisattva becomes angry at one who is, the virtue created over one thousand eons is undermined. Since we are not always able to identify who is a bodhisattva and who is not, it is to our advantage to restrain our anger toward all beings.

If a bodhisattva becomes angry at a non-bodhisattva, the disadvantages are not as great. For example, the *Lion's Roar of Maitreya Sūtra* (*Maitreya-mahāsiṅhanāda*) says that if a bodhisattva holds animosity toward the number of ordinary beings living in many world systems, and rebukes or strikes them, he does not have to wear the armor from the beginning of the path. Nevertheless, if an ordinary being becomes angry at another ordinary being, their virtue is undermined.

In the *Questions of Upāli Sūtra* (*Upālipariprcchā*) the Buddha said that he does not see the same detrimental effects from other nonvirtues as he does from anger. Anger inhibits the virtue included in the collection of merit. It seems that it does not destroy the virtue from cognizing selflessness, but Tsongkhapa says that this needs to be analyzed further.

The purpose of explaining the disadvantages of anger, especially when it is directed at a bodhisattva, is not to threaten us with suffering or to enforce a hierarchy in which we cannot disagree with a bodhisattva without being punished. The extremely harmful effects of anger described above are a natural result of being hostile toward someone who has dedicated their existence to attaining awakening for the benefit of all sentient beings. The law of karma and its effects is a natural law, like the laws of nature that indicate a barley sprout will grow from a barley seed when the right conditions are present. No one is punishing or threatening us. To the contrary, these teachings were given with compassion, to make us aware of potential harm so that we could avoid it.

With this knowledge, we should do our best to avoid animosity, resentment, belligerence, hatred, and all other forms of anger toward any sentient being and especially toward bodhisattvas. If we hold ill will toward any sentient being, we are the ones who will suffer. What has happened to our mind when we see those who are working to benefit all sentient beings—including us—as enemies? Clearly our mind is in a confused state; such a mental state cannot create the causes for happiness.

Candrakīrti summarized other defects of anger and benefits of fortitude (MMA 34–35):

> It creates an ugly body, leads to the unholy,
> and robs discrimination that knows right and wrong.
> Through non-fortitude (anger), one is quickly cast into a bad
>   migration.
> Fortitude creates qualities opposite to those explained above.
>
> Through fortitude comes beauty,
> dearness to the holy, skill in discriminating
> between the right and wrong, birth afterward as a human or god,
> and the extinguishment of nonvirtues.

Just as a person is unattractive when angry during this life, anger creates the cause to be ugly and repugnant to others in future lives. Let alone be able to benefit others, we will find it difficult to have friends. "The unholy" refers to nonvirtue; anger inclines us toward destructive actions. Anger also makes it difficult to listen to others and to think clearly, which, in turn, impedes our ability to discriminate what to practice and what to avoid. Many people find themselves in prison due to acting under the influence of malice: anger blurred their discrimination between wholesome and unwholesome actions and they engaged in actions that they wouldn't have, had they been thinking clearly. Unfortunate rebirths follow from negative karma as well. Once born in such a rebirth, generating virtuous karma becomes difficult, and that presents many obstacles to taking a fortunate rebirth in the future.

Cultivating the ability to remain calm in the face of suffering and harm leads to the opposite effects. Others find us attractive, we will be close to holy beings, our discriminating wisdom will be keen, future rebirths will be fortunate, and nonvirtues will be eliminated. Understanding this, let's practice the antidotes to anger by cultivating fortitude.

The perfection of fortitude is of three types: (1) fortitude that is undisturbed by harm from others, (2) fortitude of voluntarily accepting suffering, and (3) fortitude of certitude about the Dharma.

The Fortitude That Is Undisturbed by Harm from Others

Anger makes us unhappy. No one is happy when they are angry. Given this, it's quizzical that we tend to hold on to our anger and even bolster it by ruminating on the event that provoked it. It would be much better to release the anger and return to a balanced mental state. Śāntideva tells us (BCA 6.3, 5, 6):

> My mind will not experience peace
> if it fosters painful thoughts of hatred.
> I shall find no joy or happiness;
> unable to sleep, I shall feel unsettled.
>
> By it, friends and relatives are disheartened;
> though drawn by my generosity, they will not trust me.
> In brief, there is nobody
> who lives happily with anger.
>
> Hence the enemy, anger,
> creates sufferings such as these;
> but whoever assiduously overcomes it
> finds happiness now and hereafter.

An American journalist once asked me, "Given the devastation in Tibet and the trauma to your life after 1959 when communist Chinese forces took control of Tibet, how come you aren't angry?" I responded that if I were angry, I couldn't eat or sleep well; I couldn't think clearly, and my happiness would vanish. I think she was puzzled by my reply; many government leaders would have taken the opportunity to speak about the horror of their suffering and to harshly criticize the opposition. But I could not think of even one benefit of being angry at the communist Chinese.

The first type of fortitude involves not retaliating when others harm us, those dear to us, or our possessions. The *Prātimokṣa Sūtra* says:

> Fortitude is the first and foremost path.
> The Buddha regarded this as supreme in his teachings.
> One who has left the household life
> yet annoys others is not called a renunciant.

To abandon retaliating, seeking vengeance, blaming, criticizing, and holding grudges is indeed an austerity for a mind that selfishly sees our own happiness as foremost. In fact, we are unhappy and miserable when anger rules our mind, and in turn, our actions make others unhappy. For these reasons, cultivating fortitude brings peaceful liberation from the scourge of anger.

Practicing fortitude challenges us to avoid judging others, abandon becoming angry at whatever we do not like, and look at others' harmful actions in a new light. This does not mean ignoring or rationalizing others' harm, misdeeds, or mistakes. Rather, we look inside ourselves and investigate why anger arises. Instead of believing that anger is the only way to react to situations we don't like or speech we disagree with, we question our anger and research what button was pushed so we can begin to handle such circumstances. Dealing with the situation with a clear, calm mind is more effective.

Some people doubt, "Isn't it justified to become angry at someone who harms us or those we care about?" Distinguishing between an action and the person who does the action is essential. While we can say an action is harmful, wrong, or inappropriate, saying that the person who did it is evil and despicable is mistaken. That person has the potential to become a buddha. They wish to be happy and to overcome suffering. Their mistakes and destructive actions do not negate their good qualities. In fact, once their harmful behavior stops, they may later become our friend. The real troublemaker is the afflictions that make them act in harmful ways. Those afflictions harm them as much as, if not more than, they harm us.

We can censure an action without hating the person who did it. For example, we Tibetans fight the injustice of the Chinese communists, but

I am not against them as human beings, even those who are ruthless. I cultivate genuine compassion for them, although I still oppose their actions. It is possible to point out a person's harmful behavior or negative qualities and at the same time respect them as a human being. By acting in this way, there is no danger of creating negative karma. As always, our motivation is key. Speaking out of hatred or desire for revenge is wrong. However, if we know that by not speaking out their destructive behavior will continue and we remain silent, that is also wrong. It is incumbent on us to release destructive thoughts and emotions and strive to communicate clearly with the other person.

The Buddha recommended that, because we cannot be sure who is a bodhisattva and who is not, avoiding criticizing anyone is the best policy. In that light, Mao Zedong can be seen as a bodhisattva; I view him in my own mind on a private level in that way and do not hate him. But in terms of Tibet and the well-being of the Tibetan people, I cannot say Mao's policies were good—they destroyed our religion and our country! There is no conflict between these two views. In fact, when I consider the karmic results he will experience as a result of the harm he caused us Tibetans as well as the Chinese people, I can only feel compassion.

Some people believe that practicing fortitude and being compassionate means our external actions must always be passive and pleasing. That is incorrect. In certain circumstances, passive behavior can be harmful—for example, not interceding to stop harm when it is possible to do so with a good motivation. Refraining from anger does not mean we don't protect ourselves or that we allow another person to do dreadful actions. The point is that it is not necessary to be angry in order to divert harm. We should use our creative abilities to think of solutions to problems rather than flying into a rage.

"Righteous anger," as people usually think of it, doesn't mean that our anger has suddenly become virtuous. If it did, since we always believe our view is correct, then all our anger would become virtuous! The problem, however, is that everyone else in the situation thinks that their view is correct, which makes everyone's anger virtuous!

If we discern the difference between our internal emotions and external actions, we'll see that it's possible to internally feel compassion for someone who is harming us or others, yet externally act in an assertive manner to quell the harm. There is no malice in our mind. In certain situations, the skillful way to benefit others could involve acting aggressively, motivated by such "righteous anger." It is extremely important, however, to ensure that no malevolence or spite pollutes our motivation, for if it did, we would have succumbed to actual anger, which is an affliction. "Righteous anger" is not biased toward our own side, and we should not use "righteous anger" as an excuse to mask a very real sense of hostility inside ourselves.

The fierce-looking tantric deities exemplify the possibility of forceful actions done with compassion. They also symbolize taking strong action against our own anger and negative emotions. That doesn't mean suppressing or repressing our anger or feeling guilty for having anger. Rather, they symbolize wisdom that recognizes the disadvantages and dangers of our own anger and wrath and wants to overcome them.

When any of the usual antidotes fail to quell our anger, a skillful method to deal with it is to generate ourselves as a fierce deity (if we have the proper empowerment) and be aggressive toward our own anger. When doing this, it's important to remember that our anger is not us; the force is directed toward the anger plaguing our mind, not toward us as a human being. Once the anger has been subdued, we can choose whatever is the best way to communicate with the other persons(s). We may choose to use forceful speech, but it is backed by compassion, not malice. Transforming the energy of anger in such a way is a technique unique to Vajrayāna.

In the Pāli canon, the Buddha advised Śakra, the lord of the gods, when he asked the Buddha, "Whose killing do you approve?" (SN 11.21):

> Having slain anger, one sleeps soundly; having slain anger, one does not sorrow;
> the killing of anger with its poisoned root and honeyed tip:
> this is the killing the ariyas praise for having slain that, one does not sorrow.

In the same text (SN 11.22) the Buddha tells the story of a grotesque *yakṣa* (nature spirit) who sat on the seat of Śakra. Horrified by this audacity, the other gods threw malicious criticism at the yakṣa. But with each nasty word spoken, the yakṣa did not budge, but grew more and more handsome. Finally Śakra himself came, and kneeling before the yakṣa, he put his palms together reverentially and humbly introduced himself. As Śakra uttered each word of the introduction, the yakṣa became uglier and more grotesque until he disappeared on the spot. It's truly amazing what kindness can accomplish.

When someone harms us and then, realizing his error, sincerely apologizes, it is crucial that we forgive him and do not hold a grudge. Continuing to remind the person of his error or secretly wishing for harm to befall him runs counter to the bodhisattva spirit. Nursing a grudge also may impair our physical health and our mental well-being, not to mention creating destructive karma. The Buddha says (SN 11.24):

> There are two kinds of fools: one who does not see a transgression as a transgression; and one who, when another is confessing a transgression, does not pardon him in accordance with the Dhamma... There are two kinds of wise people: one who sees a transgression as a transgression; and one who, when another confesses a transgression, pardons him in accordance with the Dhamma.

Forgiveness—letting go of anger—is an important quality that leads to our own and others' well-being. The more we practice fortitude, the easier it will become to release grudges and feel tranquil in our hearts about events that previously caused us pain.

As for other antidotes to counter anger, please refer to those that Buddhaghosa proposed in chapter 1 of *In Praise of Great Compassion*, which are almost identical to those Śāntideva spelled out in chapter 6 of *Engaging in the Bodhisattvas' Deeds*. Also refer to the section on transforming adversity into the path in chapter 10 on mind training in *In Praise of Great Compassion*. Please read Śāntideva's text as well as *Healing Anger* and *Working with Anger*, which are commentaries on it.

Reading will give you new ideas of how to look at situations, but change comes through applying those ideas in your meditation practice. Recalling previous situations in which your anger flared up and then applying these new perspectives familiarizes you with them. Slowly these new perspectives will become a natural way to view interactions with others, and you'll find that you get angry less often and even when you do, you can resolve it in your mind more quickly. This requires practice—there are no shortcuts and you can't hire someone else to change your mind—so with an awareness of the benefits, work with your mind.

REFLECTION

Fortitude (patience) is the ability to remain undisturbed in the face of harm or suffering. It does not entail being passive. Rather, it gives the clarity of mind necessary to choose with wisdom whether to act or not to act.

1. If someone points out a fault you have or accuses you of doing something you didn't do, there's no reason to get angry. Acknowledge your faults and mistakes, just as you acknowledge having a nose if someone points that out. On the other hand, if someone blames you for something you didn't do, it's as if they said you have horns on your head. There's no reason to be angry over an accusation that is untrue; simply give them the correct information.

2. Bring to mind a recent situation where you and another were in conflict. Examine how you got involved in the situation. This has two parts:
   - What actions did you do recently to prompt the disagreement? Examining this helps to understand why the other person is upset.
   - Recognize that unpleasant situations are due to your having harmed others earlier this life or in previous lives. Seeing this as the principal cause, learn from past mistakes and resolve to act differently in the future.

3. Examine the disadvantages of anger and grudge holding.

4. Recognize that the other person's unhappiness and confusion is making him harm you. Since you know what it's like to be unhappy, empathize and have compassion for him.

The Fortitude of Voluntarily Accepting Suffering

Physical and mental pain will arise in our lives—it's a natural occurrence for beings like us in saṃsāra. There is no escaping it, but Dharma practitioners can take these experiences into the path by practicing the fortitude of voluntarily accepting suffering. This does not entail gritting our teeth while repressing our anger and fear, but rather actively transforming the situation and using it to develop positive qualities.

For example, when experiencing the physical pain from illness or injury or the mental pain from injustice or betrayal, remember that this pain is the result of causes—the destructive karma you created. The bacteria, virus, car, weapon, or other person is the cooperative condition; if we hadn't created the principal cause—harming others motivated by the self-centered attitude—the painful result would not have occurred. This is not blaming the victim or saying that someone with a severe illness caused themselves to be ill; saying such things is certainly not compassionate! Rather, it means that actions done in a previous life can bear results in this life. The fact that you have good health care and skilled health care professionals who help you is a result of virtuous karma created in previous lives.

Our karma doesn't make others behave the way they do; it doesn't make them harm us. Their afflictions cause them to harm others, and they are responsible for those actions. We suffer in a certain situation because our previously-created karma ripens at that time, but that karma is not what made others harm us. Our karma causes our suffering in a situation, but others' afflictions cause their actions. Do not have a fatalistic attitude toward karma, thinking that events are predetermined. You can and should act to prevent harm or intervene while harm is occurring, but don't do that motivated by anger.

If we respond to suffering with anger, our actions create the causes to experience pain again in the future. If we refrain from anger, the previous destructive karma is exhausted and constructive karma from practicing fortitude is created. Understanding this helps us to accept our present experience and to be more conscientious and mindful of our actions in the future. In addition, considering that this destructive karma could have ripened in a series of horrible rebirths, undergoing a much smaller suffering in this life becomes acceptable.

It is possible to willingly and even happily bear suffering. For example, a woman in labor willingly bears the pain because she wants the baby. Someone who is ill voluntarily bears injections or even surgery, knowing that it will bring about healing. We have the capacity to bear suffering patiently without becoming angry or resentful because we know that doing so will prevent future suffering and will enable us to progress on the path to awakening, a state free from all duḥkha whatsoever.

Usually we think that suffering has no benefit at all. However, although we definitely should not deliberately bring misery to ourselves, when it does arrive unasked, contemplating its benefits helps us to avoid increasing our suffering by falling into anger and despair. For example, suffering can strengthen our determination to be free from saṃsāra because we understand that as long as we're in saṃsāra, such suffering will occur. Suffering also can dispel conceit and make us a kinder and humbler person. While crushing our arrogance isn't necessarily pleasant, it is beneficial—as we're happier and have better relationships when we don't consider ourselves above others.

Undergoing misery also opens our hearts in compassion to others who are in similar situations. We understand them better, and sharing a common experience, we feel closer to them. We begin to care about their suffering as much as we care about our own, and in our heart we begin to understand that suffering is to be eliminated; it doesn't matter whose it is.

When practicing the Dharma, on occasion we may have to go through hardship while relinquishing habitual harsh speech or other bad habits and not acting according to our dysfunctional emotional habits. We may be very attached to certain things, thinking that we *must* have them. When we begin to let go of such craving, mental uneasiness may arise. At other times we may lack food, clothing, shelter, or companions. It is important to be able to face such hardship and strengthen our mind by continuing to practice the Dharma. With the fortitude of voluntarily accepting suffering, we accept the short-term difficulties of this life without despair because we have a higher aim and purpose. Our determination is strong, as Śāntideva counsels (BCA 6.9,10):

> Whatever befalls me,
> I shall not disturb my mental joy;

> for having been made unhappy, I shall not accomplish what I wish, and my virtues will decline.
>
> Why be unhappy about something
> if it can be remedied?
> And what is the use of being unhappy about something
> if it cannot be remedied?

The last verse makes so much sense, but we need to stop and reflect on it during times of stress, strife, and other problematic events. If we can do something about a painful situation, let's do it. There's no reason to complain, blame, or be upset and angry. On the other hand, if there's nothing we can do to remedy the situation, let's accept it, maintain a balanced mind, and turn our attention to something useful where we can contribute to the well-being of others.

REFLECTION

1. Contemplate the benefit you can derive from voluntarily accepting suffering:
    - Your understanding of the disadvantages of saṃsāra will increase and, along with that, so will your renunciation of saṃsāra's suffering and your aspiration to be free from saṃsāra.
    - You will understand the experience of others who are suffering so your compassion will increase.
2. Ask yourself, "Can I do something about it?" If you can, anger is out of place because you can improve the situation. If you can't, anger is useless because nothing can be done.
3. Reflect that karma that could have brought long-lasting and intense suffering in an unfortunate rebirth is now ripening as something that you can easily accept and endure.

The Fortitude of Certitude about the Dharma

Understanding the vast and profound meanings of the Dharma is not easy, but cultivating the fortitude of gaining certitude about the Dharma—also called the fortitude of definitely thinking about the Dharma—makes it easier. This fortitude gives us the ability to happily continue to learn and practice for however long it takes in order to fathom the Dharma's deep and detailed meanings.

Meditation on emptiness challenges the very root of our self-grasping ignorance, which puts up a fight when its sovereignty is challenged. It is said that when one first has a glimpse of the emptiness of true existence, fear arises in the mind and one wants to withdraw from that experience. It is important at this time not to capitulate to the fear and to continue meditating on emptiness.

The fortitude of practicing the Dharma brings appreciation for the bodhisattvas' activities and strengthens the wish to become bodhisattvas ourselves. Fear and resistance may arise all along the path because the Dharma challenges our dearly held but afflictive assumptions, preconceptions, and prejudices. It takes fortitude not to retreat into habitual emotions and behavior that are the very source of our misery, and instead to arouse courage and continue to practice.

By cultivating the fortitude of practicing the Dharma, we will learn, reflect, and meditate on the teachings, and by doing so we gain certainty in the meaning of the teachings. This conviction is gained through reflecting on the qualities of the Three Jewels, of the path, and of the awakened state; by contemplating the selflessness of persons and of phenomena; and by delving into the meaning of the profound and vast scriptures. In this way, our confidence in the Dharma will grow, enabling us to integrate it in our lives.

While the fortitude of not being disturbed by others' harm can only be practiced when someone harms us, the fortitude of practicing the Dharma can be practiced at other times—for example, when we don't feel like doing the practices we have promised to do, when a teaching is going on for a long time, or when we are studying a difficult passage or concept in the scriptures. At such times, the fortitude of voluntarily accepting hardship and of practicing the Dharma is useful to get us over the bumps in the road.

In the *Bodhisattva Grounds*, Asaṅga specified eight objects to cultivate certitude on:

1. The *object of faith and confidence* is the excellent qualities of the Three Jewels.
2. The *object to be realized* is the emptiness of persons and phenomena.
3. The *object of aspiration* is the magnificent powers of the buddhas and bodhisattvas, such as the power of the superknowledges, the six perfections, and the innate power.
4. The *object to be adopted* is the causal virtuous actions and the resultant attainments.
5. The *object to be abandoned* is the causal misdeeds and their resultant obstacles and duḥkha.
6. The *object of meditation that is the goal to attain* is awakening.
7. The *object of meditation that is the means for attaining the goal* includes the training paths engaged in with bodhicitta.
8. The *object of further practice through learning and reflection* is the twelve branches of scriptures—all the teachings and meanings contained in them.

Engaging in the Bodhisattvas' Deeds explains the fortitude of definitely thinking about the Dharma as contemplating the impermanent nature and lack of self-power of the causes of duḥkha. For example, although we don't wish to fall ill, sickness arises as a result of causes and conditions. Similarly, although people don't think "I want to be angry" and anger doesn't think "I will arise," when the causes and conditions come together anger arises in our mind. All the destructive actions we and others do under the influence of afflictions likewise don't think "We will arise"; rather, they come into being because of causes and conditions. They have no self-power.

For example, someone rear ends our car at a stoplight. Did the car think "I will hit the vehicle in front of me"? Did the driver have that intention? When we become angry and shout at the other driver because our car is dented, do we think "I'm going to become as angry as possible"? When the other driver becomes angry because he was shouted at and blamed for something that was an accident, did he have the intention "I will get angry too"? All of these components of the situation arose as a result of causes and conditions. None of them arise under their own power. All of them are transient; as soon as their causal energy is exhausted, they too will end.

Perhaps it's easier contemplating this in terms of a toddler. Does a young child have the intention to cry and create a fuss? It happens due to causes and conditions—the external situation and the internal state of the child's mind. When big children—whom we call "adults"—create their version of a fuss, it similarly arises due to causes and conditions. Like the fussy toddler, adults too are under the control of their afflictions, and afflictions arise due to other conditions.

As we gradually build up the fortitude born from reflecting on the Dharma—"Dharma" meaning either reality or the teachings—we become able to tolerate things that we could not tolerate before. Then when a situation occurs in our life, we remember what we have learned before and apply it. For example, our spiritual mentor instructed us on the impermanent nature of all conditioned things. Then, when a dear one dies, we remember that teaching and, applying it to this situation, we accept our friend's death and calm our mind. In other words, this fortitude provides us with deeper resources to draw upon as we go through life, deepen our understanding of the Dharma, and work to benefit others.

The fortitude of the nonarising of phenomena (*anutpattika-dharma-kṣānti*) is the direct realization of emptiness and pertains to the fortitude of certitude about the Dharma. The *King of Concentration Sūtra* (*Samādhirāja Sūtra*) says (SR 6.8, 10):

> But if a person maintains a fortitude that is great,
> even were they cut up, for ten million eons,
> into tiny pieces as numerous as the Ganges sands,
> their mind will never regress.
>
> Their fortitude being for the selfless nature of phenomena,
> those who perceive selflessness have no afflictions.
> They know that all phenomena are like space.
> That, therefore, is what is termed "fortitude."

This fortitude also becomes the perfection of wisdom.

Distinguishing Factors of the First Three Perfections

Regarding the perfections of generosity, ethical conduct, and fortitude, Candrakīrti said (MMA 39):

> The Sugata praised mainly the three practices
> of generosity, and so forth [ethical conduct and fortitude] for
> householders.
> These are also the collection of merit, the cause
> of a buddha's form body.

To become a buddha, we need to create the causes for both a buddha's body and a buddha's mind. The first three perfections pertain principally to the collection of merit and are the predominant causes of a buddha's form body. Of course, bodhisattvas also accumulate the collection of wisdom on the first three grounds and integrate wisdom of the ultimate nature with these three perfections by contemplating that the agent engaging in the perfection, the action of that perfection, and the object or recipient of that action are empty of inherent existence. The buddha's form body is of two types: the enjoyment body in which a buddha teaches ārya bodhisattvas in the highest pure land and the emanation body in which a buddha appears in an ordinary form to us ordinary sentient beings.

The perfections of generosity, ethical conduct, and fortitude are easier than the later three perfections for householders to practice. Householder bodhisattvas live active lives in society, and since the first three perfections involve interacting with sentient beings, they are more suitable for householders. Monastic bodhisattvas tend to have a less active life in terms of directly relating to people, so the more introspective practices of meditative stability and wisdom, which are undertaken with joyous effort, are more compatible with their lifestyle. Of course all bodhisattvas—be they householders or monastics—practice all six or ten perfections and attain the same full awakening.

3 | Living as a Bodhisattva: The Remaining Seven Perfections

THE SIX PERFECTIONS can be expanded to become ten because the sixth perfection, wisdom, is said to also include the four perfections of skillful means, unshakable resolve, power, and pristine wisdom. Having spoken of generosity, ethical conduct, and fortitude in the previous chapter, we will now turn to the remaining seven perfections: joyous effort, meditative stability, wisdom, skillful means, unshakable resolve, power, and pristine wisdom.

The Perfection of Joyous Effort

The perfection of joyous effort is a mind that takes delight in developing virtuous qualities. It does not refer to effort in general, because people may make great effort to accomplish nonvirtuous aims and that is definitely not included here!

Joyous effort is extremely important because it enables us to engage in difficult work or sustained Dharma practice and bring it to fruition. By assessing an activity well before committing to do it, and then once committed, carrying it through to completion, our confidence will increase and become stable. In addition, practices or tasks that were previously difficult will become easier because we are now familiar with them, and with sustained joyous effort, we will be able to accomplish them. Joyous effort enables our spiritual development to progress smoothly as we gradually gain realizations of the path. As Candrakīrti said (MMA 41ab):

> All attainments follow after effort,
> the cause of the two collections of merit and wisdom.

Once our goal of buddhahood is clearly understood, we have more energy to attain it. When it is not very clear, laziness easily sneaks in. To remedy this, think about the qualities of awakening and the possibility to attain it. This will inspire our effort to fulfill the two causes of full awakening, the collections of merit and wisdom.

The joyous effort that takes delight in mental transformation and the bodhisattvas' practices enables us to easily fulfill the two collections. Because these two are the essential causes to attain the truth body and form body of a buddha, joyous effort is said to be the source of all auspicious attainments.

At initial stages of practice, your ability to practice is naturally weak, but with repeated practice your capacity will increase. When it becomes strong, you will look back at your original state and see that what initially seemed almost impossible has now become possible and you have accomplished what you did not think you could. Your inner capabilities have grown through the passage of time because you made effort.

For example, at the beginning, engaging in just one practice on the method side of the path—let's say subduing your anger through the practice of fortitude—may seem almost inconceivable; let alone doing a practice in which method and wisdom are combined, by contemplating that you, your anger, the action of being angry, and the person you're angry at are empty of inherent existence but exist dependently. However, as you joyfully put energy into cultivating one good quality, then another, and another, you will eventually be able to do a practice of combined wisdom and method. Each new quality will increase your capacity, and because you remain steadfast and continue to practice, your progress will increase exponentially and realizations will automatically dawn.

A mind with joyous effort is very confident, and bodhisattvas cultivate three types of confidence:

(1) With *confidence in action*, they are prepared to act alone without others' help. This confidence enables bodhisattvas to do solitary retreat and to engage in vast actions to benefit sentient beings without feeling insecure. This confidence additionally boosts them to complete whatever projects, studies, or retreats they begin.

(2) With *confidence in their capacity* to work for others, bodhisattvas engage in beneficial activities without self-doubt or hesitation. This confidence arises from understanding, "Other sentient beings are under the influence of afflictions and can't accomplish their own welfare. I've seen the harm of afflictions and won't let myself be influenced by them, so I am capable of working for the benefit of sentient beings." With firm confidence in their abilities, bodhisattvas are mindful, and by monitoring their mind, they make sure they act in accord with the Dharma.

(3) With the *confidence to oppose afflictions*, bodhisattvas are determined not to allow themselves to fall under the sway of afflictions. Highly motivated to progress on the path, they combat afflictions whenever they arise.

The stages of the path literature speaks of three types of the perfection of joyous effort:

(1) *Armor-like joyous effort* is enthusiasm for learning, reflecting, and meditating on the Dharma that enables you to do these three without falling prey to the laziness of procrastination, the laziness of pursuing meaningless activities, and the laziness of discouragement. Armor-like joyous effort is bold so that bodhisattvas take a long-term viewpoint and make the determination to dedicate themselves for eons to benefit even one sentient being.

(2) With the *joyous effort of acting constructively*, we so deeply aspire to benefit sentient beings that our mind is energetic and delighted to engage in virtuous actions—both those done in meditation and those accomplished by directly relating to sentient beings.

(3) The *joyous effort of benefiting sentient beings* supports us to reach out and help others in need, in particular the eleven groups of sentient beings mentioned in the ethical conduct that benefits others.

The *Ornament of Clear Realizations* speaks of three types of joyous effort that counteract the three types of laziness spoken of in the above section on armor-like joyous effort:

(1) The *joyous effort of not becoming fatigued* opposes the *laziness of sleep, lethargy, and procrastination*. Contemplating death wakes us up to appreciate the opportunity afforded by our present precious human life and dispels the mind that thinks there's plenty of time to practice Dharma later and thus wants to sleep and lounge around now.

(2) The *joyous effort of not being attached to destructive or frivolous actions* counteracts the *laziness attached to worldly activities* that centers around the

happiness of only this life. We are so busy nowadays and are easily distracted by the hustle and bustle of our lives. There's so much to do—career opportunities, exciting people to meet, beautiful places to visit, adventures to have, new digital devices to explore. But in terms of practicing the Dharma, laziness rules because we have no time. What are we busy doing? Thinking about how to get what we want, how to get even with the people who have harmed us, how to get our way, how to win an argument. There is plenty of time to ruminate and to worry, but we can't make time to learn their antidotes. Remembering the disadvantages of cyclic existence jolts us out of this complacent distraction.

(3) The *joyous effort of thoroughly upholding the path* is the counterforce to the *laziness of discouragement*. Discouragement arises by thinking, "I am incapable of practicing the Dharma and will never succeed," "The path is too difficult. It's impossible to accomplish," or "The goal of awakening is too high. I can't attain that." Although these discouraging thoughts seem so real and truthful, if we examine them, we discover that they are false. It's important to monitor this kind of self-talk and refute its nonsensical arguments. It's just another manifestation of the self-centered attitude that sabotages our confidence and abilities.

Discouragement destroys joyous effort. It may arise for several reasons. Sometimes we want to develop a certain skill or to help others, but our work does not turn out as we wished or planned. This happens to me too. But when I recall my motivation, my confidence returns. I began with a sincere desire to benefit. Regardless of what others may say, my motivation was genuine, and knowing that gives me courage and inner strength. If my motivation is pure, even though my activities may not succeed as I would have liked, I still feel satisfied. If I try my best and act with integrity and kindness, even if I fail, it doesn't matter. On the other hand, if my motivation is not sincere and truthful, then even if others praise me and I become famous, inside me discomfort and self-doubt will still be present. If that happens, I have to back up and establish a genuinely compassionate motivation.

It's very important not to dwell in the laziness that is a sense of inferiority, thinking that we're incapable. To overcome this, reflect on the fact that you have the buddha nature—the potential to become a fully awakened, omniscient buddha. Your buddha nature can never be taken away. Also reflect on the marvelous situation of freedom and fortune that you have attained.

Your precious human life provides enough time to practice as well as the proper conditions to do so. By reflecting on this, your despondency will lift.

REFLECTION

1. Which of the three types of laziness do you fall prey to most often?
2. Which types of joyous effort are the antidotes to bolster your strength?
3. Imagine a situation where you apply one or more of the types of joyous effort to overcome that laziness.
4. By imagining this repeatedly, you'll develop the confidence to be able to do it. Make a strong determination to follow up on this.

In *Engaging in the Bodhisattvas' Deeds*, Śāntideva speaks of cultivating four powers to counteract the laziness that inhibits joyous effort. If you suffer from laziness, look into these:

(1) Generate *appreciation of and interest in virtue*. These come through comparing the results of nonvirtue and the results of the bodhisattva deeds. Understanding that the bodhisattva path is long and may entail formidable deeds such as giving away our body in charity, we appreciate and aspire to engage in these practices in the future. But we can approach these activities gradually and do them when we are mentally and physically ready. When we are fully prepared, we will not experience physical pain due to our merit and will not experience mental distress due to our wisdom. Śāntideva shares the vision of what we will be able to do as high level bodhisattvas (BCA 7.28):

> As their bodies are happy due to their merit and
> their minds are happy due to their wisdom,
> even if they remained in saṃsāra for the sake of others,
> why would the compassionate ones ever be upset?

(2) With *steadfastness* we are self-confident and continue whatever virtuous activities we have begun until they are completed. This self-confidence

is not unrealistic, inflated arrogance, but comes from an inner awareness of our buddha nature and the opportunities provided by this precious human life. Śāntideva encourages us (BCA 7.59):

> Whoever seizes self-confidence in order to conquer the enemy of arrogance—
> they are the self-confident ones, the victorious heroes [vanquishing afflictions].
> In addition, whoever definitely conquers the spread of this enemy, arrogance,
> completely [wins] the fruit of a buddha, fulfilling the wishes of the world.

When your mind is realistic and clear-sighted before starting a virtuous activity, you'll be able to restrain impulsivity and carefully assess if you possess the ability, time, knowledge, and other conditions necessary to complete the task. If you do not, then do not commit yourself at this time.

If you start a virtuous practice or project and discontinue it in the middle, neither you nor others will receive the beneficial results that come from completing it. In addition, you will feed the habit of leaving things undone, a habit that will have deleterious effects in this life as well as future lives. If you begin an activity and then see that continuing it would involve acting contrary to your precepts, then back away. Otherwise, carry through whatever you begin.

However, if an unexpected circumstance arises and you are unable to complete the task, notify everyone who is depending on you to finish it. Remembering that others will need to make other plans if you're unable to complete the project, inform them as soon as possible and help them find a replacement.

Steadfastness also includes being firm and counteracting afflictions as they arise, without giving up in despair. Śāntideva recommends (BCA 7.60–62):

> If I find myself amidst a crowd of disturbing conceptions,
> I shall endure them in a thousand ways.

Like a lion among foxes,
I will not be affected by this disturbing host.

Just as people will guard their eyes
when great danger and turmoil occur,
Likewise, I shall never be swayed by the disturbances within my mind,
even at times of great strife.

It would be better for me to be burned,
to have my head cut off and to be killed,
rather than ever bowing down
to those ever-present disturbing conceptions.
So likewise, in all situations, I should do nothing other than what is fit.

Sometimes our mind proliferates with distorted conceptions. Seeing their faults, we remain firm in applying the antidotes. If we cannot do that while in the situation, we excuse ourselves, calm our mind, and then return to work out the situation with those involved.

Being steadfast in the face of dangers, such as the afflictions that can send us to unfortunate rebirths if we give them leeway, we can subdue them. While it may seem easier to give in to the afflictions in order to stop our internal discomfort, in the long-term this is not advisable. Knowing that the storm of afflictions will eventually subside, we avoid making any bad decisions while under their influence. We remain committed to following the correct path to happiness.

(3) With *joy* we consistently and continuously act according to bodhicitta. Just as an elephant scorched by the midday sun in India plunges into a cool pool, with the same joy bodhisattvas are filled with joyous energy when it comes to creating virtue. Rather than impatiently anticipating the goal, they enjoy the process of creating the causes for full awakening. Śāntideva says (BCA 7.64–65):

Although [worldly] people work in order to be happy,
it is uncertain whether or not they will find it.

But how can those whose work itself is joy
find happiness unless they do it?

If I feel that I never have enough sensual objects,
which are like honey smeared on a razor's edge,
then why should I ever feel that I have enough
merit which ripens in happiness and peace?

The image of honey on a razorblade is strong. Who would ever lick such honey, even if it were the most delicious in the world? But following attachment to sensual objects is like doing this; it simply brings problems in this life and creates nonvirtuous karma that ripens in future lives. Remembering our long-term cherished goal of buddhahood, we maintain a joyful mind that doesn't get distracted.

(4) *Rest* is important to maintain a balanced body and mind so that you will be able to benefit sentient beings over a long period of time. When you are tired after engaging in virtuous activities, take a break, rest, and begin again when you feel refreshed. By resting at appropriate times before your joy has dissipated, you'll be refreshed and have great joy and enthusiasm when it is time to begin again.

Some people push themselves to practice, doing this and that virtuous activity until they are so exhausted that they stop doing any Dharma practice at all. This is not wise. We should practice joyfully because we see the benefits of the Dharma, not because we think we "should" or because we are trying to show what good disciples we are. With joyous effort, our capacity will gradually increase. Becoming wisely sensitive to what our body and mind need at any particular time, we will gratefully rest and relax when necessary.

However, if you push yourself to the point of exhaustion, the delight in virtuous activities will evaporate and your joyous effort will vanish. It is essential to be skillful and rest before becoming completely drained, so that you can continue practicing over a long period of time. Learning to become a balanced person by knowing when to take a break and when to continue will prevent the difficulties that come with burnout.

Having completed a virtuous activity or project, rejoice in the merit created and the benefit others have received, and then take a break and rest. In that way, you will be able to engage in subsequent activities with enthusiasm. Śāntideva counsels (BCA 7:67):

> When my strength declines, I should leave whatever I am doing
> in order to be able to continue it later.
> Having done something well, I should put it aside
> with the wish [to accomplish] what will follow.

REFLECTION

Contemplate the four powers to counteract the laziness that inhibits joyous effort. Think of how to integrate these in your life.

1. Generate *appreciation of and interest in virtue*, which come from comparing the results of nonvirtue and the results of the bodhisattva deeds.
2. Cultivate *steadfastness* that gives you the self-confidence to continue whatever virtuous activities you have begun until they are completed. This self-confidence is not unrealistic arrogance but is practical. It comes from an inner awareness of your buddha nature and the opportunities provided by this precious human life.
3. With *joy* consistently and continuously act with bodhicitta.
4. After you have completed a project or when you need a break, take time to *rest* and refresh yourself so you can engage in more virtuous actions and beneficial projects with renewed enthusiasm.

The Perfection of Meditative Stability

In the perfection of meditative stability, concentration or one-pointedness of mind is developed through the nine stages of sustained attention that culminate in serenity (*śamatha, samatha*). One-pointedness is the ability to focus one-pointedly on a chosen object of meditation with mental stability and clarity. The ability to do this exists within us right now, but it is undeveloped. By learning the correct methods to cultivate one-pointedness and practicing them our concentration will increase. The benefits of doing this are great: By focusing more clearly and consistently on virtuous meditation objects without being disrupted by restlessness and laxity, the various meditations we do will more swiftly bring results. For example, by sustaining concentration on impermanence or emptiness, we will be able to break through the ignorance that grasps permanence and inherent existence. By strongly focusing the mind on the experience of compassion, it will become integrated in our mindstream and will arise more easily in the future.

The practice of serenity and the higher meditative absorptions of the form and formless realms are found among both Buddhists and non-Buddhists. However, in the perfection of meditative stability, it becomes a bodhisattva's practice because it is based on refuge in the Three Jewels, motivated by bodhicitta, and aimed at actualizing the wisdom realizing emptiness in order to attain full awakening.

In general, āryas' supramundane path consciousnesses resemble mundane dhyānas in that they contemplate their object with full, single-pointed absorption and their dhyānic factors (investigation, analysis, joy, bliss, and one-pointedness) are as intense as those in the mundane dhyānas. However, they differ from the mundane dhyānas in several significant ways. First, the way they affect the defilements differs. Mundane dhyānas temporarily repress the coarse defilements but do not eliminate their seeds whereas supramundane path dhyānas forever uproot their respective level of defilements and their seeds. Second, their result in terms of rebirth differs. Mundane dhyānas lead to rebirth in the form realm, and the practitioner continues to cycle in saṃsāra; supramundane path dhyānas result in nirvāṇa, perfect freedom from saṃsāra. Third, they differ in terms of their balance of concentration and wisdom. In the mundane dhyānas, concentration is dominant and wisdom is used to analyze the faults of the lower levels of dhyāna and the benefits of the higher level, so that the practitioner will seek the higher level. In the supramundane path dhyānas, concentration and wisdom are balanced. Concentration focuses on emptiness and wisdom realizes it.

To attain serenity, a practitioner must observe ethical conduct, be pure in her habits and behavior, and have joyous effort to continue to cultivate serenity. Once serenity has been attained, a bodhisattva uses it to cultivate insight into emptiness. Through such training, the union of serenity and insight observing emptiness is attained, marking the beginning of the Mahāyāna path of preparation. From there she progresses through the remaining bodhisattva paths to buddhahood.

The higher training in concentration and the perfection of meditative stability were elaborately discussed in the previous volume, *Following in the Buddha's Footsteps*, chapters 6–10. Here is a summary of a few important points.

Residing in an isolated and peaceful place, living a simple lifestyle with few distractions, and being content with what you possess facilitate the development of concentration. While living in the city, you may like to do some serenity meditation every day—that will help your concentration—but do not expect to develop quick or complete results in that milieu. The Buddha described a wide variety of possible meditation objects, so consult your spiritual mentor regarding an appropriate object and then listen to teachings from your spiritual mentor on how to reduce the five hindrances of sensual desire, malice, lethargy and sleepiness, restlessness and regret, and deluded doubt. Also learn the methods to overcome the five faults—laziness, forgetting the meditation object, restlessness and laxity, nonapplication of the antidote, and overapplication of the antidote—by employing the eight antidotes—faith, aspiration, effort, pliancy, mindfulness, introspective awareness, application of the antidotes, and equanimity.

Serenity involves cultivating a mind that can abide one-pointedly on an object. In addition, the mind perceiving that object must be fresh and clear. The two principal hindrances to concentration are mental restlessness, which impedes the stability of the mind—its capacity to remain one-pointedly on the object—and laxity, which impedes the clarity and freshness of the mind. Restlessness arises when the mind is distracted outward toward objects of attachment, and laxity occurs when the mind is withdrawn inside too much.

Detailed instructions describing how to counteract these and other hindrances and how to progress through the nine stages of sustained attention are found in the great treatises. After completing the nine stages of sustained attention, mental pliancy, physical pliancy, physical bliss, and mental bliss are attained, each depending on the preceding one. Based on those, serenity and a mind of the first dhyāna are attained. Practitioners can now choose whether to attain the higher meditative absorptions of the form and formless realms through the mundane path or to contemplate the sixteen aspects of the four truths and unite serenity and insight to attain the supramundane path. The mundane path leads to rebirth in those meditative states that are still within cyclic existence. The supramundane path leads to liberation and full awakening. Almost all Buddhist practitioners choose the supramundane path because they aim for liberation and awakening.

REFLECTION

1. Set up a daily meditation practice. Begin with fifteen minutes and gradually increase the time when you are ready.
2. Instructions on how to set up sessions are in chapter 6 of *The Foundation of Buddhist Practice.* Do analytical meditation, for example meditating on the reflections found in this and other volumes of *The Library of Wisdom and Compassion.* Alternatively, do stabilizing meditation using either the image of the Buddha or the breath as your meditation object, as described in chapters 6 and 7 of *Following in the Footsteps of the Buddha.*

The Perfection of Wisdom

Buddhism emphasizes the development of wisdom, intelligence, and knowledge. This does not mean we must have a high IQ or a college degree to learn the Dharma or to be liberated from cyclic existence. Rather we must be open-minded, have the ability to learn and analyze clearly, be sincere in our spiritual aspirations, and have created sufficient merit. Some people who are neither brainy nor clever have the necessary focus, power, and effort for spiritual advancement. By following their teachers' instructions and practicing properly, they accomplish high levels of the path. Our intelligence and ability to understand can be increased in this life through learning, thinking, and meditating. It is not the case that we are born with a certain level of intelligence that cannot be improved, expanded, and deepened.

The value of developing wisdom is incalculable. In his *Hundred Verses of Wisdom* (*Prajñāśataka*), Nāgārjuna says (LC 212):

> Wisdom is the root of all good qualities
> seen and not yet seen.
> To achieve both of these,
> embrace wisdom.

Āryaśūra praises wisdom in the *Compendium of Perfections* (*Pāramitāsamāsa*, LC 216):

> The ten powers of the sugata, most excellent of strengths,
> all superior activities without parallel,
> and all other collections of virtues in their entirety
> arise based on wisdom as their cause.
>
> The arts and the best treasures in all worlds,
> the variety of sacred learning that is like an eye,
> protections, awarenesses, mantras, and so on,
> the different attributes of the teachings that set these forth,
>
> the multitude of enumerations and the doors to liberation,
> all such types of service to the world
> that display the great power of the bodhisattvas—
> all arise from the power of wisdom.

With compassion, Āryaśūra then points out what hinders us from cultivating wisdom so that with joyous effort we will work to free ourselves from these impediments (LC 218):

> Laziness, indolence, and reliance on bad friends,
> being governed by sleep, no feeling for discernment,
> no interest in the Sage's most sublime wisdom,
> inquiring under the influence of false pride,
>
> lacking the faith to rely on learned persons
> due to attachment to self from feelings of inadequacy,
> the great poison of false concepts that are wrong views—
> these are the causes of confusion.

It's clear why preferring to lie around and do nothing and oversleeping impede the development of wisdom. Contemplating death and impermanence remedies this. Relying on bad friends who encourage us to join them in worldly activities distracts us from what is important. Thinking about the disadvantages of saṃsāra overcomes this. Not having interest in cultivating wisdom, not seeking out qualified spiritual mentors, and the pride of thinking that we already know something when we actually do not—these three prevent us from attending teachings and studying. Contemplating the benefits derived from wisdom will overcome these. Belittling ourselves and telling ourselves that we can't learn or cultivate wisdom stops us from even trying. To counteract this, remember your buddha nature and the opportunities afforded by your precious human life.

Use the above methods to chip away at and finally abolish these hindrances. Then engage in the three types of the perfection of wisdom:

(1) The *wisdom understanding the ultimate*, emptiness, abolishes all obscurations.

(2) The *wisdom understanding the conventional* involves learning five fields of traditional knowledge—logic, grammar and poetry, medicine, the arts, and self-knowledge. To communicate with and teach others, we must have knowledge of worldly topics so that we can teach the Dharma using contemporary language and examples. By understanding grammar and poetry we can express ourselves well; with knowledge of medicine we will be able to assuage sentient beings' physical suffering in this life; with knowledge of the arts and sciences we'll arouse others' interest in self-knowledge. Today bodhisattvas may also want to learn communication and mediation skills, computer science, neuroscience, psychology, cultural anthropology, sociology, physics, biology, and other topics. In short, bodhisattvas learn whatever is useful for benefiting sentient beings.

(3) The *wisdom understanding how best to work for the benefit of sentient beings* is skilled in the diverse ways to benefit sentient beings. With it, bodhisattvas reach out to all beings to help them with both worldly and spiritual concerns. This wisdom is effective in working with the eleven types of beings mentioned in the ethical conduct of benefiting sentient beings.

The wisdom understanding the ultimate is emphasized because it is the key to awakening and the only way to free ourselves and others from saṃsāra. This perfection of wisdom is an ārya bodhisattva's direct perceiver of emptiness that is supported by the method side of the path (bodhicitta). While those who have not entered the bodhisattva path may gain nondual wisdom and actualize the paths of śrāvakas or solitary realizers, theirs is not the perfection of wisdom, which arises only after generating bodhicitta. This wisdom will be the principal topic of future volumes of the *Library of Wisdom and Compassion*.

The Buddha explained sixteen aspects of the four truths. Of the four aspects of the truth of duḥkha, two are emptiness and selflessness. The meaning of these has different interpretations according to the four tenet systems—the Vaibhāṣika, Sautrāntika, Yogācāra (Cittamātra), and Madhyamaka. Here we will follow the Madhyamaka view, and among its two branches—Svātantrika and Prāsaṅgika—we will explain the latter. Through combining the method aspect of the path (exemplified but not limited to the aspiration to be free from saṃsāra, compassion, and bodhicitta) and the wisdom aspect of the path (the realization of emptiness and selflessness according to the Prāsaṅgika view), we will attain full awakening, which does not abide in either cyclic existence or the pacification of saṃsāra that is an arhat's nirvāṇa. Maitreya says in the *Ornament of Clear Realizations* (LC 2.19):

> Through wisdom you do not abide in cyclic existence.
> Through compassion you do not abide in [an arhat's] peace.

The Madhyamaka, or Middle Way, texts explain ultimate truth—the emptiness or lack of inherent existence—and describe how realizing emptiness acts as the main and final counterforce that eliminates grasping inherent existence.

Interestingly, scientists are now reaching similar conclusions about the ultimate nature of phenomena. For example, physicists studying quantum theory are sometimes hesitant to use the term "absolute reality" because it connotes that things exist independently, from their own side. Through investigation, scientists have been unable to find such independent or inherent existence, because everything exists in dependence on the observer and a multiplicity of other factors. Instead of saying "absolute reality," they now say "probability." It will be interesting to see in which ways Buddhist reasoning and meditative experience and scientific investigation will approach the same point. But whether scientists will meditate on the view of the emptiness of inherent existence and attain awakening remains to be seen!

The Three Understandings

The three understandings (three wisdoms) are those arisen from learning (studying or hearing), reflecting (thinking, contemplating), and meditating. They come into play with respect to all Dharma topics and are especially important when we seek to realize emptiness. These three are the mental factor of wisdom (*prajñā*) and are developed progressively, beginning with the understanding arisen from learning, progressing to the understanding arisen from reflection, and finally the understanding arisen from meditation. When advancing to the next one, however, we do not abandon the previous understandings but continue to develop them. The example of cultivating the understanding of emptiness clarifies how this works.

The *understanding arisen from learning* comes through hearing and/or studying teachings, for example on emptiness. In the case of someone who is newly cultivating the understanding of emptiness, the understanding arisen from hearing is essential to developing the later wisdoms; we must first learn about emptiness before we can think or meditate on it. Here we hear the reasonings that prove that all phenomena lack inherent existence. We learn the three criteria of a syllogism—the property of the subject, pervasion, and counter-pervasion—and begin to counteract doubts by gaining a general understanding of them. After some time, we will gain a correct assumption of the meaning of emptiness.[10] For example, we hear the syllogism "Consider the I, it is empty of inherent existence because it is a dependent arising." The property of the subject is that the I is a dependent arising; the pervasion is that whatever is a dependent arising is necessarily empty of inherent existence; the counter-pervasion is that whatever is not empty is necessarily not dependent arising.

In the case of someone who has previously understood emptiness, hearing teachings on it can trigger the previous understanding or spark a new understanding to arise in her mind. In that latter case, the understanding arisen from learning can induce a reliable cognizer of emptiness as in the story of the monk who realized emptiness while listening to his spiritual mentor's discourse on it.

The *understanding arisen from reflection* is present when an inferential reliable cognizer of emptiness is generated based on ascertainment of the three criteria of a correct syllogism. This understanding is very powerful. Practitioners continue to meditate on emptiness based on this inferential understanding, and when they attain serenity focused on emptiness, the *understanding arisen from meditation* is present. This understanding comes from meditative experience and enables practitioners to develop deep familiarity with emptiness, such that the realization of emptiness arises easily in their minds. As they continue to practice, they reach a point when the analysis of the nature of existence induces special pliancy and serenity. At this time, the union of serenity and insight on emptiness is attained. According to the *Ornament of Clear Realizations*, a fully qualified insight observing emptiness and a union of serenity and insight observing emptiness are synonymous, and they mark the beginning of the path of preparation.

Depending on her level of spiritual development, one person may have these three understandings present in her mind at different times. For example, during and after listening to teachings, the understanding arisen from hearing is present. If the practitioner has already thought a great deal about emptiness, the understanding arisen from reflection may also be present at that time. Otherwise, it is developed when she debates and discusses the Dharma and gains a correct inference of emptiness. Based on that inference, she cultivates single-pointed meditation on emptiness and gains deep familiarity with it. This is the understanding arisen from meditation.

Space-Like and Illusion-Like Meditation on Emptiness

Meditation on emptiness on the ārya paths is of two kinds. The first is *space-like meditation*, which is āryas' actual meditative equipoise on emptiness. This is preceded by gaining the correct view of the Middle Way, free from the extremes of absolutism and nihilism. Absolutism is the view that all phenomena exist inherently; nihilism is the view that phenomena are totally nonexistent or that the law of karma and its results is nonexistent. Space-like meditation on emptiness is the wisdom realizing the selflessness of persons and phenomena in nondual meditative equipoise.

The second type of ārya meditation on emptiness is *meditation on the illusory nature of phenomena*, which is cultivated subsequent to sessions of space-like meditation. Through it comes the wisdom understanding that although things appear to exist inherently, they do not. Like illusions, phenomena do not exist in the way they appear.

The selflessness of persons and the selflessness of phenomena is usually explained in the context of space-like meditation. Since the selflessness of persons is easier to realize, it is explained first. Although the term "self" often refers to the person—the mere I that exists dependently—in the term "selflessness," "self" means inherent existence, the object of negation, which does not exist at all. The object of negation in the context of the selflessness of persons is the independent or inherent existence of the person, that is, a person existing from its own side, without depending on its basis of designation—the body and mind—or on the mind designating it. Since no such inherently existent person exists, the object of negation is totally nonexistent, and the wisdom realizing emptiness knows the emptiness of the person.

Before refuting the existence of an inherently existent I, we must first have a sense of what the ignorance grasping an inherently existent I holds as existent. If such an I did exist, what would it be like? To our innate self-grasping ignorance, the I appears as inherently existent, existing under its own power. There seems to be a real ME, a person who is independent of all factors, such as parts and its causes and conditions. It seems to exist independent of the mind perceiving it. An inherently existent I stands alone, with an essence that is seemingly unchanging and indestructible.

But if we reflect using reasoning, we find that even though the I appears to exist inherently, it cannot exist in that way. It is dependent on other factors. I depend on my body and mind, on the causes and conditions that produced me; I do not exist under my own power as a self-enclosed entity. Thus, a discrepancy exists between the way the I appears and the way it exists. By using reasoning, this discrepancy is brought to light and the existence of an inherently existent I is refuted.

Realizing emptiness is not a matter of repeating to ourselves, "The I is empty of inherent existence." We must examine how the I actually exists. If it existed inherently, it would not depend on anything, but we know the I depends on its causes and conditions and is constantly changing.

After gaining insight that the inherently existent I that ignorance apprehends is actually nonexistent, we focus our mind one-pointedly on the mere absence of independent existence of the I. Concentrating on the absence of an independent I is not focusing on nothingness or blankness. We must know the difference between the emptiness of inherent existence and nothingness and keep the mind alert, with clear and strong focus on emptiness. If we are unable to maintain such mindfulness on the emptiness of inherent existence but let our mind slip into focusing on mere nothingness, we may think we are meditating on emptiness, although we are not. Such incorrect meditation on emptiness does not eradicate afflictions, and getting stuck in such a view is dangerous.

To do space-like meditation on emptiness, analyze to discover the emptiness of inherent existence and then focus one-pointedly on it. Atiśa says (LP 56):

> Therefore the Subduer also has said
> that the great ignorance of conceptuality
> makes us fall into the ocean of cyclic existence.
> Resting in nonconceptual stabilization,
> space-like nonconceptuality manifests clearly.

In this context, "conceptuality" refers to inherent existence. Space-like nonconceptuality is free of both the grasping at inherent existence and the appearance of inherent existence. The emptiness of inherent existence is clear, open, and limitless like space. The mind meditating on emptiness is very spacious; it is not cluttered by the appearances of inherently existent objects and is free from discursive conceptualizations of "this and that." There is a sense of tremendous expansiveness and the bliss of freedom from the constraints of self-grasping ignorance.

Meditating on the selflessness of phenomena is similar to meditating on the selflessness of persons—the object of negation (inherent existence) is the same—but the base now is all phenomena other than persons. Because all phenomena—be they impermanent or permanent—depend on the parts that compose them, they do not exist independently. Being dependent, they are empty of independent or inherent existence. For example, the mind is dependent on a continuity of tiny moments of consciousness. Atoms are composed of ever-smaller particles. Emptiness, too, is merely designated by mind and depends on parts. It is not an independently existent absolute that either permeates all phenomena or exists in another dimension. Emptiness is here, right now. In dependence on the emptiness of the table, the emptiness of the chair, and so on, the generality "emptiness" is designated. In dependence on the person, the emptiness of the person exists.

When we do not examine and analyze, things appear to have an independent intrinsic nature from their own side. For example, when meditating on the Buddha, how does he appear? To the innate, non-analytical mind, the Buddha appears as something solid, independent, and objective. Similarly, when meditating on the suffering of sentient beings, sentient beings appear to exist from their own side without depending on anything else. It seems there are sentient beings "out there," unrelated to our mind. This is how things appear to our normal, innate mind that operates in daily activities. This mind does not analyze how things exist. Rather, things appear inherently existent to it, and ignorance accepts this appearance as true.

However, if we investigate the real nature of the Buddha, no independently existent Buddha can be found. The Buddha exists dependently. He depends on causes and conditions, parts, and the mind that designates the term "Buddha" to his aggregates. As you repeatedly investigate how the Buddha or any other object exists, the object of negation will become clearer, and you will be able to refute it. Combining this insight with serenity, the mind then remains one-pointedly focused on the absence of inherent existence. Speaking of how bodhisattvas actually exist, the *King of Concentration Sūtra* says (SR 6.17–19):

> Just as when a person has a child born to him
> and gives the child a name, saying, "This is his name!"
> but that name cannot be found anywhere,
> and that name did not come from anywhere,
>
> in that way the name "bodhisattva" is given,
> but if one seeks for this bodhisattva,
> that name will not be found anywhere.
> One who knows that is a bodhisattva.
>
> The bodhisattvas do not believe in the existence of a self
> any more than that a fire can burn in the middle of the ocean.

> Since they have developed the aspiration for awakening
> they do not have the view that there is a soul within.

In generating the correct view of emptiness, we investigate how persons and phenomena exist using ultimate analysis. That is, we search for the ultimate mode of existence of an object. What is this object really? Through such examination, the inherent existence of the object is not found. This non-finding of an inherently existent object by reasoning analyzing the ultimate does not contradict the conventional existence of the object, because we were investigating the object's ultimate mode of existence, not its conventional existence. In general, with inherent existence refuted, all that remains is a mere nominally existent object, a conventionality. Ultimate analysis does not refute existence; it only refutes inherent existence. It is obvious from our experience that things exist and have their various functions in the world. They exist through the power of imputation.

After meditators arise from space-like meditation on emptiness, the false appearance of inherent existence arises as a result of the latencies of ignorance. Meditators recognize this appearance is false and is like an illusion in that things appear one way but exist in another. This illusion-like meditation on emptiness is done while meditators go about their daily activities such as eating, walking, talking, and so forth. The Buddha says (SR 9.6):

> Bodhisattva mahāsattvas should know that all phenomena are like illusions. They should know that all phenomena are like dreams, like mirages, like echoes, like optical illusions, like the [reflection of the] moon on water, like hallucinations, like reflections, and like space.

Illusion-like meditation helps to avoid getting carried away by all the seemingly attractive and repulsive things that bodhisattvas encounter, and in that way counteracts attachment and anger. Mindfulness of the illusion-like nature reinforces their realization of emptiness and facilitates entering into meditative equipoise on emptiness in future formal meditation sessions.

Whether we practice Pāramitāyāna or Vajrayāna, whether we are on the śrāvaka, solitary realizer, or bodhisattva path, the realization of emptiness is necessary to complete that path. Since śrāvakas and solitary realizers meditate on emptiness to eliminate afflictions and attain liberation, they do not need to accumulate the vast amount of merit that bodhisattvas do. Bodhisattvas' vast accumulation of merit acts as a solid support for cultivating the wisdom realizing emptiness and enables that wisdom to eliminate even the subtle cognitive obscurations from the mind.

Various tenet systems have different views on the selflessness that has to be realized to eliminate the afflictive obscurations. Some systems do not assert a selflessness of phenomena, and claim that afflictive obscurations can be eliminated merely by realizing the selflessness of persons. In actuality, only by following the Madhyamaka view of the emptiness of inherent existence of both persons and phenomena can we generate the kind of wisdom that is capable of removing both the afflictive and cognitive obscurations.

Similarly, all four classes of tantra emphasize the need to generate the correct view of emptiness. In the practice of deity yoga, practitioners meditate on nondual profundity and clarity. Clarity refers to generating themselves as the deity and having a clear visualization of this. At the same time, they meditate on the profound nature of the deity—its emptiness of inherent existence. In this way they have the clear appearance of themselves as the deity and simultaneously reflect that the deity is empty. Based on this and other practices unique to Vajrayāna, it is possible to make manifest an extremely subtle mind that is then used to realize emptiness. The ensuing wisdom becomes a powerful counterforce that removes the afflictions and their latencies forever.

REFLECTION

1. Think of your car (bicycle, subway car, or any other vehicle). Does it appear to be a car by nature—that is, is there something in the object that makes it a car and not a turkey?
2. If it indeed exists in that manner, you should be able to find and draw a line around what is the car. The car must be either identical with one of its parts or with the collection of parts, or completely separate from them. There is no third choice.
3. Look at each part of the car and investigate if it is a car.

4. It is tempting to think the collection of parts is the car, but that would be like having a collection of non-apples and thinking it is an apple.

5. Conclude that the car cannot exist as an inherently existent thing. That absence of inherent existence is its empty, space-like nature.

6. Nevertheless, when you don't analyze, a car appears and you can drive it. It appears but is empty of inherent existence. That is its illusion-like nature.

Serenity and Insight

The ability to concentrate and to discern and investigate things are innate qualities of our mind. We already have some ability to pay attention to and to focus on a chosen object. When we enhance this mental factor of concentration, it can lead to serenity and the deep states of meditative absorption of the form and formless realms. Similarly, we already have some ability to discern various characteristics. When increased and refined, this leads to insight and wisdom. Mindfulness, introspective awareness, and effort are needed to do this, and because these mental factors and the mental factors of concentration and wisdom are conditioned phenomena, it is possible to develop and enhance them through practice.

In general, serenity and insight are common to all ancient Indian traditions. What makes them unique in Buddhism is that they are cultivated following the teachings and guidance of the awakened Buddha, his teachings (the Dharma), and his disciples (the Saṅgha) who have realized the nature of reality. In addition, they are directed toward realizing selflessness and eliminating both the afflictive and the cognitive obscurations.

Both serenity and insight are needed to generate meditative equipoise that realizes selflessness. Serenity brings stability and deep meditative concentration, while insight probes, investigates, and ascertains the ultimate nature of phenomena. Without serenity we are unable to focus single-pointedly on emptiness, and without insight we are unable to discern emptiness clearly. A union of the two is needed to realize emptiness directly and to empower that realization so that it can overcome our mental defilements.

Serenity (*śamatha*, *samatha*) is a concentration (*samādhi*) arising from meditation and accompanied by the bliss of mental and physical pliancy (*praśrabdhi*, *passaddhi*) in which the mind abides effortlessly and without fluctuation, for as long as we wish on whichever virtuous object it has been placed. Serenity is cultivated through the higher training in concentration, and for those following the bodhisattva vehicle by the practice of the perfection of meditative stability.

Serenity is necessarily the mental factor of concentration, but all concentrations are not necessarily serenity, because the mental factor of concentration is also found in the nine sustained attentions preceding the attainment of serenity. Of the two types of meditation—stabilizing (*sthāpyabhāvanā*) and analytical (*vicārabhāvanā*)—serenity is necessarily stabilizing meditation.

Insight (*vipaśyanā*, *vipassanā*) is a wisdom of discerning or analytical discrimination (*so sor rtog pa'i shes rab*) of phenomena conjoined with special pliancy induced by the power of analysis. It is an analytical wisdom that may be either conceptual or nonconceptual, and it may be either mundane or supramundane. The next several chapters speak specifically about how to cultivate supramundane insight that is focused on emptiness and leads to liberation and awakening.

Insight is a special "seeing." It is a mental factor that thoroughly analyzes phenomena and clearly distinguishes their features. Developed by practitioners of all three vehicles—the Śrāvaka, Solitary Realizer, and Bodhisattva Vehicles—insight is necessarily a wisdom consciousness. Of the two types of meditation, it is analytical meditation.

In general, serenity and insight are mental factors that are mutually exclusive; that is, there is nothing that is both of them. Concentration and wisdom are also distinct mental factors. But the higher training of concentration does not refer to just the mental factor of concentration. That is, when "concentration" is used with other words or in other phrases it may refer to a specific meditative state. For example, the *Heart Sūtra* (*Prajñāpāramitāhṛdaya Sūtra*) recounts that the Buddha was meditating on the "concentration of the countless aspects of phenomena called Profound Illumination."

While serenity and insight are lofty mental states that have specific attributes, various virtuous mental states may fall under the general category of one or the other. Tsongkhapa explains (LC 3:14):

> However, concentrations that at least involve single-pointedness on a virtuous object are classified with serenity; virtuous cognitions that distinguish an ultimate or conventional object are classified with insight.

Although these mental states may not be full-fledged serenity or insight, by cultivating them over time they will become so.

A practitioner who seeks liberation and has generated the union of serenity and insight in his or her mind is called a "yogī" or "yoginī." In some Dharma centers, anyone who attends a meditation retreat is called a "yogī." Perhaps this is done to inspire people to become actual yogīs, but if misunderstood, it could be misleading. The realizations of actual yogīs greatly exceed our own understanding.

Serenity must be generated before insight, even though someone may have an inferential realization of emptiness before attaining serenity. Tsongkhapa says (LC 3:95–96):

> If you do not first establish in your mindstream the concentration of serenity explained previously, it is not possible for the actual knowledge of insight, which is focused on either the ultimate nature or the diversity of all phenomena, to arise...
>
> In summary, you must first develop serenity and then on this basis, you may proceed on a graduated path up the peak of cyclic existence by means of insight bearing the aspect of grossness and peacefulness; or you may proceed along the five paths to liberation or omniscience by means of insight bearing the aspect of the reality of selflessness. This constitutes the general seal of the Conqueror's teachings, so no yogī can depart from it.

Without serenity, neither mundane nor supramundane insight can be attained. Mundane insight traverses the four dhyānas of the form realm and the four formless realm absorptions. Here a practitioner progresses by contemplating the peacefulness of the next level of meditative absorption and the grossness of their present level. This insight—which is common to Buddhists and non-Buddhists alike—leads to the peak of cyclic existence, the highest stage of saṃsāra, but not to liberation. While these meditative absorptions are very pleasing and it is tempting to rest in them without cultivating insight, all Buddhist teachers warn us against this. In his *Praise in Honor of One Worthy of Honor* (*Varṇāhavarṇastotra*), Mātṛceṭa says (LC 3:95):

> Those opposed to your (the Tathāgata's) teachings
> are blinded by affliction.
> Even after venturing to the peak of cyclic existence,
> duḥkha occurs again, and cyclic existence is maintained.
> Those who follow your teachings—
> even if they do not achieve actual dhyāna—
> turn away from cyclic existence,
> while under the steady gaze of the eyes of Māra.

Even if the Buddha's disciples do not immediately attain dhyāna, they bear in mind the disadvantages of cyclic existence and enrich the determination to be free from it in their minds. As they continue to practice, they will attain access concentration[11] to the first dhyāna as well as the other dhyānas that they can then conjoin with insight. This supramundane insight is focused on emptiness and leads to liberation and awakening.

The Importance of Insight

Direct realization of emptiness is necessary to remove both the afflictive and the cognitive obscurations and to attain liberation and full awakening. Although the aspiration to be free from saṃsāra, bodhicitta, and concentration are necessary qualities to gain awakening, they are not sufficient for its attainment. Only the wisdom gained from insight into emptiness has the power to cut ignorance, the root of saṃsāra. While learning about selflessness and cultivating the right view, we may use antidotes specific to each affliction to pacify it temporarily. However, these antidotes do not have the ability to remove an affliction from its root, nor does the antidote for one affliction necessarily overcome another. For example, meditating on love or patience can temporarily subdue anger, but it cannot completely eliminate the seed or potential for future anger from the mindstream. In addition, meditating on love or patience does not counteract attachment, just as meditating on the unpleasant aspects of the object—the antidote to attachment—does not lessen our anger.

Concentration and serenity are necessary to enhance all other Dharma practices. However, they are not uniquely Buddhist practices and may be gained by those of other faiths. Concentration and serenity alone cannot bring liberation because they are not combined with the wisdom realizing the emptiness of inherent existence and thus cannot cut the ignorance that grasps inherent existence. Our mind may be very peaceful and blissful while in a concentrated state because disturbing attitudes and negative emotions have been temporarily suppressed. However, because their seeds have not been removed from our mindstream, once our meditation ends, these afflictions can and will surface again.

We may gain many good qualities and even superknowledges as a result of concentration, but the danger exists of seeing these qualities as an end in themselves, which could possibly cause us to become arrogant. Such pride is a huge obstacle on the path. To avoid these pitfalls, before practicing serenity we must clearly understand that the purpose of doing so is to use it as a basis for generating insight into emptiness, and that insight and wisdom are the qualities that will liberate us from the two obscurations.

In the past, and even today, some people believe that blank-minded meditation leads to liberation. They advocate clearing all thoughts—be they correct or incorrect, beneficial or harmful—from the mind and abiding in contentless state. Such a state, however peaceful it may be, is neither liberation nor realization of emptiness. Why? Nothingness is not the meaning of emptiness, and focusing the mind single-pointedly on it is not the realization of the lack of inherent existence. Although nonconceptual meditation on nothingness temporarily suppresses afflictions so that they are not manifest at that moment, it has not eliminated the seeds or the latencies of afflictions from the mindstream. The person is still exposed to the vagaries of saṃsāra.

A person may have extraordinary meditative experiences, such as seeing deities or knowing their previous rebirths, but still not be free from cyclic existence. Although such events are wonderful, we should not be overly impressed with them, for as long as we have not cleansed all afflictions and their seeds from our mindstream through consistent meditation on the correct view of reality, we are not beyond saṃsāra. Many a practitioner has cultivated the dhyānas and the absorptions of the formless realm only to have their afflictions reappear later because self-grasping ignorance still exists in their mindstream. One may have samādhi on the conventional nature of the mind—its clarity and cognizance—but lack direct perception of its ultimate nature and thus still be trapped in saṃsāra. These days, when many people claim spiritual realizations and advertise such in the media, the point cannot be emphasized enough: only insight on the emptiness of inherent existence can eliminate the cause of saṃsāra from its root.

REFLECTION

1. Why is realizing emptiness directly important?
2. Why is blank-minded meditation or meditation on nothingness not meditation on emptiness?
3. What is serenity? What is insight?
4. Why is it important to combine serenity and insight?

The Perfection of Skillful Means

Skillful means are essential for achieving our own purposes as well as for benefiting others, and for that reason they must be perfected. In some Mahāyāna sūtras, such as the *Lotus Sūtra* (*Saddharmapuṇḍarīka Sūtra*), "skillful means" indicates the way in which, motivated by compassion, buddhas and bodhisattvas adapt their teaching method and their own behavior according to the needs and capacities of different sentient beings. In other Mahāyāna sūtras, such as the *Sūtra of the Perfection of Wisdom in 8,000 Lines* (*Aṣṭasāhasrikāprajñāpāramitā Sūtra*), skillful means applies to bodhisattvas' ability to attain deep states of concentration without getting waylaid by attachment to rebirth in the form and formless realms and to their ability to see all phenomena as empty without abandoning sentient beings.

In *Bodhisattva Grounds*, Asaṅga describes two groups of skillful means:

(1) To accomplish all the qualities of a buddha within themselves, bodhisattvas practice the skillful means of:

1. looking upon all sentient beings with compassion,
2. knowing the ultimate nature of all conditioned phenomena,
3. desiring the pristine wisdom of unsurpassed awakening,
4. not abandoning saṃsāra by looking upon all sentient beings with compassion,
5. taking rebirth in saṃsāra with an unafflicted mind that knows the reality of conditioned phenomena and is motivated by great compassion,
6. spurring their own enthusiasm to fulfill their desire to attain full awakening.

(2) To ripen all other living beings, bodhisattvas cultivate the skillful means to:

1. cause even the smallest virtuous roots in living beings to ripen into immeasurable results by teaching sentient beings how to transform small actions into great virtue,
2. cause living beings to accomplish great roots of virtue without undue hardship—for example, by teaching them to rejoice in the virtues of all beings,
3. eliminate anger in those who dislike the Buddha's doctrine—for example, by encouraging them to be tolerant of people who practice the Dharma even if they themselves do not wish to practice it,
4. encourage those who have a neutral attitude toward the Buddha's doctrine to enter into it,
5. ripen the mental continuums of those who have entered into the doctrine,
6. cause those whose minds and roots of virtue are ripened to attain liberation.

The Perfection of Unshakable Resolve

The Sanskrit term *praṇidhāna* (T. *smon lam*) is often translated as "prayer" by Tibetan translators and as "vow" by Chinese translators. This is an unshakable resolve—something more than a wish, an aspiration, or a prayer—to do particular great deeds for the benefit of sentient beings. In other words, this perfection is about making strong resolutions that we act on for the benefit of sentient beings. It is not about making prayers to the Buddha or taking ethical vows. The Medicine Buddha made twelve unshakable resolves, Amitābha Buddha made forty-eight, Samantabhadra made ten,[12] Mañjuśrī made 141 resolves,[13] and so on. Of the ten unshakable resolves of Samantabhadra, seven comprise the seven-limb prayer that is found in many practices. In the *Array of Stalks Sūtra*, another three are added to become ten resolves:

1. Pay homage and respect to all buddhas.
2. Praise all the buddhas.
3. Make abundant offerings.
4. Confess misdeeds and destructive actions.
5. Rejoice in one's own and others' merits and virtues.
6. Request the buddhas to turn the Dharma wheel.
7. Request the buddhas to remain in the world.
8. Follow the teachings of the buddhas at all times.
9. Accommodate, benefit, and live harmoniously with all living beings.
10. Dedicate all merits and virtues universally to all sentient beings.

Bodhisattvas make unshakable resolves to accomplish activities for sentient beings that cannot be actualized, at least not in the near future—for example, resolving to go to the hell realms to benefit even one sentient being or promising to lead all sentient beings from saṃsāra's duḥkha. Making such unshakable resolves is not a useless pursuit, nor is it fantasy. Rather, it strengthens bodhisattvas' determination to be of whatever benefit they possibly can to whichever sentient being is in need, regardless of the difficulties it may entail for them personally. As ordinary beings who have limited physical and mental abilities, we have to assess what we can actually do before acting. Nevertheless, making such wonderful unshakable resolves, even if they seem unrealistic, expands the scope and strength of our mind so that gradually and steadily we will be able to increase our capacity to be of benefit to others.

Bodhisattvas cultivate unshakable resolves and extraordinary aspirations to benefit all sentient beings. In his *Differentiation of the Three Vows*, Sakya Paṇḍita says that bodhisattvas have two types of aspirations: those that can be accomplished and those that cannot. For example, in *Engaging in the Bodhisattvas' Deeds*, Śāntideva aspires for many outcomes that cannot actually occur (BCA 10.2, 10.41):

> May all beings everywhere
> plagued by sufferings of body and mind,
> obtain an ocean of happiness and joy
> by virtue of my merits.
>
> May no living creature suffer,
> commit evil, or ever fall ill.
> May no one be afraid or belittled,
> with a mind weighed down by depression.

And Samantabhadra makes these unshakable resolves in the "King of Prayers" in the *Flower Ornament Sūtra* (*Avataṃsaka Sūtra*):

> Purifying the power of all polluted actions,
> crushing the power of disturbing emotions at their root,
> defusing the power of interfering forces,
> I shall perfect the power of the bodhisattva practice...
>
> Limitless is the end of space,
> likewise, limitless are living beings,
> thus, limitless are karma and afflictions.
> May my aspiration's reach be limitless as well.

Generating such unshakable resolves and magnificent aspirations is valuable because it enhances our determination to transcend our present hindrances. Such resolve gives us great courage to overcome self-centeredness and integrate bodhicitta with our mind. In addition, when we are in the position to help someone directly, we won't hesitate out of laziness or lack of confidence.

Aspirational prayers and unshakable resolves set our intention and clarify our aims. It's important to dedicate the merit from working to actualize them for the same aims. By doing so, the merit won't be exhausted until we attain full awakening. The Buddha said in the *Sūtra Requested by Sāgaramati* (*Sāgaramatiparipṛcchā Sūtra*):

> Just as a drop of water that falls into the great ocean
> will never disappear until the ocean itself runs dry,
> merit totally dedicated to supreme awakening
> will never disappear until supreme awakening is reached.

The Perfection of Power

The ninth perfection is the perfection of power. This is the strength to not be overcome by afflictions and other obscurations. Abhayākaragupta's commentary on the *Ornament of Clear Realizations* (*Abhisamayālaṃkāra*) entitled *Ornament for the Subduer's Intention* (*Munimatālaṃkāra*) speaks of thirteen kinds of power that bodhisattvas perfect:

1. The power of thought is the power of no longer indulging in the afflictions, because they have been abandoned.
2. The power of superior thought is to train well in the pristine wisdom of the bodhisattva grounds.
3. The power of retention is to remember all the Dharma teachings they have heard or read.
4. The power of meditative stability is the ability to remain in deep concentration without being distracted, no matter what they are doing.
5. The power of perfect endowments is knowing distinctly the behavior of each sentient being in the countless realms.
6. The power of fulfillment is to be able to fulfill all their aims.
7. The power of self-confidence is being skilled in distinguishing and examining all the Buddha's qualities.

8. The power of unshakable resolve is not to give up engaging in the activities of all the buddhas.
9. The power of perfection is to completely ripen the Buddha's qualities within themselves and sentient beings by teaching them, and not to give up deeds to benefit sentient beings.
10. The power of great love is to not relinquish the supreme effort to protect all sentient beings without being biased.
11. The power of great compassion is to eliminate all suffering of all sentient beings without being biased.
12. The power of ultimate reality is to actualize within themselves the experience of the ultimate reality that is like an illusion.
13. The power of being blessed by all the tathāgatas refers to approaching the pristine wisdom of omniscience by all means.

As part of the "King of Prayers: The Extraordinary Aspiration of the Practice of Samantabhadra" in chapter 40 of the *Flower Ornament Sūtra*, the bodhisattva Samantabhadra spoke of actualizing ten powers and overcoming the power of adverse factors:

> May I achieve the power of swift, magical emanation,
> the power to lead to the Great Vehicle through every approach,
> the power of always beneficial activity,
> the power of love pervading all realms,
> the power of all-surpassing merit,
> the power of supreme knowledge unobstructed by discrimination,
> and through the powers of wisdom, skillful means, and samādhi,
> may I achieve the perfect power of awakening.
>
> Purifying the power of all contaminated actions,
> crushing the power of disturbing emotions at their root,
> defusing the power of interfering forces,
> I shall perfect the power of the bodhisattva practice.

Contemplating these powers of ārya bodhisattvas gives us a glimpse of the qualities we will gain by practicing the Mahāyāna path. Creating the causes for such powers and using them to benefit ourselves and others will bring us great satisfaction, confidence, and exuberance to practice.

REFLECTION

1. Contemplate the various types of powers that bodhisattvas perfect. Imagine what it would be like to have each one.
2. Aspire to create the causes to one day attain these powers and use them to work for the well-being of all sentient beings.

The Perfection of Pristine Wisdom

In some cases the words "wisdom" (*prajñā*) and "pristine wisdom" (*jñāna*) are synonymous, while in other contexts their meanings differ.[14] In the context of the perfections, Asaṅga differentiates wisdom and pristine wisdom in *Bodhisattva Grounds*:

> That knowing the presentation of all phenomena as they are is the perfection of pristine wisdom. The wisdom that engages in apprehending the ultimate is the perfection of wisdom. That engaged in apprehending the conventional is the perfection of pristine wisdom. These are the particularities of the two.

In the first sentence, "all phenomena" refers to the diversity of phenomena and connotes conventional truths. These are the objects of the perfection of pristine wisdom. In the second sentence, "ultimate" refers to emptiness, and the wisdom engaged in directly perceiving it is the wisdom of meditative equipoise on emptiness, also called the "perfection of wisdom." The perfection of wisdom is defined as an exalted knower that is conjoined with a union of serenity and special insight that serves as the means for proceeding to or remaining in nonabiding nirvāṇa.[15] "The conventional" in the following sentence refers to the method or the vast aspect of the path.

In summary, reflect on the meaning and purpose of each of the ten perfections as presented by the *Ten Grounds Sūtra* (*Daśabhūmika Sūtra*, DBS 143):

> In each successive moment, this bodhisattva carries on the complete implementation of the bodhisattva's ten pāramitās and the ten grounds' practices. And how is this the case? This is because this bodhisattva mahāsattva takes the great compassion as foremost in each successive moment and because, as he cultivates all of the excellent qualities of the Buddha, he dedicates it all to the realization of the Tathāgata's wisdom.
>
> As for his cultivation of the ten pāramitās:
>
> The bodhisattva's bestowing on all beings all roots of virtue he cultivates in pursuit of the path to buddhahood constitutes the perfection of generosity.
>
> His ability to extinguish all heat associated with the afflictions constitutes the perfection of ethical conduct.
>
> His taking kindness and compassion as foremost and refraining from harming any being constitutes the perfection of fortitude.
>
> His insatiable striving to acquire ever more supreme roots of virtue constitutes the perfection of joyous effort.
>
> His maintaining an unscattered mind dedicated to cultivating the path even as he constantly progresses toward omniscience constitutes the perfection of meditative stability.
>
> His realization of acquiescent fortitude of the eternal nonproduction of all phenomena constitutes the perfection of wisdom.
>
> His bringing forth of countless expressions of wisdom constitutes the perfection of skillful means.
>
> His aspiration to develop the supreme wisdom constitutes the perfection of unshakable resolve.
>
> His ability to remain invulnerable to obstruction or ruination by any followers of non-Buddhist paths or by any demons constitutes the perfection of power.
>
> His accomplishment of knowing the characteristic features of all phenomena in accordance with reality constitutes the perfection of pristine wisdom.

Ultimate Bodhicitta

Many texts refer to the "two bodhicittas"—conventional bodhicitta and ultimate bodhicitta. The former is actual bodhicitta, the altruistic intention that is a primary mind held by two aspirations—the aspirations to work for the well-being of sentient beings and to attain full awakening in order to do so. This is the bodhicitta spoken about so far in this chapter.

Ultimate bodhicitta is the wisdom directly realizing emptiness. While it is called "bodhicitta," it is not actually bodhicitta. Bodhi means "awakening" and citta means "mind," so bodhicitta is the mind of awakening. Ultimate bodhicitta is the direct perceiver of the emptiness of awakening. Its observed object is awakening, and it realizes the emptiness of awakening. Conventional bodhicitta also focuses on awakening, but it aspires to actualize it for the benefit of all sentient beings. Nāgārjuna wrote a beautiful work entitled *Commentary on Bodhicitta*. Its main topic is ultimate bodhicitta, so there is much discussion of emptiness. As an aside, toward the end of the work, conventional bodhicitta is taught.

Ultimate bodhicitta can be understood in two ways, the way in common with the Sūtra Vehicle and the way unique to the Tantric Vehicle. In the Sūtra Vehicle, it is the mind that is a union of serenity and insight that directly perceives emptiness and is conjoined with conventional bodhicitta. In highest yoga tantra, the fundamental innate clear-light mind that is focused on emptiness is called "ultimate bodhicitta."[16] Its object is the subtlest object, emptiness, and the mind is the subtlest subject, the fundamental innate clear-light mind. In both the Perfection Vehicle and the Tantric Vehicle, the object of ultimate bodhicitta—the emptiness of inherent existence—is the same; the difference is in the subject—the mind realizing it.

In the *Treatise on the Middle Way*, Nāgārjuna speaks of the pacification of elaborations. Bodhi is the state in which all elaborations have been pacified. In the Sūtra Vehicle, these elaborations are the appearance of inherent existence, whereas in highest yoga tantra, elaborations are not only the appearance of inherent existence but also the white appearance, the red increase, and the black near-attainment. These are three levels of mind that are subtler than our sense consciousnesses and waking mind but are coarser than the subtlest mind—the fundamental innate clear-light mind.

Subtler than these three appearances is the fundamental innate clear-light mind. This subtle innate clear-light mind exists in all beings and is the basis of all coarser levels of mind. The coarser minds such as our sense consciousnesseses and everyday mental consciousness emerge from it and dissolve back into it. When coarser minds are active, the subtlest innate clear-light mind is dormant. In Tantra, advanced practitioners who understand emptiness can activate this subtlest mind and use it to apprehend emptiness.

In Tantra, ultimate bodhicitta—the subtlest innate mind that is absorbed nondually in emptiness—is not only free from the appearance of subject and object, the appearance of conventional phenomena, and the appearance of inherent existence but is also free from the white, the red increase, and the black near-attainment appearances. Here ultimate bodhicitta is the fundamental innate clear-light mind that directly perceives emptiness.

Because the subtle innate clear-light mind pervades all coarser states of mind and because it is their basis, it is said to exist at all times. Still, according to Tantra, these coarser states of mind must dissolve and the subtle innate clear-light must manifest alone and realize emptiness for it to be called "ultimate bodhicitta," the final cause of awakening.

A meditator is first able to make this mind manifest on the completion stage of highest yoga tantra, immediately before the arising of the impure illusory body. It is also manifest on the following levels, the meaning clear light and the union of clear light and illusory body. Although the Sūtra Vehicle does not speak of this subtle innate clear-light mind, the topic of buddha nature (*tathāgatagarbha*) in the Sūtra Vehicle hints at it and leads practitioners to then explore Tantra.

The *Guhyasamāja Root Tantra* says:

> One's mind is primordially unborn;
> it is in the nature of emptiness.

Interpreted from the viewpoint of the Sūtra Vehicle, this means that the mind has been empty of inherent existence from beginningless time. There has never been a time when it has inherently existed. Thus it is not the case that realizing emptiness changes the nature of the mind from inherently existent to non-inherently existent. Rather, the wisdom mind of ultimate bodhicitta realizes what has always been the ultimate nature of the mind.

In the unique Tantric interpretation of these lines, "primordially unborn" means that the mind—specifically the innate clear-light mind—is primordially devoid of all coarser states of mind. This subtlest mind changes moment by moment, is pure from adventitious grosser minds, and travels to awakening.[17]

Regardless of whether ultimate bodhicitta is spoken of from a Sūtra or Tantra perspective, it is a wisdom that directly realizes emptiness. But not every wisdom directly realizing emptiness is ultimate bodhicitta, because for a wisdom to become ultimate bodhicitta, it must be complemented by conventional bodhicitta. Thus the wisdom nondually perceiving emptiness in the mindstream of a śrāvaka or solitary-realizer learner is not called "ultimate bodhicitta"—although it is a true path and the wisdom of an ārya—because it is not complemented by conventional bodhicitta.

Conclusion

The Buddha said there is no second door to liberation—only the wisdom realizing emptiness can remove all obscurations. To have a deep understanding of emptiness, in addition to studying and meditating on the stages of the path (*lamrim*), we should study and reflect on the view as propounded in the four philosophical tenet systems. By practicing the stages of the path, we will develop a proper motivation for studying and meditating on emptiness and will accumulate the merit necessary to realize it. By studying the tenet schools, we will be challenged to think deeply about the nature of reality. The understanding of emptiness we gain from this will in turn help our meditation and practice of lamrim. Thus I recommend that lamrim and tenets be taught together in Dharma centers and monasteries.

A big difference exists between having an intellectual understanding of a Dharma topic and gaining realization or experience of it. Intellectual understanding is not sufficient. Whatever we understand we should put into practice and try to integrate into our daily life so that it transforms our mind and heart. That is the purpose of spiritual practice.

I suggest that you spend some time reflecting on the meaning of each of these perfections and then examine how to apply them in daily life. Reading about these wondrous thoughts and deeds is inspiring, but even better is embodying them in the way you live. Contemplate when and how you can practice the ten perfections. Then resolve to do your best to put them into practice.

As ordinary beings, we select role models and fashion our goals and behavior by their example. Since we aim to cultivate compassion and make a positive contribution to society and to all sentient beings, I recommend taking ārya bodhisattvas as our role models. Maitreya describes bodhisattvas (RGV 1.70–71):

> Though they are beyond all worldly matters,
> these [bodhisattvas] do not leave the world.
> They act for the sake of all worldly beings
> within the world, unblemished by its defects.
>
> As a lotus will grow in the midst of water,
> not being polluted by the water's [faults],
> these [āryas] are born in the world,
> unpolluted by any worldly phenomenon.

Contemplating their attitudes and actions inspires and uplifts us. It will take time to become like them, but can we think of anything more valuable to do?

4 | Sharing the Dharma

THE BODHISATTVA PRACTICE IS based on benefiting others. As many scriptures in both the Pāli and the Sanskrit canons attest, "The gift of the Dharma is the highest gift." The Dharma can be shared with others in a variety of ways. The way we live and conduct ourselves in everyday interactions is a subtle but powerful way to arouse people's interest in the Buddha's teachings. The behavior of a person who is humble, courteous, and loving touches the hearts of those who come in contact with them. Someone who speaks the truth without backing away is also a strong force for good in the world.

The most obvious way of sharing the Dharma is by giving teachings. However, teaching the Dharma is a great responsibility that must be approached gradually, with the correct motivation, and skillfully. In addition, not everyone is inclined to be a teacher. Some people prefer to lead meditations, counsel others using Dharma principles, or be socially engaged with projects that directly benefit others in this life. This can range from working in an animal shelter to aiding the elderly and infirm to volunteering in a homeless shelter. Each of us must discover our individual talents and inclinations and share the Dharma accordingly. The Buddhist community needs people to share the Dharma through a wide range of activities. No matter which way we choose, it is essential to respect others who show their love and compassion in different ways.

The Tibetan, Pāli, and Chinese scriptures all speak of four ways of attracting people in order to benefit them; these are also called the four all-embracing virtues.

Four Ways of Gathering Disciples in Tibetan Buddhism

Learning and practicing the Dharma for our own benefit alone is limited: we are only one person. Sharing what we have learned with others so that they will benefit is important, especially for those aspiring to become buddhas. To do this, in addition to working on our own practice, it is necessary to establish good relationships with others. In Tibetan Buddhism, the process of attracting people so that they will be interested in learning the Dharma is traditionally described by the four ways of gathering or assembling disciples (*saṃgrahavastu, saṅgahavatthu*). These four are directed toward building suitable conditions to be able to teach the Dharma and lead others on the path.

The six perfections are taught from the viewpoint of how to attain awakening ourselves, whereas the four ways of gathering disciples are given from the perspective of how to lead others on the path to awakening. The four are (1) being generous and giving material aid, (2) teaching the Dharma according to the capacity of the disciples, (3) encouraging them to practice, and (4) acting congruently and living the teachings through example.

The first, *being generous*, involves helping others materially by supplying them with what they need. Others will be attracted by our generosity and that opens the door for us to teach them the Dharma. Also, giving them things ensures that those who are impoverished have the material requisites—food, shelter, clothes, and medicine—necessary to learn the Dharma. Without these basic needs being fulfilled, sincere disciples will be unable to practice. The Vinaya speaks directly to this by saying that the preceptors who give monastic ordination are responsible for not only teaching the Dharma to their monastic students but also providing them with food and shelter.

But more broadly, being generous entails giving what others need. When there are natural disasters, endemic poverty, or outbreaks of diseases, Buddhist organizations such as temples, monasteries, and Dharma centers can step forward and assist as they are able. There are now some Buddhist charity organizations that do this, and I encourage their good work.[18] This indicates to the public that as Buddhists we don't just talk about generosity and kindness but we also act in that way.

Of course, generosity begins at the individual level. Whether we give to charity organizations or give a Dharma book to a friend who has questions about life, whether we give food to a beggar or small gifts to children, generosity opens our heart, benefits others, and, because we are Buddhist, attracts others to the Dharma.

Some religions have used material generosity as a way to convert people to their faith. As Buddhists, this should never be our motivation. If sentient beings have needs and we can fulfill them, we should do that, without any expectation that they become Buddhist. However, if they are then attracted to us and wish to learn what we practice, we should fulfill their wish and teach them the Dharma.

The second way to gather disciples is to *teach the Dharma in a way that appeals to them*. This may involve various ways of speaking and different topics, depending on the situation. For example, when talking with strangers in a public place, ask about what interests them in order to make their acquaintance. When a friend who has just undergone a breakup or someone who is grieving the death of a dear one approaches you, speak in a way that consoles them and broadens their perspective. When you encounter those in difficult circumstances, give advice pertinent to their problem and teach them Dharma methods that will help them in that situation.

When someone asks Dharma questions, respond as best you can; and when they request teachings, teach what you are capable of teaching. This is the gift of the Dharma. It is said that this excels all other gifts because through learning the Dharma, others become capable of creating the causes for fortunate rebirths, liberation, and full awakening. Without bias, teach anyone who is sincere—common people and intellectuals, the poor and the rich, female and male, ordained and lay. Teach only the Dharma that you know well and can explain without error. It's also important to teach when the other person's mind is ripe and the circumstances are suitable—that is, to discern their disposition and interest and teach them accordingly to lead them on the path to virtue.

There is nothing better than to speak about and listen to the Buddha's teachings. The scriptures speak of twenty benefits of teaching the Dharma. For example, when we teach with a pure heart and good motivation, then as the students' intelligence and understanding increase, a corresponding increase in our understanding will occur as well. Natural sounds are neutral, and much of our ordinary speech triggers afflictions, whereas the Buddha's teachings lead us from all duḥkha. Instead of chatting to enhance our ego or for amusement, let's use language for beneficial purposes.

The third is to *encourage others* to practice the Dharma they have learned. This entails guiding and supporting others on the path. To do this requires great patience and diligence. Sometimes people will appreciate the help you give, other times they may turn their back even though you have guided them for a long time. Cultivate the ability to accept all responses patiently, knowing that sentient beings are under the influence of afflictions. With compassion, remain open should their mental states change, and with forgiveness, welcome them if they sincerely want to return.

Fourth, *act in ways congruent with what you teach*. Being a good example inspires others to practice and increases their faith in the Three Jewels. They feel inspired and want to learn and practice the Dharma more. If you are in the role of a meditation guide, a Dharma instructor, or a spiritual mentor, it is essential to embody the Dharma in your actions. Practicing what you preach and living your life according to the Buddha's teaching—that is, doing what you instruct others to do—is essential in order to be worthy of others' trust and to be able to continue to benefit them.

There have been a few scandals as a result of the improper behavior of Dharma teachers. This may occur because the teacher's practice lacks depth and their Dharma knowledge is only intellectual. It may occur because teachers become infatuated with the devotion of their students or don't apply antidotes to the afflictions. There are no "days off" when a Dharma teacher can forget about the Buddha's teachings and act like a worldly person. Whatever the reason, it is essential to act with conscientiousness, mindfulness, and introspective awareness. Then people will develop genuine appreciation and respect. If the teacher says one thing and does another, how can the student respect him or her? Without earning the students' respect, a spiritual mentor cannot lead others on the path and creates the cause for their own suffering and unfortunate rebirth.

Four Ways of Sustaining Favorable Relationships in the Pāli Tradition

The four ways of sustaining favorable relationships (note the difference in translation of the same Pāli and Sanskrit term) appear several times in the

Aṅguttara Nikāya of the Pāli canon. Here is one passage describing them (AN 9.5):

> There are four ways of gathering disciples: (1) by giving, (2) by friendly and endearing speech, (3) by encouraging acts and beneficent conduct, and (4) by acting impartially, in a way equal [to one's words]. Among gifts, the best is the gift of the Dhamma. Among types of endearing speech, the best is repeatedly teaching the Dhamma to one who is interested in it and listens with eager ears. Among types of beneficent conduct, the best is when one encourages, settles, and establishes a person without faith in the accomplishment of faith, an unethical person in the accomplishment of virtuous behavior, a miserly person in the accomplishment of generosity, and an unwise person in the accomplishment of wisdom. Among types of impartiality or equality, the best is that a stream-enterer is equal to a stream-enterer, a once-returner is equal to a once-returner, a nonreturner is equal to a nonreturner, and an arahant is equal to an arahant. This is called the power of sustaining favorable relationships.

The above passage is oriented toward leading others to the Dharma. In the first two ways of gathering disciples we find the famous quotation, "The best gift is the gift of the Dharma." Of all the things to give to others, the Dharma alone will lead them out of duḥkha and to joy. Giving the Dharma of course does not preclude giving other necessities of life, especially to support those who sincerely want to practice the Dharma. In the third way, to encourage others to practice, we arouse, instill, and strengthen their good qualities, helping their mental, verbal, and physical actions become virtuous. Finally, whatever our level of practice and realizations, we should act equal to that. Becoming complacent or arrogant so that our actions are not equal to our words or our actions are not equal to our level of practice disillusions others and is the opposite of establishing and sustaining productive Dharma relationships. "Impartiality" also refers to treating others as we would like them to treat us—in other words, establishing a feeling of closeness that is free from all feelings of superiority or inferiority.

These four apply to whatever type of relationship we would like to establish and sustain with others. The *Commentary to the Aṅguttara Nikāya* says (AN n.687):

> Some people are to be sustained by a gift, so a gift should be given to them. Others expect endearing speech, so they should be addressed with pleasant words. Beneficent conduct is talk on increasing goodness; these people should be told, "You should do this, you shouldn't do that. You should associate with this person, not with that person." Impartiality is being the same in happiness and suffering. This means sitting together with them, living together, and eating together.

One day Hatthaka of Āḷavī, one of the Buddha's foremost lay disciples, together with over five hundred lay followers, went to meet the Buddha. The Buddha asked Hatthaka how he sustained such a large group of lay followers, to which Hatthaka cited the four ways of sustaining favorable relationships as taught by the Buddha (AN 24.24).

Four All-Embracing Bodhisattva Virtues in Chinese Buddhism

In Chinese Buddhism the four ways of attracting are known as the four all-embracing (bodhisattva) virtues:

(1) To *be generous* necessitates counteracting selfishness and extending ourselves to others. Generosity takes three forms. The first is giving material and financial support. Even if we do not have many possessions or a lot of money ourselves, we can still share and give something. A generous heart is free and comfortable, whereas a miserly heart is tight and fearful. Second is giving sentient beings confidence and freedom from fear, worry, and anxiety. This may take the form of reassuring a child afraid of the dark, a student worried about passing exams, or a person fearing for their life due to illness or assault. Giving them confidence can also be done by instructing them in a particular skill or field of knowledge. Third is teaching living beings the Dharma of the Three Baskets. Of course, to give this to others, we must know it well ourselves; otherwise we run the risk of teaching wrong views that can harm people for a long time to come. However, we can share what

we do understand and also let people know how much we have benefited from studying and practicing the Buddha's teachings.

(2) *Affectionate speech* includes speaking politely to others, consoling them, and giving them wise advice, without forcing our ideas on them. Bodhisattvas respect others and listen carefully to what they say. They praise, encourage, and comfort others, and always think about how to influence others so that they will grow in virtue. As with practicing generosity, genuinely affectionate and friendly speech will attract people to us so that we will be able to teach and guide them in the Dharma, which will help them in the long term.

(3) *Conducting ourselves in a profitable way* entails keeping our body, speech, and mind in line with the Dharma. Such behavior inspires those around us, no matter what field we work in. For example, one bodhisattva spent most of his life repairing roads, building bridges, and carrying things for the elderly without ever losing heart in the face of difficulty. Social welfare projects run by Buddhist individuals or organizations show the public that we care and that our compassion is not merely at the level of words. Acting in ways that directly benefit others attracts them to us and thereby to the Dharma. Bodhisattvas extend help to others impartially and maintain an attitude of equal care and concern for all, no matter how someone acts in return. This opens the door for bodhisattvas to engage with people from all social classes, races, religions, ethnic groups, sexes, and so on. It also enables them to work continuously for others because they do not delight in praise and appreciation or become discouraged due to blame and criticism.

(4) *Cooperating with others* and adapting ourselves to what benefits them involves providing them with a good example of how to live ethically and with kindness. For example, while being employed in an office or factory, we work together with others without straying from our ethical values. At parties we are friendly and have a good time without drinking or taking drugs. Living in accord with our precepts can occur naturally. We don't draw attention to it, but others observe and it makes them think. This can exert a powerful influence on others who usually go along with the crowd without first examining the effects of their actions. Seeing someone who is happy without being egocentric could attract them to the Buddha's teachings or inspire them to live in accordance with the values of their own religion. In either case, they will create virtue and avoid nonvirtue.

Practicing the four all-embracing virtues benefits us, the people we interact with, and society in general. These four are methods used by bodhisattvas to inspire others' interest in the Dharma and persuade them to learn and practice it.

REFLECTION

Practicing the four ways of attracting others so that we can teach them the Dharma and inspire them in goodness is prudent advice for relating to others, no matter what the situation. Those who aspire to spread the Dharma to new regions and to sustain it where it already exists should take these four to heart.

1. Being generous opens the door to establishing good relationships.
2. Speaking pleasantly in a way that connects with others and being friendly and caring about them establishes a good relationship.
3. Encouraging others to conduct themselves in a wholesome way helps them take a good direction in life. One way to do this is by teaching the Buddhadharma and creating conditions in which others can practice. Another is by living an exemplary life yourself.
4. Behaving according to your words and living according to the Dharma shows others that you are trustworthy, consistent, and wise in your decisions. Cooperating with others and living in accord with your precepts and ethical values not only inspires them but also ensures that you do not harm them by being hypocritical and uncontrolled in your behavior.

Suggestions for Western Dharma Teachers

In addition to the four ways of attracting others that are found in the scriptures, I would like to offer some suggestions specifically for Westerners who teach the Dharma. Although what follows applies to Asian teachers as well, Westerners do not have centuries-long lineages of Buddhist teachers in their own culture to look to as examples.

I appreciate the enthusiasm of Western teachers and acknowledge how much they have done to spread the Buddhadharma, to benefit sentient beings, and to decrease suffering. As Buddhism spreads in your countries, more of you will become teachers. Nevertheless, Buddhism is new in the West, and you do not yet have a culturally suitable role model to follow for being a Dharma teacher or for a proper teacher-student relationship. You must proceed slowly and carefully. You are pioneers now, and over time such role models will naturally evolve.

Before instructing others, it is essential to cultivate your own understanding under the guidance of a qualified spiritual mentor. Listen to teachings, study hard, and relate what you learn to your life. In this way your level of understanding will grow from just gathering information to critical reflection that impacts your life and your choices. With a stable understanding derived from years of study and practice as well as humble awareness that there is much more to learn, you will be able to explain the Dharma well. Otherwise, as Dharmakīrti said, how can you explain something to others that is just words to yourself? If you can speak from experience and deep understanding, your words will make a difference to others.

Western teachers have asked me: What qualities must we cultivate to become a reliable spiritual mentor to others? Who and how should we teach? The Buddha gave a vast variety of teachings; which ones are most suitable for us to teach? How do we work with students without becoming emotionally entangled with them? How do we ensure that we remain balanced so that our practice progresses? I will respond to these thoughtful questions below.

Qualities to Develop

Chapter 4 of *The Foundation of Buddhist Practice* described the qualities students should look for in prospective Dharma teachers. These qualities remain the same, no matter the country, culture, or person. You must try to develop those same qualities in your practice and apply those same standards to yourself to become a qualified teacher. Skimping on the development of your good qualities while expecting to be treated as a spiritual master won't do.

Before beginning to teach, you must have mental stability derived through your Dharma practice, so that your life is calmer. Students see teachers as role models who have the possibility to help them. If the teacher is a happy and peaceful person, they will admire her and want to learn from her. If she is distracted and anxious, students will wonder whether Dharma practice actually subdues the mind. In addition, if the teacher is always preoccupied, disorganized, and stressed, she won't have time to pay attention to students' needs or to teach them in a serious, consistent manner.

If you wish to teach the Dharma, you must examine to what extent you possess the ten qualities of a Mahāyāna spiritual mentor: look closely at your ethical conduct, meditative experience, understanding of emptiness, and knowledge of the scriptures. To what extent do you care about the well-being, temporal and ultimate, of the students? Are you irascible, surly, and quick to anger, such that students are afraid to approach you? Are you content and patient, or do you constantly complain about one thing or another? It's important to be conscientious and with mindfulness and introspective awareness monitor our attitudes and behavior in order to benefit and not harm the people who sincerely turn to us for help.

Do not be satisfied with knowing only one meditation technique, one scripture, or one tantric practice, but for the benefit of others, strive to overcome your limitations and expand your knowledge. In his *Great Treatise*, Tsongkhapa says (LC 3:349–50):

> Each Mahāyāna scripture—from summaries to [the most extensive texts]—gives a great many teachings on the profound meaning, but also leaves many things out. So you must draw points that are not taught [in certain texts] from [other] texts that do teach them, and you must draw points that are not [taught] extensively [in certain texts] from [other texts] where they are [taught] extensively. You should understand that this is true for the category of the vast [bodhisattva deeds] as well.[19] A partial [path], in which either the profound or the vast is missing cannot be considered [complete]. This is why it is often said that one [must be] skilled in all vehicles in order to be a spiritual mentor who is fully qualified to teach the path.

You must be able to discern the difference between an intellectual understanding of the teachings, which is comparatively easy to gain, and realization and experience of them, which is more difficult to cultivate and requires years of continuous practice. Do not be infatuated with a few blissful or unusual meditative experiences and think that you have become a great sage qualified to teach the masses. Rather, continue to see yourself as a student. After all, until you attain full awakening you are the Buddha's disciple. Once in a while you may temporarily be in the role of teaching the Dharma. Improving the state of your mind is your principal occupation, not becoming a famous teacher or building a big Buddhist organization with yourself at the head.

Social status, wealth, or charisma are not qualities that make a good Dharma teacher. Rather, it is the ability to show someone what to practice and what to abandon; a teacher must practice such instructions themselves.

Motivation

Be aware of the audience's buddha nature and feel honored to share the Dharma. When you teach, you must embody the Dharma. You are not just relaying information. Recite the text clearly and explain it with compassion. Always cultivate a motivation of compassion, care, and concern for the students. The Buddha comments (SN 16.3):

> A monastic teaches the Dhamma to others with the thought "Oh, may they listen to the Dhamma from me! Having listened, may they gain confidence in the Dhamma! Being confident, may they show their confidence to me!" Such a monastic's teaching of the Dhamma is impure.

This person ostensibly wants others to gain confidence in the Dharma, but he is not necessarily wishing for the students to understand or practice and receive the benefit of doing so. This person lacks humility and does not respect the Buddha and Dharma. His principal wish is more to receive offerings, reputation, and status.

Some religious leaders, both Buddhist and non-Buddhist, use religion as a way to procure money or to earn a living. Doing this not only harms the teacher, it also damages the faith of others, causing them to turn away from spiritual teachings that could benefit them. For this reason, Dharma teachers and leaders must continuously check their motivation to make sure one of the eight worldly concerns has not crept in.

In the above passage, the Buddha was speaking to monastics, who were the principal teachers of the Dharma at the time. Nowadays many lay practitioners—who have families and children to support—also teach, making the issue of earning one's livelihood through offerings from teaching the Dharma even more delicate. This requires a great deal of thought and care, so that one's motivation remains pure while sharing the Dharma with others.

Someone with the correct motivation genuinely respects the Dharma and recognizes that she has the good fortune to share it with others. Her wish is for others to learn, understand, practice, and realize the Dharma. She teaches with compassion and sincere concern that wishes the students to be free from cyclic existence. The Buddha says (SN 16.3):

> A monastic teaches the Dhamma to others with the thought "The Dhamma is well expounded by the Blessed One, directly visible, immediate, inviting one to come and see, applicable, to be personally experienced by the wise. Oh, may they listen to the Dhamma from me! Having listened, may they understand the Dhamma. Having understood, may they practice accordingly!" Thus he teaches the Dhamma to others because of the intrinsic excellence of the Dhamma; he teaches the Dhamma to others from compassion and sympathy, out of tender concern. Such a monastic's teaching of the Dhamma is pure.

Sincerity is an important quality to have when teaching the Dharma. The statue of the Buddha—emaciated when he was fasting for six years—illustrates his inner strength and determination. He was sincere and willing to undergo hardship to accomplish his spiritual aims. We are followers of this great master, but sometimes we do not listen to his advice. Some people use the Buddha's name and his teachings for their own personal gain, without taking them seriously. This is sad. It is better to remain a nonbeliever than to distort the Buddha's teachings or use them to become famous or wealthy. That would be more honest. Some so-called Buddhists are hypocrites. They present themselves as followers of Buddha Śākyamuni, but live and think differently than he did.

If we are sincere, what others say does not matter. For example, some people say I'm a living Buddha; others think I'm almost like a devil. I always remember that I'm a simple Buddhist monk. If I'm honest, even though others do things against me, gradually the truth of the situation will become clear. If we are cunning and manipulative, we may seem to be successful for a while, but when we die we will have to face what we have done. No one can help us at that time, even the Buddha. Our future is in our own hands, so we must check our motivation and our actions well.

To be a Dharma teacher you must not only know the Dharma well and teach with a compassionate motivation, you must also be humble. Generally speaking, people in the West who are educated, wealthy, or powerful tend to be proud. Although their knowledge may be limited, their confidence is often inflated. If a teacher knows a lot about Buddhism but practices little, pride may easily arise. Therefore do not become so busy teaching that you neglect your own practice. If your practice is successful, you will become more modest and thus more suitable to teach others.

Dharma teachers must also cultivate deep patience. Because students are under the influence of afflictions and karma, they will make mistakes. They will not always practice what you instruct or follow your advice. Sometimes they may act out their emotional needs. Be careful to act wisely in these situations and be patient with students when they do not meet your expectations. Do not give up on others; remember that this is an excellent opportunity to increase your compassion.

As teachers become more well-known and popular, they should become more humble. If you become arrogant, demanding, or controlling, it is a sure sign that you have neglected your Dharma practice. Śāriputra once described the awe-inspiring qualities of the Buddha while the Buddha sat humbly listening. Afterward, Venerable Udāyi, who witnessed this, marveled (DN 28.20):

> It is marvelous how content the Blessed One is, how satisfied and restrained, when being endowed with such power and influence he does not make a display of himself! If the wanderers professing other doctrines were able to discern in themselves even one of such qualities, they would proclaim it with a banner!

However many people may gather around you to learn the Dharma, remember that your first job is that of a practitioner, a disciple. Maintain a good relationship with your teachers and practice as they instruct. For the purpose of instilling humility and of not being spoiled by praise or fame, bow to the Three Jewels and to the lineage of teachers as well as reflect on impermanence before sitting on the Dharma seat.

How to Teach

Promoting Buddhism in a non-Buddhist society with the idea to convert people is not right. Religion should not be forced on anyone. However, when people want to learn about Buddhism, our responsibility is to teach them or refer them to teachers. Some people will find the Buddhist approach more suitable and will naturally grow in the Dharma. Others will find other religions or no religion at all more fitting for their minds.

When people are new to Buddhism, teach them the qualities to look for in a spiritual mentor. Encourage people to be responsible and wise when they select their teachers. Do not tell them that they should become your student.

When I teach, I first think about my own experience. For example, before teaching the four truths, I consider the fact that I am impermanent and then explain impermanence according to my own experience. I do not pretend to be Avalokiteśvara or drop hints that would lead people to believe that I have high realizations. Similarly, when teaching about the afflictions and the methods to combat them, I first think about the way I deal with anger or face attachment and give myself as an example when explaining afflictions and their antidotes. In that way, while teaching others, I do analytical meditation at the same time. This way of teaching is very useful. However, this is not the case when making presentations on the high levels of the path, because I cannot talk about those based on my own experience. We must be honest when we teach. If we pretend to have realizations that we do not have, teaching will not benefit us and at best will be of limited benefit for others.

When you do not know the answer to a student's question, clearly say so. Evading the question, humiliating the person who asked, or making up an answer to avoid losing face are damaging to both the teacher and the student. Later, ask your teachers to explain these unclear points, discuss them with Dharma friends, and research them in the scriptures.

When you encounter difficulty, seek the help and guidance of others, and do not think that simply because you have the name "teacher" you should know everything. In addition, seek the advice of your teachers and the support of Dharma friends to handle difficulties that arise when working with students.

Although Tibetan custom is to be humble and say one does not know something even when one does, in some cases this is not wise. It could discourage students because they would think the teachings are just stories and lack a living tradition of realized practitioners. If we have some knowledge or experience, we should tell others that we gained this through continuous practice. For example, if we used to have a very bad temper, but that has lessened through our Dharma practice, people will be encouraged to hear that. My style is to express openly the little experience I have on a topic so students do not think Dharma is merely an academic pursuit. In that way, they will be inspired to practice and develop realizations themselves.

However, we should not publicly say that we have insight into emptiness or have generated bodhicitta. Nor is it advisable to state that we have attained single-pointed concentration or tantric realizations. For monastics, lying about one's Dharma realizations is a root downfall, which means one is no longer a monastic. Boasting about one's realizations even when it is true is also a transgression, but a lesser one.

In general, it is better to tell students of your own internal struggles—that confronting anger, attachment, doubt, and so on requires persistence. Describe how you use the Dharma to purify and transform your mind. This level of discussion of your personal practice is permitted and advantageous. However, when doing this, avoid going to an extreme and turning a teaching situation into a tale about your emotions.

I avoid giving prescriptions to others as if the same advice did not pertain to me. Rather, I include myself—for example, saying, "When we get angry..." This reminds students that I am sincere and honest and expect the same from them.

In the sūtras, we read many dialogues that occurred between the Buddha and his disciples. The Buddha didn't simply lecture while his disciples listened passively. This system of questions and answers is good for both the teacher and the students. Ask the students questions and encourage them to be broadminded and creative when exploring various topics. In Tibetan monasteries it is said the most learning occurs in the debate yard—that is, students must discuss with one another. Sometimes they must struggle to understand a difficult point; in the end this gives them confidence. Learning the Dharma is not about remembering facts and concepts; it is about learning how to think properly, how to assess the state of our mind and improve it.

Don't expect yourself to answer everyone's questions. A hundred students will produce a hundred questions and a hundred problems. Today you answer one question and tomorrow another one arises because of that answer. Although the Buddha lived for eighty years, he was not able to answer all his disciples' queries. Even all the sūtras, treatises, and commentaries in the Kangyur (the Buddha's teachings) and the Tengyur (the major Indian commentaries) cannot quench all queries. But if you know the structure of Buddhadharma through having a deep understanding of the four truths, you will be able to investigate and find the answer. For this reason, encourage students to discuss and debate the teachings so that they learn to think for themselves and gain clarity on complex issues through using their own wisdom.

In this way, invigorate students so that they develop faith on the basis of reason, inquiry, and analysis. Dharma students in the West are educated and intelligent. They must use their analytic abilities to develop understanding, and consequently trust and confidence, in the Buddha's teachings. Blind faith is not our objective in teaching them. If such faith were sufficient to attain nirvāṇa, the Buddha and the great Indian sages would not have explained the Dharma and analyzed the nature of reality in such detail.

REFLECTION

Cultivating certain virtuous qualities is essential for those who wish to share the Dharma. Reflect on these well and take them to heart.

1. You must study the Dharma and put it into practice under the guidance of qualified Buddhist spiritual mentors.
2. Cultivate the qualities that the Buddha set forth for the various types of spiritual mentors (see *The Foundation of Buddhist Practice* for these).

3. Keep good ethical conduct. Don't tell yourself that because you're in a teaching role you are exempt from ethical precepts.

4. Constantly check your motivation so that it doesn't degenerate into seeking reputation, offerings, and service from others. If your motivation degenerates, so will your behavior, and then everything good you have done will become moot in the face of the scandals you have brought on.

5. Remember that until attaining full awakening, you are always the student of the Buddha. Once in a while, according to conditions, you may perform the role of a teacher, but it is only a temporary role and is not who you are. Don't construct an identity around it.

6. Cultivate deep patience, fortitude, and compassion. Don't expect people to respect you. Remember you are the servant of others.

7. Teach only what you know and understand. If you don't know the answer to a student's question, say that. Then research the answer and reply to the student later.

8. Do not look to students to fulfill your emotional needs and do not try to fulfill theirs. You are not their therapist, the loving parent they never had, or their best friend. Your job is to teach and encourage them in the Dharma with kindness and compassion.

9. Be careful not to change the explanation of the path so that it corresponds to what you like or what feels comfortable to you.

The Essence of the Dharma and Its Cultural Forms

The following sections were compiled from discussions His Holiness had with Western teachers. When I (Chodron) read them to His Holiness, he was concerned that people could mistakenly think he was setting a policy for the Buddhist world. This is not at all the case. Some people who are not familiar with Tibetan society incorrectly believe that the office of the Dalai Lama is similar to that of the Pope. They think that His Holiness can dictate policy to all Buddhists, or at least to all Tibetan Buddhists. This is far from the truth. Buddhism has never had the type of hierarchy found in the Catholic Church, and while there may be various national or international Buddhist organizations within each Buddhist tradition, they each have their own policies and internal rules. While some groups or organizations tend to rely more than others on the advice of a leader, the Buddha established the monastic saṅgha as a type of democracy where the voice of each fully ordained monastic could be heard and where decisions were made by consensus.

Thus while His Holiness offers his ideas about cultural adaptation, Dharma centers, and teachers, he is not setting down rules or telling all Buddhists how to conduct their lives or the internal affairs of their temple, center, or monastery. If common policies are to be established, he insists it must be done by a gathering of representatives of the concerned parties.

Returning to His Holiness's words: The actual Dharma Jewel—the true cessations of duḥkha and its causes and the true paths that exist in the mindstreams of āryas—does not depend on culture and is the same for all realized beings, no matter when or where they lived. However, the teachings that we study and learn, as well as the rituals and customs in Buddhist communities, were taught in the cultural context of ancient India and passed down for centuries in Asian cultures. This Dharma does not and cannot exist independently of culture because it is shared by and influenced by many people in a particular place.

Distinguishing the Buddha's teachings from cultural overlays is not as easy as it may appear for either Asians or Westerners. Many Asian teachers are not aware of the extent to which their culture has mixed with Buddhism over the centuries, and vice versa. Few Western students are aware of their own cultural preconceptions and assumptions and how these influence their understanding of the Dharma and Buddhist practices. Buddhism is new in the West and many questions exist regarding how and what to adapt to Western cultures while maintaining the authenticity of the path. For these reasons, time, care, and education are needed rather than quick change.

People who accept a new idea or religion, such as Buddhism, should take the essence and adapt it to their own culture. Sometimes I visit places where Western Zen practitioners have Japanese furniture and Western Tibetan Buddhist practitioners have Tibetan furniture. This makes me uncomfortable. Of course, if they like that type of furniture in their homes, that is one thing, but they should not feel that adopting Asian culture or customs is necessary for practicing Buddhism. I often joke with my Western students that even if they wear Tibetan clothes, speak the Tibetan language, and eat tsampa, they are not Tibetan; they still have a big Western nose!

Reform and adaptation of Buddhist customs and rituals are possible and necessary, but we must understand the Dharma well in order to not discard the essence. Some people believe they understand the Buddha's teachings well when in fact they are following their own opinions and preferences. Making up your own brand of teachings and claiming that it is Buddhism is extremely dangerous for both the individual and those he teaches. This happens when people do not correctly understand the Buddhadharma and yet assert themselves to be authentic teachers. Therefore, studying the sūtras and the great treatises, as well as contemplating their meaning and putting them into practice, are essential. People who teach and guide others must be rooted in what the Buddha taught. This is extremely important. The Tibetan master Tsongkhapa always cited quotations from well-known Indian Buddhist texts and commentaries when making reforms. In this way he maintained the authenticity of what he taught.

We must differentiate between what is essential in the Buddhist traditions and what is not, and then be sure to preserve the former. Cultural aspects that arise as a product of society change with time and need not be maintained. The essence to preserve is that which directly leads to liberation and awakening and is useful in daily life.

The four truths, the two truths, the eightfold path of the āryas, rebirth, karma and its effects, and the nature of the mind are not concepts made up by the Buddha. They reflect the nature of reality and the process through which a person can be perfected. Whether people are from Asia or the West, whether they live in ancient times or the present, all people have the same basic human nature, human suffering, and human potential. Since Dharma teachings address these, there is no need to change them. If such teachings were omitted, one would no longer be teaching the basis, path, and result described by the Buddha.

Buddhism came from India, and by adapting to the circumstances and culture in Tibet, it came to be called "Tibetan Buddhism." Such a process will occur in the West as well, although since many Western cultures exist—Spanish, American, French, and so on—a uniform "Western Buddhism" will not exist. Even within one country, there will be many different Buddhist traditions. Although such adaptation is important, it needs to be well-thought-out and evolve over time. We cannot legislate, "This is Western Buddhism and this is not." Neither Asian teachers nor Western students alone can adapt the forms: a joint effort is needed. Qualified Asian teachers are the source of the tradition and sincere Western practitioners will adjust the expression of the teachings to a new culture. Then profound and reliable new forms of Buddhism will develop.

Propagating the Dharma

I pray for the Buddhadharma to flourish in the ten directions; however, I do not aim to propagate the Dharma to everyone. If someone sincerely requests teachings, it is our duty to explain the Dharma to them. Billions of people, who have different dispositions and interests, live on this planet. For some, Buddhism is effective; for others, another religion is a better fit. This was true at the time of the Buddha as well.

The main aim of Buddhism is to benefit others, not to convert people to Buddhism. You should think about how to benefit others with the Dharma, not how to spread your tradition and gain the greatest number of followers. Dharma practice is more than building a Buddhist center, although some teachers seem to have the opposite priority. Great masters in the past did not have big institutions, big hats, or high titles, yet they had deep experience of the Dharma. Nowadays people look for great titles, high thrones, and big temples, and some gurus comport themselves in a pompous manner. This is a sad situation.

Sometimes we are a bit idealistic and think that if the Buddha himself were alive now, all seven billion people on this planet would become Buddhists. But even during the Buddha's time, the entire population didn't follow the Buddhadharma! If someone feels that Buddhism is not logical or suitable for them, trying to convince them is foolish. Instead, pray that they find a path that will benefit them.

Westerners tend to be very sensitive; sometimes a small incident or slight provocation causes great upset. You need to develop great patience to bring Dharma to the West and set up centers, temples, and monasteries. As long as we are in saṃsāra and haven't attained liberation, there will be difficulties.

Even if the Buddha were alive and gave teachings today, he would not be able to resolve all of these problems.

Buddhadharma must be preserved in terms of the individual and the society. As individuals we preserve the Dharma through our study and practice. Teachers and students engaging in Dharma discussions together also constitute preserving the Dharma on the level of the individual.

To preserve Buddhadharma on the societal level, we need to work together in groups. In the Buddha's time, as well as today, the preservation of the Dharma in society depends on the saṅgha, the monastic community that practices the Vinaya. The Vinaya lists over a hundred rites and activities of the saṅgha, from ordination to the manner of expelling someone from the community. These are based on a *saṅghakarman*, a group decision made by the consensus of a saṅgha. One individual alone does not have the power to make these decisions or do these practices. Therefore establishing and supporting Buddhist monasteries in the West is important.

Nowadays lay practitioners in the West go to Dharma centers to learn and practice. Decisions in these communities should be made only after discussion by the whole community. When conclusions regarding certain topics are reached through discussion, write them up as guidelines for the community. Of course, as a community changes and grows, some of these guidelines will need to be altered. This too can be done following discussions in the group.

At present, many Buddhist centers exist even in a single city in the West. Each tradition and even each teacher within a tradition has his own center. I would like to see some nonsectarian Buddhist centers with teachings from all traditions. Of course, the method to actualize this ideal in practical terms requires further thought. I can imagine a single Buddhist temple in a city, with statues of Buddha Śākyamuni for the Theravāda; Padmasambhava, Sakya Paṇḍita, Tsongkhapa, and either Gampopa or Milarepa for the four Tibetan traditions; Mañjuśrī for Zen practitioners; and Tārā as a balance for women. Familiarizing people with all these figures could reduce sectarianism. On the other hand, if you prefer simplicity, a temple with simply a Buddha statue will suffice, and various Buddhist groups in the area could meet there.

Some monasteries in India and some Dharma centers in the West have many beautiful Buddha images and religious objects. At times I wonder if they are in competition with one another to display their wealth. I also wonder if the practitioners' understanding of the Dharma is as elaborate as their buildings. I prefer that the richness of the Dharma be in our heart, not outside ourselves in the environment, and therefore encourage simplicity in the décor of monasteries, Dharma centers, and retreat centers.

We should follow Milarepa's example: he had just an empty cave. Nearby lived a lama who gave teachings to large crowds. He sat on a large throne with ornate parasols all around. One day, Milarepa's sister came and said to Milarepa, "Your way of practicing is very strange and sad. You have nothing, just an empty cave; you live like a beggar. Other lamas have many disciples. They teach a lot and enjoy many luxurious items offered by their disciples. How stupid you are!" To this, Jetsun Mila responded, "I could do elaborate shows but have no time for them because the most important practice is to check our inner world, our mind."

If people wish to build elaborate monasteries and temples, that is fine. I don't oppose it. However, the donors should know that offering money to support the health and education of monastics within the monasteries will bring results that are equally as good as offering funds for statues or temple decorations. I encourage donors to make offerings to monasteries where genuine studies take place, not to monastics who do not study or meditate. Although donors still get a good result from making offerings to them because they hold precepts, the funds are better used to support those who are sincerely trying to improve their mind through study and practice.

The sūtras say that one who offers gold and jewels to the Buddha—or to a Buddha statue that represents the buddhas—accumulates great merit. But the Vinaya Sūtra says that if a monastic is sick and has no one to look after them and no money, then selling ornaments from a buddha statue to buy medicine is permissible. After the person recovers, the money should be repaid. Here the Buddha demonstrates his deep concern for practitioners. If someone has extra money and doesn't have any other way to use it, buying ornaments for Buddha statues is fine. However, if people are in need, preference should be given to them and the money offered to improve their situation.

Traditionally Tibet did not have many secular schools, and what schools there were prior to 1959 were owned by the government or by the wealthy.

So Tibetans did not have the custom of donating money to construct and operate schools and health clinics. Today we need to change this.

Although the Buddha's teachings are based on compassion, some people are more concerned about their own upper rebirth and liberation and less with others' welfare. Therefore they think chiefly of creating merit by offering to the Three Jewels. However, those who practice bodhicitta should be more concerned with benefiting sentient beings than with creating merit for themselves, and thus they should support schools, healthcare facilities, old-age homes, and other social services, as well as help genuine practitioners have the food, clothing, shelter, and medicine they need to continue their Dharma practice.

What to Teach in the West

Teachers should teach people what is suitable according to their level, interest, and disposition. For example, although emptiness is the essence of the Dharma and understanding it is crucial for awakening, it should not be taught to everyone. People need a firm foundation in conventional truths—such as karma and its effects and the nature of saṃsāra—so that they do not misunderstand the teachings on emptiness and think that nothing exists or that "there's no good and no bad because everything is empty." Nāgārjuna says in *Treatise on the Middle Way* (MMK 24.11):

> By a misperception of emptiness
> a person of little intelligence is destroyed,
> like a snake incorrectly seized
> or a spell incorrectly cast.

For this reason, the bodhisattva ethical restraints warn against teaching emptiness to people who are not prepared. They need first to gain firm understanding of the conventional world by studying karma and its effects, the disadvantages of saṃsāra, and love and compassion.

Practical teachings, such as the stages of the path to awakening and mind training, are more effective for a general audience in the West than the sophisticated philosophical texts studied in monastic universities. Most non-Buddhists come to the Dharma to seek help in calming their afflictions and creating better relationships with people in their life. What you teach should reflect this need.

As students grow in the Dharma, gradually introduce more topics, remembering to teach according to their level. They may initially have resistance to certain topics, so answer their questions and, if they have objections, encourage them to put those topics on the back burner for the time being and return to them later. Don't change the Dharma teachings by saying the Buddha didn't teach a particular topic simply because the students initially find it difficult to understand. When students are ready to hear more advanced topics, teach them, but explain them initially in an easy-to-understand manner without a lot of complicated language. The meaning of the Buddha's teachings should be accessible to everyone, not just to a learned minority.

Nevertheless, study of the philosophical texts can deepen students' understanding of the Dharma and help their meditation practice. This level of study should be available for Westerners who find it valuable, and I hope that Westerners will continue the tradition of this deep philosophical study that Indian and Tibetan sages have found beneficial for so many centuries. I also hope that Westerners can invigorate traditional debate by bringing Western concepts onto the debating courtyard. For example, practitioners could debate Buddhist versus scientific views of the nature of mind, Buddhist and Judeo-Christian views of creation and causality, and soul versus selflessness. This would be extremely valuable for Buddhists, scientists, and followers of other faiths.

The Buddhist approach must be based on fact and investigation. The Buddha himself and the Indian masters have made that clear. If we find anything in the Buddha's words that does not comply with reality, we should not accept it literally. In the Abhidharma, there are statements saying that the world is flat and Mount Meru is at the center of the universe. If it were necessary to accept this literally in order to be a Buddhist, then I would not be considered a Buddhist! These statements of the structure of the universe were incorporated from the prevailing worldview in society during the time of the Buddha. They are not the Buddha's unique teachings and liberation from saṃsāra does not depend on accepting them.

The sequence of the stages of the path to awakening as taught in Tibetan Buddhism needs to be reconsidered when Dharma is introduced to non-Buddhists. Teaching beginners about relying on a spiritual master confuses them. This topic comes at the beginning of Tibetan texts because the traditional Tibetan audience for those texts is Buddhist. Such an audience already has some knowledge and belief in topics such as rebirth, karma, and the Three Jewels. In some cases, the audience for this teaching consisted of practitioners who were about to receive tantric empowerment. Clearly, how the teachings are given to trained Tibetan monastics who grew up in a Buddhist culture is different from the presentation for Western spiritual seekers who are not Buddhist and simply want to learn the basic Buddhist approach and begin a meditation practice. To help the latter group, beginning with the four truths and the two truths (conventional and ultimate) is more skillful. In this way, newcomers will build a firm foundation in the Dharma and gradually come to understand more difficult subjects.

How extensive should a teaching be? On the one hand, simplicity and brevity keep students focused on the important points. Because they can understand and practice what they learn, they don't feel lost. On the other hand, if the teaching is too concise, the students may lose sight of the wider picture and be unable to understand certain points in their proper context.

Sentient beings have so many distorted thoughts and disturbing emotions that one teaching or one practice cannot address all of them. One day this thought is more active, so we need one practice. Another day another is stronger, and a different antidote is needed. Our mind is complicated, and transforming it requires practices that are sophisticated and complex. By understanding this, we will appreciate the various levels on which the Buddha taught and will be able to reconcile the diverse interpretations of his teachings.

The main factor for transforming our minds is reflection on the four truths, the two truths, loving kindness, and altruism. Without reflecting first on these points, the benefit of watching our breath or visualizing tantric deities is limited. Similarly, simply saying to ourselves that things are impermanent is not enough to change our entrenched misconceptions. We must analyze and use reason to convince ourselves. For this reason, I recommend that newcomers as well as seasoned students continually engage in analytical meditation on these teachings.

Some Westerners have asked if skipping the preliminary practices such as prostrations, Vajrasattva mantra, refuge, maṇḍala offering, and guru yoga in order to proceed directly to the higher practices would be an acceptable adaptation in the West. The purpose of the preliminaries is to make the mind more receptive so that meditation will bring realizations. If our mind is obscured, doing the preliminaries will remove obstacles and create conducive conditions so that we can gain realizations of the path and integrate the Dharma in our mind and life. If someone has already done sufficient purification and accumulation of merit in the past and is able to attain realizations without doing the preliminaries, that is fine. But if they cannot, doing these practices is highly recommended.

Teaching according to the Audience

A good teacher will be aware of the interests, dispositions, and Dharma background of the audience and will explain various points in a variety of ways in order to meet the audience's needs. For example, sometimes I speak to non-Buddhists who are curious about Tibet and the Dalai Lama. In this case, I emphasize secular ethics and the importance of compassion, forgiveness, and harmony. I describe patience, kindness, seeing the best qualities in others, and self-confidence that is directed in a positive way. Sometimes I bring in scientific findings to reinforce a point—for example, citing studies that have shown that a mother's compassion is critical for the proper development of the child's brain and that patients' trust in the doctor speeds their recovery. In the talks I include some antidotes for disturbing emotions. By applying these, they will see the positive effects of the Dharma on their lives and relationships. I also explain that basic human nature is gentle, kind, and compassionate. The reasons given to support these beliefs are based on common daily experiences, so I do not speak about rebirth, karma, nirvāṇa, or buddhahood. In this way, these people will hear ideas that will help them to live a good life now and receive a good rebirth in the future. Thinking about good values sets a foundation for them to become better people and better citizens of this world.

A second type of audience has keen interest in Buddhism but does not know about or understand some of the basic beliefs or assumptions on which the path to awakening is based, such as rebirth, countless sentient beings, and infinite eons. Most non-Buddhists did not grow up with these notions. Therefore a more academic approach is better for these people. Explain the two truths, the four truths, rebirth and karma, and the structure of the path. Talk about dependent arising and the way to apply it to many fields and disciplines. Then let them reflect. Time is needed to think about these topics and to gain some certainty. It does not happen quickly after hearing one explanation or reading one book. After hearing and reflecting upon teachings for a while, some people will begin to think that future lives are possible. They will accept this way of thinking, develop genuine interest, and continue studying. On this basis, then teach them how to practice the Buddhadharma.

A third audience consists of people who have some idea of rebirth, karma and its effects, and the four truths. They accept the existence of saṃsāra and nirvāṇa; they have heard a little about emptiness and dependent arising and are eager to learn more. The usual Buddhist approach is suitable for these people. We can teach a Dharma text or explain a topic from the perspective of the Buddhist worldview.

When teaching Buddhism to these people, teach the four truths, the three higher trainings, and the four immeasurables; do not explain the visualization of deities and maṇḍalas as found in Vajrayāna. Many people are exposed to Vajrayāna too soon. Some people are put off by it because they lack a proper foundation of the Buddhist worldview. Others started visualizing deities and reciting mantras, but because their understanding of the path is vague, they don't understand the purpose of such practices or the correct way to do them. The Buddha began by teaching his disciples the four establishments of mindfulness and the thirty-seven harmonies with awakening. He did not begin with guru yoga, which comes in a particular context and is only one part of the path.

Tantra is an advanced practice, and to do it people must receive empowerments. Since this cannot be received from a book, they must seek a living spiritual master with a valid lineage to give the empowerment. From this perspective, guru yoga becomes important. Tantric practice comes later in a practitioner's development, after sufficient preparation. Empowerments and tantric teachings are not for everyone who attends a Dharma center. They should not be among the initial topics a newcomer is exposed to.

Many Westerners who want to explore Buddhism grew up with faith in God. It is not wise to teach them deity and protector practices at the beginning, for they easily project notions of God onto these Buddhist figures, seeing them as external, truly existent beings. They then may have blind faith in them or, conversely, may feel guilty or fearful if they act negatively, thinking the protectors will punish them. According to Buddhism, we are our own master, as the teaching on the twelve links of dependent origination shows. Only introduce devotional practices when the people have received sufficient preparation, and then explain them well so that people gain the proper understanding.

The Buddha as well as the great Indian masters taught according to the students' mental dispositions and interests, and we should do the same. For example, they presented diverse philosophical tenets according to the students' aptitude. What and how they taught was also influenced by the conditions in society at that time. For this reason, if we look carefully, we will discern differences in how the Indian and the Tibetan masters guided their disciples on the path, due to the differing circumstances in which they lived. In ancient India, non-Buddhist teachers and their teachings had a strong influence in society. Thus Indian sages such as Nāgārjuna, Āryadeva, Dignāga, Dharmakīrti, Candrakīrti, and Śāntideva emphasized reasoning as the way to distinguish correct beliefs from incorrect ones.

In Tibet, on the other hand, the situation was different. From the time Buddhism came to Tibet, there have been no strong rival philosophical systems. Although Bön, an indigenous spiritual tradition, pre-dates Buddhism in Tibet, Bön practitioners gradually adopted many elements from Buddhism. Points that were debated extensively in India were automatically accepted in Tibet. The Vajrayāna, which was not practiced publicly in India, became popular in Tibet, where it was taken for granted that almost everyone would participate in certain permissory rituals (T. *rjes snang*) qualifying them to do the practices of such deities as Avalokiteśvara or White Tārā. Also, in the latter centuries of Indian Buddhism, Buddhism was largely confined to the monastic universities; the laypeople in the villages mostly followed Hinduism or Jainism. In Tibet, Buddhism spread throughout the country—with the exception of a small Muslim population—and was practiced in the home. Because of this difference in society, the approach Tibetan masters used in guiding their students differed from that of Indian masters. While monastics follow a rigorous program of study, reflection, and meditation, lay followers do devotional practices and daily recitations of prayers.

Since Buddhism is new in the West, and a multiplicity of philosophical, religious, scientific, and psychological views exist in Western countries, it is best for us Buddhists to return to the way of the Indian masters. According to these sages, first one studies, and on the basis of correct understanding, one comes to have faith. In other words, Western students should not be encouraged to have devotion for the teachings or the teacher from the very beginning. Instead, they should be encouraged to learn, investigate, and reflect upon the teachings. Through their own examination, they will see the validity of the teachings and the faith they subsequently generate will be based on knowledge, not blind belief.

I tell people who attend my Dharma talks not to think of me as their guru, but simply as a spiritual friend. Of course, later if someone takes monastic precepts, the bodhisattva vow, or tantric empowerment from me, it's a different situation. Devotion to the Buddha or to a teacher is not simply saying, with big eyes, "The Buddha and my teacher are so wonderful!" Therefore I encourage people new to Buddhism to listen, think, and assess the validity of the Dharma for themselves. They should practice what they learn and experience it themselves. On that basis, they will know that the Buddha's teachings benefit them and will develop genuine interest in the Dharma. Through this, they will naturally admire the Buddha and respect the person who explains the teachings to them. Guru yoga comes later, after ten, fifteen, or even twenty years.

Teach only what you have conviction in. For example, I have doubts about the geographical location of the hells as described in the *Treasury of Knowledge*, so I do not include this topic in my teaching. In addition, do not teach everything you have learned, but only those things with which you have had experience and which will benefit the audience.

If your teacher asks you to instruct a group, you may do so. If some people ask you to teach, ask permission from your spiritual mentor. Do not set yourself up as a teacher without permission. At each step, as you assume more responsibility for instructing others, consult your teacher. For example, if someone requests you to give refuge, check with your teacher, receive their approval, and then request them to instruct you on the proper way to conduct the refuge ceremony and give the five lay precepts. Should someone request you to give the bodhisattva vow, make sure that you keep the bodhisattva precepts well. Know the difference between aspiring and engaging bodhicitta and be familiar with the ceremonies for each. If you are not familiar with this or if you do not know the eighteen root and forty-six auxiliary transgressions well, it is better to refer the person to your teacher or another practitioner who will bestow the bodhisattva vow.

If you are requested to give a tantric empowerment, check with your tantric spiritual mentor. Make sure you have received that empowerment and have completed the requisite retreat and fire pūjā. Giving an empowerment and guiding students in tantric practice are big responsibilities, so you may wish to refer people to your teachers for these. As Buddhism evolves in the West, the empowerment texts will be translated into various languages. Then you can learn how to perform empowerments properly and ensure that the rituals are complete.

As time goes on, sincere and wise Western practitioners will write texts and ceremonies in their own language and a body of literature will gradually build up. To ensure that this process proceeds well, those of you who are first-generation Buddhist teachers in the West must be very conscientious.

Asian teachers should try to be aware of Westerners' specific problems so they can adapt their teaching methods. Learning about Western culture and values will help them to avoid teaching in an inappropriate way that results in misunderstanding or disappointment.

It is not skillful for Asian teachers to teach Western audiences as if they were speaking to Asian Buddhists. If an Asian teacher displays a culturally chauvinistic attitude toward Western practitioners, the Westerners should simply not pay attention. However, Westerners too should avoid cultural arrogance, thinking that because some of their societies are more advanced technologically they can improve everything they come in contact with.

For both Asians and Westerners, the establishment of teachers' training programs would be helpful. These programs should emphasize teaching skills as well as communication, mediation, and counseling skills. For teachers who are not familiar with government regulations, learning how to observe those is also important so that the Dharma center, temple, or monastery conducts all affairs—be it constructing a new building, remodeling an old one, or procuring visas for teachers or monastics—according to the law.

Translations and Rituals

The texts and sādhanas we chant are designed to assist us in visualization and meditation. The purpose of reciting the words is to contemplate their meaning. Without knowing the meaning of the words you chant, the value of your recitation declines sharply. Therefore, unless you know Tibetan, you should do your recitations in your own language. In that way, you will understand what the text says and will be able to visualize and meditate accordingly. Mantras, however, are recited in Sanskrit; we believe there is a special blessing from doing this.

In general, we Tibetans do not pronounce Sanskrit correctly. When I hear some Indian scholars, especially those in Varanasi University, recite the Sanskrit mantras and texts, I find it very touching and inspiring. Some of the melodies are truly remarkable; we Tibetans cannot recite this way. Maybe in a previous life I was a lazy disciple of a great Indian master, and that is why I feel so attracted to this chanting.

At the moment, translation terms and translation styles vary considerably from one translator to another. To standardize translation terms, scholars and practitioners could meet and gradually come to a consensus. Asian scholars cannot decide this. Much thought is required to select appropriate terms, and this selection should be done by those knowledgeable in the language and in the meaning of the Buddha's teachings.

Of course, each translator has his or her own style and getting a group of translators to agree on standard terms would be quite an undertaking! Let's see how the situation evolves. It could be that everyone will employ their own terms and styles, and gradually over time most people will gravitate toward one.

Westerners do not need to use Asian names or religious titles such as "lama." Much confusion can arise from not properly understanding the meaning of such Asian words, and because no uniform way of acquiring Tibetan titles exists, people with different levels of qualities use the same title. If it is beneficial to use a title at all, a Western one that conveys the correct connotation would be better.

If Westerners would like to have Buddhist ceremonies for births, rites of passage to adulthood, marriage, and funerals, meetings can be held to create them. Simple ceremonies for Buddhists of all traditions would be good. However, if a Buddhist marriage ceremony is created and its performance involves fully ordained monastics, care must be taken not to cause an infraction of the precept prohibiting monks and nuns from matchmaking. Monastics could perform an offering ritual with the couple and their dear ones in attendance, enabling the couple to create merit as an auspicious way to begin their marriage. However, it would be more appropriate if a lay Buddhist performed the actual marriage ceremony.

Many Ways to Benefit Sentient Beings

In addition to teaching, counseling, giving precepts, and enhancing our own Dharma practice, there are many ways to benefit sentient beings. These include chanting protective scriptures and mantras, performing offering ceremonies, reciting words of truth, enabling sentient beings to contact holy objects, and recollecting the Buddha. All of these rely to some extent on the power of the Three Jewels to bless and inspire our minds, and all Buddhist traditions engage in these in one way or another.

Followers of the Pāli tradition often recite the *Protective Discourses*, or *Paritta Suttas*. Followers of the Mahāyāna chant the names or mantras of Amitābha Buddha, Medicine Buddha, Chenrezig (Kuan Yin), and other bodhisattvas. They also do pūjās (offering ceremonies) to create merit and eliminate obstacles. Both traditions meditate on recollection of the Buddha (*Buddha-anusmṛti*, C. *nien-fo*) and recite words of truth.

Because results arise dependent on many factors, the effects of these practices are undoubtedly contingent on the motivation of the practitioners and their mental states and level of concentration when doing the practice. These more devotional practices work in a psychological and mysterious way—mysterious meaning that our rational mind and present level of knowledge are not fully able to grasp the dependently arising way these causes bring their effects.

Chanting Protective Scriptures and Mantras

Protective discourses (*paritrāṇa*, *paritta*) express basic Dharma principles. Chanting and hearing them reminds people of these principles so that they can practice them in their daily lives. Monastics from the Pāli tradition often recite them to teach the Dharma as well as to create auspiciousness and receive blessings for new activities, such as blessing a new residence, opening a business, and beginning a marriage. The *Jewel Sutta* (*Ratana Sutta*, Sn 2.1) expresses the qualities of the Three Jewels, the *Sutta of Great Blessings* (*Mahāmaṅgala Sutta*, Sn 2.4) teaches how to live a good life, the *Sutta on Loving-Kindness* (*Mettā Sutta*, Sn 1.8) focuses on developing a kind and caring attitude toward others. All three sūtras promote harmony in society and faith in the Three Jewels.[20]

Using the example of the *Jewel Sutta*, we see how protective discourses inspire and bless the mind. This sūtra was taught at Vaiśālī, when the city was undergoing great hardship due to famine, evil spirits, and the plague. The citizens, who were from the Licchavi clan, invited the Buddha and Saṅgha to come, hoping they could remedy the situation. To remedy this harm, prevent future harm, and increase the safety and well-being of all, the Buddha taught this sūtra on the qualities of the Three Jewels[21] with a heart of loving-kindness and compassion for the spirits causing the difficulties, for the devas living in the area, and for the human beings experiencing hardship. Through the power of his reciting this and of the citizens contemplating its meaning and generating faith in the Three Jewels, the demons causing the havoc fled. Good conditions were restored to the city, its citizens took refuge, and the town later became a stronghold of the Dharma.

In the present day, the sūtra is often recited for similar purposes and brings similar results. Reciting the verses connects our minds to the qualities of the Three Jewels. This draws the spiritual power (P. *ānubhāva*) of the Buddha, Dharma, and Saṅgha into our mind. This spiritual power comes from the Buddha's practice—his accomplishment of the ten perfections and his complete cultivation of the thirty-seven harmonies with awakening—and the results of this practice—the ten powers of a tathāgata, the four fearlessnesses, and his wisdom and compassion. It also arises from the Dharma—true cessations and true paths—and from the Saṅgha and its marvelous qualities. By calling these qualities to mind, devotion, confidence, and trust arise in our mind, and we are imbued with inspiration. That transformation of our mind is the blessing.

Words of Truth

With that virtuous state of mind, we then declare words of truth (*satyavacana, saccavacana*). In this case, with loving-kindness and compassion, we generate the strong wish for the happiness, well-being, safety, and security of ourselves and others. One way of explaining this is that our mind becomes a channel for the blessing power of the Three Jewels—a power that arises due to their virtuous qualities. By reflecting on their qualities, we draw their spiritual energy into our mind and then express it in a strong determination for the welfare of self and others. Another way of explaining it is that our mind becomes transformed into virtue by reflecting on the wonderful qualities of the Three Jewels, and the power of that virtuous mind is expressed in the determination of truth. In both cases, spiritual power arises due to the virtues of the Three Jewels and the transformation that has occurred in our mind; in both cases, the result is compassionate wishes for the well-being of self and others.

Initially, our words of truth may not have much power because our mind is not yet strong in the Dharma. However, as we continue to practice—living ethically, being generous, generating loving-kindness, listening to and reflecting on the Buddha's teachings—the power of our declaring words of truth increases. In the case of the Buddha, it increased to such an extent that the evil spirits at Vaiśālī could not endure the force of his virtue and realizations and left the town. The healing of Vaiśālī was not due to the Buddha's magical powers or to his being omnipotent, because the Buddha is neither omnipotent nor a performer of magic. The effect a buddha can have on us sentient beings and the world is dependent on our mental states and our karma.

Found in both the Pāli and Sanskrit traditions, words of truth are spoken with a strong virtuous intention motivated by love and compassion. They are not a promise to do an action, but a statement of fact. The truth of this fact assures the occurrence of an event. Often the person who utters words of truth appeals to natural forces to validate their statements. For example, after attaining supreme awakening under the bodhi tree, the Buddha declared his attainment and, putting his right hand on the ground, asked the earth goddess to validate its truth. She appeared and did so.

Another example of a paritta in which words of truth are uttered occurs in the *Aṅgulimāla Sutta* (MN 86), in which the terrifying bandit and murderer was subdued and converted by the Buddha. After he was ordained as a monk but before he became an arhat, Aṅgulimāla was on alms round when he saw a woman giving birth to a deformed child. Overwhelmed with compassion, he thought, "How beings are afflicted!" He told the Buddha what he saw, and the Buddha instructed him to return and say to the woman, "Sister, since I was born with the noble birth [that is, when he became an ārya], I do not recall that I have ever intentionally deprived a living being of life. By this truth, may you be well and may your infant be well!" Aṅgulimāla did as instructed—what an amazing, truthful, and compassionate declaration this was, made by someone who had murdered 999 people! By the force of this truth spoken by a virtuous monastic, both the mother and child were healed. Nowadays people recite the same words of truth found in the scriptures. In Theravādin countries, Aṅgulimāla's words of truth are often recited by a monk when a pregnant woman is ready to give birth.

The power of words of truth depends on the sincerity, compassion, and truth of the person who utters them. Knowing this, it is essential to pay special attention to the state of our mind when reciting words of truth. The *Questions of King Milinda* (*Milindapañha* 4.1.42) relates an event that occurred when the Ganges overflowed its banks and a city was threatened. The king brought many sages to the site, but the water continued to rise even after each one declared words of truth. The prostitute Bindumatī heard of the danger to the city and went to the riverbank, where she uttered words of truth. Much to everyone's surprise the waters subsided. The townspeople questioned how she could do this, to which she replied, "Since I have been in this profession, I have never distinguished between my clients. I treat them all equally, without discrimination based on their caste, physical appearance, or wealth. I used this truth as the basis for my words of truth."

The *Sivi-Jātaka* (*Jātaka* 499) recounts how King Sivi gave both his eyes to the god Śakra, who, disguised as a blind brahmin, tested the king's determination to give what was most dear to him by requesting his eyes. To illustrate the purity of his motivation in giving both his eyes, the king spoke words of truth, by which one eye was restored. When the king again spoke words of truth, saying, "A greater joy and more delight that action did afford. If these my solemn words be true, may the other eye be restored!" his second eye was restored.

In the *Smaller Amitābha Sūtra*, the Buddha uttered words of truth several times. The first time he said:

> Śāriputra, as I perceive that such blissful benefits are matters of great importance, I pronounce these words of truth: Good men and good women of pure faith who hear Amitāyus Buddha's name of inconceivable merits and also learn of the Pure Buddha Land of Great Bliss (Sukhāvatī) should all receive [the teaching] with faith, arouse aspiration, practice the method as prescribed, and attain birth in that buddha land.

The buddhas of the ten directions then uttered the words of truth:

> Sentient beings should all receive in faith this gate of the Dharma concerning praise of the inconceivable merits of the buddha land and protection by all buddhas.

As stated by the Buddha in the sūtra itself, the purpose of these words of truth are to "urge sentient beings to receive this teaching in faith, in order to guide and benefit them and give them peace and bliss."

In Tibetan Buddhism, words of truth are expressed when making offerings to the Three Jewels:

> By the power of the truth of the Three Jewels, the power of the inspiration of all the buddhas and bodhisattvas, the great might of the completed two collections [of merit and wisdom], and the power of the intrinsically pure inconceivable sphere of reality, may [these offerings] become suchness.

Throughout history, Tibetan masters have written words of truth. In the last century, Jamyang Khyentsé Chökyi Lodrö wrote "The Sage's Powerful Words of Truth,"[22] and His Holiness the present Dalai Lama composed "Words of Truth," a prayer for the freedom of the Tibetan people.[23]

Offering Ceremonies

In Mahāyāna countries, people often request monastics to conduct offering ceremonies in order to create merit that is dedicated for a specific purpose in addition to dedicating for the full awakening of all sentient beings. The Medicine Buddha pūjā is done to remedy illness, and the

Green Tārā pūjā is performed to counteract obstacles and hindrances or to bring success when beginning a new project. The *Amitābha Sūtra* and Amitābha's name are recited to help the recently deceased to be born in Sukhāvatī pure land. Kuan Yin's name is often recited for this purpose, and in Tibetan Buddhism people recite and contemplate the *Guru Pūjā* and other sādhanas to create merit for many different occasions, ranging from beginning a marriage to wishing someone to be born in a pure land in their next life.

Holy Objects

Just hearing Dharma words that express goodness or seeing Dharma objects sets good latencies on sentient beings' minds, even if they lack the ability to understand them. These latencies will ripen in their having a connection with the Dharma in the future. For this reason, many spiritual mentors encourage their students to make statues of various buddhas and bodhisattvas, to circumambulate stūpas, and to recite mantras, sūtras, and other Dharma texts.

In the *Path of Purification*, Buddhaghosa tells the story of a frog who was in the vicinity when the Buddha was teaching on the banks of the Gaggara Lake. While the frog was hearing the Buddha speak the Dharma, a cowherd put a stick on the frog's head and crushed it. The frog was born in the Celestial Realm of the Thirty-Three (Trāyastriṃśa, Tāvatiṃsa). Seeking the cause of this wonderful rebirth, he saw that it was due to having heard the Buddha's voice. With gratitude, the former frog went to pay respects to the Buddha, who again taught him the Dharma, whereby he became a stream-enterer.

The Nālandā tradition tells the story of Sthiramati (Sāramati), a great Abhidharma scholar, who in his previous birth was born a pigeon that often perched outside Vasubandhu's cave. There he heard Vasubandhu recite the entire Abhidharma. In his next life, the pigeon was born as a boy in the area. He ordained as a monastic and became a renowned Abhidharma scholar due to having had the seeds of this topic planted in his mindstream when he was a pigeon.

In the pure-land practice, just hearing the name of Amitābha can have a powerful effect on a person's mindstream, causing merit created in previous lives to ripen. Ou-i says:[24]

> No matter what your station in life, all you have to do is hear the Buddha's name and the good roots you have accumulated over many eons immediately ripen, and all forms of negativity and perversity are transformed into virtues.

However, Ou-i continues by clarifying that for inspiration and wisdom to arise, the reciters must have refuge in the Three Jewels, meditate on the bodhicitta aspiration, and maintain ethical conduct:

> Merely hearing the name of Amitābha [without faith and vows] may become a long-term causal basis [for one's awakening], but it cannot be called the wisdom that comes from hearing. Reciting the Buddha's name is a matter of being mindful of the Buddha's name from moment to moment—thus it is the wisdom that comes from reflecting [on what you have heard].

Although what we are exposed to may influence us in subtle and profound ways, we don't want to remain ignorant and leave our spiritual progress to such rare occasions as serendipitously hearing the Dharma. Practice is essential.

Recollections of the Buddha

The formal recollection of the Buddha entails reflecting on the Buddha's qualities one by one. This recollection is much deeper and has more impact on the mind than reciting sūtras quickly. Done in a meditative manner, it can lead to samādhi.

The Pāli and Sanskrit traditions both speak of the recollections of the Buddha, Dharma, Saṅgha, ethical conduct, generosity, and deities.[25] In the Sanskrit tradition, recollection of Amitābha Buddha or Akṣobhya Buddha generates faith in these buddhas and increases our aspiration to be born in their pure lands. They also inspire us to generate the qualities of the holy beings, such as compassion.

Areas of Caution

Buddhism is new to the West; it is still in the process of finding its footing in Western culture. As such, there are many areas where caution is needed.

First, students may have unrealistic projections on and expectations of Dharma teachers. Many people tend toward a black-and-white way of thinking, with little appreciation for gray areas. If they admire someone, they praise him or her to the skies. This can lead to idolizing Dharma teachers and having unrealistic expectations of them. To avoid this, when you teach, make it clear from the beginning that you are an ordinary practitioner, not a superhuman.

When a student seeks guidance, the teacher should respond and help. But if there is danger—for example, that the student will become emotionally attached to the teacher or overly dependent on the teacher's guidance—then for the benefit of all parties the teacher should keep some distance. Each case must be looked at individually; a general statement can't be made that will apply to all situations.

Once a woman who attended teachings told me she loved me. I responded, "Nāgārjuna said, 'Like the earth, water, wind, and fire, medicinal herbs, and trees in the wilderness, may I always be an object of enjoyment for all beings, just as they wish,' so if you want to think of me like that, it's okay." I didn't let what she said affect my mental attitude or behavior toward her. Another time a Russian lady said she wanted to marry me. To her I said, "Do not think like that. I'm a monk and will remain one!"

I have had the experience of people coming to me, publicly and privately, thinking "The Dalai Lama will bless me." It is not wise for them to think like this. I can't do this. Sometimes people think "The Dalai Lama will heal me." This way of thinking is also dangerous, for both the teacher and the student. The teacher may be tempted to act as if he had some extraordinary ability, and the student may worship the teacher instead of practicing the teachings. Personally, I am skeptical of those who claim to heal diseases; I make sure not to present myself in that way. To avoid misleading others or becoming inflated myself, even when people look with devotion and ask, "Are you awakened?" I always reply, "I am a simple Buddhist monk. No more, no less."

Second, there may be the temptation to dilute the Buddha's teachings in order to make them acceptable to a larger number of people. In other words, a teacher may have faith in a certain teaching but not teach it because he or she is concerned that students will not find them pleasing and will stop attending the Dharma center. Although you should teach according to people's dispositions, it is harmful to leave out certain aspects of the Dharma because you are more concerned with the number of students than with the purity of the teachings. As I mentioned before, our purpose is not to celebrate that many people call themselves Buddhist. We are not out to win converts or to become well-known teachers. Our purpose is to benefit sentient beings.

Third, a teacher may have deep doubt about some points and omit these teachings or say that the Buddha didn't really mean that or teach that. Simply because certain points do not agree with our opinions, we cannot say that the Buddha never taught them or that they are not part of the Buddhist worldview. Especially when teaching others, a person cannot dismiss parts of the teachings that he does not agree with and still say he is explaining the entire path of the Buddhadharma. To do so is very dangerous, because without extensive learning, thinking, and meditating, we are unable to properly discriminate what is correct and what is not. We could easily fall into picking and choosing from various teachings, putting them together, and inventing a spiritual path that agrees with our ideas. Not only would this harm us but it would also cheat students and lead to the degeneration of the Buddha's teachings in our world.

Fourth, a teacher may become emotionally dependent on his or her students. When you are in the position of teaching the Dharma, be conscientious about how you present yourself. Learn to work with your emotions and your wish for companionship by applying the mind training teachings. Don't expect your students to take care of you emotionally and don't draw them into fulfilling your personal needs for validation, appreciation, or love. Try to emulate the great practitioners such as Milarepa, who, due to their renunciation, have great love for sentient beings. Because their compassion is free from attachment, everyone is their friend. Such a practitioner has no needs arising from attachment and prefers no companions. Of course such people are rare, but we must emulate these good examples. Maybe this year we cannot be like that, but next year or after ten or fifteen years, we too can cultivate this kind of attitude.

Lay teachers should also have appropriate friends with whom they can discuss their emotions and their difficulties. Their students should not be put in the position of having to support the teacher emotionally or solve the teacher's personal problems.

Fifth, a teacher and student may be sexually attracted to each other. Due to afflictions and karma, we now have this body that tends toward attachment—including sexual desire—and anger. When the body is weak, anger comes more easily; when it is well, more sexual desire arises. Even if you control the sexual desire, on subtle levels attachment still persists. Much depends on your practice. Even though you may not be able to eliminate your sexual desire, if you have enough conviction and spiritual strength, you will remain balanced and not get distracted from your spiritual goals and the precepts that will guide you to them. I include myself on this level.

The layperson's precepts do not prohibit sexual relations, so there is more danger of lay followers misusing sexuality. Therefore it is best for lay teachers to be married upāsikās or upāsakas and to live according to the five precepts, which include abandoning unwise or unkind sexual behavior. Monastic teachers must be celibate. Both monastic and lay teachers must avoid touching students inappropriately—in a sexual manner or in a manner that someone could misinterpret to be sexual in nature.

Another area of caution is the tendency for the eight worldly concerns to pollute your mind. For example, I was reading the works of Tsukang Lama Rinpoché, a respected and learned practitioner, and noticed that his way of explaining the process for taking refuge was the same as I use. On the one hand I was happy, knowing that I wasn't teaching my own fabrication and that there was sound basis in the writing of an authentic sage. Meanwhile, in one corner of my mind was the thought of the eight worldly concerns, "I want all the credit for this excellent explanation. If other people read Tsukang Lama's book, they'll think that I copied my explanation from him and my reputation as the originator of this explanation will be lost!"

The Tibetan tradition emphasizes the threefold process of listening to the teachings, reflecting on their meaning, and meditating to integrate them into our lives. Thus practitioners need to balance responsibilities of teaching others with their own practice. When I teach, my daily meditation is shortened because of time constraints, but at the same time the Dharma becomes more effective in my mind because I am thinking deeply about it. Also, when students ask questions, I must reflect on the meaning of the Dharma in order to answer them properly.

If a teacher is sincere and dedicated to helping others without concern for fame, problems will not arise. But if a teacher has great status yet lacks the corresponding spiritual realizations, there is the danger of creating an image to protect oneself. For that reason, I advise those who teach the Dharma to spend a few months each year focusing on their personal practice and a few months teaching others. They must have time to develop their own practice and deepen their understanding to effectively teach others.

In conclusion, teaching the Dharma is a wonderful opportunity to share what is precious, to help others, and to create boundless merit. However, we must approach it seriously and responsibly so that we create benefit, not damage, for ourselves and others.

Respect for the Dharma

The Dharma is our real refuge; the Dharma is the object of our highest respect. Śākyamuni Buddha is the product of the Dharma Jewel, which is the true paths and true cessations of duḥkha and its causes. The resultant awakening that he attained is so magnificent that since we venerate and admire it, we should also esteem its causes, the Dharma teachings. To indicate this, before the Buddha taught the Perfection of Wisdom sūtras, he himself arranged the seat on which he sat when giving these teachings.

Similarly, to show respect for the path to liberation, when five hundred arhats gathered after the Buddha's parinirvāṇa at the First Council to recite the teachings they had heard the Buddha give, they stacked their saffron upper robes to make a throne on which the reciter would sit. Such veneration was accorded not to the person but to the teachings that explained the true paths and true cessations. Similarly, nowadays a teacher sitting on a throne or high seat to teach indicates that the teaching he or she gives is worthy of admiration and reverence.

To signify the preciousness of the Dharma teachings and to prevent arrogance, before sitting on the Dharma seat, the teacher makes three prostrations to the seat as well as to the lineage of teachers and to the Dharma teachings. While sitting down, the teacher recites a verse from the *Dia-*

mond Sūtra (*Vajracchedikā*) to recall the transient and empty nature of phenomena:

> A star, a visual aberration, a flame of a lamp,
> an illusion, a drop of dew, or a bubble,
> a dream, a flash of lightening, a cloud—
> see conditioned things as such.

Recalling the insubstantial nature of the world helps the teacher to sustain a pure motivation for teaching, one that is not defiled by worldly concerns, such as the wish to receive offerings, praise, reputation, or a large and devoted following.

The danger of arrogance arising when one sits on a high seat is real. In Tibet some lamas succumbed to what I call the "high-throne syndrome," competing to see who had the highest throne and was thus the highest lama. To counteract this, the Fifth Dalai Lama stipulated that the thrones of the lamas in the audience should all be exactly the same height. However, some clever attendants of one lama managed to slip a slate under the cushion of their teacher's throne. After a while, when all the others' cushions had compressed because lamas were sitting on them, the lama sitting on the seat with the slate underneath appeared higher than the others. He and his disciples shined with pride.

Buddhadharma in Asia

Buddhism contains vast and profound teachings that are set forth in detail. It is scientific and logical. But in many Buddhist countries the people do not seriously study the Dharma; for them Buddhism is just part of the tradition and culture of their country. They engage in ancestor worship, perform the practices of folk religions, and pray to the Buddha and to worldly gods without distinguishing between them. As the younger generation reexamines these old traditions, they sometimes discard Buddhism along with ancestor worship and turn to other religions. Considering oneself a Buddhist simply because it is part of one's family tradition without understanding it does not have much meaning to them. If someone introduces a new and different religion, it may seem more attractive, and that person may adopt the new faith. Of course, this is their personal decision, but it is sad that this is done because they were ignorant of the Buddha's teachings.

As with Westerners, people in Asia and in Asian communities in the West would benefit greatly from more Dharma study as a prelude to practice. Buddhists should conduct seminars on Buddhism in these places so that people have accurate information about the religion of their family. Initially, an informative approach could be used, giving a general explanation to raise interest. For example, the teacher could explain Buddhist beliefs in a more academic way, describe Buddhism as it is found in various countries, have courses on comparative religion, or speak of the relationship of Buddhism to science. In this way, people will receive correct information about the Buddha's teachings. With this general knowledge, some will want to learn more, and at that point, more explanation about how to practice should be given.

Two types of people take an interest in religion. One type wants help for this life and protection from harm. These people are not interested in and do not think much about the philosophy behind a religion. They simply accept what they are told. Some Asian Buddhists unfortunately have this attitude. Another type of person thinks more about human nature and investigates the nature of the mind, the purpose of life, and what happens after death. They are looking for a deeper explanation. When such a person studies the Buddha's teachings, they will be attracted to them. By employing their analytical abilities, they will find answers in the Buddhadharma. They will also find a practical method for transforming the mind from negative states to positive ones. This is the proper way for people to be Buddhists, for their faith and practice is based on understanding.

I am happy to note that when I visit Chinese Buddhist communities—for example, in Taiwan—more people are showing interest in studying the Buddhadharma. Still, more needs to be done along this line. For example, in my visit to Taiwan in 2001, about eight thousand people attended the four days of teachings, but nearly twice as many attended the last two days when I gave the Avalokiteśvara empowerment. Nevertheless, I am glad that more people in traditionally Buddhist countries see the importance of study and understand that Buddhism involves transforming our own disturbing emotions, not seeking blessings from an external teacher or deity.

Buddhism can coexist with the Confucian values found in Asia. For example, Confucius instructed people to respect their elders and parents. The Buddha gave similar advice when he spoke to ordinary people, and he encouraged monastics to respect those senior in ordination. Respecting those more experienced and wiser than we are is good advice that everyone should follow.

However, if we ask, "According to Confucius, why do we respect elder people?" people may not know how to answer. For that reason, some young people think, "The elderly managed when they were young, and they can manage alone now too. Young plants grow, and the old plants will go. That is part of nature." With that attitude, they neglect their parents. But explaining the reason for helping elders according to the Dharma does not allow for such self-centered thinking. Instead, we see that the elderly want happiness and not suffering just like everyone else. If we serve and help them, they will be happy, and we will accumulate merit. We are sentient beings with consciousness, and our minds continue on to future lives. To create the causes for happiness in future lives, we need to keep pure ethical discipline and not harm others. Thus helping others benefits them and ourselves, and brings happiness now as well as in future lives.

Dharma Centers

The purpose of having Dharma centers, retreat facilities, and temples is to benefit sentient beings by giving them correct information about the Buddhadharma, meditation instruction, and access to qualified spiritual mentors and Dharma friends who can support them on the path. We need to remain true to this purpose and resist measuring success by the size of our institutions, the number of followers, or the beauty of our altars.

Buddhism has three parts: (1) Buddhist science, (2) Buddhist philosophy and metaphysics, and (3) Buddhist religion or spirituality. Buddhist science has to do with our theories about particles, the levels of mind, the process of cognition, and so on, whereas Buddhist philosophy focuses on impermanence, emptiness, and interdependence. Buddhist religion deals with awakening and the path to attain it. Although Buddhist religion is only for Buddhists, Buddhist science and philosophy can be shared with non-Buddhists. These are academic topics that can be taught in Dharma centers to Buddhists, non-Buddhists, and nonbelievers alike. We present the Buddha, Nāgārjuna, and the great Indian masters as astute philosophers and professors at Nālandā University. One time I gave a Buddha statue to a close friend who was not a Buddhist and told him to regard the Buddha as a great thinker and philosopher. Twenty-six centuries ago, the Buddha was one of the chief philosophers who debated with many other philosophers and dispelled their untenable views. My friend appreciated this perspective.

Dharma centers can serve a variety of people in society: those who are interested in Buddhist science and philosophy, those who seek a method to calm their mind, and those aspiring for liberation and awakening.

Dharma Events, Dharma Teachers, and Finances

It is better if resident Buddhist teachers at Dharma centers are not involved with the finances of the center. They must concentrate on teaching while the members manage the center's finances. Neither the teacher nor the members of the Dharma center should be influenced by benefactors who make large donations. Sometimes it happens that sincere practitioners who do not have a lot of money are denied teachings or access to the teacher, while those with funds are honored and respected. This is wrong. When wealthy students wave promises of sponsorship in front of teachers, monastics, or members of a Dharma center with the thought to gain special attention, teachings, or privileges, we should ignore this behavior and treat them as we would everyone else.

Traditionally, Dharma teachings are freely offered, and students, knowing that their teachers need food, shelter, clothing, medicine, and travel expenses, offer their support according to their ability. This custom is not well-known in the West, where people are used to being charged a specific amount for an event. This, however, goes against the spirit of generosity and can lead to holding Dharma events with the motivation to make money.

Nevertheless, given the reality of the situation, teachers may at times be forced to charge for teachings to cover the expenses involved—rent, travel, and food—but they should clarify with the students that the minimum is being charged and that it is just for what is needed. At the same time, we should educate Westerners that giving freely from our heart, not in payment for receiving teachings, is part of our practice of generosity, or *dāna*.

Sometimes when I teach in the West, the organizers use this as an opportunity to raise funds. They also give me a large offering, which I either give back to the Dharma center or to worthwhile projects. I do not need these offerings. The Indian government kindly gives me a modest stipend, which is sufficient for my needs. I encourage the organizers of the teachings to give the offerings to those in need instead. Even though the organizers or I donate such funds to good causes, my preference is that my Dharma teachings not be used for fundraising. Organizers should estimate the cost of the event based on past experience and not charge more than is necessary to cover these expenses. In this way people who cannot afford costly tickets will not be turned away from the teachings. In addition, the teachings should be made accessible to a wider audience so that people who are physically challenged, have minimal income, or are deprived of educational opportunities are able to attend my talks. Now I do not accept any offering from the organizers of my teachings in the West. Instead, at the conclusion of teachings I ask them to announce the income and expenditures to the audience, including where they will donate any surplus income.

The Buddha instructed monastics on the cultivation of modest needs and desires and inner contentment. He advised them to avoid a lifestyle of either extreme luxury or asceticism. This advice should apply equally to lay practitioners, especially if they teach the Dharma. It is crucial that we ensure that whatever income we receive is not from wrong livelihood.

Supporting oneself by teaching the Dharma becomes a complex issue for lay teachers, especially those who need to provide for their family. It raises many questions: Are Dharma students responsible for supporting a lay teacher's family? How much is enough to support a family, especially in Western culture where children want designer clothing and the latest digital devices? This subject needs much thought and discussion.

Some lamas go to Taiwan, Singapore, or the West to teach or give empowerments in order to raise funds for their monasteries. Teaching the Dharma only with the thought of raising money is not correct. Those who need to raise funds for their monastery should be straightforward. Instead of simply asking an audience for offerings for a nebulous purpose, they should show people the architectural designs, the estimated budget, and an outline of the various phases of the project. With everything clearly presented and well-organized, they can then explain, "This is the project. This is the amount we need to complete it. We appreciate whatever you are able to contribute." Do not make people feel obliged to give; give them the space to be moved by a generous thought so that they feel inspired to contribute and give an amount that feels comfortable.

Profit from the sale of Dharma materials is a sensitive issue. In Tibet this issue is taken so seriously that it is said you should avoid eating at the home of a person who lives on the proceeds from selling Dharma books and statues. In addition, giving the proceeds from selling Dharma books and statues to a monastic community to buy food or clothing is not appropriate. If possible, avoid using this money to pay fees to attend teachings. Perhaps the money could be used for charitable works or given to a hospital or school, but best is to use it to print more Dharma materials. Motivation is extremely important. For example, using money from selling Dharma books to stay at a center so that you have a place to live is not appropriate. But if your motivation is to spread the Dharma teachings and you need money to live on and to run the Dharma center, then perhaps it is all right.

5 | The Ten Perfections in the Pāli Tradition

THE *Basket of Conduct* (*Cariyāpiṭaka*)[26] tells the story of the Buddha's previous life as King Sivi, when he desired to give his eyes to someone who asked. The god Śakra, lord of the devas, wanted to test this desire and so appeared as a decrepit, blind old man who asked the king for his eyes. With great joy, King Sivi immediately had a doctor remove his eyes to give to the old man. After doing this, he uttered these words (CP 1.8.15–16):

> While I was desiring to give, while I was giving, and after the gift had been given by me, there was no contradictory state of mind; it was for the sake of awakening itself. The two eyes were not disagreeable to me nor was I disagreeable to myself. Omniscience was dear to me; therefore I gave the eyes.

Such is the pure motivation of a bodhisattva.

The Pāramīs

In addition to the Pāli texts mentioned in the previous chapter, *A Treatise on the Pāramīs*, written by the great Pāli commentator Dhammapāla around the sixth century, explicitly explains how to engage in the ten bodhisattva practices. This text is found at least twice in the Pāli commentarial literature: once in a commentary to the *Basket of Conduct* and a slightly shorter version in a subcommentary to the *Brahmajāla Sutta* (DN 1). Dhammapāla drew on the *Chronicle of Buddhas* (*Buddhavaṃsa*) for his description of the bodhisattva aspiration, the eight qualities for its success in attaining buddhahood, and the enumeration of the ten perfections. He drew on the *Jātakas*,[27] the *Path of Purification*, and other Pāli sources for other material included in his treatise. While the presentation of selflessness, wisdom, and the structure of the path in *A Treatise on the Pāramīs* accords with the presentation in the Pāli canon, some passages in the text were adopted from the Sanskrit treatise the *Bodhisattva Grounds* (*Bodhisattvabhūmi*)[28] by Asaṅga and included in Dhammapāla's treatise.[29]

The audience Dhammapāla had in mind is indicated by the first sentence of his treatise:

> We now undertake a detailed explanation of the pāramīs for clansmen following the suttas (P. *suttantikas*) who are zealously engaged in the practice of the vehicle to great awakening (P. *Mahābodhiyāna*), in order to improve their skillfulness in accumulating the collections (requisites) for awakening.

Here "suttantikas" does not refer to followers of the Sautrāntika tenet system but to Theravāda practitioners who aspire for full awakening and seek instruction in the sūtras on how to attain it. Dhammapāla's treatise fills out the instructions they need. "Mahābodhiyāna" does not refer to Mahāyāna as a school but to the vehicle (*yāna*) or mind leading to the noble spiritual goal of great awakening (*mahābodhi*) aspired to by bodhisattvas.

Just as in the Sanskrit tradition, the ten perfections are the collections (requisites, *sambhāra*) needed to attain the full awakening of a buddha. They are also good qualities to cultivate no matter which of the three paths we follow, and in the Pāli tradition are not considered unique practices reserved only for bodhisattvas. Theravāda practitioners of all inclinations practice these ten, the difference being that bodhisattvas have to practice them more intensely and for a longer period of time in order to attain their spiritual goal. Buddhaghosa comments (Vism 1.33), "The virtue of the pāramīs done for the deliverance of all beings is superior." In this way, he praises the Buddha for having completed the bodhisattva path and having become a *sammāsaṃbuddha*, a fully awakened buddha.

It is said that by practicing the perfections all merit and goodness comes about. Disciples in Theravāda countries frequently praise their teachers for their great accumulation of perfections. These ten are generosity (P. *dāna*), ethical conduct (P. *sīla*), renunciation (P. *nekkhamma*), wisdom (P. *paññā*), joyous effort (P. *viriya*), fortitude (P. *khanti*), truthfulness (P. *sacca*), determination (P. *adhiṭṭhāna*),[30] love (P. *mettā*),[31] and equanimity (P. *upekkhā*).

After Sumedha (the person in the previous continuum of Śākyamuni Buddha) first generated bodhicitta, he examined the factors that would bring about buddhahood and found that they were the ten perfections. At that time, he gave a concise explanation of each (BCA 119–20, 124–25, 129–30, 134–35, 139–40, 144–45, 148–50, 154–55, 159–60, 164–65):

> (Generosity) As a full jar overturned by whatever it may be discharges the water completely and does not retain it there, so, seeing supplicants—low, high, or middling—give a gift completely like the overturned jar.
>
> (Ethical conduct) As a yak, if her tail is caught in anything, does not injure her tail, but goes to death there, so, fulfilling the ethical habits in the four planes,[32] protect ethical conduct continuously like the yak [does] her tail.
>
> (Renunciation) As a person who for long has lived painfully afflicted in a prison does not generate attachment there, but seeks only freedom, so do you see all becomings (rebirths in saṃsāra) as a prison. Be one turned toward renunciation for the utter release from becoming.
>
> (Wisdom) As a monastic seeking alms, do not avoid low, high, or middling families [but go in successive order] to acquire sustenance. Then by questioning discerning people [about what is virtuous and what is not] at all [possible] times, go on to [practice] the perfection of wisdom and attain full awakening.
>
> (Joyous effort) As a lion, the king of beasts, whether he is lying down, standing, or walking, is not of sluggish energy but always exerts himself, so you too firmly exert energy in every becoming.
>
> (Fortitude) As the earth endures all that is thrown on it, both pure and impure, and shows no repugnance (or) approval, so you too have fortitude toward all respect and disrespect.
>
> (Truthfulness) As Osadhi is balanced[33] for devas and mankind in [all] times and seasons and does not deviate from her course, so you too must not deviate from the course of the truths.

> (Determination) As a mountain, a rock, stable and firmly based, does not tremble in rough winds but remains in precisely its own place, so you too must be constantly stable in resolute determination.
>
> (Love) As water pervades with coolness good and evil people alike and carries away dust and dirt, so you too develop love for friend and foe equally.
>
> (Equanimity) As the earth is indifferent to the impure and the pure thrown on it and avoids both anger and attachment, so you too must be balanced always in the face of the pleasant and unpleasant.

Etymologically, "pāramī" could mean "supreme," referring to the supreme qualities bodhisattvas develop on their way to buddhahood. Or, similar to the Sanskrit, "pāramī" could mean "to go beyond," indicating that bodhisattvas' practices enable them to reach far beyond saṃsāra. The ten perfections in the Pāli and Sanskrit traditions are not exactly the same. Generosity, ethical conduct, fortitude, joyous effort, and wisdom are identical in their terms, whereas determination (*adhiṭṭhāna*) in Pāli and resolve (*praṇidhāna*) in Sanskrit are different terms, but the description of that perfection in both traditions is similar. Bodhisattvas need strong resolve and determination to complete the path and to benefit sentient beings. The other four perfections differ in their terms and in their meaning: in Pāli, renunciation, truthfulness, love, and equanimity; in Sanskrit, meditative stability, skillful means, power, and pristine wisdom. However, both traditions teach these eight excellent qualities as part of the overall presentation of the path to liberation and full awakening.

Dhammapāla says that when seen according to their nature, the ten perfections become six: generosity, ethical conduct, fortitude, joyous effort, meditative stability, and wisdom—the six perfections listed in the Sanskrit tradition (TP 12).

> The perfection of renunciation, as the going forth into homelessness, is included in the perfection of ethical conduct; as seclusion from the hindrances in the perfection of meditative stability; and as a generally wholesome quality, in all six pāramīs.

> One part of the perfection of truthfulness—its aspect of truthful speech or abstinence from falsehood—is included in the perfection of ethical conduct, and one part—its aspect of truthful knowledge—in the perfection of wisdom. The perfection of love is included in the perfection of meditative stability, and the perfection of equanimity in the perfections of meditative stability and wisdom. The perfection of determination is included in all.

The order of the ten perfections indicates a sequence of practice. Buddhaghosa explains the progression from one perfection to the next (Vism 9.124):[34]

> For the Great Beings' minds retain their balance by giving preference to beings' welfare (love) by dislike of beings' suffering (compassion), by desire for the various successes achieved by beings to last (empathic joy), and by impartiality toward all beings (equanimity). And to all beings they (1) give gifts that are a source of pleasure without discriminating thus: "It must be given to this one; it must not be given to this one." And to avoid doing harm to beings they (2) undertake the precepts of ethical conduct. They practice (3) renunciation[35] for the purpose of excelling in ethical conduct. They cleanse their (4) wisdom for the purpose of nonconfusion about what is good and bad for beings. They constantly arouse (5) effort, having beings' welfare and happiness at heart. When they have acquired heroic patience through supreme energy, they have (6) fortitude with beings' many kinds of faults. They (7) do not deceive when promising, "We shall give you this; we shall do this for you." They have unshakable (8) determination for beings' welfare and happiness. Through unshakable (9) love they place others first. Through (10) equanimity they expect no reward. Having thus fulfilled the [ten] pāramīs, these [divine abidings] then perfect all the good states classed as the ten powers, the four kinds of fearlessness, the six kinds of knowledge not shared [by śrāvakas], and the eighteen unique qualities of the Awakened One.[36] This is how they bring to perfection all the good states beginning with generosity.

Unlike in the Sanskrit tradition, Pāli sages did not develop a schema of bodhisattva grounds that correlate to each of the perfections. Also, they assert that even when Gautama was an advanced bodhisattva just prior to attaining awakening under the bodhi tree, he had not yet abandoned the fetters abandoned by a stream-enterer. He traversed all four stages of stream-enterer, once-returner, nonreturner, and became a buddha arahant during one meditation session while seated under the bodhi tree. In the Pāli presentation, the bodhisattva path is open to anyone who wishes to practice it. However, it is especially crucial for those who are to become wheel-turning buddhas—buddhas who will teach the Dhamma when it is not yet present in a particular world system.

Dhammapāla's treatise speaks of the perfections in a comprehensive way in sixteen sections:

1. their definition
2. the reason for calling them pāramīs
3. their number
4. their sequence
5. their characteristics, functions, manifestations, and proximate causes
6. their condition
7. their defilement
8. their cleansing
9. their opposites
10. how to practice them
11. how to analyze them
12. how to synthesize them
13. how they are accomplished
14. time needed to accomplish them
15. their benefits
16. their results

We'll begin by looking at how to practice the ten perfections. The characteristic they all share is that they function to benefit others. They are all motivated by the aspiration to attain buddhahood and are done with a mind unpolluted by craving, conceit, and wrong views. Great compassion and skillful means are their proximate causes and accompany each of them.

Here "skillful means" (*upāyakauśalya, upāyakosalla*) refers to the wisdom "that transforms giving (and the other nine virtues) into requisites of awakening." Without compassion and skillful means, the perfections would be mere virtuous activities. Dhammapāla does not define the meaning of "wisdom" in this context any further.

Generosity

Generosity is the giving of ourselves and our belongings. Based on nonattachment and the relinquishing of miserliness, generosity enables us to willingly give our possessions, body, and life for the well-being of others. In terms of the object given, there are three types of generosity: the giving of material possessions, the giving of fearlessness, and the giving of Dharma.

Regarding being *generous with material possessions* or money, bodhisattvas give whatever is needed to whomever needs it. They give even if not asked, and they give a suitable amount, not just a little so that the other person will leave them alone. They give without expecting to receive a gift, praise, or fame in return, and when there is not enough to go around, they distribute it equitably among all those in need. Things that can cause harm or that can stimulate afflictions to arise in the other person's mind—for example, weapons, intoxicants, poisons, pornography, dangerous chemicals, and amusements that can lead to lack of conscientiousness—are not given. If a person is sick, they do not give food and drink that could hinder recovery or increase the illness, even if the sick person requests it. In other words, they give only what is conducive for the other's well-being, especially in the long term. They give what is appropriate to the recipient—for example, they do not give monastic robes to householders or lay clothes to monastics.

Should bodhisattvas notice that they are becoming attached to a particular object, they immediately find someone to give it to. When asked for something, bodhisattvas contemplate the disadvantages of clinging to things: destructive karma is created to acquire and protect them, they spark quarrels and disputes, they cause worry, possessiveness, and inevitably grief because everything is left behind at death. Instead they see the person asking as a close friend who is helping free them from bondage to these items, someone who is giving them the opportunity to practice the perfection of generosity.

In addition to giving external possessions, bodhisattvas give their own body. They may do this by serving others or, if needed, by giving parts of their body. But they give their own body only when it will be used well; they do not give it to someone who is mentally unstable or sociopathic. If they hesitate to give their body, they should think that if people in need of the various parts of a medicinal tree—the root, trunk, branches, leaves, and fruit—were to come and take them, the tree would not complain, "You're taking my belongings!" Similarly, since this body is in the nature of duḥkha and since they have entrusted their body to the service of others, there is no sense of clinging to it, thinking, "This is mine, this am I, this is my self." Contemplating in this way, they give whatever is required with a joyful heart, knowing that through relinquishing attachment and giving generously, they will attain full awakening.

The *generosity of fearlessness* involves offering protection to those who are frightened, lost, or in danger. Aiding others in this way calms their mind and shields them from physical suffering. One of the *Jātaka* tales (407) recounts the story of one of the Buddha's previous lives as a bodhisattva who was a monkey. As the leader of a group of 80,000 monkeys, he saved them from the brutality of the human king, even though he was being tormented by another monkey, who was a previous incarnation of Devadatta. Witnessing the monkey-bodhisattva's willingness to sacrifice his body and life to save the other monkeys and his virtuous actions done for the sake of others, the king was inspired to change his ways, to rule his kingdom with compassion and justice, and to do kind deeds to benefit others.

Giving the Dharma is to give correct Dharma teachings that lead to well-being and peace in this life and future lives, and to liberation and awakening. In this way bodhisattvas enable sentient beings who have not met the Dharma to meet it and mature the minds of those who are already practicing. Bodhisattvas give discourses on the vehicles of the śrāvakas, solitary realizers, or bodhisattvas in accordance with the dispositions of those in the audience.

Bodhisattvas do not give out of fear, shame, coercion, or obligation. They do not give unwillingly or by inconveniencing others and causing them problems. They give respectfully, with their own hands, a pleasant expression on their face, and kind words from their hearts. After they have given they do not pride themselves on their generosity, nor do they regret having given. They behave amicably, without drawing attention to their generous action or the gift.

When giving, bodhisattvas reflect on the symbolism of the gift. For example, when giving beverages, they think, "May I cease the thirst of sensual attachment," and when they give medicines, they think, "May I give sentient beings nirvāṇa, which is free from aging, sickness, and death." When they give monasteries and beautiful natural environments, they aspire, "May I and all others attain the dhyānas."

While giving, bodhisattvas recall the impermanence of the possessions and their life. They consider their possessions as things that are shared in common with others. They give with no sense of loss, not being concerned that now they will lack what they need. Bodhisattvas dedicate the result of their generosity to the happiness and peace of all beings and to their awakening.

To whom should we give? The wanderer Vacchagotta told the Buddha that he heard some people say that gifts should be given only to the Buddha and his disciples because great merit is created by doing this, but gifts should not be given to other teachers and their disciples because little merit is created by doing this. The Buddha replied that he had been misrepresented, and he clarified (AN 3:57):

> Vaccha, anyone who prevents another person from giving alms causes obstruction and impediment to three people: he obstructs the donor from doing a meritorious deed, he obstructs the recipient from having the gift, and prior to that, he undermines and harms his own character... Even if one throws away the rinsings from a pot or cup in a village pool or pond, wishing that the living beings there may feed on them—even this would be a source of merit, not to speak of giving a gift to human beings.
>
> However, I do declare that offerings made to the virtuous bring rich fruit, whereas not so much those made to the unethical.

The Buddha then continued to explain that the virtuous are those who have abandoned the five hindrances—sensual desire, malice, lethargy and sleepiness, restlessness and regret, and doubt—and who possess ethical conduct, concentration, wisdom, liberation, and the knowledge and vision of liberation of one perfect in training. The merit created by giving depends on both the intention of the donor and the ethical purity of the recipient. For example, an act of generosity done with humility, respect, and kindness by someone who abandons the ten nonvirtues creates more merit than the same gift given by someone who does not maintain ethical conduct or someone who gives with indifference. Furthermore, giving to those intent on accomplishing the path and those who have realized the path creates more merit than giving to someone who hunts or exterminates insects. This does not mean, however, that we should neglect the poor and needy and give only to spiritual practitioners. We should help whomever we can. In addition, we should not discourage people who want to give to good causes or worthy people.

Ethical Conduct

Ethical conduct is pure and blameless physical and verbal conduct. Based on personal integrity and consideration for others, it is restraint from destructive actions and engagement in beneficial actions.

Contemplating the benefits of ethical conduct encourages us to practice it. It cools the fires of anger and greed, prepares the mind to attain higher states of meditative absorption, is the path leading to the awakenings of all three vehicles, and brings about the fulfillment of our wishes. Abiding in ethical conduct prevents guilt, remorse, and anxiety. It averts fear and reproach from others and is the basis for rejoicing in our own merit and goodness. It is a contribution to world peace, for others feel safe around a person who abandons even the wish to harm others. Good ethical conduct cannot be stolen by thieves or embezzled by manipulators; it is the basis for having a fortunate rebirth that enables us to continue practicing the Dharma.

Restraint from destructive actions is the best protection from being harmed ourselves; it is more effective than thousands of warheads and the best bodyguards. While ethical conduct governs actions of body and speech, it gives sovereignty over our mind. It is said that those with pure ethical conduct exude the "fragrance of virtue," which makes them more attractive to others, and thus more effective in benefitting them, than any perfume. The *Dhammapada* counsels (110):

> Better it is to live one day
> virtuous and meditative
> than to live a hundred years
> unethical and uncontrolled.

If afflictions arise in the mind threatening their virtue, bodhisattvas ask themselves, "Didn't you resolve to attain awakening for the benefit of all beings?" Then they remind themselves, "I cannot be successful in mundane affairs, let alone attain supramundane states, without ethical conduct. I should always behave well and safeguard my ethical conduct, otherwise others won't want to be around me. If I want to benefit others and lead them on the paths of the three vehicles, I must teach the Dharma. But someone with dubious ethical conduct cannot be trusted; to be trustworthy I must have a pure character. In addition, to guide others, I should have attainments such as the dhyānas and wisdom, and these are founded upon pure ethical conduct. Therefore I should protect my ethical conduct as a hen does her eggs."

Bodhisattvas wish for others to live ethically so that they will have temporal and ultimate happiness. Thus they teach others and model themselves on four activities to purify ethical conduct:

1. Purifying inclinations for nonvirtue. Some people have strong personal values and goals and naturally have revulsion toward nonvirtue. Having personal integrity, they purify their inclinations for nonvirtue. Other people are more inclined to see the harmful effects of their nonvirtuous actions on others, and with consideration for others, purify those inclinations.
2. Taking precepts. Taking lay or monastic precepts helps bodhisattvas maintain their ethical conduct.
3. Not transgressing their precepts. Cultivating mindfulness and introspective awareness regarding their actions of body, speech, and mind helps bodhisattvas to establish themselves in virtue by not transgressing their precepts.
4. Purifying any transgressions that do occur. They invoke their sense of integrity and consideration for others and purify any transgressions using the proper means to do so.

There are two types of ethical conduct, that of restraint from negativity and that of enacting virtue—that is, abandoning what should not be done and doing what should be done. Regarding the first, having great confidence in the law of karma and its effects and considering the karmic results of their actions before doing them, bodhisattvas abandon the ten nonvirtues. This frees them from all their disadvantages, and they receive the benefits of fulfilling the ten virtues. For example, because bodhisattvas do not harm others physically, all beings feel safe around them. In addition, their meditation on love excels without obstacles, and they are healthy, live long, and are free from the pain of hatred and animosity. By abandoning lying, their speech becomes authoritative and others trust them, thus facilitating instructing sentient beings and guiding them on the path. By abandoning disharmonious speech, they have companions and assistants who are harmonious among themselves and who help them to spread the Dharma. By exercising mindfulness and introspective awareness, bodhisattvas restrain their sense faculties, have honest and right livelihood, and are thoughtful in their use of requisites such as food, clothing, shelter, and medicine.

Regarding the second type of ethical conduct, enacting virtue, bodhisattvas respect their spiritual mentors and those worthy of respect, offer service to them, and care for them during illness and old age. They appreciate advice and instructions of the wise and rejoice in the merit of others. With gratitude for those who have helped them, they benefit and honor the worthy ones in return.

Furthermore, bodhisattvas care for the ill and injured, comfort the grieving, and give wise advice to the reckless, thereby directing them toward wholesome actions. Bodhisattvas aid the elderly, the blind, the deaf, and those who are physically or mentally challenged. They help those without faith to cultivate it, teach the lazy how to be energetic, and instruct those plagued by the five hindrances in the means to dispel them. Bodhisattvas rehabilitate those whose ethical conduct has degenerated, those who have succumbed to addictions, and those whose criminal behavior has harmed themselves and their families. Bodhisattvas are there to offer help when others experience misfortunes such as natural disasters, poverty, or social disorder. In short, in whatever way their companionship, knowledge, or abilities can benefit others, they employ these without hesitation.

Being judicious, bodhisattvas are accessible to others, but only at the right time, in a suitable place, and in an appropriate situation. They neither push their help and advice on others nor refuse to offer them when needed. In guiding others to virtue, bodhisattvas behave only in ways that increase others' good qualities and virtuous actions. They never abuse, harm, or humiliate others, or lead them to act harmfully. When with others, bodhisattvas do not antagonize them by praising those they resent or criticizing those they hold dear. They encourage others to continue cultivating their good qualities and virtue.

When hearing of the wondrous deeds and spiritual accomplishments of previous bodhisattvas, they do not become discouraged, restless, or alarmed, but reflect, "Those great beings were once human beings like me, too. They attained their great abilities by training in the perfections and fulfilling the collections. I will train as they did and attain the same realizations and abilities to benefit others." In this way, bodhisattvas generate faith and encourage themselves.

Bodhisattvas conceal their virtues and good qualities and reveal their faults. They are content, do not complain, and are not conceited or manipulative. They are honest and direct, yet tactful. Seeing the disadvantages of the afflictions, they counteract them and do not let them interfere with their ethical conduct. Avoiding complacency, they continue to train in a balanced way that brings success, without discouragement or pushing themselves.

Buddhaghosa details the practice of ethical conduct in the first chapter of the *Path of Purification*. Although his explanation is specifically directed to those seeking the awakening of a śrāvaka, they also pertain to bodhisattvas' practice of the perfection of ethical conduct. The difference is that bodhisattvas' ethical conduct is motivated by bodhicitta and the merit from this practice is dedicated for full awakening. Dhammapāla concludes (TP 10):

> They dedicate it only for the purpose of becoming an omniscient buddha in order to enable all beings to acquire the incomparable adornment of ethical conduct.

Renunciation

Renunciation is founded on realizing the unsatisfactory nature of everything in saṃsāra. Based on a sense of spiritual urgency (P. *saṃvega*), practitioners abandon attachment to sense pleasures and to existence in any realm of saṃsāra. Renunciation protects bodhisattvas from extreme asceticism, involvement in the afflictions of others, and indulging in sense pleasures.

To generate renunciation—the determination to be free from cyclic existence—bodhisattvas reflect on the dangers of sensual pleasures, the distractions of the householder's life, and the benefits of the left-home life of monastics. The Buddha spoke about this often (MN 27.12):

> Household life is crowded and dusty; life gone forth is wide open. It is not easy while living in a home to lead the holy life utterly perfect and pure as a polished shell.

In response to a king who questioned why he left his wealthy and prestigious family to practice the Dharma as a monastic, the Buddha's disciple Raṭṭhapāla replied (MN 82.42):

> Sensual pleasures, varied, sweet, and delightful,
> in many different ways disturb the mind.
> Seeing the danger in these sensual ties
> I chose to lead the homeless life, O King.
>
> As fruits fall from the tree, so people too,
> both young and old, fall when this body breaks.
> Seeing this too, O King, I have gone forth.
> Better is the monastic's life assured.

Bodhisattvas see that work and family life lead to numerous entanglements that occupy time and stimulate afflictions to arise uncontrollably. They know the deceptive nature of sense pleasures (TP 10):

> Sense pleasures, like a drop of honey smeared over the blade of a sword, give limited satisfaction and entail abundant harm. They are fleeting like a show perceived in a flash of lightning, enjoyable only through a perversion of perception like the adornments of a madman, a means of vengeance like a camouflaged pit of excrement, unsatisfying like a thin drink...subject to the duḥkha of

> change like the enjoyment of a festival, inwardly burning like the fire in the hollow of a tree, intensifying thirst like a drink of salt water, and giving little satisfaction like a necklace of bones.

Seeing the disadvantages of living immersed in and preoccupied with sense pleasures, bodhisattvas contemplate the benefits of renunciation, simplicity, and solitude, and request monastic ordination. Then, living in ethical conduct, they establish themselves in three of the traditions of āryas—contentment with robes, alms food, and shelter—and in this way they attain the fourth āryan tradition—delight in meditation. Although meditative stability is not listed as a separate perfection, it is subsumed under renunciation. The first level of renunciation leads to monastic ordination and pacification of the mind through ethical conduct. The second level of renunciation leaves behind the afflictions of the desire realm to attain the dhyānas.

The thirteen ascetic practices[37] that the Buddha set out for some of his disciples and the forty meditation objects for the cultivation of concentration and serenity[38] are discussed under the topic of renunciation. These are found in the *Path of Purification* (Vism 2.1) and should be practiced as explained there, the only differences being that here they are practiced with the bodhicitta motivation by those aspiring for the full awakening of buddhahood, and they are conjoined with compassion and the skillful means of wisdom.

Wisdom

Wisdom understands the general and specific characteristics of phenomena. It illuminates phenomena and banishes ignorance and confusion; it arises based on concentration and knowledge of the four truths.

Wisdom purifies all other virtues and perfections, enabling them to serve as the causes for the omniscient mind of a buddha. Wisdom enables bodhisattvas to give even their own bodies and frees ethical conduct from afflictions such as craving. Wisdom recognizes the dangers of immersion in sensual pleasures and the householder's life; it knows the benefits of monastic ordination, meditative stability, and nirvāṇa. Wisdom properly directs joyous effort, enabling it to accomplish all virtues, and it enables bodhisattvas to be patient with others' wrongdoings and inappropriate or offensive behavior. One who has wisdom speaks truthfully, has firm determination, cares for the welfare of all beings with love, and maintains equanimity when serving and guiding them. Wisdom enables bodhisattvas to remain equanimous while still abiding with the continuous vicissitudes of cyclic existence.

To cultivate the wisdom arising from learning, bodhisattvas fully study the five aggregates, twelve sources, eighteen constituents,[39] four truths, twenty-two faculties, twelve links of dependent origination and its cessation in their forward and reverse orders, four establishments of mindfulness, and classifications of phenomena such as the virtuous and nonvirtuous, and so forth. Bodhisattvas also learn worthy fields of secular knowledge that could be useful in benefiting sentient beings: science, writing, and so forth. Bodhisattvas learn through studying, listening to teachings, memorizing, and asking questions. They are ingenious in developing ways to lead others on the path and provide the temporal conditions others need in order to better themselves and their situation.

Bodhisattvas then cultivate the wisdom arising from thinking by reflecting on the specific characteristics of those phenomena, such as the aggregates, that they have studied.

Following that, they engage in the preliminary portion of the wisdom arising from meditation, which is included in the mundane kinds of full understanding (P. *pariññā*), beginning with discernment of the general and specific characteristics of the aggregates. The general characteristics are the three characteristics that all things share—impermanence, duḥkha, and not-self. In this regard, bodhisattvas understand all internal and external phenomena as follows: This is mere name and form, which arise and cease according to conditions. There is no agent or actor here. They are impermanent because they change in every moment; they are in the nature of duḥkha because they oppress sentient beings by coming and going. They are not-self because they cannot be mastered or controlled.

Through this understanding bodhisattvas abandon attachment and lead others to do so too. They mature sentient beings' minds in the paths of the three vehicles, helping them to attain the meditative absorptions, deliverances, concentrations, attainments, and mundane direct knowledges. They continue doing this until reaching the peak of wisdom and the qualities of the Buddha are in sight.

The wisdom of meditation may be spoken of in two ways. The first is the mundane superknowledges and their auxiliaries. These are the first five superknowledges—supernormal powers, divine eye, divine ear, knowledge of others' minds, and the knowledge of recollecting past lives.[40] The second is the five purifications—purification of view, purification by overcoming doubt, purification by knowledge and vision of what is and is not the path, purification by knowledge and vision of the way, and purification by knowledge and vision, which is the supramundane knowledge of the four ārya paths.[41] These topics have been explained for those following the śrāvakas' path to arhatship. As before, bodhisattvas should do them with the motivation of bodhicitta and to make these the collections or requisites for full awakening. Learning, thinking, and meditating should be imbued with compassion and the skillful means of wisdom and dedicated for the awakening of all sentient beings.

Bodhisattvas develop insight up to and including purification by knowledge and vision of the way. They must wait to attain purification by knowledge and vision because this pertains to the four ārya paths that realize nirvāṇa in stages. However, bodhisattvas must first complete the requisites for awakening—the perfections—before entering the ārya paths so that their realization of nirvāṇa coincides with their full awakening. Thus before entering the ārya paths, bodhisattvas must balance their development of compassion and skillful means on the one hand and wisdom on the other, and only when the perfections are complete do they enter the ārya paths and attain full awakening.

Joyous Effort

Joyous effort involves employing our body and mind to willingly and happily work for the well-being of sentient beings. Free from laziness, restlessness, and hounding ourselves with unrealistic expectations, joyous effort is untiring. Without energy, accomplishing even worldly goals is not possible, let alone actualizing our spiritual aspirations. With joyous effort we will happily practice the path for our own and others' welfare, without becoming discouraged or exhausted. With indefatigable effort, we will undertake liberating all sentient beings from saṃsāra and will not give up.

Bodhisattvas reflect, "Have I accumulated the collections today? What have I done to benefit sentient beings today?" In this way, they remember their heartfelt spiritual aspirations and encourage themselves to energetically act upon them. Bodhisattvas willingly take upon themselves the suffering of all beings and rejoice in their merit and virtues. They frequently recall the Buddha's great qualities and abilities and do all actions motivated by bodhicitta. In this way, day by day, they accumulate the requisites for buddhahood.

In addition, bodhisattvas seek remedies for sentient beings' suffering from hunger, thirst, loneliness, oppression, cold, heat, separation from loved ones, sickness, injury, poverty, warfare, betrayal, and so forth. Whatever happiness they experience—from enjoyable environments and companions, to the blissful meditative absorptions, to the happiness they gain from helping others—all these they wish for all beings to experience as well.

Bodhisattvas frequently meditate on the duḥkha experienced by sentient beings in all saṃsāric realms and generate compassion, which instigates their joyous effort to reach out and help. Speaking especially of bodhisattvas who have actualized levels of concentration, Dhammapāla describes how they meditate on compassion (TP 10):

> [Bodhisattvas] contemplate the whole world of sentient beings immersed in the great suffering of saṃsāra, with the sufferings of afflictions and karma at its base. They see the beings in hell experiencing violent, racking, agonizing pain uninterruptedly over long periods as they are cut up, dismembered, split, pulverized, and roasted in scorching fires; the great suffering of animals owing to their mutual hostility as they fight, harass, and kill one another, or fall into captivity at the hands of others; the suffering of the various hungry ghosts who go about with their bodies aflame, consumed and withered by hunger, thirst, wind, and sun, weeping and wailing as their food turns into vomit and pus.
>
> They contemplate as well the suffering experienced by human beings, which is often indistinguishable from the suffering in the unfortunate realms: the misery and ruin they encounter in their search [for means of sustenance and enjoyment]; the various punishments they meet, such as the cutting off of their hands, and so forth; ugliness, deformity, and poverty; affliction by hunger and thirst; being vanquished by the more powerful, pressed into the

> service of others, and made dependent upon others; and when they pass away, falling into the hell, hungry ghost, or animal realms.
>
> They see the celestial beings of the desire realm being consumed by the fever of lust as they enjoy their sense objects with scattered minds; living with the fever [of passions] unextinguished like a mass of fire stoked with gusts of wind and fed with a stock of dry wood; without peace, dejected, and dependent on others. They see form and formless realm gods after a long lifespan in the end succumb to the law of impermanence, plunging from their heights back down into the round of birth, aging, and death, like birds swooping swiftly down from the heights of the sky or like arrows shot by a strong archer descending in the distance. Having seen all this, bodhisattvas arouse a sense of spiritual urgency and suffuse all beings universally with love and compassion.

Needless to say, meditating in this way will arouse us to practice the perfections without cowardice, hesitation, or self-indulgent laziness, and with joyous effort to attain full awakening for the benefit of all beings. Such energy brings incredible spiritual courage and power to enact the glorious bodhisattva deeds. Thus from the time of generating the initial aspiration for full awakening until the time we become fully awakened buddhas, we should reflect on the benefits of joyous effort and permeate our practice of the perfections with it.

Fortitude

Fortitude is the ability to endure hardship and suffering. With fortitude, we do not give up on beings no matter how they treat us. Fortitude regarding the Dharma involves accepting Dharma concepts that our wisdom has not yet completely penetrated. Unlike blind faith, this fortitude trusts the Buddha's word because we have already benefited from practicing some of the Buddha's teachings. With fortitude we continue to investigate the teachings, knowing that time is needed to fully understand them. Fortitude in the Dharma prevents restlessness.

Acceptance and tolerance contribute to fortitude, for fortitude accepts the desirable, the undesirable, and emptiness. Fortitude vanquishes anger, the destroyer of happiness and merit. Fortitude and patience are the basis for a pleasant personality and a good reputation, which enables us to benefit others. People with little fortitude are demanding and continually unhappy. They create a lot of nonvirtuous karma due to harsh speech and spiteful actions, and they consume much time in complaining and being disagreeable.

There are many ways to think to prevent ourselves from becoming angry, resentful, or belligerent when others harm us. Dhammapāla suggests contemplating these.[42]

- Although this suffering arises from the harmful deeds of others, this body of mine is the field for that suffering, and the karma that made me take it was created by me alone.
- What am I angry at? The hair on his head? His nails? Bones (and other body parts)? The feeling aggregate? Discrimination aggregate? Miscellaneous factors aggregate? Consciousness aggregate?
- This suffering will consume my destructive karma so that it no longer obscures my mind.
- This person who is harming me is my teacher because she enables me to accomplish the perfection of fortitude.
- Although this person is harming me now, in the past he has been my friend and benefactor and has given me great help.
- All beings are like my young children. How can I be angry at their misdeeds done through unknowing?
- The harmful action, the one who did it, and the one to whom it was done—all these have ceased at this very moment. They are past. With whom, then, should I be angry? And who is becoming angry? Since all phenomena are not-self, who can harm whom?
- This harm is showing me the suffering nature of saṃsāra. How I wish others and myself were free from it! I must work toward that end.
- It is the nature of the sense faculties to encounter pleasant and unpleasant objects. I must maintain equanimity.
- The Buddha looks at all these beings as dear ones. How can I hate someone the Buddha loves?

- Nothing beneficial ever comes from anger: Due to it, my good qualities and happiness decline. I cannot sleep or eat well.
- Anger is the real enemy because it destroys all that is good, perpetrates harm, and spreads negativity.
- Enemies are the result of angry thoughts and preconceptions. To free myself from enemies, I must relinquish anger.
- Anger destroys my ethical conduct and merit. Without these how can I fulfill my bodhisattva aspiration? And until I do that, all sentient beings will be immersed in duḥkha.
- Mere phenomena alone exist, devoid of self or of anything pertaining to a self. They arise and pass away due to causes and conditions. They do not come from anywhere, they do not go anywhere, they are not established anywhere. There is no agency in anything whatsoever.

By applying whichever way of thinking works best at any particular moment, release anger and cultivate fortitude and compassion for your own and others' benefit.

A deep understanding of conditionality and impermanence is also effective for releasing anger, even in difficult or terrifying situations. Someone who has done intensive meditation on the various components that make up an experience can dissect an event or experience into its parts and see that each component arose dependent on its causes and that each one is also transient, arising and passing away in the briefest moment. Śāriputra says in the *Greater Discourse on the Simile of the Elephant's Footprint* (MN 28.8):

> If others abuse, revile, scold, or harass a monastic, he understands thus: "This painful feeling born of ear-contact has arisen in me. That is dependent, not independent. Dependent on what? Dependent on contact." Then he sees that contact is impermanent, that feeling is impermanent, that discrimination is impermanent, that miscellaneous factors are impermanent, and that consciousness is impermanent. And his mind...acquires confidence, steadiness, and decision.

The Buddha said that to retaliate when abused, criticized, insulted, or even beaten is not the practice of his disciples. Therefore, whether or not we have erred, guarding the mind against anger when accused is an important practice. One way to do this is to examine the conditioned and conditioning factors involved in the experience. For example, first you recognize a painful feeling that comes from hearing unpleasant words. That feeling is not a given; it arises due to conditions. In this case, there was contact—the coming together of the auditory consciousness and the sound by means of the auditory sense faculty—all of these being conditioned and impermanent factors that played a role in the arising of that painful feeling. The contact arises and passes away in a micro-moment; there is nothing enduring about it at all. Similarly, the auditory consciousness that heard the sounds, the conditioning factors that interpreted their meaning, the mental consciousness that understood them, and the discrimination that this person is an enemy—all of these are conditioned, dependent phenomena. Being conditioned, they are impermanent; when their cause ceases, they too cease. They cannot endure on their own or by their own power.

Being impermanent, all these factors are also unsatisfactory, and being both impermanent and unsatisfactory, they are not suitable to be considered mine, I, or my self. That is, none of those factors is a self that is being insulted or criticized. There is no person who is being criticized and no person who is feeling hurt due to being criticized.

If we are beaten or physically attacked, we should recall (MN 28.9): "This body is of such a nature that contact with fists, clods, sticks, and knives assail it." Even if we did not go looking for violence, it may happen that we were caught in the middle of it. At this time we should remember that this is the nature of physical existence and cultivate love toward the assailant. Remembering that the Buddha would not want us to respond with wrath or self-pity is also effective in warding off harmful emotions that otherwise could arise in us.

The *Aṅgulimāla Sutta* relates a beautiful example of practicing fortitude by seeing suffering as a ripening of our karma and thereby accepting and feeling happy about the situation. After Aṅgulimāla, the detested and feared bandit and murderer, was subdued and ordained as a monastic by the Buddha, he attained arhatship. One day while he was on alms round, the townspeople saw him and scornfully threw things at him and struck him. Bleeding, with his alms bowl shattered and his robes torn, Aṅgulimāla approached the Buddha, who advised him, "Bear it, brahmin! You are experiencing here and now the results of deeds because of which you might have been tortured in hell for many years, for many hundreds of years, for many thousands of years."

Taking that advice to heart, Aṅgulimāla accepted his situation and generated love and compassion for those who tormented him. He then said (MN 86.18):

> Who checks the evil deeds he did
> by doing virtuous deeds instead,
> he illuminates the world
> like the moon freed from a cloud...
>
> Let my enemies hear discourse on the Dhamma,
> let them be devoted to the Buddha's teachings,
> let my enemies wait on those good people
> who lead others to accept the Dhamma.
>
> Let my enemies give ear from time to time
> and hear the Dhamma of those who preach fortitude,
> of those who speak as well in praise of kindness,
> and let them follow up that Dhamma with kind deeds.
>
> For surely then they would not wish to harm me,
> nor would they think of harming other beings,
> so those who would protect all, frail or strong,
> let them attain the all-surpassing peace.

The Buddha gave excellent advice for dealing with painful, pleasant, and neutral feelings when he spoke to sick patients at an infirmary. In daily life we often blindly react to these three feelings, but when we are ill or injured, painful feelings occupy our attention. Without mindfulness and introspective awareness at that time, we easily fall prey to anger and aversion toward the unpleasant feelings and to craving for pleasant, or at least neutral, feelings. The Buddha advises (SN 36.7):

> When a monastic dwells thus, mindful and introspectively aware, diligent, ardent, and resolute, if there arises in him a painful feeling, he understands thus: "There has arisen in me a painful feeling. Now that is dependent, not independent. Dependent on what? Dependent on just this body. But this body is impermanent, conditioned, dependently arisen. So when the painful feeling has arisen in dependence on a body that is impermanent, conditioned, dependently arisen, how could it be permanent?" He dwells contemplating impermanence in the body and in painful feeling; he dwells contemplating vanishing, contemplating fading away, contemplating cessation, contemplating relinquishment. As he dwells thus, he abandons the underlying tendency to aversion in regard to the body and in regard to painful feeling.

The Buddha makes similar points regarding how to contemplate pleasant feelings so as to give up the underlying tendency to sensual desire and how to contemplate neutral feelings in order to abandon the underlying tendency to ignorance.

This is excellent advice to follow whenever we do not feel well or whenever the mind is unhappy or filled with painful feelings. First, be aware that a painful feeling is present. Instead of thinking, "I don't like this. It shouldn't happen to me. I want it to go away," turn your attention to the feeling itself and contemplate it. A painful physical feeling does not exist independent of all other factors. Among other factors, it depends on having a body. The body itself is transient and dependent. It depends on the various physiological systems that compose it. It arose dependent on ignorance, karma, and the consciousness taking rebirth. The body is conditioned by karma as well as by environmental factors. Painful feelings that arise in such an impermanent, conditioned body cannot be permanent. These feelings, too, are conditioned and dependently arise. They are impermanent—arising and vanishing in each split second. Furthermore, the painful feelings are not I or mine; they are not a substantial self, nor do they belong to such a self. What is "mine" about these feelings?

To be balanced in your attitude toward all feelings, do this contemplation when you experience pleasant or neutral feelings as well. Wanting to overcome painful feelings yet craving to indulge in pleasant ones will not bring wisdom or liberation. All feelings in saṃsāra are marked by the three characteristics of impermanence, duḥkha, and not-self.

When meditators with strong concentration and wisdom contemplate in this way, they naturally begin to contemplate vanishing, fading away, cessation, and relinquishment. That is, they use the wisdom gleaned in meditation to reduce and eventually abandon the underlying tendency to aversion. Then all their future pleasant, painful, or neutral feelings will be experienced with nonattachment. The Buddha says (SN 36.6):

> The wise one, learned, does not feel
> the pleasant and painful [mental] feeling.
> This is the great difference between
> the wise one and the worldling.
>
> For the learned one who has comprehended Dhamma,
> who clearly sees this world and the next,
> desirable things do not provoke his mind;
> toward the undesired he has no aversion.
>
> For him attraction and repulsion no more exist;
> both have been extinguished, brought to an end.
> Having known the dust-free, sorrowless state,
> the transcender of existence rightly understands.

Truthfulness

Truthfulness is speaking without deception. To benefit sentient beings, they must trust us, and being honest enables them to do so. Not only do we train ourselves to be patient when confronted with others' wrongdoings, abuse, and ungrateful actions, we must remain true to our word to benefit them. Through speaking truthfully and acting according to our word, we do not abandon sentient beings, and they will come to see that we are reliable. Being truthful builds the foundation for all good qualities and opens the door to be able to enact the welfare of all beings.

Bodhisattvas speak what is true, whether others react by helping or harming them. This is true not only in ordinary affairs but in teaching the

Dharma as well. They teach the Dharma skillfully and according to the inclination of the audience, but they do not alter the Buddha's words so that others will like them. Thus sentient beings can trust that when bodhisattvas teach they are receiving the actual Dharma, not something adjusted or made up in order to win their favor and receive more offerings.

With truthfulness bodhisattvas accept the empty nature of beings. Not being deceived about the true nature of phenomena, they complete all the collections and requisites for awakening and accomplish the bodhisattva path.

The *Basket of Conduct* (CP 3.9) relates the story of the Buddha's previous life as a bodhisattva who was born as a quail. As a tiny chick, he was completely dependent on his parents for food and protection. However, when a forest fire approached, they were forced to abandon him for fear of their own lives. Terrified and without any ability to fly away, the chick reflected on the power of the Dharma and remembered the strength of the truth as demonstrated by previous buddhas. The baby quail made a declaration of truth, whereby the fires receded and he was saved.[43]

Determination

Determination is the unshakable resolve to fulfill our promise to liberate sentient beings and to perfect the ten perfections. It gives us the courage to remain steadfast in the practice, even when afflictive mental states attempt to sway us to do the opposite. As long as we are in saṃsāra, afflictions will arise and interfere with practicing the perfections. With determination and energy we must remain constant, doing what we know is right.

The *Temiya Jātaka* tells the story of the Buddha's previous life as a bodhisattva born as the much-longed-for son of the king and queen of Kasi. As an infant, one day he heard his father sentence some robbers to a harsh punishment, and that caused him to remember a past life in which he had been a king and had acted similarly. Subsequent to that life, he had been born in the hell realm due to the harmful karma he had created. Temiya desperately did not want to rule a kingdom again and followed the advice of a goddess who counseled him to pretend to be dumb and incapable. This he did for sixteen years, and while his parents knew this was a pretense and did everything they could to break his resolve, he was determined not to assume the throne. Finally at wits end, his parents ordered a charioteer to take him to a cemetery and club him to death. Temiya remained resolute, thinking (CP 3.6.17–18):

> I did not break that resolute determination that was for the sake of awakening itself. Mother and father were not disagreeable to me, nor was self disagreeable to me. Omniscience was dear to me; therefore I resolutely determined on that itself.

When Temiya told the charioteer his wish to become an ascetic, the charioteer wanted to join him in spiritual pursuits. But first he returned to tell Temiya's parents, the king and queen, what had happened. They came to Temiya's hermitage, where he taught the Dharma to them and their retinue, after which all of them renounced and became ascetic spiritual practitioners.

Love

Love is the aspiration to give happiness to all sentient beings and create the conditions whereby they will be happy. Free from resentment or expectation, love lies behind our determination to fulfill the aspiration to awakening and to complete the practices of the perfections. Someone who is self-centered lacks genuine love; they harm others and have many enemies in this life and are not happy in future lives. Someone lacking in love and compassion cannot lead all beings to nirvāṇa. The Buddha says (AN 11.16):

> When the liberation of the mind by love is developed and cultivated, frequently practiced, made your vehicle and foundation, firmly established, consolidated, and properly undertaken, eleven blessings may be expected. What eleven?
>
> You sleep peacefully; you awaken peacefully; you see no bad dreams; you are dear to human beings; you are dear to nonhuman beings; you will be protected by devas; fire, poison, and weapons cannot injure you; your mind becomes easily concentrated; your facial complexion will be serene; you will die unconfused; and if you do not penetrate higher, you will be reborn in the Brahmā-world.

To illustrate the peace that love brings, the *Basket of Conduct* tells the story of the Buddha's previous life as Sāma, a lad who lived in the forest, taking care of his blind parents (CP 3.13):

> When in a wood I was Sāma...I brought the lions and tigers in the forest to love. Surrounded by lions and tigers, by leopards, bears, buffaloes, and by spotted deer and wild boar, I lived in the wood. No one was frightened of me, nor did I fear anyone. Sustained by the power of love, I delighted in the forest then.

Bodhisattvas think, "It is good to wish for the happiness of others, but that alone will not provide them with happiness. I must act with love and employ joyous effort to accomplish the welfare of others." Bodhisattvas also reflect that sentient beings are the incomparable, supreme field of merit with which they can cultivate virtue and fulfill the collections. In that way, they always maintain a mind that cherishes sentient beings and never abandons them. With an unbounded heart they reach out to give happiness to others. To do that, they must eliminate sentient beings' pain, misery, and their cause—the afflictions. In this way, compassion, which is a principal cause of buddhahood, arises and expands in their minds.

Equanimity

Equanimity is impartiality with respect to the desirable and pleasing and the undesirable and displeasing. It is an inner attitude that doesn't oscillate according to either the people or the objects we encounter. Remaining equanimous, bodhisattvas are able to continue to practice no matter what comes their way. Equanimity enables us to benefit sentient beings impartially, not sliding into attachment for those who benefit, praise, and give us offerings, and not falling into animosity for those who don't fulfill our expectations or wishes or who inflict harm on us. Without equanimity our mood resembles a yo-yo that constantly goes up and down.

The mind is reactive to the external environment and controlled by the sense objects in it. This lack of balance impedes developing concentration, disturbs ethical conduct, and obstructs acting in ways that benefit sentient beings. Without equanimity, we cannot complete the perfections well, and we find difficulty in dedicating the virtue from practicing the perfections for the awakening of all sentient beings. But imbued with equanimity, we can face whatever comes in a balanced way, free from worry and fear regarding our life. Equanimity overcomes discontent, and being unconcerned about either the praise or the insults of others, bodhisattvas' determination to serve them never flags. In short, equanimity supports the practice of all the perfections.

The *Basket of Conduct* relates the story of the Buddha's previous life as a bodhisattva who, being impoverished, lay down in a cemetery and piled up bones to use as a pillow. Wondering who he was, some children approached. Some of them gave him gifts, others cruelly ridiculed him. Toward them all, the bodhisattva maintained equanimity.

The Sequence of the Perfections

There are several reasons to explain why each perfection follows its preceding one; a summary of them will suffice. To develop our understanding of the perfections, it is helpful for us to reflect and see additional connections among them. In most cases, the preceding or subsequent perfection helps to perfect or purify the one immediately before or after it.

Generosity is first because (1) it is comparatively easy to practice, and (2) all beings—religious and nonreligious—respect and practice it.

Ethical conduct follows because (1) although generosity benefits others, ethical conduct stops us from harming them, and (2) generosity is the cause of wealth, and to enjoy that wealth in the most suitable conditions a fortunate rebirth is needed. Ethical conduct is the principal cause for good rebirth.

Renunciation comes next because (1) although ethical conduct entails having good physical and verbal conduct, renunciation involves good mental conduct, (2) one who has renunciation can develop the dhyānas without difficulty, and (3) after abandoning harmful physical and verbal actions, we should abandon mental obsessions.

Wisdom is spoken of now because (1) in the absence of the dhyānas, wisdom is difficult to develop, and (2) skillful means, which is wisdom in working for others' welfare, arises as a result of meditation focused on their well-being.

Joyous effort follows because (1) bodhisattvas undertake wonderful deeds to benefit sentient beings on the basis of understanding their emptiness with wisdom, and (2) joyous effort follows upon the careful consideration and understanding involved in wisdom.

Fortitude comes next because (1) it can balance the energy produced by joyous effort so that restlessness is calmed, (2) those with joyous effort must also persevere to accomplish their spiritual aims, (3) bodhisattvas must patiently endure hardships while joyously working to benefit sentient beings, and (4) bodhisattvas who energetically aid sentient beings do not crave award or acknowledgment as they cultivate fortitude with respect to the Dharma.

Truthfulness is mentioned now because (1) truthfulness sustains the resolve to practice fortitude, (2) while fortitude endures the harms of others, truthfulness keeps the bodhisattva's promise to benefit them, (3) bodhisattvas remain steady with fortitude when confronted with abuse, and with truthfulness they do not give up on others, and (4) this shows the truth of the wisdom that was developed through the fortitude understanding the emptiness of sentient beings.

Determination follows because (1) whereas truthfulness is nondeceptive speech, determination is commitment to fulfill the bodhisattva practices without wavering, (2) after gaining the truthfulness of wisdom knowing things as they really are, bodhisattvas have strong determination to complete the requisites (collections) for awakening.

Love is mentioned next because (1) it sustains and supports the determination to work for the welfare of sentient beings, (2) after making a strong determination to work for others' welfare, love provides for their well-being, and (3) undertaking activities to benefit sentient beings proceeds well only with an unshakable determination.

Equanimity is next because (1) when bodhisattvas are actively working to benefit sentient beings with love, they must remain equanimous to any harm or insults they receive, (2) equanimity evolves from love, and (3) bodhisattvas remain equanimous and impartial even to those who wish them well and treat them well.

The perfections are defiled by afflictions, preconceptions, and mental proliferations. They are cleansed by applying the antidotes to the afflictions. When contemplating the perfections, it is helpful to reflect: What afflictions do I need to particularly guard against when practicing each perfection? What are the antidotes to that affliction? How can I energize mindfulness and introspective awareness to recognize the afflictions and apply their antidotes?

How to Accomplish the Perfections

The perfections can be related to other categories of phenomena as a way of helping to penetrate the meaning of each and to understand the relationships among them. The ten perfections are related to the four foundations of truth, relinquishment, peace, and wisdom.[44]

1. Bodhisattvas practice the *foundation of truth* by acting in accordance with what they have vowed and understood. Through this they maintain their practices of generosity, ethical conduct, and so on.
2. They practice the *foundation of relinquishment* by giving up the opposite of each perfection—for example, relinquishing stinginess, unethical behavior, and so on.
3. They practice the *foundation of peace* by pacifying obstacles to each perfection—for example by abandoning ignorance, anger, attachment, and fear toward recipients and objects of generosity, by pacifying physical and verbal misconduct, and so on.
4. They practice the *foundation of wisdom* by applying each perfection at the proper time, place, in a suitable manner, and so forth.

The perfections are actualized by four methods:

1. Enthusiastically accumulating the collection of merit for the sake of full awakening by practicing the perfections without discouragement or lack of interest.
2. Engaging in them completely with respect and esteem.
3. Doing them uninterruptedly with perseverance.
4. Continuing to do them over a long time without stopping part way.

To develop the inner strength to complete the path, bodhisattvas offer themselves and their possessions to the buddhas—for example, when they receive something, they immediately resolve to share it with others and use only what remains for themselves. Having done that, they may still encounter four shackles that impede their generosity. Fortunately there are counterforces that break these shackles:

(1) Lacking the habit of giving in the past. When a bodhisattva has something to give and a potential recipient is nearby but he does not immediately think to give it, he counteracts this by thinking, "This complacency is due to my lack of familiarity with generosity in the past. In order to overcome this, I will give now, and give with delight." In this way, he trains himself and develops the habit of giving with joy.

(2) Having only poor-quality goods to give. If a bodhisattva has only substandard objects to offer, she reflects, "The lack of good items to offer is due to my not having practiced generosity in the past. Therefore, even though what I have is poor quality, I will give it so that in the future excellent items will come my way and I can practice generosity with them."

(3) Being attached to the good qualities of the object. When a bodhisattva is reluctant to give because he finds the object very attractive, he admonishes himself, "You vowed to attain the most excellent state of awakening. For that noble purpose, you need to give excellent and beautiful gifts. Now that you have the chance to do this, do it!"

(4) Feeling a sense of loss or worry after giving. If a bodhisattva worries about suffering from not having the object or feels the pang of loss from giving even though she has enough, she thinks, "Possessions are transient. There is no way I can own this forever, so I should use it to create merit and give it now. Because I was stingy in the past, now my belongings are depleted; I do not want to create more karma like this. Therefore, whatever I have, be it a lot or a little, I will give so that I can perfect the quality of generosity."

In all four instances, the bodhisattva then gives generously, openhandedly, and with delight. In this way he destroys the four shackles to giving. Similarly, whenever he faces a hindrance in completing any of the other perfections, he thinks in whatever way is helpful to dispel it, for most of the hindrances are in the mind.

Sometimes bodhisattvas will encounter difficulties in their practice of the perfections: they may be deprived of means of support, be insulted or abused, face physical illness or injury, or feel low-spirited and exhausted. At this time, they reflect, "I have given myself to the buddhas for the sake of the awakening of all beings. Whatever comes, comes." In this way they trust the Three Jewels and have confidence in the law of karma and its effects. They do not succumb to fear or worry and remain unshaken and determined to continue on the bodhisattva path. Dhammapāla concludes:

> In brief, the destruction of self-centeredness and the development of love for others are the means to accomplish the pāramīs.

By contemplating sentient beings as their precious children or relatives, bodhisattvas increase their love, compassion, and affection. Having subdued their own ignorance, attachment, and animosity, they mature others' minds with the four ways of gathering disciples—generosity, loving speech, encouragement, and acting congruently. These were described according to both traditions in the chapter "Sharing the Dharma." With these four ways of gathering disciples, bodhisattvas cause sentient beings to enter and then reach the end of whichever of the three vehicles they choose. Bodhisattvas treat all beings as equal to themselves in importance, and emotionally they remain stable under all circumstances, be they pleasant or unpleasant, helpful or harmful. After they become buddhas, their ability to benefit others and lead them on the path is perfected due to having practiced these four ways of gathering disciples while they were bodhisattvas.

Bodhisattvas can be grouped according to which factor is prominent in them. In some bodhisattvas wisdom is predominant, in others faith, and in others energy is principal. These bodhisattvas attain full awakening, respectively, in four countless and a hundred thousand great eons, eight countless and a hundred thousand great eons, and sixteen countless and a hundred thousand great eons. Since full awakening is attained by the power of wisdom, those bodhisattvas inclined toward wisdom proceed more rapidly.

The three types of bodhisattvas all receive predictions of their awakening directly from a buddha. When they first generate bodhicitta, the length of time they will practice to fulfill the perfections and attain full awakening is not part of their aspiration. However, they perfect the perfections in the amount of time that corresponds to their respective type. It is not possible for them to attain full awakening quicker than that time period because it takes that length of time for their knowledge to mature and for them to accumulate the collections for full awakening. Just as fruit ripens after the length of time required for its growth and not sooner, so too a bodhisattva's mind ripens in the length of time required for their type.

Benefits and Results of Practicing the Perfections

The benefits of practicing the perfections are countless. In Theravāda countries today, practicing them is highly respected, so much so that people who aspire for arhatship engage in ten wonderful practices similar to the perfections.

However, doing these practices with the motivation of bodhicitta and sealing them with the understanding of not-self make these practices unique. Rather than being ordinary generosity that leads to wealth in future lives, those factors make the bodhisattvas' perfections causes for full awakening. Other benefits that accrue to bodhisattvas are that they become like kind and compassionate parents of all beings. They are worthy of offerings and reverence and become supreme fields of merit. Humans and nonhumans hold them dear and they are protected by deities. Bodhisattvas cannot be harmed by wild animals and will have excellent conditions in whatever rebirth they take. They become energetic, mindful, concentrated, and wise. Their afflictions are tamed so they are easy to get along with, easy to admonish, and are hospitable and cooperative. Bodhisattvas' manifest malice, jealousy, competitiveness, hypocrisy, miserliness, stubbornness, and arrogance have greatly decreased.[45] Needless to say, they have many friends and helpers, and as a result of their compassion, others treat them well. Their presence in an area prevents danger and disasters. Even when bodhisattvas are born in unfortunate realms, they are not oppressed by suffering, but instead their sense of spiritual urgency increases as they transform all experiences into methods that increase their resolve to attain buddhahood.

More benefits of bodhisattvas' perfections are:

They have a *long life* in whatever state of existence they are born, and as a result, they can accumulate many virtuous qualities, deepen their meditation, and bring to fruition many virtuous actions to benefit sentient beings.

By having an *attractive form*, bodhisattvas attract others to them and inspire confidence and reverence in those who value and respond to attractive forms.

Bodhisattvas are born in *excellent families*, who steer them to the Dharma when they are still children. Being from families that are well-known and well-respected in society, bodhisattvas can guide those who are attached to social status.

Bodhisattvas have *sovereignty* in their lives. They are influential and have many helpers who assist them in accomplishing their virtuous works, especially in enacting the four ways of gathering disciples and using the Dharma to subdue those who are rash and unrestrained.

Bodhisattvas have *credibility*. Because they are trustworthy and reliable, sentient beings value their advice and direction and give them authority. This enables them to protect others from making unwise or brash decisions and to steer them to increase their virtuous qualities.

As dedicated practitioners, bodhisattvas have the *greatness of spiritual power*. Because their minds have been transformed into the Dharma, bodhisattvas cannot be conquered or subjugated by others, but instead subdue them through their noble qualities.

Not all bodhisattvas will have the above conditions in every birth, but those who seek to benefit sentient beings through these noble qualities gain them as results of their great accumulation of merit and wisdom. Through these accomplishments, bodhisattvas' practice of the perfections increases and they become more capable of guiding others in the Dharma of the three vehicles and have more opportunities to do so.

In understanding these benefits, we should not expect each and every bodhisattva to display them. For example, it is incorrect to think, "That person does not have an attractive form, so he must not be a bodhisattva" or "That person is from a lower social class, so he cannot be a bodhisattva." Bodhisattvas manifest in whatever ways can benefit sentient beings, according to their karma. So bodhisattvas may appear as lepers, homeless people, refugees, or people who are physically challenged. They do this in order to benefit others. Since we do not know who is and isn't a bodhisattva, we should avoid judging and discriminating against others but instead view all sentient beings as teachers. After all, we can learn important things from interacting with and listening to everyone.

The benefits of practicing the perfections can be found in the Pāli sūtras. In the *Sutta on the Wonderful and Marvelous* (*Acchariyaabbhuta Sutta*, MN 123), the Buddha asks Ānanda to describe the Tathāgata's wonderful and marvelous qualities, and in the *Sutta on the Great Passing* (*Mahāparinibbāna Sutta*, DN 16.3.15–20) the Buddha speaks of eight causes of the great trembling of the earth, six of them related to events in the Buddha's life. The *Jātakas* and the *Buddhavaṃsa* mention other benefits of practicing the perfections. While many of the stories of the Buddha's previous lives in the *Jātakas* sound like legends and folktales, the points that they illustrate can be applied to our lives. On a deeper level, these stories illustrate the level of commitment to compassion and to fulfilling the perfections that bodhisattvas have; pondering them will inspire us to think and act in that way.

The result of bodhicitta and the bodhisattvas' perfections is buddhahood, with the magnificent form body (*rūpakāya*) that possesses the thirty-two marks and eighty signs of a great person[46] and the truth body (*dharmakāya*),[47] glorious with its wondrous qualities such as the ten powers, the four fearlessnesses, the six kinds of knowledge not held in common with others, the eighteen unique qualities of a buddha,[48] and so forth. The qualities of a buddha are too numerous to ever finish describing. Dhammapāla concludes his treatise:

> And it is said: If a buddha were to speak in praise of a buddha, speaking nothing else for an eon, the long eon would end but the praise of the Tathāgata would still not be finished.

Part II. The Three Vehicles and Their Fruits

HAVING BEEN INTRODUCED to the bodhisattva perfections in both the Sanskrit and Pāli tradition, we'll now turn to the paths and fruits of the three vehicles. The paths are consciousnesses that are developed in stages as we boost our concentration and deepen our understanding and realization of the ultimate truth. Knowing these enriches our practice in multiple ways. Our understanding of the Three Jewels will expand, especially our understanding of the progressive practices of the Saṅgha Jewel and their specific result. But we cannot understand these without increasing our understanding of the Dharma Jewel—the true paths and true cessations. And since the final result of the path is supreme buddhahood, our appreciation of the abandonments and realizations of the Buddha Jewel will also grow. With this, our feeling when we take refuge in the Three Jewels will be transformed and our faith in their ability to guide us on the path will increase exponentially.

6 | Breakthrough to Nirvāṇa: The Pāli Tradition

LEARNING ABOUT THE PATHS and fruits of the three vehicles gives us a road map of the practices that we must engage in and the results that will come about according to the vehicle we enter. This will guide us in our practice and will enable us to check our progress on the path. Of course, conferring with our spiritual mentor is undoubtedly necessary, but this road map is helpful to keep us going straight on the path.

In addition, as we learn the paths and fruits of our chosen spiritual vehicle, we will begin to imagine gaining those realizations and qualities. Such imagination is important in Dharma practice since it inspires us to engage with joyous effort in the practices to cultivate these realizations and qualities. In addition, while we engage in Dharma practice, imagination will spark small glimpses of those realizations and qualities, which further fuels our effort to create the causes to attain them. In short, learning the paths and grounds not only plants seeds in our minds but also affects how we think about the paths and grounds now.

The remainder of this chapter will present the paths and fruits of Fundamental Vehicle practitioners from the viewpoint of the Pāli tradition. The next chapter will cover the same material from the perspective of the Sanskrit tradition.

The Three Vehicles

The oldest Pāli sūtras speak of three types of individuals who attain awakening: a fully awakened buddha (*samyaksaṃbuddha*, *sammāsaṃbuddha*), a solitary realizer (*pratyekabuddha*, *paccekabuddha*), and a śrāvaka (P. *sāvaka*).

All of them were seen as having attained the same awakened state of nirvāṇa, although each of them had different characteristics. A fully awakened buddha realizes awakening without a teacher in his last life. He teaches the Dharma to others and begins a dispensation (*śāsana, sāsana*)—that is, he turns the Dharma wheel in a time when the Buddhadharma is not present in the world. A solitary realizer attains awakening without the aid of a teacher, does not generally teach others verbally,[49] and does not begin a dispensation. A śrāvaka attains awakening through following the guidance of a teacher. All three have realized the fourfold path knowledge (P. *magga ñaṇa*)—that is, they have realized the four truths and are arhats.

With the passage of time, each of the three became known as practitioners of different vehicles. Practitioners of the Pāli tradition continued to follow the early sūtras, thus aiming for the śrāvaka awakening that they speak of. Nevertheless, the bodhisattva ideal was revered in the *Buddhavaṃsa*, a later text that was added to the Sūtra Piṭaka. This text also spoke of the bodhisattva's great aspiration (*ābhinīhāra, abhinīhāra*) and put forth ten perfections practiced by a bodhisattva, and the *Jātaka* tales illustrate a bodhisattva's practice of the perfections. Meanwhile, practitioners in some of the other early schools, such as the Sarvāstivāda and the Mahāsāṃghika, came to speak of three vehicles leading to awakening that were differentiated by the difficulty and length of practice.

As time went on, in addition to the characteristics described above, new terms came about to describe these three types of individuals and their respective states of awakening. A buddha attains full awakening (P. *sammā-saṃbodhi*) and is all-knowing. Here "all-knowing" does not mean a buddha knows everything, but that he could know anything if he turned his mind to it. A buddha has eradicated all defilements as well as latencies (habitual tendencies, *vāsanā*). Practitioners with a strong motivation to attain full awakening are called *sammā-sambodhisattas*. Those with a virtuous aspiration to attain a solitary realizer's awakening (P. *pacceka-bodhi*) are known as solitary realizer bodhisattvas (P. *pacceka-bodhisattas*), and those aspiring to attain śrāvaka awakening (P. *sāvaka-bodhi*) are known as śrāvaka bodhisattvas (P. *sāvaka-bodhisatta*).[50] All three practice the āryan eightfold path and attain the path that realizes the four truths.

A commentary on the *Buddhavaṃsa* speaks of *arhat-bodhi* (the awakening of a śrāvaka arhat) and *sabbaññu-bodhi* (the awakening of a buddha).

Present-day Theravāda practitioners regard the perfections as practices done by all three types of practitioners because they bring about qualities that are requisites for awakening. However, someone aspiring for a buddha's awakening cultivates the perfections both for a longer period of time and in more depth than practitioners aspiring to become śrāvaka or solitary realizer arhats.

Dhyānas and the Destruction of Pollutants

Several modes of progressing to liberation exist and a general map is given here, but as with any map, there are smaller roads that are not shown. Similarly, there are a diversity of ways of progressing through the four stages of liberation—stream-enterer (*srotāpanna, sotāpanna*), once-returner (*sakṛdāgāmin, sakadāgāmi*), nonreturner (*anāgāmin, anāgāmi*), and arhat (P. *arahant*).

The dhyānas and formless realm absorptions are states of deep mental tranquility in which the defilements are temporarily suppressed but not eradicated. The Pāli commentaries say that a meditator who has developed access concentration (P. *upacāra samādhi*), which is prior to attaining the first dhyāna, can develop insight wisdom and then gradually progress through the stages of stream-enterer, once-returner, and nonreturner to attain arhatship. These are called "dry-insight arhats" (P. *sukkhavipassaka*) because their minds are not moistened and softened by the deep concentration of the dhyānas. The Sarvāstivāda Abhidharma, followed in the Tibetan tradition, speaks of similar arhats.

Those who go beyond access concentration and gain the first dhyāna can use that as the basis to attain the destruction of pollutants. They do not need to cultivate any levels of concentration beyond that. However, some meditators also develop the second, third, and fourth dhyānas and then use the latter to attain the destruction of pollutants. When describing how he attained the destruction of all pollutants, the Buddha said he attained the fourth dhyāna and then realized the three higher knowledges: recollection of previous lives, knowledge of the death and rebirth of sentient beings, and knowledge of the destruction of all pollutants.

Each level of dhyāna gives power, precision, and clarity to the mind, and the mind of the fourth dhyāna in particular is described as being "purified, bright, unblemished, free from imperfections, malleable, wieldy, steady, and attained to imperturbability." This mind is free from the imperfections of the minor corruptions and minor defilements and can be molded according to the meditator's needs. It doesn't waver and is completely still.

To actualize the knowledge of the destruction of all pollutants, meditators first cultivate insight wisdom (P. *vipassanā pañña*) by meditating on the three characteristics—impermanence, duḥkha, and not-self. Based on a meditation practice such as the four establishments of mindfulness, they refine their mindfulness, and with the practice of dhyāna, the mind has become very sharp, clear, and pliant. They direct their mind to the factors of their experience—the five aggregates, six sense sources, and so on—as they are occurring. What is within the realm of awareness of this highly trained and focused meditative mind is far beyond what we can discern with our ordinary awareness. These meditators investigate the factors of their body and mind at a microscopic level, directly witnessing their subtle impermanence as they arise and pass away in the briefest moment. Seeing that everything in their present experience is arising and passing away, they know that the mind is just a process of events that are arising and passing away. What is taken to be the mind is actually a stream of events—feelings, discriminations, various miscellaneous factors, and consciousnesses—and each of them no sooner comes into being than they cease. This is the realization of the first characteristic, subtle impermanence.

The meditators then realize that whatever is impermanent—especially their cherished body and mind—cannot be relied upon for security and is not a basis for lasting happiness. This is the realization of the second characteristic, duḥkha, which the commentaries define as "oppression due to arising and passing away."

Furthermore, whatever arises and passes away and is made of constituents is not a solid, stable self. It is not I, it is not a true self—the third characteristic. The meditators now directly perceive the entire field of their experience in terms of these three characteristics of saṃsāric existence.

This insight wisdom, which contemplates things as they really are, serves to weaken the underlying tendencies of the defilements that have been together with the mind since beginningless time. Insight wisdom brings "specific-factor abandonment"—that is, it temporarily overcomes a particular misunderstanding or wrong conception.

As insight wisdom matures and when practitioners' faculties are ripe, the mind momentarily turns away from all conditioned phenomena and realizes the unconditioned, ultimate peace that is not impermanent and unsatisfactory. When they have a clear realization of this, they gain the true understanding of four truths and know: this is duḥkha, this is the origin of duḥkha, this is the cessation of duḥkha, this is the path to the cessation of duḥkha. At arhatship, this clear realization is called "knowledge of the destruction of the pollutants," which also knows: these are the pollutants, this is their origin, this is their cessation, this is the path leading to their cessation. With the wisdom of a clear realization that knows nirvāṇa directly, the defilements are eradicated in "eradication abandonment." This clear realization is a sudden experience in that meditators see what they have never before seen—nirvāṇa, the unconditioned, the deathless. This experience is a total transformation of consciousness. In general, practitioners arrive at this through the gradual practice of the three higher trainings. However, the sūtras tell of some people who encounter the Buddha or an accomplished disciple and attain the path and fruit just by hearing a discourse, without prior practice in that life. However, they undoubtedly cultivated the three higher trainings in previous lives.

According to the Pāli commentaries, clear realization occurs at a single moment. A practitioner penetrates the third truth, nirvāṇa, as the object of their meditation, and simultaneously realizes the other three truths by way of their function. Through the realization of nirvāṇa they fully understand the five aggregates, the six sources, and so on as the truth of duḥkha, and they abandon some defilements that are the cause of duḥkha. Through their own experience they know that cultivating the eightfold path is the way to the cessation of duḥkha.[51]

With the experience of the wisdom of a clear realization, the destruction of the fetters (*saṃyojana*) begins. With the first realization of nirvāṇa, the first three fetters—view of a personal identity, deluded doubt, and view of bad rules and practices—are eradicated and the disciple becomes a stream-enterer. With the weakening of two more fetters—sensual desire and malice—the disciple becomes a once-returner. With the eradication of those two additional fetters, all five lower fetters have been removed and the disciple becomes a nonreturner. With the destruction of the remaining fetters—desire for existence in the form realm, desire for existence in the formless realm, conceit, restlessness, and ignorance—and the three pollutants (of sensual desire, existence, and ignorance), the disciple attains arhatship. In the *Greater Discourse at Assapura* (*Mahāassapura Sutta*), the Buddha describes this experience (MN 39:21):

> When he knows and sees thus, his mind is liberated from the pollutant of sensual desire, from the pollutant of existence, and from the pollutant of ignorance. When it is liberated there comes the knowledge: "It is liberated." He understands: "Birth is destroyed, the holy life has been lived, what had to be done has been done, there is no more coming to any state of being."
>
> Just as if there were a lake in a mountain recess, clear, limpid, and undisturbed, so that a person with good sight standing on the bank could see shells, gravel, and pebbles, and also shoals of fish, swimming about and resting, he might think: "There is this lake, clear, limpid, and undisturbed, and there are these shells, gravel, and pebbles, and also shoals of fish, swimming about and resting." So, too, a monastic understands as it actually is: "This is duḥkha... This is the origin of duḥkha... This is the cessation of duḥkha... This is the way leading to the cessation of duḥkha..." He understands: "Birth is destroyed, the holy life has been lived, what had to be done has been done, there is no more coming to any state of being."

Direct Knowledge, Full Understanding, and Realization

Direct knowledge (*abhijñā*, *abhiññā*), full understanding (P. *pariññā*), and realization (*sākshāt-kriyā*, *sacchi-kiriyā*) are terms that are often found together but have slightly different meanings. Understanding their specific meanings and limits fine-tunes our understanding of the path to liberation.

Direct knowledge is insight wisdom that knows the specific or unique characteristics of an object as well as its general or common characteristics. Specific characteristics are what distinguish one object from another. For example, the specific characteristics of a bird are its attributes that enable us to distinguish it from a table. But both a bird and a table also share some common characteristics: they are impermanent, unsatisfactory, and not-self. Direct knowledge is possessed by both learners—stream-enterers, once-returners, and nonreturners—and arhats.

Direct knowledge leads to understanding, and understanding is enhanced along the path until it culminates in the full understanding of an arhat. What is to be fully understood? In his first teaching, the Buddha talked about how to engage in each of the four truths. True duḥkha is to be fully understood, true origin is to be abandoned, true cessation is to be realized, and true path is to be cultivated. The object that we want to fully understand is true duḥkha, which is in essence the five aggregates. The process of cultivating understanding begins as ordinary beings, progresses during the stages of stream-enterer, once-returner, and nonreturner, and culminates in full understanding at arhatship.

Understanding implies having extensive knowledge, but knowledge does not mean simply knowing terms and concepts. It is gained by investigation, contemplation, and gradually building up an expansive and deep understanding, specifically of conditioned phenomena such as the five aggregates. The five aggregates must be fully understood to attain liberation; a partial understanding will not suffice.

Realize is to see "with your own eyes" or to witness. While understanding and knowledge are developed gradually in the course of practicing the path, realization is seeing in a markedly different way than before. When knowledge and understanding of the five aggregates reach completion, the clear realization of nirvāṇa occurs and the practitioner sees what had not been previously seen—the unconditioned—and enters a totally new "world" that is free of phenomena conditioned by ignorance and craving. Here nirvāṇa is the object of realization. By fully understanding the nature of the five aggregates, practitioners can see nirvāṇa, which is beyond the five aggregates. The realization of nirvāṇa does not occur without causes such as the knowledge and understanding gained previously as well as practice and meditation. Like full understanding, complete realization is the province only of arhats. With stream-entry the realization of nirvāṇa is partial. Stream-enterers must continue to sharpen their insight to see the impermanent, unsatisfactory, and selfless nature of conditioned phenomena more clearly. By developing their faculties, nirvāṇa appears more clearly to their mind. The quality of that realization increases as they progress to the levels of once-returner and nonreturner, and it culminates with complete realization of nirvāṇa at arhatship.

The *Path of Purification* says that at each point of clear realization at the four stages, the four ways of engaging with the four truths occur whereby meditators fully understand duḥkha, abandon its origin, realize true cessation, and cultivate the true path. At the lower levels, these four ways of engaging occur to some extent and are completed at the time of becoming an arhat.

Insight knowledge knows the three characteristics and can arise without having previously attained dhyāna. None of the ārya paths or fruits are the result of concentration alone; they are the outcome of insight and the cultivation of wisdom. One who follows the vehicle of insight can begin meditation to attain insight even without attaining serenity, by meditating with mindfulness on mental and physical phenomena, such as done in the four establishments of mindfulness. After cultivating insight knowledge over time, path knowledge—the knowledge of nirvāṇa—arises with the clear realization of nirvāṇa. When nirvāṇa is the object of the meditator's mind, mental factors such as equanimity and love, which relate to sentient beings, are not manifest. Only nirvāṇa is perceived.

The Four Pairs of Āryas

The four types of āryas are stream enterers, once-returners, nonreturners, and arhats. In relation to each, there are two phases—one in which the person is practicing to attain the corresponding fruit, which they are certain to attain in that life, and a second phase in which they have attained it. The Pāli commentaries call these two phases the "path" (*mārga*, *magga*) and the "fruition" (*phala*). In the Sanskrit tradition, they are called "approachers" and "abiders." The Buddha speaks highly of these holy beings (AN 8.59):

> These eight persons are worthy of gifts, worthy of hospitality, worthy of offerings, worthy of reverential salutations, the unsurpassed field of merit for the world. What eight? The stream-enterer, the one practicing for the realization of the fruit of stream-enterer; the once-returner, the one practicing for the realization of the fruit of once-returner; the nonreturner, the one

practicing for the realization of the fruit of nonreturner; the arahant, the one practicing for arahantship.

These eight āryas are differentiated based on the strength of their faculties (faith, effort, mindfulness, concentration, and wisdom), the defilements they have eradicated, and the number and type of rebirths remaining before they attain arhatship. When asked if there were monks and nuns who had attained arhatship, the Buddha responded that there were not just one hundred or five hundred, but many more who in this life entered upon and dwelt in the liberation of mind, liberation by wisdom that is unpolluted.[52] In general, liberation of mind (P. *cetovimutti*) is the result of serenity, and liberation by wisdom (P. *paññāvimutti*) refers to wisdom and is the result of insight. When the two are conjoined and described as unpolluted, they are the result of the eradication of pollutants by an arhat's supramundane path.[53]

All of us begin as uninstructed ordinary beings. Then we encounter the Dharma and listen to teachings, undertake ethical conduct, begin meditating, and gradually develop wisdom. As we do so, we become a virtuous ordinary person (P. *kalyāṇaputhujjana*) who aspires for stream-entry. Four factors are important to actualize this aspiration and generate extensive, vast, profound, unequaled, great, abundant, quick, buoyant, joyous, swift, sharp, and penetrative wisdom:

1. *Associating with superior persons* is to be near a qualified teacher and Dharma friends who are intent on liberation and will spur us on to study and practice.
2. *Hearing the true Dharma* is essential before embarking on the practice of the path. We must know what the path is, what potential detours and roadblocks there are, how to work around them, and so on.
3. *Appropriate and wise attention* enables us to focus on what is important in a way that helps us to see the three characteristics.
4. *Practicing in accord with the Dharma* indicates that only by integrating the Dharma with our lives and our minds will realizations come about.

Practitioners enter the path to **stream-enterer** when, having diligently practiced insight, their wisdom faculty becomes strong enough to break through mundane reality. Their meditation on the three characteristics—especially again and again seeing that there is no findable self—leads to a radical elimination of the notion of self, to the point where they cannot hold any mistaken view of self at all. Whereas prior to this they have seen with insight the aggregates are not mine, not I, and not my self, at the time of breakthrough any idea of a substantial self is forever uprooted. Their wisdom now reaches beyond insight to seeing (vision, P. *dassana*) nirvāṇa as well as realizing the four truths. Their minds go beyond perceiving conditioned phenomena and they briefly experience the unconditioned, the deathless state, nirvāṇa. Simultaneous with this clear realization of the unconditioned, they eradicate the first three fetters and their seeds, thereby becoming stream-enterers.

The first three fetters are the view of a personal identity, deluded doubt, and the view of bad rules and practices. The *view of a personal identity* grasps at a self that can be identified with the five aggregates.[54] Since a stream-enterer has directly seen the truth of the Dharma, he no longer harbors *deluded doubt* concerning it. Having seen the truth, a stream-enterer knows that liberation is possible only by following the three higher trainings and no longer possesses the *view of bad rules and practices.*

According to the Abhidharma concept of the "cognitive process," the stream-enterer's momentary breakthrough to nirvāṇa is followed by a few mind-moments that also experience nirvāṇa. This is the fruition; it enjoys the results of the path, experiencing the peace of nirvāṇa right after those three fetters have been eradicated. For example, the path is like a person who is shackled breaking free from the chains, and the fruition resembles the freedom he feels just afterward. Stream-enterers are so called because they have entered the stream of the Dharma, the stream of the supramundane eightfold path. They have attained the clear realization of the Dharma (P. *dhammābhisamaya*) and the vision of the Dharma (P. *dhammacakkhu-paṭilābha*). This clear realization is called "the arising of the Eye of Dharma" because they see the Dharma as the truth of the Buddha's teaching.

Because of this realization, a stream-enterer will never do any of the five heinous actions: killing his mother, killing his father, killing an arhat, causing a schism in the saṅgha, or maliciously drawing blood from a buddha. Stream-enterers observe ethical conduct well: Lay stream-enterers keep the five precepts and monastic stream-enterers keep monastic precepts. While they may still commit transgressions such as harsh speech, they never conceal their transgressions and confess and make amends as soon as possible.

Stream-enterers have four defining characteristics: unshakable confidence in the Buddha, the Dharma, and the Saṅgha, and firm commitment to observe at least the five precepts. Because they have seen nirvāṇa directly, all doubt about the path, the teacher, and those who have experienced the truth has been removed. Their confidence and faith in the Three Jewels are immoveable and arise as a result of their direct experience of the Dharma. Their confidence in the law of karma and its effects is also firm, and thus they are committed to keep whatever level of precepts they have taken. Stream-enterers who are householders may marry and be attached to their families, and they may enjoy praise, compete in business deals, and become angry when criticized. Nevertheless their afflictions are weaker than those of ordinary people who are not āryas.

The Buddha says that monastic āryas are far better off than wheel-turning monarchs who have great power in this life and a luxurious life as devas in the next. Even though monastic āryas maintain themselves with lumps of alms food and wear rag-robes, they are free from rebirth in unfortunate states and possess the four defining characteristics mentioned above. Sovereignty over the four continents—one of the powers of a wheel-turning monarch—is worthless in comparison to obtaining those four qualities.

The wisdom eye of a stream-enterer has been opened, and she is irreversibly headed for liberation. Having had direct insight into reality, she will never regress on the path and will never lose her understanding of the Dharma even when she dies; the Dharma is now part of the fabric of her being. She will be reborn as a human being or a deva a maximum of seven times before attaining nirvāṇa and can no longer be born in the unfortunate realms or as a demi-god. While this first direct realization of the unconditioned is not sufficient to eradicate all defilements and must be enhanced through cultivating the seven awakening factors, a stream-enterer has made an irrevocable shift. To illustrate this, the Buddha once asked monastics to compare the little bit of soil under his fingernail with all the soil on the Earth. Similarly, he said, the duḥkha that remains for those who have gained the Eye of Dharma is very small compared with the former mass of duḥkha that has been destroyed.

After a path and its fruits have been attained, the yogī engages in subsequent periods of meditation called "fruition attainment" (P. *phala-samāpatti*) during which nirvāṇa is again perceived and experienced, but the understanding is not yet deep enough to attain the next path. For example, after attaining both the path and fruition of stream-enterer, a person may again meditate on nirvāṇa and reexperience the fruit of stream-enterer without again having to attain the path of a stream-enterer. Nevertheless, her understanding may not yet be deep enough to progress to the path of a once-returner.

Some stream-enterers may attain arhatship in that very life, as did Śāriputra, Maudgalyāyana, Ānanda, and many others. Otherwise, they will be reborn as humans or devas in saṃsāra, but never in unfortunate realms. Stream-enterers with sharp faculties will take only one more rebirth, those of middle faculties will take two to six rebirths, and those of dull faculties will take at most seven more rebirths before attaining final nirvāṇa.[55]

Someone who has attained stream-entry in this life may not want to stop there and may seek to become a **once-returner**. Accordingly, she continues to practice, enhancing her samādhi and insight. When her faculties mature to a certain point and her seeing of nirvāṇa deepens, she attains the path and fruit of once-returner and then comes back to normal consciousness as a once-returner. At this point her sensual desire and malice have been substantially reduced, although not totally eliminated. The three poisons of attachment, anger, and confusion have also been reduced.

A once-returner will be reborn in the desire realm at most only one more time. The Pāli commentaries say there are several types of once-returner. In one case, the person is a human being who becomes a once-returner. He takes rebirth as a deva and attains final nirvāṇa as a deva. A second case is someone who becomes a once-returner as a human, is reborn in the human realm, and attains nirvāṇa in that rebirth as human. A third possibility is a deva who becomes a once-returner, is reborn as a human, and attains nirvāṇa as a human being. In a fourth scenario, a deva becomes a once-returner, is reborn again as deva, and attains nirvāṇa in the deva realm. In a fifth case, a human being becomes a once-returner, is reborn as a deva, is reborn again as a human, and attains nirvāṇa in the human realm. As we can see, there are several permutations. Someone with ripe faculties can actualize stream-enterer and once-returner in rapid succession in the same human life.

A once-returner with sharp faculties and good supporting conditions then aspires to become a **nonreturner** and practices intensely for this. Having deepened his samādhi to the point of mastering one of the four dhyānas or one of the first three formless absorptions, he now turns his mind to examine the state of samādhi itself and sees that it is made up of various factors, all of which can be included in the five aggregates (or four aggregates if it is a formless absorption). With insight wisdom, he sees that all these factors, however sublime, are still impermanent and in the nature of duḥkha. They are substanceless and selfless; they cannot be held on to or identified as self. The sūtras themselves do not specify whether he must emerge from the meditative absorption in order to engage in the above examination. Seeing the meditative absorptions as being marked with the three characteristics is important to eradicate the desire for rebirth in these realms. No matter how sublime these states may be, holding even the slightest ignorant desire to remain in them inhibits the attainment of liberation.

Extending the insight of the three characteristics from the meditative absorption to all conditioned phenomena, he sees all of them as impermanent, unsatisfactory, and not-self. When his faculties reach a particular level of maturity, his mind goes beyond conditioned things and touches the unconditioned, nirvāṇa. Those with very ripe faculties who can relinquish all attachments can attain arhatship then and there, whereas those whose faculties are not as sharp cannot yet let go of all attachments and thus become nonreturners.

While on the path of a nonreturner, a person completely eradicates sensual desire and malice. When she is successful, she experiences the fruit of nonreturner and is never again born as a human or a desire-realm god. If she does not attain nirvāṇa in that life, she may be reborn in a pure abode—one of five special levels of the fourth meditative stabilization where only nonreturners take birth.[56] A nonreturner born there is born spontaneously, without conception or gestation in the womb, and will attain final nirvāṇa in that pure abode. Although the pure abodes are connected with the fourth dhyāna, nonreturners who have not attained the fourth dhyāna may still be born there.

Some cases are recorded in the sūtras of people who are ordinary beings with no attainment. They meet the Buddha, hear his discourses, and due to the ripeness of their faculties developed in previous lives, they seem to go directly to nonreturner. The commentary says they pass through stream-entry and once-returner in brief instants, thus becoming nonreturners quickly. While we would all like to think that we have such sharp faculties and will have quick attainments, we should note that such cases are due to someone having practiced very diligently in previous lives. Such occurrences are rare nowadays.

If a nonreturner wishes to attain arhatship in this life, she again cultivates insight, progresses through the stages of insight realizations, and gains a clear realization of nirvāṇa once again. At this point, she attains the path approaching arhatship and eradicates the five higher fetters: desire for existence in the form realm; desire for existence in the formless realm; the conceit of "I am," which is a subtle conceit of being an existing I; restlessness, which is present in any mind that is not liberated; and ignorance.

Having eliminated these five fetters, she abides in the fruit of arhatship. She is totally free from saṃsāra and lives in the experience of nirvāṇa. This is called nirvāṇa with remainder, because the polluted physical and mental aggregates remain. When she passes away from that life, she attains the final goal, nirvāṇa without remainder, and has actualized the end of the path.

Both monastics and lay followers can practice the path and attain the fruit of stream-enterers and once-returners. Some of those lay followers continue to live at home in a couple relationship. The Buddha speaks of them as (MN 73:12) "lay followers...clothed in white, enjoying sensual pleasures, who carry out my instruction, respond to my advice, have gone beyond doubt, become free from perplexity, have gained intrepidity, and become independent of others in the Teacher's dispensation."

Although the sūtras do not specify this, it seems that yogīs practicing to become nonreturners would be celibate. To become nonreturners they must overcome sensual desire, and for this celibacy is necessary. Lay followers who attain the fruit of nonreturner can still live at home, but they would abide in celibacy because their sensual desire has been eliminated. After they pass away, these nonreturners may then be born in a pure abode where they attain arhatship.

The scriptures record some instances of lay followers attaining arhatship, but they are either just about to die or they ordain as monastics very soon after becoming arhats. Because arhats have severed all craving, they have no interest in a householder's lifestyle.

The Four Āryas

DISCIPLE	FETTERS JUST ABANDONED	REMAINING REBIRTHS	WHO CAN ATTAIN THIS
Stream-enterer	View of a personal identity, deluded doubt, view of bad rules and practices	Seven at most; all will be either as a human or a deva	Someone who has first realization of nirvāṇa, unshakable faith in the Three Jewels, firm commitment to observe at least the five precepts; lay followers (who may or may not be celibate) and monastics
Once-returner	None, but sensual desire and malice are reduced, as are attachment, anger, and confusion	One more birth in the desire realm	Lay followers (who may or may not be celibate) or monastics
Nonreturner	Sensual desire and malice	No more birth in the desire realm, born in the form realm and attain arhatship there	Monastics or lay followers who are celibate
Arhat	Desire for existence in the form realm, desire for existence in the formless realm, conceit, restlessness, ignorance	None—while alive, they abide in nirvāṇa with remainder; after they pass away, they attain nirvāṇa without remainder	Male and female monastics; some lay followers have attained arhatship but they either were on the brink of death or became monastics shortly after becoming an arhat

The Pāli commentaries say that it is possible for someone to become a stream-enterer, once-returner, nonreturner, and arhat without having attained dhyāna. Dhyāna meditation is said to moisten and relax the mind; thus these practitioners are said to become "dry-insight" arhats.[57]

There are several ways in which arhats are distinguished from ordinary beings. Contemplating these inspires our effort to practice because we see that we too can attain the same results. Speaking of an arhat, the Buddha says (MN 140:28):

> Formerly, when he was ignorant, he experienced covetousness, attachment, and sensual desire...he experienced anger, malice, and hatred...he experienced ignorance and confusion. Now he has abandoned them, cut them off at the root, made them like a palm stump, done away with them so that they are no longer subject to future arising. Therefore a bhikkhu possessing (this peace) possesses the supreme foundation of peace, for this is the supreme noble peace, namely, the pacification of sensual desire, hatred, and confusion.

Arhats do not worry about whether they will lose their temper or become depressed when they encounter hardship. They are not apprehensive about not getting what they want, nor do they succumb to the jealousy of others. They do not handle difficulties by drinking and drugging, or by shopping and gambling. They still encounter people who insult them, mock them, and pressure them to act in destructive ways, but because their minds are free from defilements, they do not fall prey to these influences and maintain their independence.

There are different types of arhats. As noted above, some have not attained dhyāna, while others have attained the dhyānas and have developed the five supernormal powers, which are considered mundane knowledges that depend on samādhi. Samādhi makes the mind powerful, malleable, and agile, so that when meditators generate the intention to develop supernormal powers, such as multiplying their body, they will be able to successfully develop them. Meditators who have attained the dhyānas can also use this powerful mind of samādhi to gain the divine ear, know others' minds, recollect previous lives, or develop the divine eye that knows how other sentient beings die and are reborn according to their karma. The Buddha followed this path of samādhi, developing these supernormal powers before attaining arhatship.

Someone with samādhi at the levels of the dhyānas may aspire (MN 6:19), "May I, by realizing for myself with direct knowledge, here and now enter upon and abide in the liberation of mind, liberation by wisdom that is unpolluted with the destruction of the pollutants." This refers to a mental state that is a liberation of mind just like the dhyānas and formless absorptions, but it differs in that it is also a liberation by wisdom. This wisdom destroys all pollutants and thus brings ultimate liberation. Such a person becomes an arhat and is never again born in cyclic existence.

Having eliminated all defilements, arhats are incapable of doing nine actions (AN 9:7): killing, stealing, engaging in sexual activities, deliberately lying, storing up or hoarding things to use later, and making bad decisions because of sensual desire, anger, confusion, or fear. In addition, arhats' minds cannot be moved by seeing either the most enticing or the most horrific objects of the five senses or of the mental consciousness. Their minds remain steady, peaceful, and calm, free from fear, personal distress, clinging, or repulsion. Knowing all these to be impermanent, they contemplate their disappearance and are unperturbed.

In addition, arhats have ten powers that prove they have destroyed all pollutants: (1) they have seen all things as they really are with correct wisdom as impermanent and thus do not crave them; (2) they have seen all sensual pleasures as they really are with correct wisdom as similar to a pit of burning charcoal and thus are not enticed by them; (3) their minds are inclined toward seclusion, delight in renunciation, and disinterest in things that are a basis for pollutants; and (4–10) their four establishments of mindfulness, four right strivings, four bases for spiritual power, five spiritual faculties, five spiritual powers, seven awakening factors, and eightfold path have been well developed.

REFLECTION

1. In your practice, how can you increase the four factors to actualize your aspiration for liberation and gain great wisdom by (1) associating with a qualified teacher and Dharma friends, (2) hearing true Dharma teachings, (3) cultivating appropriate and wise attention, and (4) practicing in accord with the Dharma?

2. Review the four pairs of āryas: the paths and fruits of stream-enterer, once-returner, nonreturner, and arhat. What fetters have they eliminated? How many future lives in saṃsāra will they have? What are their special features?

Those Who Have Work to Do with Diligence and Those Who Do Not

Usually the Buddha talks about four types of disciples—stream-enterers, and so forth—based on their current level of development on the path. However, in the *Kīṭāgiri Sutta* (MN 70), the Buddha speaks of seven kinds of disciples, subsuming them into two main categories: those who have completed the path and have no more work to do with diligence, and those who have work to do on the path with diligence. The first group, *those who have no more work to do with diligence*, are arhats, which are of two types: those liberated in both ways (P. *ubhatobhāgavimutta*) and those liberated by wisdom (P. *paññāvimutta*). Arhats are bhikkhus (MN 70:12):

> with pollutants destroyed, who have lived the holy life, done what had to be done, laid down the burden, reached the true goal, destroyed the fetters of existence, and are completely liberated through final knowledge.

Arhats have destroyed the pollutants of sensual desire, attachment to existence in saṃsāra, and ignorance. They have lived the holy life (*brahmacarya*) as monastics perfected in ethical conduct and have attained the ārya path. Having laid down the burden of the defilements, when they pass into nirvāṇa without remainder, they also lay down the burden of the polluted body. They have reached the true goal of the path—liberation by destroying all fetters that could lead to continued existence in saṃsāra. Having attained the final knowledge of the four truths and realized nirvāṇa directly and fully, they have attained the liberation that was their spiritual goal. Having done the "work" of practicing the path and attaining the goal with diligence, they are not capable of being negligent. Arhats are called *asekhas*—those who require no-more-learning or training on the path.

Arhats liberated in both ways are liberated from the physical body because of having gained the formless absorptions; they are also liberated from the mind-body (*nāma-kāya*)—the four unliberated mental aggregates—by the path of arhatship. The Buddha lauds them as the most excellent type of arhat because their faculties of wisdom and concentration are both strong. Their wisdom has destroyed the pollutants, and their concentration dwells in the formless absorptions just prior to attaining arhatship, freeing them from the limitations of both desire-realm and form-realm consciousnesses. Because they have attained the fourth dhyāna, which is the basis for developing the superknowledges, most of these arhats have also cultivated supernormal powers, the divine ear, knowledge of others' minds, recollection of past lives, and the divine eye prior to having attained the sixth superknowledge—knowledge of the destruction of the pollutants.

There are different degrees of arhats liberated in both ways. The lowest degree has attained arhatship based on the meditative absorption of infinite space, the first formless absorption. Others have attained arhatship depending on the absorptions of infinite consciousness, nothingness, and neither-discrimination-nor-nondiscrimination (the three remaining formless absorptions).

The most excellent is the one who has gone beyond the four dhyānas and the four formless absorptions to attain the cessation of discrimination and feeling (*saṃjñā-vedayita-nirodha, saññā-vedayita-nirodha*)—also known as the *absorption of cessation* (*nirodha-samāpatti*)[58]—which is an extremely refined state that only nonreturners and arhats can attain. Proficient in all four dhyānas and four formless absorptions prior to attaining liberation, these meditators can go up and down through various meditative absorptions whenever they want and dwell in them for as long as they wish. They know with insight wisdom—which is the special cause for the cessation of discrimination and feeling—that all these meditative absorptions do not go beyond being impermanent, duḥkha, and not-self. Beginning with the first dhyāna, they enter into that meditative absorption, master it, and after emerging from it, contemplate and know with the eye of insight that it is in the nature of the three characteristics. After meditating in this way up to neither-discrimination-nor-nondiscrimination, they go back to the absorption in nothingness, dwell in it for some time, emerge from it and contemplate it as impermanent, unsatisfactory, and selfless. They then set a determination to go into cessation of discrimination and feeling and to remain in that state for a certain period of time. After that they enter neither-discrimination-nor-nondiscrimination for a few moments and then their discrimination and feeling ceases and they are in the cessation of discrimination and feeling.

Arhats liberated by wisdom destroy their pollutants by seeing with wisdom, although they do not attain the formless absorptions. Although their samādhi is not as strong as the arhats liberated in both ways, the Buddha does not urge these arhats to attain those absorptions, because they have already attained liberation.

In short, although all arhats have destroyed their pollutants by wisdom, they are dissimilar in other respects. One of these is the level of samādhi through which they attain liberation. Those liberated by wisdom could have attained any of the four dhyānas or they could have attained only access concentration and become "dry-insight arhats," their minds not softened by the moisture of dhyāna.[59]

In contemporary Theravāda circles, some meditation masters emphasize attaining dhyāna first, then developing insight. Others teach a system of meditation that focuses on insight and also increases concentration, but not to the level of dhyāna. This is because the investigation and analysis necessary for insight meditation is not conducive for the depth of calm and stability necessary to attain dhyāna. For example, the four establishments of mindfulness do not highlight the attainment of dhyāna, although some of the methods in it can be used to do so. Its emphasis is the cultivation of insight wisdom, which does not require dhyāna.

Disciples in the second group—*those who still have work to do with diligence*—have reached at least the path to stream-enterer. They are *sekhas*—trainees or learners—because they are still learning and training in order to gain realizations. When they reside in a conducive environment, associate with wise Dharma friends, and balance the five faculties (faith, effort, mindfulness, concentration, and wisdom), they will attain the final goal of arhatship. These disciples are of five types—body-witnesses (P. *kāyasakkhi*), ones attained to view (P. *diṭṭhippatta*), ones resolved through faith (P. *saddhāvimutta*), Dharma followers (P. *dhammānusāri*), and faith followers (P. *saddhānusāri*). They are distinguished principally by their dominant faculty. The first three have reached at least the fruit of stream-enterer.

Body-witnesses possess some or all of the formless absorptions, and some degree of the pollutants have been removed by seeing with wisdom. When these ārya disciples gain wisdom strong enough to destroy all pollutants, they become arhats liberated in both ways. As a general group of āryas, they are more admirable because their faculties of both wisdom and concentration are strong. Among body-witnesses, there are those who have attained the fruit of stream-enterer, the path to once-returner, the fruit of once-returner, the path to nonreturner, the fruit of nonreturner, and some are on the path to arhatship. The body-witnesses proceed to arhatship by cultivating insight wisdom in relation to the formless absorptions.

Ones attained to view have destroyed some degree of pollutants by seeing with wisdom. They have not attained the formless absorptions. They have reviewed, investigated, and analyzed the Buddha's teachings with wisdom and have understood the four truths. The principal difference between the ones attained to view and the arhats liberated by wisdom is that the former have eliminated only a portion of their pollutants, while the latter have removed all of them. It is not guaranteed, however, that when the ones attained to view attain liberation they will become arhats liberated by wisdom. It could be that they make effort and gain some or all of the formless absorptions between now and then, and thus become arhats liberated in both ways. Among ones attained to view are the same individuals as above, ranging from ones who have attained the fruit of stream-enterer to ones on the path to arhat.

Ones resolved through faith (or ones liberated by faith) have not attained the formless absorptions although some of their pollutants have been destroyed by seeing with wisdom. In this way they resemble the ones attained to view. However, wisdom is the dominant faculty for the ones attained to view and they emphasize investigation and analysis of the teachings, whereas faith is the dominant faculty for the ones resolved through faith and they are motivated to practice because their faith is "planted, rooted, and established in the Tathāgata." Their strong devotion and love for the Buddha spurs them on the path. They may become arhats liberated by wisdom, or if they make effort to gain the formless absorptions, they may become arhats liberated in both ways. The ones resolved through faith include the same six types of individuals as above.

The last two types of the ārya disciples are both on the path leading to stream-enterer.[60] *Dharma followers* have not gained the formless absorptions and their pollutants have not yet been destroyed by seeing with wisdom. But due to having learned, thought about, and meditated on the Buddha's teachings, they accept them, are eager to practice, and have cultivated all five faculties. When they attain the fruit of stream-enterer, Dharma followers will become ones attained to view.

Faith followers also lack the formless absorptions, and their pollutants have not yet been destroyed by wisdom. However, they have sufficient faith, devotion, and love for the Buddha, which motivates them to practice, and they have cultivated all five faculties. When they attain the fruit of stream-enterer, faith followers will become ones resolved through faith.

The main difference between the Dharma followers and faith followers is the faculty to which they are inclined. Both have all five faculties, which include faith and wisdom. To be on the path to stream-entry, both must have heard teachings on the three characteristics and so forth, and have cultivated insight and wisdom, and both must have faith in the Buddha.

Both Dharma followers and faith followers are incapable of creating karma that would cause them to be born in an unfortunate rebirth, and both are guaranteed to attain the fruit of stream-enterer before they pass away. When their insight wisdom reaches the point where the clear realization of the unconditioned occurs, they have direct knowledge of the four truths and become stream-enterers. Faith followers and Dharma followers accept the teaching due to either faith or rough investigation, whereas those attained to view and those resolved through faith are stream-enterers who know and see the Dhamma directly through their own experience.

The following chart summarizes the key points regarding the seven types of disciples as presented in the *Kīṭāgiri Sutta*.

REFLECTION

1. Review the seven types of disciples and their relationships to one another (see the chart on the facing page).
2. What are the benefits of becoming an arhat liberated in both ways?
3. Why would a practitioner wish to become a dry-insight arhat?

Seven Types of Disciples

TYPE OF DISCIPLE	LEVEL ON PATH	FORMLESS ABSORPTIONS	POLLUTANTS DESTROYED BY WISDOM	DOMINANT FACULTY	SPECIAL FEATURE	WORK WITH DILIGENCE
Ones liberated in both ways	Arhat	Yes	All	Wisdom and concentration, maybe faith	Liberated from physical body and mind-body	No
Ones liberated by wisdom	Arhat	No	All	Wisdom	May have any of the four dhyānas or be dry-insight arhats	No
Body-witnesses	Fruit of stream-enterer to path to arhat	Yes	Some	Wisdom and concentration, maybe faith	Will become arhats liberated in both ways	Yes
Ones attained to view	Fruit of stream-enterer to path to arhat	No	Some	Wisdom	Have investigated and analyzed the Buddha's teachings with wisdom	Yes
Ones resolved through faith	Fruit of stream-enterer to path to arhat	No	Some	Faith	Faith in the Buddha is planted, rooted, and established	Yes
Dharma followers	Path to stream-enterer	No	None	Wisdom	Have reflective acceptance of the Buddha's teachings, will become ones attained to view	Yes
Faith followers	Path to stream-enterer	No	None	Faith	Have sufficient faith in and love for the Buddha, will become ones resolved through faith	Yes

Purification and Knowledge

An overview of the path that points out the stages of insight knowledge that are cultivated prior to realizing nirvāṇa is a helpful guide to know how our mind will develop and how to access that development as we progress. Although the following section is concise and contains a lot of terminology, it provides a clear way to discern the steps of the path to arhatship. The seven purifications spoken of below form the structure for Buddhaghosa's pivotal work, the *Path of Purification* (*Visuddhimagga*), which explains them elaborately by relying on the commentarial tradition.[61]

Wisdom is the direct antidote that frees us from saṃsāra. To describe how to cultivate it, Buddhaghosa gives the analogy of a tree—its soil, roots, and trunk. The soil is the object of analysis, and the seven purifications comprise the roots and trunk.

The *soil* in which wisdom will grow is wisdom's field of examination: the five aggregates, twelve sense sources, eighteen elements, twenty-two faculties, four truths, and dependent origination.[62]

Just as *roots* of the tree ground it and make it stable, so too do the first two purifications form the foundation for wisdom: (1) the purification of ethical conduct (P. *sīla-visuddhi*)[63] and (2) the purification of mind (P. *citta-visuddhi*).[64]

Just as from the *trunk* of a tree grow the branches, leaves, flowers, and fruit, so too do many qualities of the āryas grow from wisdom, including the next five purifications:[65] (3) purification of view (P. *diṭṭhi-visuddhi*), (4) purification by overcoming doubt (P. *kaṅkhāvitaraṇa-visuddhi*), (5) purification by knowledge and vision of what is the path and what is not the path (P. *maggāmaggañāṇadassana-visuddhi*), (6) purification by knowledge and vision of the way (P. *paṭipadāñāṇadassana-visuddhi*), and (7) purification by knowledge and vision (P. *ñāṇadassana-visuddhi*). The seven purifications are practiced in order, each one depending on the preceding ones. The first six are mundane, the last is supramundane.

1. *The purification of ethical conduct* is the higher training of ethical conduct. There are four factors to accomplish:

(1) The ethical conduct of restraint by the prātimokṣa entails taking and living by the precepts: the eight one-day precepts, five lay precepts, precepts of a novice monastic, precepts of a training nun, and precepts of a fully ordained monastic. These precepts function to prevent us from physical and verbal nonvirtuous actions. To do this, we must work with the mind that motivates these nonvirtues. Taking precepts is not sufficient; we need to use them as guidelines to train our speech and physical actions and do our best to keep them well.

(2) The ethical conduct of restraining the sense faculties involves practicing mindfulness and introspective awareness so that the mind does not get entangled in having attachment for attractive sense objects and aversion toward unattractive ones.

(3) The ethical conduct of pure livelihood is to receive the requisites to stay alive in an honest and nonharmful way.

(4) The ethical conduct of proper use of requisites is for a monastic to use the four requisites—food, clothing, shelter, and medicine—after reflecting on their purpose, shedding attachment to them, and dedicating for the welfare of the donors.

2. *The purification of mind* is the higher training of concentration. This involves subduing the five hindrances by the two types of concentration: access concentration and absorption concentration, which includes the four dhyānas and the four formless absorptions.

Practitioners may cultivate insight in two ways. Some follow the vehicle of serenity and attain access concentration, the dhyānas, or the formless absorptions and then use that meditative absorption as the base for generating insight. Here, the meditator emerges from the absorption, sees the factors of that absorption in terms of the five aggregates, understands their conditions, and then examines them to see that they are marked by the three characteristics. The purification of mind for these people is whatever degree of concentration they have developed from access concentration on up.

Others follow the vehicle of pure insight, do not cultivate concentration specially, but go directly to observing the mental and physical process of their own experience with mindfulness. Here concentration is developed on the ever-changing physical and mental events, producing a level of concentration called "momentary concentration," which is comparable in strength to access concentration. Momentary concentration is the purification of mind for practitioners who follow the pure insight approach. They have "dry" insight in that it is not moistened by the calm of the dhyānas.

The five following purifications are included in the higher training of wisdom.

3. *The purification of view* begins the process of cultivating wisdom by discerning the characteristics, functions, manifestations, and proximate causes[66] of the five aggregates. Through doing this, meditators discern that what is called a person is a collection of interdependent mental and physical factors. This purifies the wrong view of a monolithic permanent self. This purification is also known as the analytical knowledge of mind and matter.

4. *Purification by overcoming doubt* discerns the conditions of mind and matter. Building on the purification of view, it discerns the conditions for mind and matter in the past, present, and future and eliminates doubts concerning them. By meditating on dependent origination, meditators view the present collection of mental and physical aggregates as dependently arisen, conditioned phenomena. They understand that their body-mind complex did not come into being through the work of an independent Creator, is not a manifestation of a primal or permanent cosmic substance, and did not appear causelessly. This purification is also called "the knowledge of discerning conditions," because the understanding of conditionality is primary here.

5. *Purification by knowledge and vision of what is the path and what is not the path* is the next step. During this and the purification by knowledge and vision of the way, ten insight knowledges occur, the knowledges of (1) comprehension, (2) arising and passing away (with two phases, [a] initial and [b] mature), (3) dissolution, (4) fearfulness, (5) danger, (6) disenchantment, (7) liberation, (8) contemplation, (9) equanimity toward formations, and (10) conformity.

Knowledge of comprehension (1) and the first phase of the knowledge of rising and passing away (2a) both occur during the purification by knowledge and vision of what is and is not the path. The remaining knowledges occur during the purification by knowledge and vision of the way.

Now that meditators have discerned the mind and matter of the three realms—desire, form, and formless—and their conditions, they prepare to cultivate the knowledge of comprehension by thinking of the three realms in terms of the five aggregates. All matter—be it past, present, or future, internal or external, near or far, coarse or subtle, inferior or superior—is subsumed in the form aggregate. Similarly, all the feelings in the three realms are consolidated in the feeling aggregate, all discriminations in the discrimination aggregate, all the other diverse mental factors in the miscellaneous factors aggregate, and all consciousnesses in the consciousness aggregate.

(1) *The knowledge of comprehension.* To cultivate the knowledge of comprehension, meditators apply the three characteristics to the five aggregates. The aggregates are characterized by impermanence in that they disintegrate when they arise and do not keep the same identity in the next moment. They are marked with duḥkha in that, being momentary, they do not give any security or constancy. They lack a self because they are without an inner core or identity. Meditators apply the three characteristics to the five aggregates in specific periods of time, first a longer time—for example, the body of this lifetime is impermanent—then in increasingly shorter periods of time—for example, the feelings of this year are unsatisfactory and the discriminations of this month are not a self. Finally they see that in every split second, the body, feeling, discrimination, miscellaneous factors, and consciousness are transient, unsatisfactory, and not-self. They apply this same contemplation to the continuity of the aggregates as well as to individual moments of each aggregate.

(2a) *Knowledge of arising and passing away (initial phase).* The knowledge of arising and passing away is developed by contemplating that conditioned things arise and pass away. Both their arising and their ceasing depends on the presence or absence of their respective conditions. They contemplate this not in a theoretical or conceptual manner but by observing the very moment in which arising and passing away occur. In each split second everything is arising and passing away, giving way to the next moment that will arise and cease.

The knowledge of arising and passing away happens in two phases. In the first, as the meditation deepens, ten imperfections of insight (P. *vipassanā-upakkilesa*) may arise in the meditators' minds: (1) an aura of light radiating from their body; (2) joy, (3) pliancy, (4) and bliss in a way not previously experienced; (5) stronger resolution; (6) exertion in practice; (7) more mature knowledge, (8) stable mindfulness, (9) immovable equanimity, and (10) subtle enjoyment, clinging, and attachment to these experiences. This last factor is why they are called "imperfections": the mind is relating to the first nine in an incorrect way. These "imperfections" indicate that one's meditation is going well; but difficulties arise if, because of these experiences, meditators assume they have attained a superior stage of insight—a path or fruition of stream-enterer, and so forth—when they haven't.

Those who lack discernment will mistakenly think that they have attained the supramundane path and fruit. Leaving insight meditation aside, they will instead enjoy these experiences without recognizing their attachment to them. This is clearly poisonous for their progress on the path.

Someone with discernment will see these experiences as natural byproducts of insight and recognize the disadvantages of being attached to them. Reflecting that they too are impermanent, unsatisfactory, and not-self, they relinquish attachment to them and continue with insight meditation.

Purification by knowledge and vision of what is the path and what is not the path is the ability to discern that these ten imperfections, no matter how fascinating they may be, are not the path to liberation and that insight meditation into the three characteristics is the correct path to liberation. This purification is instrumental in keeping meditators on the right track so that they will be able to actualize their spiritual goal.

6. *Purification by knowledge and vision of the way* occurs after having eliminated the ten imperfections as obstacles to practice. Meditators now proceed to generate nine insight knowledges with regard to the three characteristics. Together, these nine insight knowledges constitute the purification by knowledge and vision of the way.

(2b) *Knowledge of arising and passing away (mature phase).* Having overcome the ten imperfections of insight, the knowledge of arising and passing away continues to develop, becoming clearer and more stable.

(3) *Knowledge of dissolution.* Once the knowledge of arising and passing away is strong, meditators focus only on the phase of dissolution, cessation, and vanishing. This brings home the fact of impermanence on a much deeper level because they see the conditioned things of saṃsāra are in a continual process of disintegration. Clearly there is no stability or anything trustworthy in them; they are wholly unsatisfactory, and because they are only ceasing, how can a self exist in them?

(4) *Knowledge of fearfulness.* Continuing to contemplate that all conditioned things in the past, present, and future are constantly in the process of disintegration, meditators see them as fearful. This fear is not an emotional fear that rejects the world because the world is "bad" or because they have an unhealthy fear of relating to people or to the world. Rather, this is a healthy fear that is concerned about becoming attached to these things and remaining stuck in saṃsāra as a result. Because this fear can sometimes initially manifest in an unbalanced way, a teacher's help is crucial at this point.

(5) *Knowledge of danger.* Recognizing all conditioned things are fearful, meditators now know with certainty that conditioned things have the nature of duḥkha and lack any core of a real self. They also know that safety exists only in the unconditioned, which is free from the unpredictability and insecurity of things that are continuously arising and vanishing. This knowledge brings appreciation for nirvāṇa.

(6) *Knowledge of disenchantment.* Seeing the danger of being attached to and seeking happiness from conditioned things that are unable to provide well-being, meditators becomes disenchanted and disillusioned with them. Their delight in saṃsāric phenomenon—no matter the realm—ceases. Meditators now clearly see the disadvantages of clinging to existence in the desire, form, or formless realms.

(7) *Knowledge of desire for liberation.* Now the momentum of turning away from saṃsāra and turning to nirvāṇa increases, and the meditators have a strong motivation to be liberated from and to escape from the world of conditioned existence. This is not a psychologically immature wish to escape from difficulties but a wise motivation to seek liberation by clearly knowing what actually can provide peace.

(8) *Knowledge of reflective contemplation.* Knowing that liberation from conditioned things requires clearly seeing them as marked by the three characteristics, meditators review and again examine these things in light of their impermanence, unsatisfactory nature, and selflessness. This is an expansive way of applying the three characteristics to all conditioned things.

(9) *Knowledge of equanimity toward formations.* Seeing that there is nothing in any conditioned thing whatsoever that is suitable to be I or mine, meditators leave aside both attraction and repulsion toward those things and abide in equanimity. This mental state is one of great relief that comes from the cultivation of proper wisdom regarding the five aggregates.

(10) *Knowledge of conformity.* This knowledge arises in the desire-realm consciousness that precedes the consciousness of the change of lineage that leads to the supramundane path. It is called the "knowledge of conformity" because it conforms to the truth of the previous insight knowledge and of the supramundane path that will follow.

7. *Purification by knowledge and vision* is the only supramundane purification of the seven, according to Buddhaghosa. This purification is knowledge of the four supramundane paths: those of stream-enterer, once-returner, nonreturner, and arhat. Preceding the breakthrough to the supramundane path are some moments of transition from purification by knowledge and vision of the way as the mind "changes lineage," in that it goes from being a mundane mind with conditioned phenomena as its objects to a supramundane mind with nirvāṇa as its object.

When the meditator is engaged in insight meditation just prior to the arising of absorption of the supramundane path and the purification by knowledge and vision, the bhavaṅga consciousness stops and there are a few moments of insight consciousness that focus on either impermanence, duḥkha, or not-self. On the perfection of the knowledge of equanimity toward formations and the knowledge of conformity to the truths, "insight leading to emergence" arises. This is the culmination of insight that occurs just before the first moment of the supramundane path. This insight gives way to the supramundane path that emerges from conditioned phenomena by taking nirvāṇa, the unconditioned, as its object, and that emerges from mundane consciousness by eliminating a portion of defilements.

This last moment of insight is called the "change of lineage consciousness," and it is the proximate cause for the supramundane path. It marks the transition from being an ordinary being to being an ārya. Although the change of lineage consciousness is like the path in that its object is nirvāṇa, it is unlike the path in that it cannot dispel the defilements that obscure seeing the four truths. This transition consciousness precedes each of the four paths. Just before it transitions to the path of stream-entry, it is called "change of lineage." Before it transitions to the paths of once-returner, nonreturner, and arhat, it is called "cleansing" because it marks the transition to the next higher path knowledge.

The path consciousness[67] performs four functions: (1) fully understanding (P. *pariññā*) duḥkha, (2) abandoning (P. *pahāṇa*) the origin of duḥkha, (3) realizing (P. *sacchikiriyā*) nirvāṇa, and (4) cultivating (P. *bhāvana*) the āryan eightfold path. Each path consciousness performs these four functions, and when the corresponding level of defilements has been reduced or eradicated, that path consciousness is followed by a fruition consciousness. After each fruition consciousness, a reviewing knowledge (P. *paccavekkhanañāṇa*) looks back and reflects on the path, fruit, and nirvāṇa, and often, but not always, on the defilements that have been abandoned and those that are yet to be abandoned. There is a tremendous sense of satisfaction, relief, and joy at this time, and meditators continue to practice until they reach the fruit of arhatship. The knowledge of the four supramundane paths has been accomplished and the final goal, nirvāṇa, has been attained.

In the *Relay Chariots Sutta*, Śāriputra asked the bhikkhu Puṇṇa Mantāṇiputta if the holy life was lived under the Buddha for the sake of the seven purifications, to which Puṇṇa Mantāṇiputta responded in the negative, explaining that the holy life was lived for the sake of final nirvāṇa without clinging. Here "final nirvāṇa without clinging" refers either to the fruit of arhatship that none of the four types of clinging can grasp or to nirvāṇa, the unconditioned, that does not exist due to conditions. None of the seven purifications themselves are final nirvāṇa without clinging, but final nirvāṇa without clinging cannot be attained without them. Puṇṇa Mantāṇiputta then gave the analogy of the king going to a faraway city on urgent business by means of a series of seven relay chariots. By means of the first chariot he arrives at the place of the second, by means of the second he arrives at the place of the third, and so on until by means of the seventh chariot he arrives at his final destination. We cannot say that the king arrived at his destination by means of the last chariot or any of the other chariots individually. Each chariot was taken for the sake of reaching the next one but all had the final destination in mind. So too, each of the seven purifications will take us to the subsequent one until we reach our final destination of nirvāṇa. In short, none of the purifications are goals in and of themselves, and no single purification is sufficient to realize final nirvāṇa without clinging. But when the seven are practiced in order, each one building on the previous one, we will arrive at our spiritual destination.

Occasions for Attaining Liberation

Pāli sūtras mention five occasions or "spheres of liberation" (P. *vimuttāyatana*) that can trigger the breakthrough to liberating insight: when hearing the Dharma, teaching the Dharma to others, reciting sūtras and scriptures, reflecting on the Dharma, and meditating.

While doing any of these five activities, a practitioner may have a direct grasp of the teachings, which leads to experiencing delight and joy, which in turn bring pliancy and concentration. Of these, joy, pliancy, and concentration are awakening factors. The description of the seven awakening factors says these are preceded by mindfulness, investigation of phenomena, and effort, which lead to the direct grasp of the teachings. A mind with these awakening factors that is thus concentrated sees things as they really are, and as the Buddha often said, a concentrated mind leads to a realistic vision of things according to the four truths. Such clear insight leads to disenchantment regarding the five aggregates and dispassion, which triggers the process of eliminating ignorance, anger, attachment, and other afflictions. This process culminates in liberation.

Clearly liberation is attained not from just listening to teachings, teaching others, reciting sūtras, and so forth. Rather, these five are occasions for the ripening of previously created causes in the mindstreams of mature practitioners who have cultivated the three higher trainings. The ripening of these causes produces a breakthrough to nirvāṇa.

Four Kinds of Persons Who Attain Arhatship

The Buddha speaks of four kinds of persons who attain arhatship, differentiating them according to the strength of their five faculties and based on their inclination toward serenity or insight (AN 4:169). The path where serenity is prominent is seen as one without intentional exertion, due to the smoothness and tranquility of the dhyānas. The path in which insight is prominent is considered one with intentional exertion because practitioners meditate on topics that lead directly to disenchantment and dispassion.

The first are practitioners who attain nirvāṇa in this life through intentional exertion. They meditate on the unattractiveness of the body, the repulsiveness of food, dissatisfaction with the saṃsāric world, impermanence, and death. These meditations require effort in that they open our eyes to the terrifying reality of saṃsāric existence. The sobering effect they have on the mind leads to disenchantment with saṃsāra and releases their deep attachment to conditioned phenomena. They depend on the five powers of a trainee—faith, integrity, consideration for others, effort, and wisdom—and because their five faculties are strong, they attain nirvāṇa.

The second are those who attain nirvāṇa with the breakup of the body through intentional exertion. They do the same meditations mentioned above and depend on the same five powers. However, because their five faculties are comparatively weak, they attain nirvāṇa after death, presumably being a nonreturner when they die.

Four Kinds of Persons

TYPE OF PRACTITIONER	PRACTICE WITH INTENTIONAL EFFORT	SERENITY OR INSIGHT IS PROMINENT	DEPEND ON FIVE POWERS OF TRAINEES	STRENGTH OF FACULTIES	ATTAIN NIRVĀṆA
1	Yes	Insight	Yes	Strong	In this life
2	Yes	Insight	Yes	Weak	After death
3	No	Serenity	Yes	Strong	In this life
4	No	Serenity	Yes	Weak	After death

The third are practitioners who attain nirvāṇa in this very life without intentional exertion. Living secluded from sensual pleasures and from nonvirtuous mental states, they attain the four dhyānas. They depend on the five powers, and because their five faculties are very strong, they attain nirvāṇa in this life.

The fourth are ones who attain nirvāṇa with the breakup of the body without intentional exertion. They too live secluded from sensual pleasures and from nonvirtuous mental states and attain the four dhyānas. They depend on the five powers of a trainee, but their five faculties are weak and they attain nirvāṇa after death.

Liberation of Mind, Liberation by Wisdom

In many sūtras we come across the phrase "liberation of mind, liberation by wisdom." For example, in the *Discourse to Potaliya* the Buddha says (MN 54:24):

> Having arrived at that same supreme mindfulness whose purity is due to equanimity, by realizing for himself with direct knowledge, this ariya disciple here and now enters upon and abides in the liberation of mind, liberation by wisdom that are unpolluted with the destruction of the pollutants.

The liberation of mind, liberation by wisdom is the ultimate liberation that comes through the destruction of the pollutants. According to the Pāli commentaries, here "mind" refers to an arhat's samādhi and "wisdom" to an arhat's wisdom. When these two liberations are joined together and are unpolluted, they signify the liberation attained with the destruction of pollutants by the supramundane path of an arhat.

The mind is very pure due to the eradication of defilements and very bright due to the light of wisdom. Arhats can live and act in the world without being controlled by the defilements. They make choices and decisions without being sabotaged by the defilements. They no longer crave the attractive objects they encounter; they no longer become upset or angry when things do not happen the way that they wish. They are not troubled by confusion about what is virtuous and to be practiced and what is nonvirtuous and to be abandoned. Having realized the selfless nature of all phenomena, they have cut through the web of proliferations and become a sage at peace (P. *muni santo*).

Ānanda asks the Buddha why some monastics gain liberation of mind and some gain liberation by wisdom (MN 64:16). This is a curious question, because usually arhatship is referred to as liberation of mind, liberation by wisdom, the two not being separated out.

The Buddha replies that the difference is in their faculties. That is, arhats who are inclined toward concentration are said to have liberation of mind because they developed great skill in the various samādhis and attain supernormal powers. Other arhats have greater aptitude for understanding, analysis, and wisdom, and gain liberation by wisdom. However, they come to the same point. The Buddha's two chief disciples, Śāriputra and Maudgalyāyana, both attained arhatship through cultivating serenity and insight, but Śāriputra is known for his amazing ability in analysis and is said to have attained liberation by wisdom, while Maudgalyāyana was foremost in supernormal powers and is said to have attained liberation of mind.

Nirvāṇa and the Arhat

Nirvāṇa's nature is undifferentiated, endless ultimate reality, the deathless unconditioned that is completely outside the limits of the conditioned world.[68] Nevertheless, according to its basis (the situation of the person who has attained nirvāṇa), it can be distinguished into nirvāṇa with remainder and nirvāṇa without remainder. The Buddha states (Iti 44):

> What, monastics, is the nirvāṇa element with remainder? Here a monastic is an arahant, one whose pollutants are destroyed, who has lived the holy life, done what had to be done, laid down the burden, reached his own goal, utterly destroyed the fetters of existence, one completely liberated through final knowledge. However, his five sense powers remain unimpaired, by which he still experiences what is agreeable and disagreeable, still feels pleasure and pain. It is the destruction of sensual desire, hatred, and confusion in him that is called the nirvāṇa element with remainder.

Nirvāṇa without remainder occurs at the time an arhat passes away. The Buddha explains (SN 12:51):

> With the breakup of the body, following the exhaustion of life, all that is felt, not being delighted in, will become cool right here; mere bodily remains will be left.

While an arhat is still alive, his nirvāṇa is the nirvāṇa with the remainder of the five polluted aggregates. When someone who will become an arhat in that life is born, his aggregates were produced under the influence of ignorance and craving and are the polluted aggregates of a being who is not free from saṃsāra. After he attains liberation, he still has the same aggregates as at the time of birth; those aggregates are the "remainder." He has nirvāṇa with remainder (*sopadhiśeṣa-nirvāṇa, sopādisesa-nibbāna*) of the polluted aggregates until he passes away from that life. Because of this, he experiences pleasure and pain, but contemplating these feelings as impermanent, conditioned, and dependently arisen, he does not hold to or delight in them. Thus he does not react to them with attachment, anger, or confusion, nor does he generate more karma that will cause rebirth. Still, he must decide, choose, and act within the limits of his situation.

At the time of death, his nirvāṇa is nirvāṇa without remainder (*anupadhiśeṣa-nirvāṇa, anupādisesa-nibbāna*) because the polluted aggregates have been left behind and no new polluted aggregates will be taken up since ignorance and craving have been totally abandoned. The literal meaning of "nirvāṇa" is to go out, as in a fire being extinguished, and this is precisely what happens to feelings at the time of an arhat's death.[69] With the end of that life, there is no further rebirth, and the person is said to have become "nirvāṇa-ized" in nirvāṇa without remainder. In the commentaries nirvāṇa with remainder is called "the extinguishment of the afflictions" (P. *kilesa-parinibbāna*), and nirvāṇa without remainder is the extinguishment of the aggregates (P. *khandha-parinibbāna*).

Nirvāṇa is the state of extinguishment. Parinirvāṇa does not mean nirvāṇa after death. It is the event of passing away or extinguishment undergone by one who has attained nirvāṇa during his or her lifetime. The question of what happens to an arhat at the time of nirvāṇa without remainder, which is parinirvāṇa, has been the topic of discussion for centuries. Some people may assume that since there are no more polluted aggregates, the conventional person ceases to exist and only blank nothingness remains. However, no sūtra says that that is the case. Instead, nirvāṇa is always said to be a reality (*dharma*), a source (*āyatana*), an element (*dhātu*), and a state (*pada*).

As ordinary beings, we are used to thinking of people in terms of their aggregates and see them as real, substantial beings who are findable in relation to their aggregates. But what happens when craving and ignorance have ceased and no new aggregates are taken because there is no cause for them? Let's look at what the sūtras say.

Godhika was a bhikkhu who became an arhat just before he died. Together with a group of monks, the Buddha went to the place where Godhika had died. Pointing to a cloud of swirling smoke, the Buddha explained to the monks (SN 4:23):

> This is Māra, the Evil One, searching for the consciousness of the clansman Godhika, wondering: "Where now has the consciousness of the clansman Godhika been established?" However, monastics, with consciousness unestablished, the clansman Godhika has attained final nirvāṇa.

The commentary explains that Māra was looking for Godhika's rebirth-consciousness, but since he had passed away having ceased craving, his rebirth-consciousness was unestablished—that is, it lacked a cause for it to arise. After passing away, it is said that an arhat's consciousness is not established anywhere, meaning it has no connection with or attraction to any conditioned mode of existence. The commentary also says that "the cause for the non-establishment of consciousness was precisely the cause for his parinirvāṇa."

Some passages in the *Suttanipāta* are interesting in this regard. In *Upasīva's Questions* (*Upasīvamānavapucchā*), the Buddha says (Sn 5.6):

> As a flame blown out by a gust of wind ceases and cannot be reached by conception, in the same way the Sage (*muni*), released from name and body, ceases and cannot be reached by conception...
>
> Of him who has gone to cessation there is no measure, there is nothing in terms of which they could speak about him. When all dhammas have been uprooted, all the ways of speech have also been uprooted.

These passages indicate not only that the experience of nirvāṇa is beyond words and concepts, but also that nirvāṇa itself cannot be adequately explained with words.[70]

At the Buddha's time, people asked many spiritual leaders what happens to a tathāgata after death, and these leaders gave diverse responses. Those who believed in an everlasting self or soul that was separate from the aggregates asserted that a tathāgata ascended to an eternal state or merged with an eternal cosmic substance from which everything arises and into which everything returns. The Materialists, who believed the person was the body, asserted that a tathāgata disappeared into nonexistent oblivion when the body was given up.

The Buddha disagreed with these positions because they were based on the false assumption of a real person. Thus when the wanderer Vacchagotta asked the Buddha whether the Tathāgata is reborn, is not reborn, both, or neither, the Buddha replied that none of the four alternatives applied (MN 72). Had Vacchagotta not clung to the self and thought, "The aggregates of an arhat cease at death because when the pollutants have been destroyed, there is no cause for the reappearance of polluted aggregates in the future," that would not have been a wrong view. However, Vacchagotta was operating on the belief that a substantial being, a substantial tathāgata, was being destroyed at death. Such a substantial tathāgata never existed. In other words, it is like asking, "Does a turtle trim his moustache, not trim it, both trim it and not trim it, or neither trim it or not trim it?" Such a question cannot be answered because there is no moustache on a turtle to start with!

In response to Vacchagotta's confusion, the Buddha asked him: If a fire in front of him were extinguished, would he know that the fire was extinguished? If so, where did the fire go—to the north, south, east, or west? None of those choices apply because there is no fire that has gone anywhere. Similarly, a tathāgata has abandoned the five aggregates by which someone talking about him might describe him. However, the Buddha did not say the Tathāgata was nonexistent; he simply said the Tathāgata was beyond what our ordinary conceptual mind covered with ignorance can understand: "The Tathāgata is deep, immeasurable, hard to fathom like the ocean."

Within contemporary Theravāda, some say that after an arhat dies, there is nothing. There is not a self or soul that is annihilated; the arhat's previous existence with the five aggregates was a process and the process has come to an end. After that, nothing can be pointed to. Others say that nirvāṇa is the unborn reality. The process or the stream of consciousness continues until the passing away of the arhat, after which that stream of consciousness enters into nirvāṇa. There is no continuation in an individual form and no consciousness that continues in nirvāṇa. Nirvāṇa is the unconditioned, eternal reality, and the consciousness merges with that.

Others see both of the above positions as inadequate and say that nirvāṇa cannot be eternal because it is beyond time. Nirvāṇa is the unconditioned, unborn, deathless. It is not nonexistent. It is the timeless, imperishable, stable reality. When someone realizes this reality, the destruction of defilements and release from conditioned existence occurs. Nirvāṇa itself, however, is neither the destruction of defilements nor the release from conditioned existence because both of those are conditioned events that occur in time. These two events are stages in the full actualization of unconditioned nirvāṇa.

Tathāgatas and Arhats

How does the Buddha fit in the four stages of awakening? What are the similarities and differences between a tathāgata and an arhat? This topic is discussed in both the Pāli and Sanskrit traditions. The following is according to the Pāli tradition.

A Buddha is an arhat, as shown in all the praises recited to the Buddha. Arhats, too, are said to have attained full awakening. This shows that the Buddha and arhats have realized the same truths. On the other hand, only a tathāgata is a perfectly awakened buddha. When asked about the difference between a perfectly awakened buddha and a monastic arhat, the Buddha says (SN 22:58):

> The Tathāgata, the Arahant, the Perfectly Awakened One is the originator of the path unarisen before, the producer of the path unproduced before, the declarer of the path undeclared before. He is the knower of the path, the discoverer of the path, the one skilled in the path. And his disciples now dwell following that path and become possessed of it afterward.
>
> This is the distinction, the disparity, the difference between the Tathāgata, the Arahant, the Perfectly Awakened One and a bhikkhu liberated by wisdom.

The Tathāgata is the Teacher who first discovered the path in our world and declared it to all those who were interested in hearing. His disciples, also called "śrāvakas" because they listen to his teachings, follow that path and actualize it in their own continuums.

It appears that the practices done by those who become buddhas are the same as those who become arhats. In describing how all the tathāgatas of the past, present, and future become awakened, Śāriputra says, with the Buddha's approval (SN: 47:12):

> Whatever Arahants, Perfectly Awakened Ones arose in the past [or future or present], all those Blessed Ones first abandon the five hindrances, defilements of the mind that weaken wisdom;

> and then, with their minds well established in the four establishments of mindfulness, they develop correctly the seven awakening factors, and thereby they awaken to the unsurpassed perfect awakening.

This is the same path the Tathāgata expounds in the Pāli sūtras, through which so many of his disciples attain arhatship. On the other hand, some sūtras point out distinct qualities of a tathāgata that the arhats do not share. For example, the *Greater Discourse on the Lion's Roar* (MN 12) speaks of the ten powers of a tathāgata, the four kinds of self-confidence, and other qualities that are unique to a tathāgata. In the *Sutta on the Wonderful and Marvelous* (MN 123) Ānanda explains many marvelous and unique qualities about the Tathāgata's previous lives and his birth and activities in this life that his arhat disciples do not have. So clearly there is a difference in attainment and capability between the two. Therefore there must be a difference in the path they practice, because unique causes are necessary to produce a unique result.

It is interesting that despite the Buddha obviously possessing qualities that not one of his disciples possessed completely, and despite the fact that the Buddha's activities far outweighed those of his disciples in terms of the benefit they had for sentient beings, in the earliest texts of the Pāli canon no one is recorded as having asked the Buddha how he attained his unique state by practicing the bodhisattva path.[71] It is indeed strange that no one had the aspiration to become exactly like the Teacher, even though he was known as having been a bodhisattva and one that became perfectly awakened. It is only in later centuries that the bodhisattva path was expounded in the Pāli tradition.

In the Pāli canon, we get to know the Buddha as a human being. We see his daily habits, his way of explaining the Dharma according to the dispositions and interests of the various people he encounters. We see him being open and friendly to a host of different people—brahmins and ascetics, the wealthy and the impoverished, the free and those enslaved. We observe how he handles disputes among his followers, how he deals with people who slander him or are contemptuous, how he reacts to those who praise him and shower him with gifts and to those who distort the Dharma he teaches. In the sūtras we see the exceptional inner qualities that manifest in his daily activities, which he imbues with the greatness of a mind at peace and endowed with wisdom and compassion.

The Tathāgata knows duḥkha, has abandoned its origin, has actualized its cessation, and has perfectly cultivated the path. His mind is all-knowing and clearly sees all that is. His speech is completely reliable: as he describes something, that is how it is. As he counsels us to do, he does that as well; he is free from all hypocrisy. With compassion he fearlessly teaches the Dharma to all those who wish to hear it.

7 | Fundamental Vehicle Paths and Fruits: The Sanskrit Tradition

Bodhicitta and the wisdom realizing emptiness are like the two wings of a bird that carry us to full awakening. Combining bodhicitta and wisdom gives us inner strength and stable self-confidence. Thinking of Śāntideva, the great scholar-adept, every day I aspire as he did (BCA 10.55):

> For as long as space endures,
> and for as long as sentient beings remain,
> until then may I too abide
> to dispel the misery of the world.

When we follow Śāntideva's example and generate this noble determination, we totally dedicate our body, speech, and mind for others. This gives our existence profound meaning. We feel that every minute of our life is purposeful. I don't have this full experience, but I have enthusiasm to practice in order to generate it. Meanwhile, through my daily practice, some inner peace and satisfaction have arisen, so my talk isn't entirely empty words.

Realization of the Four Truths

The four truths of āryas are the principal objects of meditation on the path to arhatship and buddhahood, and realizing their sixteen aspects is essential.[72] The order in which the four truths are presented—duḥkha, its origin, the cessation of duḥkha and its origin, and the path to that cessation—is done from the perspective of realizing them. Contemplation of the four aspects of each truth is the means to deepen our understanding of that truth. By contemplating duḥkha we understand our present situation—that is, we, our aggregates, and the environment around us are impermanent, unsatisfactory in nature, empty, and selfless. Then we inquire into the origins of this unsatisfactory state and understand that it is produced by causes such as craving, polluted karma, and their root, ignorance. There is no external or permanent creator.

The question then arises, "Is there a possibility to end duḥkha and its causes?" This brings us to contemplate true cessations and to understand that nirvāṇa exists; it is a state of supreme peace that is irreversible. Knowing this, we become eager to know the unmistaken path to attain true cessation and learn of the three higher trainings of ethical conduct, concentration, and wisdom. The wisdoms realizing selflessness and emptiness have the power to definitively destroy the ignorance that is the root of saṃsāra and to bring nirvāṇa.

This is the order in which to contemplate the four truths and their sixteen aspects to gain a comprehensive understanding of them. Contemplation on true duḥkha and true origins leads to a strong feeling of renunciation of cyclic existence and contemplation on true cessations and true paths stimulates a strong wish to attain liberation.

After generating renunciation and the aspiration to attain liberation, the primary meditation to do is the one to realize selflessness. This involves meditation on impermanence and duḥkha as well, for these support and reinforce insight into selflessness. As Dharmakīrti says in the *Commentary on (Dignāga's) "Compendium of Reliable Cognition,"* "From impermanence arises the understanding of duḥkha, and from duḥkha arises the understanding of selflessness." Deepening of the understanding of selflessness is reflected primarily in the progression of the five paths, each of which is able to remove subtler layers of obscurations. No matter whether we follow the Śrāvaka, Solitary Realizer, or Bodhisattva (Mahāyāna) Vehicles, we need to gain the wisdom realizing the sixteen aspects of the four truths.

According to how they define ignorance, the four tenet systems have different understandings of the meanings of selflessness and emptiness in the context of the sixteen aspects of the four truths. Non-Buddhists see that conditioned phenomena are unreliable and untrustworthy and postulate the existence of a permanent, unitary, independent self that is separate from the conditioned psychophysical aggregates. For the Vaibhāṣika and

Sautrāntika systems, emptiness is the lack of such a transcendental self as asserted by non-Buddhists, and selflessness is the absence of a self-sufficient substantially-existent self that is different from the aggregates. Realizing these constitutes the wisdom realizing the selflessness of persons.

According to the Yogācāra and Svātantrika systems, the principal meditation object for śrāvakas and solitary realizers who seek arhatship is the selflessness of persons[73]—which they accept as the lack of a self-sufficient substantially-existent person—and for bodhisattvas who seek buddhahood it is the selflessness of phenomena as defined by each of those systems. For these systems the direct realization of its principal meditation object marks the attainment of the path of seeing of that vehicle.

The Prāsaṅgika system has unique assertions concerning both the object of negation in the meditation on emptiness and selflessness and the entry point to the path of seeing. Here the object of negation is the inherent existence of all persons and phenomena; to attain the path of seeing of any of the three vehicles, its practitioners must directly realize the emptiness of inherent existence of persons and phenomena.

Dharmakīrti praised the Buddha as a reliable teacher because he taught the four truths. Since he didn't hold the Prāsaṅgika view, the four truths he praised are the coarse four truths, which do not include the selflessness of phenomena and which assert the selflessness of persons to be the lack of a self-sufficient substantially-existent I. Nāgārjuna, on the other hand, praised the Buddha for his teaching of emptiness that leads to the relinquishing of all views of the inherent existence of both persons and phenomena and the realization of the subtle four truths.

According to Nāgārjuna's view, the view held by the Prāsaṅgikas, direct perception of the coarse four truths occurs prior to the path of seeing of any of the three vehicles. Realization of the subtle four truths occurs at the time of entering the path of seeing. The demarcation of entering the path of seeing of all three vehicles is the direct realization of the emptiness of inherent existence of both persons and phenomena.

To be free from saṃsāra, Prāsaṅgikas say we must realize the four truths perfectly as they are in reality. This means to realize that they are empty of inherent existence, empty of existing from their own side or by their own character. Śrāvakas, solitary realizers, and bodhisattvas all meditate on the emptiness of inherent existence of the four truths. The Buddha says in the *Sūtra on the Miserliness of One in Trance* (*Dhyāyitamuṣṭi Sūtra*, CTB 163):[74]

> Mañjuśrī, he who sees all conditioned things are unborn thoroughly knows duḥkha. He who sees all phenomena as without origin has abandoned the origins of duḥkha. He who sees them as utterly passed beyond sorrow has actualized cessation. He who sees all phenomena as totally unborn has cultivated the path.

Three Vehicles: The Paths of Method and Wisdom

Learning the systematic progression that practitioners of the three vehicles—śrāvakas, solitary realizers, and bodhisattvas—experience as they progress on their respective paths to their spiritual goals enables us to understand how the awakening of each vehicle is attained. The three types of practitioners were spoken of in the early sūtras, but the paths and grounds through which they progress to their respective awakenings were set out later, in the Abhidharma texts that arose in the centuries following the Buddha's parinirvāṇa. The authors of these early texts developed elaborate systems of classifications of afflictions and defilements, and together with that they laid out paths and grounds that lead to their abandonment. Commentators on the Mahāyāna sūtras later laid out the bodhisattva paths and grounds.

Tibetan scholar-adepts synthesized the material in these Indian treatises, composing a genre of texts called "grounds and paths" (T. *sa lam*). These texts contain definitions of the progressive stages of the path and describe practitioners' meditation objects, the defining characteristics of their realizations, and the practices they do between meditation sessions.

Although the grounds and paths texts are very technical and solicit many debates, studying them gives us a roadmap for spiritual development. They contain information that will help us to practice correctly, without taking unnecessary detours or becoming distracted by seemingly unusual meditation experiences. Having accurate knowledge derived from descriptions in the sūtras prevents us from having unrealistic expectations that lead to disappointment or wasted time.

Knowledge of the grounds and paths is also useful as a measuring stick that lets us know where we are. This keeps us humble and prevents the conceit thinking we are more advanced than we are. Because it makes us immune to further progress, conceit is a huge obstacle on the path. People who overestimate their attainments may also harm others by mistakenly teaching topics they believe they have experienced in meditation but in fact have not.

People may sometimes have strong or unusual experiences in meditation. Having heard certain terminology, but not really knowing what it means, they think they have attained particular realizations or levels of the path. By knowing the layout of the grounds and paths, we'll be able to distinguish a strong experience we have had once from a stable consciousness that is an actual path. When we have a stable experience, we'll be able to see if it has the other attendant characteristics that demarcate a certain level of the path. For example, we may sometimes have a strong experience of compassion in our meditation. This is excellent and to be cherished. Knowing that it is possible for us to experience such a state of mind is very encouraging. However, this one experience does not mean that we have attained the Mahāyāna path of accumulation and are now a bodhisattva. Entering the Mahāyāna path of accumulation requires not only a continuous feeling of renunciation of cyclic existence but also the altruistic aspiration to attain awakening that spontaneously arises whenever we see sentient beings. These are stable realizations, not brief experiences.

A man once came to me and announced that he had experienced direct insight into emptiness and was convinced he had attained the Mahāyāna path of seeing. I had to inform him that the attainment of this path also entailed other qualities, such as the ability to manifest in a hundred bodies and to go to one hundred pure lands to make offerings to the buddhas. Unfortunately, he was unable to accomplish these feats.

While the grounds and paths texts are an excellent guide, nothing can replace a close relationship with an experienced spiritual mentor. Having meditative experiences themselves, they are able to question us and guide us wisely. They will offer suggestions to fine-tune our understandings or will bring us back on track if we have come to incorrect conclusions in our meditation.

As mentioned previously, the compassionate Buddha taught three vehicles, according to the inclinations and interests of various sentient beings—

the Śrāvaka Vehicle, Solitary Realizer Vehicle, and Bodhisattva Vehicle. Each vehicle leads to its respective awakening—a śrāvaka's awakening, a solitary realizer's awakening, and the full awakening of a buddha. Those who actualize these vehicles differ in terms of their aspirations, the amount of merit they accumulate, the length of time they practice, and the other qualities they develop. According to the Prāsaṅgikas, all of them realize the emptiness of inherent existence, the selflessness of persons, and the selflessness of phenomena. Furthermore, according to most Mahāyāna tenet systems, all beings will eventually follow the Bodhisattva Vehicle and attain the full awakening of buddhahood. Some beings initially enter the Śrāvaka or Solitary Realizer Vehicle and, after becoming an arhat, begin the Bodhisattva Vehicle. Others enter the Bodhisattva Vehicle from the outset.

The śrāvakas (literally, hearers, disciples) are so called because they listen to teachings from the Buddha, practice them, and after attaining their result—the awakening of a śrāvaka—they cause others to hear about their attainment. They are also called śrāvakas because they hear the Buddha's teachings on the path and result of buddhahood and teach it to those who have the Mahāyāna disposition. However, they do not practice this path or actualize its results themselves.

Solitary realizers (*pratyekabuddha, paccekabuddha*) are so called because during their last life in saṃsāra they generate realizations on their own without depending on the instructions of a living master and during a time when no buddha is turning the Dharma wheel. Solitary realizers are also called "middling realizers of suchness" because they surpass the śrāvakas by accumulating merit for a hundred eons, whereas śrāvakas can complete their path in a minimum of three lifetimes. Although they may have compassion, it is not the great compassion of bodhisattvas. Although they have a similitude of the two collections of merit and wisdom, they are not the two collections of bodhisattvas that lead to buddhahood. Bodhisattvas are so called because they have the bodhi mind, the aspiration for full awakening.

Each of the three vehicles has the five paths of accumulation, preparation, seeing, meditation, and no-more-learning.[75] Each of the five paths that comprise one of the three vehicles is called by the name of that vehicle—for example, there is the śrāvaka path of accumulation, the solitary realizers' path of meditation, the Mahāyāna or bodhisattvas' path of preparation, and so on. The five paths in each vehicle are differentiated in terms of the power of wisdom. That is, the five paths of each vehicle are distinguished by the power of insight into emptiness and the purification of the mind that it brings.

The three vehicles are differentiated in terms of the method aspect of the path. Śrāvakas' and solitary realizers' method practices are supported by renunciation of saṃsāra; bodhisattvas' method practices are supported by bodhicitta. Practitioners of each vehicle must accumulate different degrees of merit by practicing the method aspect of their vehicle in order to support those increasingly powerful levels of wisdom.

Path, Ground, and Clear Realization

Learning some vocabulary is helpful. A path (*mārga*) is an exalted knower that is conjoined with uncontrived renunciation. Path, ground (*bhūmi*), and clear realization (breakthrough, *abhisamaya*, T. *mngon rtogs*) are generally equivalent.[76] "Path" does not refer to an external walkway or to a doctrinal path. Rather, a path is so called because it is a consciousness that leads us out of saṃsāra and to awakening. A path is called a "ground" because like the earth, the ground is the basis for the growth of good qualities and the basis for release from afflictive obscurations and cognitive obscurations. A clear realization is a consciousness that is a path because just as an external path leads a person to their destination, a clear realization leads a practitioner to a higher spiritual realization. The term "vehicle," as in Fundamental Vehicle and Mahāyāna (Universal Vehicle), refers to a consciousness. Just as vehicles bear weight and take us somewhere, these consciousnesses bear the weight of sentient beings' welfare—either our own or that of all beings—and carry us to arhatship and buddhahood.

According to the Sanskrit tradition, practitioners on all of the five paths of any of the three vehicles have path consciousnesses and clear realizations. However, in the Pāli tradition, a clear realization is a consciousness that clearly observes reality and understands existence as it actually is; it is a path wisdom that directly perceives the truth and so is a supramundane path. In the Pāli tradition, the truth is nirvāṇa; in the Nālandā tradition, the truth refers to emptiness, and in particular the emptiness of a mind that is forever free from all defilements. Since those defilements have been eliminated in the sphere of emptiness, nirvāṇa is that emptiness.

In the Pāli tradition, a clear realization is a breakthrough experience in the sense that, until that point, our understanding has not been complete, but now the obstacles preventing direct perception of the truth have been pierced and wisdom perceives the truth directly, nonconceptually, intimately. "Clear realization" is used in a technical sense on two occasions. The first is the initial clear realization of the Dharma (P. *dhammabhisamaya*), which is the initial direct seeing of nirvāṇa. This clear realization transforms a person from someone on the path into a stream-enterer, an ārya. It is equivalent to obtaining a vision of the Dharma (P. *dhammacakkhupatilabha*), to seeing the truth. The second is the full realization of the Dharma, the total eradication of conceit and the other fetters, which establishes one as an arhat. Here "clear realization" is synonymous with penetration, which refers to the four functions of a supramundane path: to understand duḥkha, to abandon its origin, to realize its cessation, and to cultivate the path to that cessation. The immediate cause of the clear realization of nirvāṇa is insight wisdom, which gives rise to the path wisdom that realizes nirvāṇa directly.

Each of the three vehicles has five paths. There are many common features of the five paths in all three vehicles, and there are many differences as well. The five paths of the Śrāvaka and Solitary Realizer Vehicles are similar, whereas the five paths of the Bodhisattva Vehicle have some features in common with the Fundamental Vehicle paths and some marked differences. For example, bodhisattvas' motivation of bodhicitta and the fruit of the full awakening of buddhahood stand in contrast to śrāvakas' and solitary realizers' motivation of renunciation of saṃsāra and their fruit of arhatship.

Approachers and Abiders

The presentation of the Fundamental Vehicle paths and results in the previous chapter was according to the Pāli tradition. We'll now look at the same topic from the viewpoint of the Sanskrit tradition. In accord with the general presentation of this series, these topics are explained according to the Prāsaṅgika system.[77]

Fundamental Vehicle āryas form four pairs of realized beings—the approacher and abider for stream-enterer, the approacher and abider for once-returner, the approacher and abider for nonreturner, and the approacher and abider for arhat. Each of these four pairs has two phases: the path and the fruit. During the path phase, one is an approacher (*pratipannaka*, *paṭipannā*) and practices to attain the fruit that is certain to be attained in that very life. During the fruit phase, one has succeeded in diminishing or overcoming that stage's corresponding fetters and becomes an abider in the fruit or result (*phalasthita*, *phalaṭṭhā*). These eight āryas may be monastics or lay practitioners. The lower tenet systems, Pāli tradition, and Prāsaṅgika system have slightly different descriptions concerning some details regarding the eight approachers and abiders.

Just as when we wash clothes the grosser dirt comes out first, while the deeper intransigent dirt requires more scrubbing and more soap, so too grosser grades of self-grasping are eliminated first and gradually the subtler grades are eliminated. There are eighty-one grades of self-grasping ignorance and its corresponding afflictions and their seeds: Each of the nine levels of saṃsāra—the desire realm, the four levels of the form realm (the first through fourth dhyānas), and the four levels of the formless realm (limitless space, limitless consciousness, nothingness, and peak of saṃsāra)—has nine grades of self-grasping. The nine grades range from gross to subtle according to the strength of self-grasping: great-great, middle-great, small-great; great-middle, middle-middle, small-middle; great-small, middle-small, and small-small.[78] The antidotes that eradicate these grades of afflictions begin with the small-small, middle-small, and so on up to the middle-great and the great-great: the small-small antidotes overcome the grossest afflictions, and the great-great antidotes eliminate the small-small afflictions. That is, the smaller antidotes are sufficient to counteract the gross afflictions, while greater antidotes are needed to overcome the subtle, more deeply entrenched afflictions. This is similar to needing a stronger cleaning agent to remove subtle stains, while a weaker soap will do for the gross dirt.

According to the general Sanskrit tradition, while abandoning the first six of the nine grades of ignorance and afflictions that are related to the desire realm, Fundamental Vehicle practitioners are approachers to once-returner. When they have fully abandoned those six grades of ignorance, they become abiders in the fruit of once-returner.[79] Approachers to nonreturner are abandoning the seventh through ninth grades of desire-realm ignorance by an uninterrupted path. Abiders in the fruit of nonreturner have attained the liberated path that has abandoned these three grades. Nonreturners receive their name because they are no longer born in the desire realm.

Then the tenth through eighty-first grades of ignorance and afflictions of the form and formless realms are also abandoned by the uninterrupted paths of the path of meditation. The practitioners abandoning them are approachers to arhat; when they have been abandoned, those āryas become abiders in the fruit of arhat. According to Prāsaṅgikas, in general the eighty-one grades are eliminated in nine steps, whereby all the great-great afflictions are abandoned at once, the middle-great afflictions at once, and so on.

Innate Afflictions Abandoned on the Path of Meditation

REALM	LEVEL	AFFLICTIVE OBSCURATIONS BEING ABANDONED	
Afflictive obscurations of the desire realm	Great	Great-great	1
		Middle-great	2
		Small-great	3
	Middle	Great-middle	4
		Middle-middle	5
		Small-middle	6
	Small	Great-small	7
		Middle-small	8
		Small-small	9
Afflictive obscurations of the form realm	First dhyāna	10–18	Each of the afflictions on the left has nine grades from great-great to small-small.
	Second dhyāna	19–27	
	Third dhyāna	28–36	
	Fourth dhyāna	37–45	
Afflictive obscurations of the formless realm	Infinite Space	46–54	
	Infinite consciousness	55–63	
	Nothingness	64–72	
	Peak of saṃsāra	73–81	

Fundamental Vehicle practitioners have a variety of ways in which they proceed on the path to liberation. This involves the topic of the twenty saṅghas, which engenders much discussion. Below is a simplified presentation of how Fundamental Vehicle practitioners progress to liberation.[80]

Simultaneous eliminators completely overcome all great-great afflictions of the three realms at once, all the middle-great afflictions at once, and so on to the small-small afflictions of all three realms. Because they work at abandoning afflictions of the peak of saṃsāra—which are usually abandoned by nonreturners—just after becoming an abider in stream-enterer, they become approachers to arhat very quickly and do not become once-returners or nonreturners. Thus simultaneous eliminators are either abiders in the fruit of stream-enterer who are seeking to become abiders in the fruit of arhat by leaping over the fruits of once-returner and nonreturner, or they are abiders in the fruit of arhat, having leapt over the fruits of once-returner and nonreturner.

Such practitioners progress using a preparation of the first dhyāna called the "capable preparation" (*anāgamya*), which is a mind of the form realm. They become "dry" or "unadorned" arhats, because they haven't attained even the first dhyāna by a worldly path of meditation. Their minds have not been moistened by meditative absorption. Although dry arhats have eradicated the afflictive obscurations, they have not abandoned the obscurations to absorption (T. *snyoms 'jug gi sgrib pa*) that prevent attaining meditative absorption. "Adorned" arhats have also accomplished all eight meditative absorptions, the absorption of cessation (T. *'gog pa'i snyoms 'jug*) as well as alternating dhyāna meditation (T. *bsam gtan spel sgom*) where they have the ability to alternate meditative absorption on polluted and unpolluted paths and in this way overcome the obscurations to concentration. Simultaneous eliminators are sharp-faculty disciples because they can overcome all afflictions in just nine steps. Being of sharp faculties, they could easily gain the meditative absorptions of the dhyānas and formless realms and become an adorned arhat.

Gradual attainers proceed serially through all eight stages of approachers and abiders and abandon all the grades of afflictions step-by-step. In general, they are approachers to stream-enterer during the last uninterrupted path of the path of seeing and become abiders in the fruit of stream-enterer at the last liberated path of the path of seeing. They first "abandon" the great-great grade of desire-realm afflictions by a worldly path that suppresses those afflictions and then abandon this grade of afflictions by a supramundane path of meditation. The worldly path suppresses some grades of afflictions by meditating on the grossness of the lower state and the peacefulness of the next higher one, while the supramundane path completely abandons afflictions by meditating on emptiness. Only the afflictions of the nothingness level of the formless realm and below can be abandoned by a worldly path;

the afflictions of the peak of saṃsāra of the formless realm cannot be abandoned in this way because there is not a higher worldly level of meditative absorption that can suppress these afflictions. Those on the path of meditation who are in the process of actualizing once-returner or nonreturner are gradualists.

Leapers bypass some of the fruits. Some leapers have suppressed the first six of the eighty-one grades of afflictions—which are desire-realm afflictions—by the worldly path before entering the path of seeing. They become approachers to once-returner and abiders in the fruit of once-returner, respectively, during the last uninterrupted path and last liberated path of the path of seeing. Other leapers have suppressed all nine desire-realm grades of afflictions by the worldly path and attained an actual dhyāna before entering the path of seeing. They are approachers to nonreturner when they attain the path of seeing and become abiders in the fruit of nonreturner upon attaining the last liberated path of the path of seeing.

REFLECTION

Review: Yogīs on the Fundamental Vehicle paths may proceed in several ways.

1. Simultaneous eliminators completely overcome all great-great afflictions of the three realms at once, all the middle-great afflictions at once, and so on to the small-small afflictions of all three realms.
2. Gradual attainers proceed serially through all eight stages of approachers and abiders and abandon all the grades of afflictions step-by-step.
3. Leapers bypass some of the fruits.

Eight Grounds of the Fundamental Vehicle

Fundamental Vehicle grounds are divided into the eight lesser grounds of śrāvakas and the grounds of solitary realizers. Here the term "realizers" refers to consciousnesses.

(1) *Grounds of lineage* are the four levels of the śrāvakas' path of preparation, which are clear realizations of common beings who are definite in the lineage of śrāvakas—that is, they will follow the Śrāvaka Vehicle to arhatship without changing vehicles. These practitioners have a union of serenity and insight observing emptiness that, as an inference, is a conceptual realization.

(2) Realizers of approachers to stream-enterer are called "the *grounds of the eighth*" by counting backward from the ground of an arhat—that is, starting with abiders in the result of arhat.

(3) Realizers of abiders in the fruit of stream-enterer are the *grounds of seeing* that first realize emptiness directly. Approachers to stream-enterer are in the process of abandoning the acquired afflictions by means of the uninterrupted path of the path of seeing. When they attain the liberated path of the path of seeing, they have eliminated the acquired afflictions and become abiders in the fruit of stream-enterer.

(4) Realizers of abiders in the fruit of once-returner are called "*grounds of diminishment*" because a once-returner has abandoned most, but not all, desire realm afflictions. Once-returners are so called because they will be reborn in the desire realm only one more time before attaining arhatship.

(5) Realizers of abiders in the fruit of nonreturner are *grounds of freedom from desire*, because that person has abandoned attachment to desire-realm afflictions. They are called "nonreturners" because, having eliminated the first nine of the eighty-one grades of afflictions, which are conjoined with the desire realm, they can never again be reborn in the desire realm due to afflictions and polluted karma.

(6) Realizers of approachers to once-returner, nonreturner, and arhat are *grounds of realizing completion*. These are śrāvakas' grounds that aren't included in the other grounds. While Fundamental Vehicle practitioners have an uninterrupted path that is abandoning the first six grades of desire-realm afflictions, they are approachers to once-returner. When they have abandoned them, they pass to a liberated path of the path of meditation and become abiders in the fruit of once-returner.

When they have an uninterrupted path that is abandoning the last three grades of desire-realm afflictions, they are approachers to nonreturner, and when those afflictions have been abandoned, they pass to a liberated path and become abiders in the fruit of nonreturner. While abandoning the afflictions of the form and formless realms, they are approachers to arhat, and when those afflictions have been totally abandoned they become abiders in the fruit of arhat.

(7) *Grounds of śrāvakas* are realizers of abiders in the fruit of arhat. This is the path of no-more-learning of the Śrāvaka Vehicle in which all afflicted obscurations have been completely and forever eradicated. As liberated beings, these arhats are no longer bound in saṃsāra and will no longer take rebirth under the control of afflictions and polluted karma.[81]

(8) Realizers of solitary realizer āryas are *grounds of solitary realizers*, practitioners of the "middle" vehicle.

The eight grounds may be condensed into two: grounds of śrāvakas and grounds of solitary realizers. The most prominent classification of śrāvakas is of the four approachers and the four abiders. Although the framework of the eight approachers and abiders is not explicitly mentioned in terms of solitary realizers in the canonical scriptures, it may be applied to them.

Five Paths of the Fundamental Vehicle

Readers who are unfamiliar with the grounds and paths will encounter many new terms as well as seemingly complex schemas in this and the next chapter. At first these may seem dry and technical, but as you become more familiar with them you will appreciate the spiritual roadmap that they constitute. Later, when you study a grounds and paths text in depth with a teacher and classmates with whom you can discuss the material, the background you gain here will come in handy.

The five Fundamental Vehicle paths are the śrāvaka and solitary realizer paths of accumulation, preparation, seeing, meditation, and no-more-learning.

The Fundamental Vehicle **path of accumulation** (*sambhāramārga*) is a clear realizer of the doctrine—"doctrine" here referring to the words of the scriptures. The śrāvaka and solitary realizer practitioners enter their respective paths of accumulation when they have developed full, unshakable renunciation of cyclic existence and a firm determination to attain liberation. This path is called "accumulation" because at this stage practitioners accumulate a great amount of hearing the doctrine and because they begin to accumulate the merit and wisdom that will lead to the goal of that vehicle. There are three stages of the path of accumulation: small, middle, and great. Before being able to enter the path of accumulation, wrong views of nihilism—such as rejecting karma and its effects and rebirth—and of absolutism—such as asserting a soul (self) or a permanent creator—must be deactivated.

The Fundamental Vehicle **path of preparation** (*prayogamārga*) is a clear realizer of the meaning—that is, of emptiness. When yogīs first attain a concentration that is a union of serenity and insight focused on emptiness, they enter the path of preparation. This path is so called because this profound conceptual realization prepares yogīs for the direct, nonconceptual perception of emptiness on the path of seeing. The path of preparation has four stages: heat, peak, fortitude, and supreme mundane dharma. The first three stages are subdivided again into small, middle, and great. However, the supreme mundane dharma path of the Fundamental Vehicle lasts only one small moment that completes an action and so is not subdivided.

The Fundamental Vehicle **path of seeing** (*darśanamārga*) is a clear realizer of the truth, the emptiness of inherent existence. Practitioners enter this path when they first develop a direct, nonconceptual perception of emptiness. At that time, they begin abandoning the objects of abandonment—in this case the acquired self-grasping and its corresponding afflictions, and their seeds. There are two clear realizers on this path, each of which has subdivisions.

1. The *pristine wisdom of meditative equipoise* (*samāhitajñāna*) of the path of seeing realizes emptiness directly and nonconceptually with a concentration that is the union of serenity and insight. It is a realizer for which dualistic appearances with respect to emptiness vanish. It has three types:

    - An *uninterrupted path* (*ānantaryamārga*) is the actual antidote to the acquired self-grasping (grasping true existence) as well as acquired afflictions and their seeds. It consists of eight forbearances, which are minds that realize the emptiness of the object (the four truths) and of the subjects (the minds meditating on the four truths). The eight forbearances occur simultaneously. Whatever is an uninterrupted path of the path of seeing is all eight forbearances. Due to the meditator's prior meditation on the antidotes, movement toward the wisdom *directly* realizing emptiness, which is the antidote, and movement toward the elimination of the last moment of self-grasping and its seeds to be abandoned by that level of that path occur at the same time. By the simultaneous arising of the antidote and the elimination of that grade of self-grasping, the uninterrupted path is attained, and that grade of self-grasping and afflictions can no longer be generated in that person's mindstream. However, she has not yet completely and forever abandoned them.

An uninterrupted path is so called because it leads the meditator uninterruptedly to liberation from those specific afflictions and their seeds. It is not that the afflictions and the uninterrupted path exist at the same time and battle each other, because an unpolluted mind and a polluted one cannot exist simultaneously.

- A *liberated path* (*vimuktimārga*) directly follows an uninterrupted path and is a wisdom that has definitely abandoned and is completely free of the acquired self-grasping. The liberated path consists of the eight knowledges, which also meditate on the emptiness of the object (the four truths) and the emptiness of the subject (the mind meditating on the four truths). The eight knowledges occur simultaneously and follow the eight forbearances. The uninterrupted path is compared to kicking the thief out of your house, and the liberated path is analogous to locking the door so he can never reenter.

Vaibhāṣikas say that these sixteen happen in a sequence—a forbearance followed by its knowledge, then another forbearance and its knowledge, and so on—whereas the Prāsaṅgikas say that the eight forbearances occur simultaneously, followed by the eight knowledges, which also occur simultaneously. This is because the Prāsaṅgikas say that when one has direct realization of the emptiness of one phenomenon, one simultaneously directly realizes the emptiness of all phenomena.

- A *pristine wisdom of meditative equipoise that is neither an uninterrupted path nor a liberated path* occurs between the liberated path of the path of seeing and the first uninterrupted path of the path of meditation. Here yogīs strengthen their realization of emptiness until it becomes strong enough to become the uninterrupted path of the path of meditation. This occurs seamlessly in the same meditation session of meditative equipoise on emptiness.

2. The *pristine wisdom of subsequent attainment* (*pṛṣṭhalabdha-jñāna*) of the path of seeing is the subsequent clear realizer of someone who has arisen from a liberated path. This wisdom does not realize emptiness directly. Conventional phenomena again appear at this time and one accumulates merit in order to attain higher paths. This pristine wisdom is of two types:

    - The *pristine wisdom concerned mainly with the method aspect of the path* supports other virtuous activities. This would be, for example, meditation on renunciation and the aspiration to attain liberation for oneself.

    - The *pristine wisdom concerned mainly with the wisdom aspect of the path* is, for example, contemplating that all phenomena are like illusions, appearing to exist from their own side but not existing in that way.

The Fundamental Vehicle **path of meditation** is a Fundamental Vehicle subsequent clear realizer. Practitioners enter this path when they attain the first uninterrupted path of the path of meditation by generating a pristine wisdom directly realizing emptiness that has the power to uproot one round of innate self-grasping. It has two divisions: the pristine wisdom of meditative equipoise and the pristine wisdom of subsequent attainment.

1. The *pristine wisdom of meditative equipoise* is a subsequent clear realizer that perceives emptiness without any dualistic appearance. It has three subdivisions: uninterrupted paths, liberated paths, and pristine wisdoms of meditative equipoise that are neither of the two.

- *Uninterrupted paths* are wisdoms that are the actual antidotes to the innate self-grasping that is its object of abandonment.

- *Liberated paths* are the wisdoms that are directly liberated from the innate self-grasping that is the corresponding object of abandonment as the uninterrupted path that induces it. Each uninterrupted path flows seamlessly to become its corresponding liberated path in the same meditation session.

Just as the grades of ignorance and afflictions number eighty-one, so do the uninterrupted paths of the path of meditation number eighty-one. Here the small-small paths of each level eliminate the great-great grades of self-grasping of each level, the middle-small paths overcome the middle-great self-grasping, and so on, until the great-great paths eliminate the small-small grades of self-grasping.

The eighty-one grades of innate afflictions are abandoned in nine steps. All nine small-small paths occur simultaneously, overcoming all nine grades of great-great self-grasping ignorance. All nine middle-small paths eliminate all nine middle-great grades of ignorance and so on until all nine great-great paths overcome all nine grades of small-small ignorance.

There are nine uninterrupted paths on the path of meditation, the last one being the vajra-like concentration, but there are only eight liberated paths on the path of meditation, because the vajra-like concentration eradicates the final levels of self-grasping and brings the path of no-more-learning, which is totally free from all self-grasping, afflictions, and their seeds.

All uninterrupted paths and liberated paths realize emptiness directly. Progressing through the nine cycles of uninterrupted paths and liberated paths of the path of meditation is akin to repeatedly washing a cloth, each time removing a more strongly entrenched level of dirt until all dirt is finally abolished. As yogīs abandon more grades of self-grasping ignorance, the ignorance gets weaker and the strength of one's assent to the appearance of true existence also declines until at the path of no-more-learning they are forever eradicated.

Śrāvaka āryas progress through the path of seeing and path of meditation in various ways, depending on whether they are simultaneous eliminators, leapers, gradual attainers, or gradual eliminators.[82]

- *Pristine wisdoms of meditative equipoise that are neither of the two* are, for example, the pristine wisdoms realizing emptiness that precede each uninterrupted path in the same meditation session.

2. The *pristine wisdom of subsequent attainment* is a clear realizer that does not realize emptiness directly. It arises after a liberated path while the yogī is engaged in daily life activities, as does the pristine wisdom of subsequent attainment of the path of seeing. It is of two types:

    - The *pristine wisdom concerned mainly with the method aspect of the path* supports other virtuous activities. This could be, for example, yogīs' thought to attain nirvāṇa for their own personal benefit.

    - The *pristine wisdom concerned mainly with the wisdom aspect of the path* is, for example, the pristine wisdom that directly realizes subtle conventionalities that appear like illusions in that they appear one way but exist in another.

The Fundamental Vehicle **path of no-more-learning** is a clear realizer of emptiness that has completely abandoned self-grasping ignorance, afflictions, and their seeds. This has two subdivisions:

1. The path of no-more-learning that is a method type of realizer is, for example, the intention of an arhat to enter meditative equipoise on nirvāṇa and not arise again.
2. The path of no-more-learning that is a wisdom type of realizer is, for example, a pristine wisdom of an arhat that directly realizes conventionalities as empty, like illusions.

These five paths can be condensed into two: the paths of ordinary beings (the paths of accumulation and preparation) and the paths of āryas (the paths of seeing, meditation, and no-more-learning). Fundamental Vehicle āryas consist of the eight approachers and abiders. Practitioners who attain the uninterrupted path of the path of seeing are approachers to stream-entry. When they attain the liberated path of the path of seeing and have fully abandoned the acquired afflictions, they are known as abiders in stream-entry. A stream-enterer is so called because they have entered the stream of Dharma flowing to liberation.

Approachers to and abiders in once-returner and nonreturner and approachers to arhat are on the path of meditation. Abiders in the fruit of arhatship are on the path of no-more-learning.

Śrāvakas and solitary realizers who are definite in their lineage abandon the self-grasping of both persons and phenomena by meditating on the emptiness of true existence of persons and phenomena. Śrāvakas accumulate merit for three lifetimes to attain arhatship; solitary realizers accumulate merit for one hundred eons to reach their goal. They use compact reasonings to realize emptiness, unlike bodhisattvas who realize emptiness by meditating on elaborate, multifaceted reasonings. Bodhisattvas who practice the Sūtra Vehicle accumulate merit for three countless great eons in order to gain full awakening. In general the paths of śrāvakas and solitary realizers are similar, as explained above; both groups have practitioners of modest and middling faculties who may take longer or shorter times to become arhats.

The Svātantrika Madhyamaka system and below say that first arhats attain a nirvāṇa with remainder and then nirvāṇa without remainder because when arhats attain nirvāṇa, they still have the remainder of their body produced under the influence of afflictions and karma. When they pass away, they separate from the remainder of the polluted body and attain nirvāṇa without remainder. Vaibhāṣikas and Sautrāntikas say that at this time the continuum of the person is severed. The Yogācārins and Mādhyamikas assert one final vehicle, saying that arhats will eventually enter the Mahāyāna and attain buddhahood.

Prāsaṅgikas identify "remainder" differently, saying it refers to the appearance of true existence. When arhats directly realize emptiness in meditative equipoise, their wisdom realizing emptiness lacks the remainder of the appearance of true existence. This is a nirvāṇa without remainder. After emerging from meditation, however, the appearance of true existence returns during the time of subsequent attainment; at that time arhats have a nirvāṇa with remainder. Thus Prāsaṅgikas say that first arhats attain a nirvāṇa without remainder followed by a nirvāṇa with remainder.

In its description of the śrāvaka path, the Pāli tradition does not use the schema of the five paths, but it does use the names of four of the five paths to refer to similar stages of development. In the later commentaries, "collection" (P. *sambhāra*) is used to refer to accumulations or requisites a practitioner must assemble for the attainment of liberation. In the Abhidharma, "seeing" (P. *dassana*) is used to indicate the path of a stream-enterer, and "meditation" (P. *bhāvanā*) is used to refer to the paths of once-returner, nonreturner, and arhat who cultivate or familiarize themselves with the view attained with the experience of stream-entry. "No training" (P. *asekha*), which refers to arhatship or buddhahood, is the last ground (P. *bhūmi*). It is called a "ground," not a "path" (P. *magga*), because it marks the end of cultivation. Here we see four terms—accumulation, seeing, meditation (familiarization), and no (more) training—referring to the same stages of development in both the Pāli and Sanskrit traditions.

REFLECTION

Review what occurs with each of the five paths of Fundamental Vehicle paths:

1. The path of accumulation is attained upon gaining firm renunciation of saṃsāra and firm determination to attain nirvāṇa.
2. The path of preparation is attained when first having the union of serenity and insight on emptiness.
3. The path of seeing is attained upon realizing emptiness directly and nonconceptually for the first time.
4. The path of meditation is attained when one's meditation on emptiness is strong enough to eradicate innate afflictions.
5. The path of no-more-learning is arhatship, when all afflictions and their seeds have been forever overcome.

Solitary Realizers

Śrāvakas meditate principally on the four truths and can attain a śrāvaka's awakening (liberation) in three lifetimes. Solitary realizers practice similar to śrāvakas, but their principal object of meditation is dependent origination, and they accumulate merit and practice for at least one hundred eons. Because of their great accumulation of merit, in their last lifetime in saṃsāra they can attain a solitary realizer's awakening (liberation) without relying on a teacher.[83]

There are two types of solitary realizers: community-based and rhinoceros-like. To learn the Dharma, all of them initially receive teachings from a buddha or Buddhist master. On that basis, they begin to practice and to accumulate merit and wisdom. Those on the penultimate learner path before they become arhats make three prayers when they are dying: (1) may I be reborn in a land where there is no buddha or bodhisattva performing the various activities, such as teaching the Dharma; (2) may I be able to teach the Dharma through the gestures of my body, without speaking; and (3) in my last existence, may I attain nirvāṇa without relying on the instructions of a master. These prayers are actualized, and in their last life in saṃsāra they live in a very solitary way. The meaning of "solitary realizer" is self-realized because they are able to achieve realizations in their last life without depending on a master. Both śrāvakas and solitary realizers benefit sentient beings through teaching them the Dharma.

According to some scholars, *rhinoceros-like solitary realizers* who are definite in their lineage practice the collection of merit as a disciple of a buddha for a hundred great eons on the path of accumulation, and then in one lifetime attain the path of preparation on up to arhatship without depending on a buddha or another teacher.

Community-based solitary realizers are of two types: The *great-assembly solitary realizers* attain all the fruits except arhatship in the presence of a buddha, and in their last lifetime attain the fruit of arhatship without depending on a buddha or another teacher. The *lesser-assembly solitary realizers* attain the first three of the four levels of the path of preparation—heat, peak, and fortitude—in the presence of a buddha and then attain the remaining paths and the fruits alone in their last lifetime.

While most śrāvaka and solitary realizer practitioners enter the path of accumulation and traverse the remaining paths of their respective vehicles and attain arhatship, some of them may choose to transfer to the Mahāyāna before becoming arhats. Those that generate bodhicitta can transfer to the Mahāyāna path from the heat and peak stages of the path of preparation of their respective vehicle. They then enter the Mahāyāna path of accumulation because as bodhisattvas they must accumulate the great merit necessary to attain buddhahood.

Those that do not generate bodhicitta follow their given path until attaining arhatship.[84] These arhats take a mental body and abide in the personal peace of nirvāṇa for a long while. It is said that at some point the Buddha will "arouse" them from their meditative equipoise on emptiness and encourage them to work for the benefit of all sentient beings and attain full awakening. They will generate bodhicitta and enter the Mahāyāna path of accumulation. Those arhats who have meditated on the four immeasurables extensively have an easier time doing this than those who have not. There is much discussion on how these arhats-cum-bodhisattvas accumulate merit. For example, to engage in the first four perfections requires having a body that lives in the world with ordinary sentient beings. Given that, why and how would those who have already accomplished their goal of arhatship take such a body?

The Variety of Dispositions and Faculties

As we know, sentient beings are not all alike, and eliminating the defilements through Dharma practice does not entail that we become replicas of some predetermined idea of a holy being. We have different inclinations (*āśaya*, *āsaya*), habits (*carita*, *cāritta*), dispositions (*adhimukti*, *adhimutti*), and levels of faculties (*indriya*). Thus the way people practice, the path they follow, and what they emphasize in their practice will vary. As a skillful teacher, the Buddha can lead all beings, no matter their personal differences.

Regarding the path to arhatship, the Pāli tradition says that some people are more inclined toward a path based on faith and devotion, while others prefer to base their practice on investigation and wisdom. While all arhats are similar in having removed all afflictions and their seeds, some are *liberated in both ways*—that is, they have attained a meditative absorption of the formless realm that liberates them from the material body and liberating wisdom that frees them from saṃsāra. Other arhats are *liberated by wisdom*; of these some have attained a dhyāna and others are "dry arhats" who have attained access concentration only. Furthermore, some arhats have supernormal powers and others do not. Some have six superknowledges, others do not. Regarding the five faculties—faith, effort, mindfulness, concentration, and wisdom—arhats may differ in terms of which faculty was stronger when they practiced the path.

The Pāli sūtras tell us about arhats with different specialties. In the *Greater Discourse in Gosinga* (MN 32), when asked what kind of monastic would illuminate or beautify the Gosinga forest, the Buddha's foremost disciples—all of whom were arhats except Ānanda—each had a different idea. Most of their ideas were consistent with their own special proclivity. Ānanda, the Buddha's attendant who had heard many teachings, suggested a monastic who had learned much through hearing teachings, had memorized and recited those teachings, had investigated and practiced them, and finally had penetrated them to realize them. Having done this, his ideal monastic then teaches others so that their underlying tendencies will be eradicated and they will attain liberation. Revata, on the other hand, suggested someone who delights in solitary meditation and who actualizes both serenity and insight while living alone. Anuruddha proposed someone who had attained the divine eye, while Mahākāśyapa recommended a monastic who engages in ascetic practice, wearing only rags and eating only alms food. Mahāmaudgalyāyana put forth monastics who discuss and debate the technical aspects of the teachings, while Śāriputra advocated a monastic who has mastery of his own mind and can abide in whatever meditative absorption he wished without clinging to I and mine. The Buddha praised each of their ideas, and he himself suggested someone who had strong resolution to attain awakening.

Likewise, those who are drawn to the bodhisattva path have different faculties. Those whose faculty of faith is strong and faculty of wisdom weaker generate bodhicitta first, enter the bodhisattva path of accumulation, and then realize emptiness in order to attain the path of preparation. Those whose faculty of wisdom is stronger first realize emptiness inferentially, and by this they are convinced that attaining liberation and awakening is indeed possible. Only then do they apply themselves to gain the full realization of renunciation and bodhicitta and enter the bodhisattva path of accumulation. On the path of accumulation they accumulate the merit necessary to progress to the path of preparation. They also perfect their serenity if they hadn't attained it previously.

Owing to the difference in their faculty of wisdom, modest-faculty bodhisattvas gain the signs of irreversibility (*avaivartika* or *avinivartanīya*) with respect to awakening and abandon all thoughts seeking liberation for themselves alone on the eighth ground, whereas middle-faculty bodhisattvas gain this on the path of seeing, and sharp-faculty bodhisattvas gain it on the path of preparation. All these bodhisattvas attain buddhahood, but their practice on the path differs according to their abilities. It is said, however, that our faculties and abilities can be sharpened, so putting ourselves in one or another category as if it were fixed is not wise.

Of practitioners who are trying to generate bodhicitta, those who are inspired more by faith and devotion prefer to meditate on the seven cause-and-effect instructions, while those whose faculty of wisdom is stronger initially generate bodhicitta by meditating on equalizing and exchanging self and others.

Although all buddhas are the same in having eradicated the two obscurations and attained omniscience, we connect to them in different ways. Medicine Buddha is the personification of healing because, as a bodhisattva, he made unshakable resolutions to cure disease. Avalokiteśvara is the personification of compassion because of the way he practiced compassion as a bodhisattva. Although each buddha has all the means to lead us to full awakening, depending on the form in which that buddha manifests, we will be more attracted to one or another due to our dispositions and inclinations.

Knowing this, it is important to respect ourselves and others while we practice as ordinary beings, when we attain the ārya path, and after we manifest the result. Some people enter the śrāvaka path, others the solitary realizer path, still others the bodhisattva path. Some people attain arhatship and then begin the bodhisattva path, others enter the bodhisattva path directly. If we can enter the bodhisattva path directly without first becoming a śrāvaka or solitary realizer arhat, that would be best because we will be able to attain full awakening and benefit sentient beings more quickly. But if we cannot, practicing to become an arhat is wonderful. What is most important is that we assist one another as we all progress.

Many topics arise in the explanation of the bodhisattva paths and grounds. You may frequently want to refer to the following outline as you read the next several chapters.

The Five Mahāyāna Paths

1. *Bodhisattva Path of Accumulation*
1.1 Small phase
1.2 Middle phase
1.3 Great phase

2. *Bodhisattva Path of Preparation*
2.1 Heat stage
2.2 Peak stage
2.3 Fortitude stage
2.4 Supreme mundane dharma stage

3. *Bodhisattva Path of Seeing*
3.1 *Pristine wisdom of meditative equipoise*
3.1.1 Uninterrupted path
3.1.2 Liberated path
3.1.3 Pristine wisdom of meditative equipoise that is neither an uninterrupted path nor a liberated path

3.2 *Pristine wisdom of subsequent attainment*
3.2.1 Pristine wisdom concerned mainly with the method aspect of the path
3.2.2 Pristine wisdom concerned mainly with the wisdom aspect of the path

4. *Bodhisattva Path of Meditation*
4.1 *Pristine wisdoms of meditative equipoise*
4.1.1 *Uninterrupted paths*
4.1.1.1 Uninterrupted paths that abandon the innate afflictive obscurations
4.1.1.1.1–6 Uninterrupted paths of the second through seventh grounds that abandon the six grades of self-grasping, their afflictions, and seeds
4.1.1.1.7 Uninterrupted path of the initial part of the eighth ground that abandons the three small grades of innate self-grasping, their afflictions, and seeds
4.1.1.2 Uninterrupted paths that abandon the cognitive obscurations
4.1.1.2.1 Uninterrupted path of the later part of the eighth ground
4.1.1.2.2 Uninterrupted path of the ninth ground

4.1.1.2.3 Initial uninterrupted path of the tenth ground
4.1.1.2.4 Final uninterrupted path of the tenth ground

4.1.2 *Liberated paths*
4.1.2.1 Liberated paths of the second ground through the initial part of the eighth ground
4.1.2.2 Liberated paths of the second part of the eighth ground, the ninth ground, and the initial liberated path of the tenth ground

4.1.3 *Pristine wisdoms of meditative equipoise that are neither uninterrupted paths nor liberated paths*

4.2 *Pristine wisdoms of subsequent attainment*
4.2.1 Pristine wisdoms concerned mainly with the method aspect of the path
4.2.2 Pristine wisdom concerned mainly with the wisdom aspect of the path

5. *Mahāyāna Path of No-More-Learning (Buddhahood)*

8 | The Paths of the Bodhisattva

Five Mahāyāna Paths

In many ways, the Bodhisattva Vehicle (Mahāyāna or Universal Vehicle) is similar to the Fundamental Vehicle. Like the Fundamental Vehicle, it also has five paths—the Mahāyāna paths of accumulation, preparation, seeing, meditation, and no-more-learning. The paths of the Bodhisattva Vehicle are usually called Mahāyāna (Universal Vehicle) paths rather than bodhisattva paths because the path of no-more-learning is possessed by a buddha, not a bodhisattva.

Like the Fundamental Vehicle, the Mahāyāna paths of seeing and meditation are classified into the pristine wisdoms of meditative equipoise and the pristine wisdoms of subsequent attainment. These, in turn, are divided into the same branches as the Fundamental Vehicle paths, so for the details about these, please refer to the preceding chapter. In this chapter, we'll discuss the ways in which the bodhisattva paths and grounds differ from those of the Fundamental Vehicle. On the bodhisattva paths of seeing and meditation, bodhisattvas also traverse the ten bodhisattva grounds (*bhūmi*). In traversing their paths and grounds, bodhisattvas abandon not only the afflictive obscurations, as do Fundamental Vehicle practitioners, but also cognitive obscurations, resulting in the attainment of full awakening, or buddhahood, with qualities surpassing those of arhats. Nevertheless, the object of meditation of both vehicles' uninterrupted and liberated paths is the same—the emptiness of inherent existence.

Among practitioners who aspire for buddhahood, those of sharp faculties settle the correct view of emptiness before generating bodhicitta. Although at this time they have not entered the path of accumulation, their inference of emptiness has a powerful impact on other areas of their practice. It strengthens their refuge, increases their determination to be free from saṃsāra, and motivates them to cultivate strong compassion for all sentient beings—the great compassion observing the unapprehendable that Candrakīrti spoke of in the homage to the *Supplement*.[85]

Several different grounds and paths (T. *sa lam*) texts are used in Tibetan monasteries. One of the most common is from the Svātantrika Madhyamaka perspective. However, here we will rely on the grounds and paths text by the Mongolian scholar-adept Losang Tayang (1867–1937), *A Brief Presentation of the Grounds and Paths of the Perfection Vehicle, Essence of the Ocean of Profound Meaning*, that is written according to the Prāsaṅgika perspective.[86] Losang Tayang's method of setting out the bodhisattva grounds and paths according to the Prāsaṅgikas accords with that of Jamyang Shepa and Ngawang Palden but differs from that of Losang Chökyi Gyaltsen.

Bodhisattva Path of Accumulation

Based on great compassion and the great resolve, when the bodhicitta of bodhisattva-aspirants becomes spontaneous, they enter the path of accumulation and become actual bodhisattvas. Those who freshly enter the bodhisattva path do so when they have gained genuine and spontaneous bodhicitta, such that whenever they see any sentient being, their spontaneous thought is "I want to attain full awakening in order to lead this being from duḥkha and bring him or her to the bliss of full awakening." At present, although we admire the bodhisattva path and even generate contrived bodhicitta in our minds, we are not yet actual bodhisattvas. Those beings who have spontaneous bodhicitta are truly admirable.

All Mahāyāna tenet systems, except the Yogācāra Scriptural Proponents, assert one final vehicle. That is, all sentient beings—including Fundamental Vehicle arhats—will eventually enter the bodhisattva path and become buddhas. These arhats enter the Universal Vehicle on the bodhisattva path of accumulation. Although they have already realized emptiness and removed all afflictive obscurations, they must still create great merit in order to progress through the bodhisattva paths and grounds. The path of accumulation is so called because during this time bodhisattvas newly or freshly entering the path—that is, those who haven't previously attained arhatship—accumulate a great deal of merit, hear many teachings on the bodhisattva practice and on emptiness, and clarify their understanding of emptiness in order to progress to the path of preparation. Before entering the path of accumulation all bodhisattvas have overcome the wrong views of nihilism—such as rejecting karma and its effects and rebirth—and of absolutism—such as asserting a soul (self) or permanent creator.

Henceforth some bodhisattvas practice the Pāramitāyāna—the Perfection Vehicle—in which they fulfill the collections of merit and wisdom in three countless great eons to become buddhas. Others follow the Tantrayāna, where if they practice properly, the time is much shorter.

In both cases, they proceed to buddhahood by cultivating method and wisdom. The Buddha succinctly laid out the path in the *Heart Sūtra* when he spoke the perfection of wisdom mantra, *tadyathā gate gate pāragate pārasaṃgate bodhi svāhā. Tadyathā* means "it is thus," *gate* means "having gone," *pāragate* is "having thoroughly gone," *pārasaṃgate* is "having thoroughly and completely gone," *bodhi* means "awakening," and *svāhā* means "may it be so." This is explained in terms of the person who is going, that to which they are going, that from which they are going, and the means in dependence upon which they are going.

Who is going? The I that is merely designated in dependence on the mindstream is the person who is going. That from which we are going is saṃsāra, the state of being under the power of ignorance, afflictions, and polluted actions. That to which we are going is the resultant truth body, the everlasting cessation of duḥkha, its origins, and their latencies. That by which we are going is a path that is a union of method and wisdom.

By saying *gate*, the Buddha tells us to go to the other shore. From our point of view, saṃsāra is the near shore and nirvāṇa is the far shore. By saying these five—*gate, gate, pāragate, pārasaṃgate, bodhi*—the Buddha encourages and instructs us to go, go, thoroughly go, thoroughly and completely go, and (go) to full awakening. These five represent, respectively, the bodhisattva paths of accumulation, preparation, seeing, meditation, and no-more-learning.

The path of accumulation is a clear realizer of the doctrine—"doctrine" here referring to the words of the scriptures gained mainly by hearing and contemplating the teachings. The bodhisattva path of accumulation is similar to the Fundamental Vehicle path of accumulation, but bodhisattvas continue to strengthen their bodhicitta and collect a great amount of merit before passing to the bodhisattva path of preparation.

While on the path of accumulation, bodhisattvas have states arisen from meditation, but they do not yet have states arisen from the union of serenity and insight realizing emptiness. It is called "the path of accumulation" because during this time, they accumulate the conditions to gain the union of serenity and insight into emptiness arisen from meditation.[87] These bodhisattvas accumulate merit through engaging in the method aspect of the path with the bodhicitta motivation and accumulate wisdom by consistent meditation on emptiness.

The bodhisattva path of accumulation has three phases: small, middle, and great. *On the small phase*, bodhisattvas do not necessarily have the correct view of emptiness. In addition, their bodhicitta is not stable; it could degenerate if those bodhisattvas are not careful. This stage is like a sick person who has taken the medicine, but it's uncertain if he will be cured. Referring to the twenty-two types of bodhicitta, the bodhicitta of small-phase bodhisattvas is like the earth.[88] Just as the earth is the basis for and provides nourishment for all that grows, this bodhicitta is the basis on which all the excellent qualities of the bodhisattva path will arise in the future.

On the middle phase, their bodhicitta will not degenerate. It is like gold—a precious substance buried under the ground for a long time. However, these bodhisattvas must still create a great deal of merit before gaining the path of preparation.

On the great phase, bodhisattvas' bodhicitta and excellent qualities grow like the waxing moon. Having the concentration called "the stream of Dharma," they are able to emanate many bodies that travel to various pure lands to listen to teachings from many buddhas.[89] Never forgetting the teachings they hear, these bodhisattvas also listen to Dharma discourses from supreme emanation bodies. Bodhisattvas who have not previously gained the correct view of emptiness attain it on either the second or third phase of the path of accumulation.

Bodhisattva Path of Preparation

The path of preparation is a clear realizer of the meaning—here "meaning" refers to emptiness. For "new" bodhisattvas—those who entered the Bodhisattva Vehicle directly—the demarcation of entering the path of preparation is having the union of serenity and insight on emptiness. Here their understanding of emptiness becomes more experiential because it is derived from insight and because they now attain a new concentration that is a clear conceptual realization of emptiness.

Bodhisattvas who had previously become Fundamental Vehicle arhats attain the bodhisattva path of preparation when they accumulate the requisite two collections of merit and wisdom on the path of accumulation necessary to advance to the bodhisattva path of preparation. This requisite is the same for those bodhisattvas until they reach the eighth ground because in order to eradicate the cognitive obscurations on the pure grounds—the eighth, ninth, and tenth grounds—they must first accumulate merit and wisdom for two countless great eons. For all bodhisattvas, the first great countless eon of merit is accumulated on the paths of accumulation and preparation, the second on the first to the end of the seventh ground, and the third on the three pure grounds.

On the path of preparation, bodhisattvas familiarize themselves with emptiness and further cultivate the method side of the path through altruistic activities. Within the path of preparation are four stages—heat, peak, fortitude, and supreme dharma—where their realization of emptiness continues to deepen and their awareness of emptiness becomes subtler and clearer. They continue to meditate using various reasonings to refute inherent existence and establish emptiness. Having correctly established the view, they then meditate on emptiness with the union of serenity and insight. The conceptual appearance of emptiness is gradually worn away, and conceptual elaborations and dualistic appearances begin to fade.

The four stages of the path of preparation are posited according to the gradual decrease of dualistic appearances during meditative equipoise on emptiness and the new ability to suppress the four manifest forms of self-grasping. Yogīs suppress the manifest self-grasping of afflictive and pure objects on the first two stages and the manifest self-grasping of subjects—the consciousnesses realizing emptiness—on the last two stages. At each stage, their conceptual cognition of emptiness becomes clearer. Each of these four stages has three phases—small, medium, and great—because bodhisattvas must create a great amount of merit on the path of preparation to advance to the bodhisattva path of seeing.

The *heat stage* is so called because one is approaching the fire of the direct realization of emptiness that burns up the afflictions.

The *peak stage* is so called because one's roots of virtues can no longer be damaged by anger and wrong views. Yogīs newly attain a concentration that is a deeper conceptual realization of emptiness.

The *fortitude stage* is so called because these bodhisattvas can "bear" emptiness without fear. From this point onward, they have certainty that they will never again be born in an unfortunate rebirth. Although the karmic seeds for such rebirths are still on their mindstream—they are not eliminated until the path of seeing—the conditions for them to ripen are now incomplete. However, these bodhisattvas do not have complete control of the rebirth process. This ability is gained on the first ground; thereafter they can take any rebirth they wish.

In the first two stages of the path of preparation, there is the appearance of subject and object during meditative equipoise on emptiness and the meditator can ascertain them. Now, although the appearance or image of emptiness is still present, it has diminished to such an extent that she no longer ascertains it. However, she does ascertain emptiness.

The *supreme mundane dharma stage* is so called because it is the highest mundane state. These bodhisattvas are still common beings (*pṛthagjana*, *puthujjana*), but upon attaining the path of seeing, they will become āryas. The veil of the conceptual appearance of emptiness is very thin, and the sense of a subject—a mind realizing emptiness—cannot be ascertained. They are on the verge of breaking through the veil of the conceptual appearance to realize emptiness directly.

Bodhisattva Path of Seeing

The *Ornament of Clear Realizations* says that the physical support—that is, the body—of those who enter the bodhisattva path of seeing directly without having first attained arhatship in the Śrāvaka Vehicle is the body of a human being[90] or the body of any of the six classes of desire-realm gods. Form- and formless-realm gods have weak renunciation of saṃsāra, and because of their attachment to the peacefulness of their meditation they are unable to attain the bodhisattva path of seeing. It is said that some form-realm gods can attain the first three levels of the bodhisattva path of preparation, but not the fourth because that leads directly to the path of seeing. The mental support—that is, the sphere (*avacara*) of consciousness—needed to attain the bodhisattva path of seeing is an actual dhyāna.[91]

When all dualistic appearances—of subject and object, of conventional truths, and of inherent existence—dissolve, yogīs in meditative equipoise on emptiness on the supreme mundane dharma phase of the path of preparation transition to the bodhisattva path of seeing. Their insight into emptiness is now direct and nonconceptual. The mind and emptiness are fused, like water poured into water, with no appearance of subject and object. As ārya bodhisattvas, these yogīs are not subject to the duḥkha of birth, aging, sickness, and death. Although they will take rebirth, it is no longer under the control of the ignorance, afflictions, and polluted karma that would give rise to this saṃsāra duḥkha. These bodhisattvas now eliminate the acquired afflictions.

The bodhisattva path of seeing is a clear realizer of the truth, emptiness; it encompasses the first bodhisattva ground and has two clear realizers: the pristine wisdom of meditative equipoise and the pristine wisdom of subsequent attainment of the path of seeing.

1. The *pristine wisdom of meditative equipoise* realizes emptiness directly and nonconceptually with a concentration that is the union of serenity and insight. That pristine wisdom has no dualistic appearance whatsoever. It has three types: an uninterrupted path, a liberated path, and the pristine wisdom of meditative equipoise that is neither.

    - An *uninterrupted path* (*ānantaryamārga*) is an exalted wisdom of the Mahāyāna path of seeing that is the actual antidote to acquired self-grasping and acquired afflictions. This uninterrupted path consists of the eight forbearances, which are synonymous with one another. This uninterrupted path leads the meditator without any interlude to liberation from the acquired afflictions. It is not that the afflictions and the uninterrupted path exist at the same time and battle each other, because an unpolluted mind and a polluted one cannot exist at the same time. Rather it is like the dawn of a new day: the approaching of radiant sunlight and the approaching of the cessation of darkness are simultaneous.

- A *liberated path* (*vimuktimārga*) directly follows the uninterrupted path and is a pristine wisdom of meditative equipoise of a Mahāyāna path of seeing that has definitely abandoned and is completely free of acquired self-grasping and acquired afflictions to be eliminated on that path. Due to the power of the antidote—the pristine wisdom of meditative equipoise—those afflictions can never again appear in the mind. Attaining a liberated path and actualizing a true cessation are simultaneous. The reality (emptiness) of the mind free from those objects of abandonment on that path is a true cessation.

  Just as the eight forbearances, which comprise the uninterrupted path, occur simultaneously and abandon the acquired afflictions, the eight knowledges, which comprise the liberated path, occur simultaneously and are the knowledge that the acquired afflictions have been abandoned. This liberated path realizes the emptiness of both subject and object with respect to the four truths.[92]

- The *pristine wisdom of meditative equipoise that is neither an uninterrupted path nor a liberated path* is, for example, the pristine wisdoms of meditative equipoise of the bodhisattva path of seeing of someone who had previously become a Fundamental Vehicle arhat. As arhats these practitioners have already abandoned all the afflictive obscurations that are the objects of abandonment of the first seven grounds. So until they reach the eighth ground, they do not have any new uninterrupted paths or liberated paths, although they still engage in meditative equipoise on emptiness. Rather, they focus on accumulating the merit necessary to support their pristine wisdoms on the pure grounds that will eradicate the cognitive obscurations.

2. The *pristine wisdom of subsequent attainment of the path of seeing* is the clear realizer of someone who has arisen from a liberated path. This wisdom does not realize emptiness directly. Conventional phenomena again appear at this time, and these yogīs engage in virtuous activities to accumulate merit in order to attain higher paths. This pristine wisdom is of two types: the pristine wisdom concerned mainly with the

method aspect of the path and the pristine wisdom concerned mainly with the wisdom aspect of the path.

- The *pristine wisdom concerned mainly with the method aspect of the path* is, for example, bodhicitta that supports virtuous activities, such as the practices of the perfections of generosity, ethical conduct, and fortitude.

- The *pristine wisdom concerned mainly with the wisdom aspect of the path* is, for example, the wisdom contemplating that all phenomena are like illusions in that they appear to exist from their own side but do not exist in that way. Derived from the realization of emptiness, this wisdom knows that although phenomena do not inherently exist, they function in the conventional world.

On the path of seeing, bodhisattvas completely overcome acquired afflictions. Their innate afflictions are weakened so that without these gross impediments, their great compassion easily expands and intensifies. However, if the influence of the realization of emptiness wanes, bodhisattvas on the first seven grounds may still experience manifest afflictions. These afflictions are weak, do not disturb their mind or create karma, and are easily neutralized by bodhisattvas' wisdom and compassion. Ārya bodhisattvas create only unpolluted karma.

Fundamental Vehicle learner āryas may still experience the unpleasant results of previously created destructive karma. Ārya bodhisattvas, however, experience neither physical nor mental suffering because of the power of their wisdom and compassion.

Since the virtuous karma ordinary beings create is considered polluted and is not a direct cause of awakening, the question arises: What happens to the seeds of this virtuous karma when the person becomes an ārya? They are gradually transmuted into seeds of unpolluted karma as the power of ārya bodhisattvas' realizations and excellent qualities increases.

In the following chapters that describe the practice of ārya bodhisattvas, you will see the power and capability of their great compassion and wisdom. This gives us confidence that our compassion and wisdom, when continuously cultivated, will likewise expand exponentially.

Bodhisattva Path of Meditation

The bodhisattva path of meditation is a bodhisattva subsequent clear realizer. Bodhisattvas transition to the path of meditation when they have accumulated enough merit and their wisdom is powerful enough to begin eradicating the innate afflictions. "Meditation" in Tibetan has the same verbal root as "to familiarize," so this is called "the path of meditation" because yogīs are mainly familiarizing themselves with the emptiness directly realized by the path of seeing. The bodhisattva path of meditation is of two types: pristine wisdoms of meditative equipoise and pristine wisdoms of subsequent attainment.

1. The *pristine wisdoms of meditative equipoise* are a bodhisattva's subsequent clear realizers in which all dualistic appearances regarding emptiness have vanished. Here, too, there are three types: uninterrupted paths, liberated paths, and pristine wisdoms of meditative equipoise that are neither.

   A. An *uninterrupted path* is a pristine wisdom of meditative equipoise that is the actual antidote to whichever of the two obscurations—afflictive obscurations and cognitive obscurations—is its object of abandonment. Uninterrupted paths of the bodhisattva path of meditation are of two types: those that abandon innate afflictive obscurations and those that abandon cognitive obscurations.

      (1) *Uninterrupted paths that abandon the innate afflictive obscurations* are, in turn, divided into seven. The first six are the uninterrupted paths of the second through seventh grounds on which the six grades of innate self-grasping and its corresponding afflictions and their seeds are eradicated. These six grades are the great-great through the small-middle grades of innate afflictions of the three realms.

      The seventh uninterrupted path occurs on the initial part of the eighth ground. For bodhisattvas who did not enter the Fundamental Vehicle first, this uninterrupted path eradicates the three small grades of innate self-grasping, their afflictions, and their seeds simultaneously, in one moment. Having pacified coarse striving and exertion, this uninterrupted path is very powerful because it can abandon in a short time the self-grasping and afflictions that could not be abandoned during many prior eons. In that way it is like a ship that sails with difficulty in channels, but once it reaches the open ocean can quickly traverse great distances. The *Ten Grounds Sūtra* says (EOM 18):

> O Children of the Conqueror, it is like this: For example, until it reaches the great ocean, a great ship that goes on the great ocean must be forcibly moved and made to go. As soon as it reaches the great ocean, it is carried by billows of wind. It goes without needing to be moved forcibly. It [traverses] effortlessly that which one could not traverse even in a hundred years by means of the previous forcible moving and going.
>
> O Children of the Conqueror, similarly, one who has thoroughly accumulated the collection of roots of virtue of a bodhisattva and achieves well the Mahāyāna, having reached the ocean of the deeds of bodhisattvas, by means of a spontaneous pristine wisdom obtains in one brief period a measure of all-knowing pristine wisdom that he could not have obtained even in one hundred thousand eons of those previous forcible deeds.

When these bodhisattvas attain the liberated path of the initial part of the eighth ground, they have totally eradicated the root of saṃsāra and have attained a nirvāṇa that is the complete exhaustion of the afflictive obscurations. They are similar to arhats who are free from desire regarding the three realms of saṃsāra. The *Ten Grounds Sūtra* says, "Here, just at this time, he passes thoroughly beyond sorrow." Candrakīrti's *Supplement* says (EOM 18–19):

> Because an awareness that is without desire does not abide together with faults, on the eighth ground those defilements are thoroughly pacified along with their root, the afflictions, are extinguished, and [one] is unsurpassed in the three realms. However, [one] is not [yet] able to attain all the fortunes of buddhas, limitless like the sky.

Although these bodhisattvas are now similar to arhats, they are not non-learners, because they haven't attained the path of no-more-learning of any of the three vehicles. Bodhisattvas that previously attained arhatship in the Fundamental Vehicle are non-learners because they attained the path of no-more-learning in the Fundamental Vehicle. However, they are not non-learners of any of the three vehicles because they are now in the Bodhisattva Vehicle.

(2) *Uninterrupted paths that abandon cognitive obscurations* are divided into four. The uninterrupted path of the later part of the eighth ground and the uninterrupted path of the ninth ground, respectively, abandon the great and middle cognitive obscurations. The initial and final uninterrupted paths of the tenth ground, respectively, abandon the coarse and subtle small cognitive obscurations.

B. *Liberated paths* are directly freed from either of the two obscurations that are the object of abandonment of the uninterrupted path that induced it. There are ten liberated paths from the second to the tenth grounds. The liberated path that corresponds to the last uninterrupted path of the path of meditation is the first moment of buddhahood. Thus on the path of meditation, there are eleven uninterrupted paths and ten liberated paths.

C. The *pristine wisdoms of meditative equipoise that are neither* an uninterrupted path nor a liberated path are, for example, the pristine wisdom of meditative equipoise in the continuum of an ārya bodhisattva who is about to attain the third through the tenth grounds. These pristine wisdoms occur between one liberated path and the next uninterrupted path. During this time, yogīs collect merit and continue to enhance their wisdom realizing emptiness. Their meditative equipoise on emptiness prepares them to attain the next uninterrupted path, and when their wisdom is strong enough to eliminate the next level of afflictions and their seeds, they seamlessly, without arising from meditation, pass into the next uninterrupted path. The actual transition from one ground to the next and from the tenth ground to the path-of-no-more-learning occurs during meditative equipoise. Similarly, the transition from the supreme mundane dharma stage of the path of preparation to the first ground occurs during meditative equipoise.

2. The *pristine wisdoms of subsequent attainment* are a bodhisattva's subsequent clear realizers that do not directly realize emptiness. These are of two types:

   A. The *pristine wisdom concerned mainly with the method aspect of the path* supports other virtuous activities such as the practices of the perfections of generosity, ethical conduct, and fortitude. It also includes the three mental engagements of aspiration, dedication, and rejoicing. Aspiration creates the roots of virtue, dedication makes them inexhaustible, and rejoicing increases them.[93]

   B. The *pristine wisdoms of subsequent attainment that are wisdom types of realizers* are exalted knowers that realize emptiness through a conceptual appearance. When yogīs arise from meditation realizing emptiness, they don't forget what they realized. The impact of that realization stays with them and influences how they perceive the objects they use in daily life. As long as their minds are informed by this realization, although people and things appear to them as inherently existent, they know that this appearance is false and that these objects are like illusions.

While on the paths of seeing or meditation, before progressing to the next uninterrupted path a yogī repeatedly generates the pristine wisdom of subsequent attainment and the pristine wisdoms of meditative equipoise that are neither. This is done because it takes time for practitioners' merit and wisdom to become strong enough to induce the next uninterrupted path. Depending on the acuity of their faculties and other conditions, they may be on a particular path for several months, years, lifetimes, or for the good part of a countless great eon. During this time, they eat, sleep, talk to people, and do other activities in their daily lives, all the time practicing bodhicitta and virtuous actions to accumulate merit. They repeatedly meditate on impermanence and emptiness with the pristine wisdoms of meditative equipoise that are neither. Only after accumulating merit and wisdom for a long time do bodhisattvas generate the next uninterrupted path. After meditating with this new uninterrupted path and its liberating path that eradicate the next grade of afflictions, they again practice for extended periods of time meditating with the pristine wisdom of subsequent attainment and the pristine wisdoms of meditative equipoise that are neither.

On the second to the seventh grounds of the bodhisattva path of meditation, progressively more subtle levels of the innate afflictions are abandoned. When their minds are still influenced by the realization of emptiness they had in meditative equipoise, they see all phenomena as like illusions. However, if the influence of their realization of emptiness wanes, ārya bodhisattvas may still experience manifest afflictions, but they are weak, do not create karma, and are easily suppressed.

The uninterrupted path of the initial half of the eighth ground eradicates the subtlest afflictive obscurations, and its liberated path marks the full abandonment of all acquired and innate afflictions and their seeds from the root. Eighth-ground bodhisattvas resemble arhats in terms of having eliminated all afflictive obscurations and being entirely free from cyclic existence. Bodhisattvas, however, have many special qualities that śrāvakas and solitary realizer arhats lack.

Objects Abandoned on the Bodhisattva Paths and Grounds

BODHISATTVA PATH	BODHISATTVA GROUND	OBJECTS BEING ABANDONED AND OBJECTS COMPLETELY ABANDONED
Path of seeing	1 UIP and LP	Acquired afflictions
Path of meditation	2 UIP and LP	Great-great innate afflictive obscurations
Path of meditation	3 UIP and LP	Middle-great afflictive obscurations
Path of meditation	4 UIP and LP	Small-great afflictive obscurations
Path of meditation	5 UIP and LP	Great-middle afflictive obscurations
Path of meditation	6 UIP and LP	Middle-middle afflictive obscurations
Path of meditation	7 UIP and LP	Small-middle afflictive obscurations
Path of meditation	8 initial UIP and LP	Great-small, middle-small, small-small afflictive obscurations
Path of meditation	8 initial LP	Liberated from saṃsāra
Path of meditation	8 later UIP and LP	Great cognitive obscurations
Path of meditation	9 UIP and LP	Middle cognitive obscurations
Path of meditation	10 initial UIP and LP	Coarse small cognitive obscurations
Path of meditation	10 later UIP	Subtle small cognitive obscurations
Path of no-more-learning		Buddhahood

UIP = Uninterrupted path

LP = Liberated path

REFLECTION

1. What are the entry points for each of the five bodhisattva paths?
2. What is the function of each of these pristine wisdoms on the bodhisattva path of meditation?
   - *Pristine wisdoms of meditative equipoise*
     - Uninterrupted paths
     - Liberated paths
     - Pristine wisdoms of meditative equipoise that are neither uninterrupted nor liberated paths
   - *Pristine wisdoms of subsequent attainment*
     - Pristine wisdoms concerned mainly with the method aspect of the path
     - Pristine wisdoms of subsequent attainment that are wisdom types of realizers
3. Imagine what it would be like to gain these pristine wisdoms and the freedom they bring. Develop a strong determination to do so for the benefit of all beings.

The Yogācāra-Svātantrikas, Sautrāntika-Svātantrikas, and Prāsaṅgikas have different ways of describing the bodhisattva paths of seeing and meditation. This is related to what they consider to be afflictive obscurations and cognitive obscurations.

Yogācāra-Svātantrikas say grasping the coarse and subtle self of persons are afflictive obscurations, and grasping the coarse and subtle self of phenomena are cognitive obscurations. The coarse self of persons is a permanent, unitary, independent self and the subtle is a self-sufficient substantially-existent person. Grasping the coarse self of phenomena—grasping the perceiving subject and perceived object as being of different substantial entities—is the coarse cognitive obscurations, and grasping the true existence of phenomena is the subtle cognitive obscurations. For bodhisattvas who enter the bodhisattva path freshly, the path of seeing abandons acquired afflictive obscurations and acquired cognitive obscurations and their seeds. Depending on the bodhisattva path of seeing (which encompasses the first ground), bodhisattvas actualize a true cessation of acquired obscurations. The remaining nine grounds of the bodhisattva path of meditation abandon the innate afflictive obscurations and innate cognitive obscurations simultaneously. Both obscurations have been completely removed at buddhahood.

Sautrāntika-Svātantrikas say grasping the coarse and subtle self of persons are afflictive obscurations, and grasping the self of phenomena are cognitive obscurations. Like the Yogācāra-Svātantrikas, they say the coarse self of persons is a permanent, unitary, independent self and the subtle is a self-sufficient substantially-existent person. Unlike Yogācāra-Svātantrikas who assert a coarse and subtle self of phenomena, Sautrāntika-Svātantrikas assert only one level of grasping the self of phenomena—grasping both persons and phenomena as truly existent. For bodhisattvas who enter the bodhisattva path freshly, acquired afflictions are eliminated by the path of seeing. Unlike Prāsaṅgikas who assert that first all afflictive obscurations are abandoned on grounds one through seven and then cognitive obscurations are abandoned on the three pure grounds, Sautrāntika-Svātantrikas assert that cognitive obscurations are abandoned on all ten grounds. All afflictive obscurations are abandoned by the beginning of the eighth ground and all cognitive obscurations have been abandoned at the path of no-more-learning, buddhahood.

Prāsaṅgikas assert that afflictive obscurations are the self-grasping ignorance of persons and phenomena, afflictions, and their seeds. Cognitive obscurations are the latencies of self-grasping ignorance and the subtle dualistic appearances that they cause. As described above, all afflictive obscurations are abandoned by the beginning of the eighth ground, and only at that time do bodhisattvas begin to eliminate cognitive obscurations. All self-grasping ignorance and afflictions, which are afflictive obscurations, must be eliminated prior to eliminating cognitive obscurations. This is because before removing the latencies of the afflictions, the afflictions themselves must be eliminated, just as before eliminating the smell of onions in a pot (cognitive obscurations), the onions themselves (afflictive obscurations) must be removed.

Three Special Times

Although all bodhisattvas have sharp faculties compared with other practitioners, among themselves they may be of sharp, medium, or modest faculties. The path of preparation (especially the heat stage), the path of seeing, and the eighth ground come up repeatedly as times that special events may occur for bodhisattvas, depending on their level of faculties.

Signs of irreversibility (*avaivartika* or *avinivartanīya*) consist of forty-four signs, such as having stopped manifest self-grasping and not engaging in worldly talk. The forty-four signs illustrate that these bodhisattvas have an internal, stable realization of method and wisdom; they are now on an irreversible course to full awakening and will proceed directly to buddhahood. They no longer fear that self-interest or the aspiration for only their own liberation will hold them back from full awakening. The *Ornament of Clear Realizations* says that sharp-faculty bodhisattvas gradually receive signs of irreversibility on the four stages of the path of preparation, middle-faculty bodhisattvas receive signs of irreversibility on the path of seeing, and modest-faculty bodhisattvas receive signs on the eighth ground.[94]

Previously it was said that after the middle level of the path of accumulation, one's bodhicitta does not degenerate. Wouldn't that mean that bodhisattvas are irreversibly on the path to full awakening at that time? Although those bodhisattvas do not reverse course from full awakening, they have not yet attained the *signs* of irreversibility because they still haven't generated the confidence that they will not succumb to any self-centered thought that would seek their own liberation. Attaining the signs of irreversibility occurs at one of the three times mentioned above.

According to a commentary on the *Ornament of Clear Realizations*, these three points on the path also correspond to the time when the respective bodhisattvas attain the fortitude of the nonarising of phenomena. Having unwavering conviction that all phenomena lack inherently existent arising or production, and developing fortitude and acceptance with respect to emptiness, bodhisattvas can now meditate on emptiness without hesitation. It is called "fortitude" because it supports bodhisattvas on the path, preventing them from backsliding into self-preoccupation and seeking only their personal liberation. Bodhisattvas realize that there are no inherently existent sentient beings to lead to nirvāṇa and no inherently existent bodhisattvas or buddhas who are leading them. All persons and phenomena, by their very nature, are free from inherent existence; all existents in saṃsāra and nirvāṇa are originally unborn and nonarisen and are empty of inherently existent birth, arising, and production.[95]

The Perfection of Wisdom sūtras and the *Ornament* say that at these three points of the path, the respective bodhisattvas may also receive a prophecy of their awakening from the Buddha. A prophecy occurs when a particular wheel-turning buddha indicates directly or indirectly the time in the future when this bodhisattva will attain full awakening.

There is some discussion about when the self-centered attitude seeking one's own liberation is overcome or no longer manifests. By one account, it may occur at these three times, according to whether a bodhisattva has sharp, medium, or modest faculties.

We can see why these and other occurrences may happen at these three times on the path: attainment of the union of serenity and insight on emptiness marks the beginning of the heat stage of the path of preparation; the first direct, nonconceptual realization of emptiness marks the beginning of the path of seeing; and the complete extinguishment of the afflictive obscurations marks the beginning of the eighth ground.

9 | Bodhisattva Grounds

Special Qualities of Each Ground

The Śrāvaka Vehicle has eight grounds and the stages of the four pairs of approachers and abiders of stream-enterer, once-returner, nonreturner, and arhat, whereas the bodhisattva path is divided into ten bodhisattva grounds. These ten commence on the path of seeing and continue through the end of the path of meditation. Nāgārjuna tells us (RA 440):

> Just as eight grounds are explained
> in [the texts of] the Śrāvaka Vehicle,
> so too, the ten grounds of bodhisattvas
> are taught in the Mahāyāna.

Candrakīrti's autocommentary to the *Supplement* defines a bodhisattva ground (CTB 131):

> When a bodhisattva's unpolluted wisdom, conjoined with compassion and so forth, is divided into parts, each part is called a "ground" because it is a base for good qualities.

These grounds are all ultimate bodhicitta—an ārya bodhisattva's wisdom directly and nonconceptually realizing emptiness conjoined with compassion. This wisdom of meditative equipoise on emptiness is unpolluted by either ignorance or its latencies. In post-meditation time, the minds of bodhisattvas on the first seven grounds are polluted by ignorance, its seeds, and its latencies because ignorance may still manifest and phenomena appear truly existent. On the eighth ground and above, ignorance and its seeds have been abolished and bodhisattvas' minds in post-meditation are polluted only by the latencies of ignorance. In this respect they are similar to arhats who have removed the afflictive obscurations but still have the cognitive obscurations.

Candrakīrti's definition of a bodhisattva ground is a general one. Ārya bodhisattvas do not nonconceptually realize emptiness every moment, but their minds are always conjoined with that realization. Although they are not explicitly conjoined as they are in meditative equipoise, since ārya bodhisattvas' wisdom realizing emptiness has not degenerated or been forgotten in post-meditation when they interact with others, their minds are always conjoined with ultimate bodhicitta.

Although the ten grounds are chiefly defined by their wisdom of meditative equipoise on emptiness, not every consciousness of an ārya bodhisattva is a ground. Ārya bodhisattvas' love, compassion, and first nine perfections also occur on the ten grounds, but they are not the wisdom directly realizing emptiness. Nor are ārya bodhisattvas' sense consciousnesses or their mental consciousnesses remembering past events considered grounds. Grasping true existence may arise on the first seven grounds, but it is quickly subdued and does not overwhelm their minds. Some manifest afflictions may also occur, although they are usually transmuted into a bodhisattva practice. An example is a bodhisattva's desire that manifests when they want to produce children who will benefit others.

Another example is that of a ship captain who was an ārya bodhisattva. Knowing that someone aboard the ship was going to kill the other five hundred passengers, with compassion he killed that man to prevent him from harming others and from creating the destructive karma of killing. Some scholars say that although his causal motivation was compassion, in order to actually take a life, there must have been a moment of anger or hatred at the time of doing the act; otherwise he wouldn't have been able to take a life. However, this is a topic of debate, with other scholars saying that if the preparation, action, and conclusion of the action were all done with compassion, no affliction was present. Still others say that on the first two grounds, bodhisattvas may have a little anger at the moment of doing the action, but on the third ground and above they would not because they have attained a surpassing practice of fortitude.

In any case, afflictions do not harm ārya bodhisattvas. It is like someone who has recovered from an illness, but slight remnants of the virus remain in their body without adversely affecting them.

Ārya bodhisattvas' unpolluted wisdom of meditative equipoise is nondual wisdom. Here "nondual" does not mean free from the two extremes of absolutism and nihilism, as it does when speaking of ordinary beings developing the right view. Instead, it means that the subject and object appear undifferentiable, not as two separate, distinct entities, that there are no appearances of veiled truths, and that there is no appearance of inherent existence. As bodhisattvas ascend the ten grounds, this wisdom purifies their minds of first the afflictive obscurations and then the cognitive obscurations. Once these pollutants have been removed, the continuity of the clear-light mind remains and buddhahood is attained.

Although ārya śrāvakas, like ārya bodhisattvas, have realized emptiness directly, their wisdom is not a bodhisattva ground due to several distinguishing factors. Ārya bodhisattvas' wisdom realizing emptiness is conjoined with great compassion and bodhicitta and possesses twelve special characteristics. In addition, ārya bodhisattvas' wisdom directly realizing emptiness arises from having meditated on emptiness during the bodhisattva paths of accumulation and preparation using a wide variety of reasonings to get at the meaning of emptiness.

Ārya bodhisattvas' one unpolluted wisdom of meditative equipoise on emptiness is divided into parts—its earlier and later moments—forming the ten bodhisattva grounds. Just as the earth is the foundation of life, each ground is the basis of certain qualities. The division of this one seamless wisdom is made due to differences in four features: the number of sets of twelve good qualities, the degree of their majesty of power, the surpassing practice of a particular perfection, and the fruitional rebirth they take. The grounds are not differentiated in terms of how they realize emptiness or the emptiness that is their object of observation.

However, there is a difference in the ten grounds in terms of seeing the true cessations that are gradually gained by eradicating the various grades of obscurations. All these true cessations are emptinesses of a mind that has overcome a certain portion of obscurations. To a mind directly perceiving these emptinesses there is no difference in the experience of perceiving the emptiness of inherent existence. However, because the mind that is the basis of each true cessation is progressively cleansed, it is said that the emptiness of that mind is also progressively cleansed as more true cessations are gained. In other words, the successive uninterrupted paths of the ten grounds have increased power and greater ability to overcome subtler defilements. As a result, the successive liberated paths that they bring about have more true cessations and increased freedom from defilements. First-ground bodhisattvas directly realize the true cessation they have attained, but not the true cessations of the higher bodhisattvas, and the higher bodhisattvas directly realize the true cessations previously attained as well as the true cessation gained on their ground. Nāgārjuna describes this as a gradual process similar to the moon gradually waxing full. *In Praise of the Dharmadhātu* (*Dharmadhātustava* 75–76) says:

> Just as the crescent moon
> is seen to increase day by day,
> similarly, those abiding on the grounds also
> are seen to increase in stages.
>
> On the fifteenth day of the waxing moon
> the moon becomes complete.
> Similarly, on the completion of the grounds
> the truth body is fully manifest.

The following four features enable us to discern the division of this one seamless ultimate wisdom into the ten grounds:

(1) The *number of sets of twelve good qualities* a bodhisattva possesses increases. In one instant, a first-grounder can see a hundred buddhas, receive the blessing of a hundred buddhas, go to a hundred buddha lands, illuminate a hundred lands, vibrate a hundred world systems, live for a hundred eons, see the past and future of a hundred eons with wisdom, enter into and arise from a hundred concentrations, open a hundred doors of Dharma, ripen a hundred sentient beings, emanate a hundred bodies, and be surrounded by a hundred bodhisattvas. These twelve good qualities arise just after the first-grounder arises from the meditative equipoise on emptiness.

The number of these sets of twelve increases with each ground. On the second ground a bodhisattva possesses one thousand sets of twelve good qualities; on the third ground, one hundred thousand; on the fourth ground, one billion; on the fifth ground, ten billion; on the sixth ground, one trillion; on the seventh ground, one sextillion; on the eighth ground, the number of atoms of a billion worlds; on the ninth ground, the number of atoms of ten sextillion worlds; and on the tenth ground, the number of atoms of an inexpressible number of an immeasurable number of buddha lands.

(2) The *degree of power increases*. Each successive ground has greater power to purify the various levels of obscurations and to advance to a higher path. The first ground abandons the acquired afflictions. The second through the seventh grounds sequentially abandon the great-great up to the small-middle rounds of afflictions. The first part of the eighth ground abandons the great-small, middle-small, and small-small rounds of afflictions. The eighth, ninth, and tenth grounds abandon the cognitive obscurations, and on the first moment of the Mahāyāna path of no-more-learning all obscurations have been totally abandoned.

(3) On each ground, bodhisattvas develop a *surpassing practice of a particular perfection*: generosity, ethical conduct, fortitude, joyous effort, meditative stability, wisdom, skillful means, unshakable resolve, power, and pristine wisdom. This occurs chiefly due to the power of wisdom that enables bodhisattvas to overcome manifest obstacles to that perfection and attain a superior level of its practice. Accomplishing this refines their body, speech, and mind. While bodhisattvas continue to practice that perfection—for example, joyous effort—on prior and subsequent grounds, on one particular ground they attain a special competence in it. In addition, all the other perfections become more excellent on each subsequent ground, even though they may not become surpassing on that ground.

(4) On each successive ground, bodhisattvas have *the choice to take higher rebirths* in which they have more power to benefit sentient beings. They do not take these rebirths because they seek fame, riches, or power, but to be able to influence an ever-growing number of beings in a positive way.

While the object and aspect of each of these wisdoms is the same, each ground should be understood not only as the unpolluted wisdom of meditative equipoise but also as the features it possesses in post-meditation. Due to the variances of these four features, the ability of the unpolluted wisdom of each ground differs. The *Ten Grounds Sūtra* says (CTB 136):

> Just as the wise cannot express or see
> the trail of any bird across the sky,
> so none of the grounds of the Conqueror's heirs
> can be expressed. Then how can one listen?
>
> However, [differences between these ultimate grounds] are explained in terms of gradual progression of a mere portion of those [grounds]:
> by way of love, compassion, and aspirational prayers,
> and not in terms of objects of activity of the mind.

Any description of each ground falls short of the actual experience of it; ultimate bodhicitta cannot be adequately expressed in words. We differentiate the grounds based on the four features above and in terms of the actualization of a new true cessation not present in the previous ground. These new true cessations come about due to the eradication of a certain portion of obscurations by the uninterrupted path of each ground. Due to this, the clarity of the mind's perception of emptiness increases, and with that increased clarity, the yogī's wisdom becomes capable of eliminating a new level of obscurations on the next ground. This progressive development of qualities and cleansing of the mind continues until nonabiding nirvāṇa, in which all obscurations have been forever eradicated, is attained.

REFLECTION

1. In general, the ten bodhisattva grounds are one unpolluted wisdom of meditative equipoise on emptiness conjoined with compassion that is divided into its earlier and later moments.
2. This wisdom is divided into the ten grounds due to differences in four features: the number of sets of twelve good qualities, the degree of their majesty of power, the surpassing practice of a particular perfection, and the fruitional rebirth they are capable of taking.
3. The grounds are not differentiated in terms of how they realize emptiness or the emptiness that is their observed object. However, in addition to the

four features mentioned above, they also differ according to the obscurations that have been overcome and the true cessations attained.

There are several ways to contemplate the qualities of the bodhisattvas on the ten grounds. One is to do so in terms of thinking of the qualities of the Saṅgha Jewel that we take refuge in. Doing this helps us to understand their abilities to protect us from saṃsāra and guide us on the path such that our faith in the ārya bodhisattvas and buddhas increases and becomes stable.

Another way to contemplate the qualities of the Saṅgha Jewel is by seeing them as the qualities we have the ability to develop and will attain as we gradually practice the path and ascend the bodhisattva grounds. This gives us great inspiration and self-confidence to practice now because we have a clearer vision of the kind of person we can become and how we can contribute to the well-being of others.

The verses below that commence the description of each ground are from Nāgārjuna's *Precious Garland* (RA 441–61). As you read the qualities and realizations of these remarkable bodhisattvas, let your mind soar and imagine what having these realizations would be like. Be aware that these are not just qualities that others possess; they are also qualities that you are capable of cultivating and bringing to completion. The *Ten Grounds Sūtra* describes the practices undertaken and perfected on the ten grounds that culminate in full awakening. The following quotations from this sūtra are from the Chinese canon.

First Ground, the Joyous

> The first of these is called "the Joyous"
> because these bodhisattvas experience great joy
> since the three fetters have been eliminated
> and they have been born into the tathāgata family.
>
> Through the maturation of that [ground],
> the perfection of generosity becomes supreme,

> they are able to make a hundred worlds quake,
> and they become the Great Lord of Jambudvīpa.

First-grounders are called "the Joyous" (*pramuditā*) because they have eliminated the portion of afflictions to be abandoned on the path of seeing—all acquired afflictions and most notably the acquired forms of three fetters: view of a personal identity, view of bad rules and practices, and deluded doubt. Vasubandhu in the *Treasury of Knowledge* explains why these three are specifically mentioned (CTB 141):

> Not wishing to go, mistaking
> the path, and doubting the path
> obstruct progress to liberation.
> Therefore the three are indicated.

If we want to go from Dharamsala to San Francisco, we must first have the wish to go there, then we must learn the correct route, and finally we have to clear all doubts about going and the route we'll take. Similarly, to attain awakening we must first eliminate the acquired form of the view of a personal identity, which hampers our aspiration to attain awakening. Afraid of losing the I and mine that the view of a personal identity clings to so strongly, we hesitate and back away even though we have the opportunity to practice the path.

Because of our immature understanding of selflessness, this fear often manifests as laziness, busyness, or a multitude of excuses that justify our resistance to learning and practicing the Dharma. Once we have overcome this and our aspiration to attain awakening is healthy and strong, we need to find and follow the correct path to accomplish our spiritual aim. Doing this necessitates overcoming the view of bad rules and practices that holds bad conduct and incorrect practices as supreme. Otherwise, there is great danger of following a wrong path that will lead us not to awakening but to the unfortunate realms.

When we find the correct path, our certainty may be weak, in which case dispelling the vacillating mind of doubt is essential to practice the path effectively. If doubt remains in our mindstream, our efforts to practice will be like sewing with a two-pointed needle, making progress impossible. The acquired form of these three fetters is abandoned on the first ground, while the innate levels of these afflictions are eliminated on the second through seventh grounds.[96]

The coarse form of the view of a personal identity grasps the I and mine to be a self-sufficient substantially-existent person, and based on that ignorance, coarse afflictions arise. The subtle form of the view of a personal identity grasps the I and mine to be an inherently existent person, with subtle afflictions arising from this ignorance. On the second through seventh grounds, different levels of both the coarse and subtle forms of the view of a personal identity and the afflictions associated with them are gradually abandoned. At the beginning of the eighth ground, they have been completely overcome.

First-ground bodhisattvas obtain a mental body.[97] The causes of a mental body are unpolluted karma[98]—the mental factor of intention that is the subtle effort supporting the motivation to assume a mental body—and the base of latencies of ignorance,[99] which is the cognitive obscurations that give rise to the subtle dualistic view. Here we see that in both Sūtra and Tantra, bodhisattvas attain a similitude of a buddha's form body before attaining buddhahood.

First-grounders are said to outshine śrāvaka and solitary realizer arhats by way of lineage. The analogy is given of a monarch's child and a senior government minister. The minister may be wise and powerful now but can never become the monarch, whereas although young, the monarch's child is of royal lineage and will one day ascend the throne. In the same way, although at this moment Fundamental Vehicle arhats are free from saṃsāra and first-grounders are not, these bodhisattvas will definitely become buddhas. At present first-grounders do not outshine Fundamental Vehicle arhats by way of their wisdom, since the arhats are liberated from saṃsāra, whereas they are not; however, these bodhisattvas outshine the arhats by way of lineage. Through generating great compassion, great resolve, a great collection of merit, and conventional and ultimate bodhicitta, first-grounders have entered the lineage of a Tathāgata Monarch of Doctrine and will not fall back to the Śrāvaka Vehicle. One day they will become fully awakened buddhas.

First-ground bodhisattvas have attained a surpassing practice of generosity. They joyfully give their possessions, wealth, and even their bodies without any attachment or sense of loss. While bodhisattvas on the paths of accumulation and preparation can freely give their possessions and wealth, they experience mental discomfort when they think of giving their bodies and they fear the physical pain of doing so. Although ordinary bodhisattvas on the path of preparation may still give their bodies, they do so with more effort and less joy than first-ground bodhisattvas, who are completely delighted.

The ripening result is that first-grounders can choose to be born as the Great Lord of Jambudvīpa, the southern continent where we presently reside according to the ancient Indian view of the cosmos.

In the *Ten Grounds Sūtra*, Vajragarbha Bodhisattva speaks of the joy of a first-ground bodhisattva (DBS 46–48):

> I have joyful thoughts due to having turned away from and abandoned all worldly states;
> I have joyful thoughts due to entering the uniform equality of all buddhas;
> I have joyful thoughts due to departing far from the grounds of the common person;
> I have joyful thoughts due to drawing close to the grounds of knowledge;
> I have joyful thoughts due to severing all vulnerability to entering any of the wretched destinies;
> I have joyful thoughts due to becoming a refuge for all beings;
> I have joyful thoughts due to drawing near to and seeing all buddhas;
> I have joyful thoughts due to being born into the domain of the buddhas;
> I have joyful thoughts due to entering the ranks of all bodhisattvas;
> and I have joyful thoughts due to leaving behind the fear of all circumstances that would cause hair-raising terror.

> Why is it that when this bodhisattva mahāsattva gains the Joyous Ground, all types of fearfulness are immediately left far behind? In particular, they are: the fear of failing to survive; the

fear of a bad reputation; the fear of death; the fear of falling into the wretched destinies; and the fear of the awesomeness of great assemblies...

It is because this bodhisattva has abandoned any perception of a self. He does not even covet his own body. How much less does he covet whatever things he happens to use. As a consequence, he has no fear of failing to survive.

His mind does not cherish any hope of receiving offerings or reverence from anyone, but instead thinks, "I should make offerings to beings of whatever they require." Therefore he has no fear of a bad reputation.

He has abandoned any view conceiving of the existence of a self. Because he has no perception of the existence of a self, he has no fear of death.

He also thinks, "When, after I have died, I am reborn, I most certainly will not take rebirth somewhere apart from the buddhas and bodhisattvas." As a result, he has no fear of falling into wretched destinies.

He thinks: "The object of my bodhicitta and that in which I delight have no equal anywhere, so how could anything be superior to it?" Consequently, he has no fear of the awesomeness of great assemblies...

Children of the Buddha, these bodhisattvas take great compassion as foremost and possess a profound and vast resolve that is solid. Thus they redouble their diligent cultivation of all roots of goodness.

Second Ground, the Stainless

The second ground is called "the Stainless"
because [bodhisattvas'] tenfold activities
of body, speech, and mind are stainless,
and they naturally adhere to those [ethical activities].

Through maturation of that [ground] the perfection of ethical
conduct becomes supreme;

they become glorious rulers with the seven treasures, wheel-turning monarchs, beneficent to beings.
Through its maturation they become monarchs that rule all four continents,
and they gain expertise in turning beings away from unethical behavior.

Second-ground bodhisattvas are called "the Stainless" (*vimalā*) due to their extremely pure ethical conduct; they restrain from engaging in the ten nonvirtuous actions and any other unethical behavior even in their dreams. Although first-grounders have no transgressions, second-grounders have attained a surpassing practice of ethical conduct and naturally abide in the ethical codes they have adopted without any difficulty. Not only do they abandon all naturally negative actions, but they also keep their precepts faultlessly, thus abandoning all actions proscribed by the Buddha. As a result they have no regret or remorse due to committing transgressions. In addition, they engage in all actions that comprise proper ethical conduct. For monastics this entails following all activities that the Buddha prescribed for monastics.

It is said that those with pure ethical conduct have the "scent of pure morality"—a delightful fragrance around them—and a peaceful radiance that comes from their having abandoned cruelty and harmful intent. Sometimes we meet people whose calm and compassionate energy immediately puts us at ease; we trust and feel safe around them because we sense that they have no intention to harm us or anyone else. This comes from subduing the actions of their body, speech, and mind by abiding in pure ethical conduct. Candrakīrti says that these bodhisattvas are serene and radiant like an autumn moon. Their serenity derives from restraining their senses and their radiance comes from having a clear body. In addition, they do not grasp their ethical conduct or precepts as inherently existent, differentiating their practice from that of ordinary beings whose minds are immersed in ignorance. Likewise, if they do the twelve austere practices, they aren't polluted by conceit because they don't see themselves or these practices as inherently existent.[100] The *Heap of Jewels Sūtra* distinguishes such bodhisattvas from other bodhisattvas whose ethical conduct appears flawless but is polluted by ignorance (CTB 195):

> Kāśyapa, some monastics have proper ethical conduct; they abide restrained by the prātimokṣa ethical code. Their rites and spheres of activity are perfect, and they view even coarse and subtle transgressions with concern. They thoroughly assume and train in the precepts and possess pure activities of body, speech, and mind. Hence their livelihood is thoroughly pure, but they propound a self. Kāśyapa, they are the first of those seeming to have proper ethical conduct that in fact is faulty.... Furthermore, Kāśyapa, even though some monastics thoroughly assume the twelve austere practices, they view them with apprehension [of inherent existence]. Abiding in the grasping of I and mine [as inherently existent], Kāśyapa, they are the fourth of those whose ethical conduct appears to be proper but is faulty.

These bodhisattvas may choose to take birth as monarchs who rule all four continents of our world system and who possess the seven treasures that we present in the maṇḍala offering—the precious wheel, jewel, queen, minister, elephant, horse, and general—that symbolize worldly power. By using this power with wisdom, these bodhisattvas lead their followers on the path.

Although the ripening results of ārya bodhisattvas may seem to be saṃsāric rebirths, they are not; they are produced by unpolluted virtue created on the bodhisattva path. This is similar to the Buddha's signs and marks arising as the ripening results of the unpolluted paths of the ten grounds.

Third Ground, the Luminous

> The third ground is [called] the Luminous
> because the light of peaceful wisdom arises,
> the concentrations and superknowledges have arisen,
> and attachment and anger have completely ceased.
>
> Through the maturation of that [ground],
> they practice supreme fortitude and joyous effort;
> they become the celestials' skilled
> great lord who averts all sensual desire.

The third ground is called "the Luminous" (*prabhākarī*) because with great fortitude that is not concerned for their body or life, these bodhisattvas seek the transmitted Dharma and share the light of the Dharma with others. The third ground receives its name because the fire of wisdom burns brightly, emitting a light that consumes all dualistic elaborations during meditative equipoise on emptiness. In addition, just as a copper-colored light appears in the sky just before sunrise, in the times of subsequent attainment a red-orange light appears, heralding the upcoming cessations of defilements. This light does not appear to the mind in meditative equipoise on emptiness, although a light appears to be shining on them when they are in this meditative state. When they arise from meditation, the copper-colored light appears to their wisdom of subsequent attainment like the radiance of red-orange light at dawn.

On this ground, bodhisattvas gain the surpassing practice of fortitude. Their practice of fortitude is supramundane because it sees the three—themselves as the one practicing fortitude, the action of practicing fortitude, and the person or suffering that is the object of their fortitude—as empty of inherent existence yet arising dependently, like reflections. Their anger and resentment are not suppressed or repressed, but have been dissolved as a result of their practice of fortitude. No matter how severely someone criticizes, rebukes, or beats them, their minds are not disturbed by anger. Instead they have deep compassion for the person who has harmed them. Wouldn't it be wonderful to have this ability?

In addition, third-grounders do not blame others for their problems, nor do they hold grudges seeking to retaliate for previous harms. Even if someone were to torture them by slowly cutting away their flesh, these bodhisattvas would have great compassion for their torturers, knowing that they will experience extreme suffering as a result of their nonvirtuous action.

In the *Supplement*, Candrakīrti discusses the way a third-ground bodhisattva who has achieved the surpassing practice of fortitude deals with suffering and harm (MMA 29):

> Though another, unjustifiably disturbed by anger,
> cuts from his body flesh and bone
> bit by bit for a long time, he generates
> strong fortitude toward his mutilator.

This example of practicing fortitude is rather extreme, and fortunately few people find themselves having to undergo such torture. Nevertheless, the example is useful to illustrate this bodhisattva's degree of fortitude and know that we can attain the same through practice.[101]

In this situation, the bodhisattva had not acted in a way to provoke such strong anger in the attacker. In addition, the harm is extreme—the flesh is being cut from the bodhisattva's body slowly, not quickly; it is being cut one bit at a time, not all at once; and the cutting lasts a long time. Most of us would react with fear or anger, but this bodhisattva has transformed his mind so thoroughly that these emotions do not arise in him. Instead he has fortitude and compassion for the perpetrator, knowing that this person's mind is overcome by tremendous ignorance and confusion and that he is creating the cause to experience intense suffering in the hell realms.

Although first- and second-ground bodhisattvas are not disturbed when their bodies are cut, the depth of the fortitude and compassion of the third-grounder is greater, and thus he attains surpassing fortitude. This bodhisattva is totally free from self-centeredness and truly cherishes others. Thus he is focused more on the situation of the other person—the other's confused state of mind and future suffering—than on his own.

The surpassing fortitude of third-grounders is also due to their realization of emptiness. Candrakīrti said (MMA 30):

> For a bodhisattva who sees selflessness,
> *who* is being cut by *whom*, at *what time*, and in *what manner*?
> Because he sees all phenomena as resembling reflections,
> he will endure [all such harms].

In other words, this bodhisattva sees all the elements of the harm—herself as the one being cut, the person cutting her, the method of cutting, and the time the cut is made—as being empty of inherent existence and existing similar to illusions in that they do not exist in the way they appear. This wisdom protects her mind from anger and enables her to bear the suffering without physical or mental pain.

When it is said that a particular perfection becomes surpassing on a certain ground, it doesn't mean the other nine perfections don't also improve at that time. They do. It is simply that the particular perfection is refined in a more notable way.

Third-grounders also excel in the higher training in concentration and develop special abilities to enter into and arise from the four dhyānas of the form realm and the four meditative absorptions of the formless realm quickly and easily. The mental control and concentration necessary to do this are difficult-to-attain feats. These bodhisattvas have also attained the four immeasurables and five superknowledges that advance their practice and enable them to benefit others in a superior way due to their profound concentration. By the power of their concentration, these bodhisattvas have suppressed the manifest afflictions of the three realms and greatly diminished the fetters of sensual desire, attachment to the form and formless realms, and ignorance.

Third-grounders have abandoned the attachment and anger to be abandoned on the third ground; further levels of these afflictions will be abandoned on higher grounds.

These bodhisattvas may choose to be born as the great lord of the Heaven of the Thirty-Three, as Indra, or as other powerful gods. In these forms, they work to benefit others.

REFLECTION

1. Imagine practicing the perfection of generosity the way a bodhisattva does. Although you may not be capable of practicing it as a bodhisattva does now, imagining it will open your mind and expand your heart.
2. Similarly, imagine practicing the perfections of ethical conduct and fortitude as those ārya bodhisattvas do.

Fourth Ground, the Radiant

The fourth is called "the Radiant"
because the radiance of true wisdom arises,

and [bodhisattvas] distinctively develop
all the harmonies to awakening.

Through the maturation of that [ground]
they become the celestial ruler in the abode of the Suyāma [deities].
They become skilled,
destroying the source of the view of a personal identity.

The fourth ground is called "the Radiant" (*arciṣmatī*) because during both meditative equipoise and subsequent attainment, these bodhisattvas radiate the light of true wisdom. This light is far superior to that of the third ground and arises owing to their increased wisdom of the subtle points of the thirty-seven harmonies to awakening: the four establishments of mindfulness, four supreme strivings, four bases of spiritual power, five faculties, five powers, seven awakening factors, and eightfold path of the āryas. The thirty-seven harmonies were extensively explained in *Following in the Buddha's Footsteps* and are wonderful practices that propel bodhisattvas on the path.

In addition, fourth-grounders attain the surpassing practice of joyous effort. This comes about because on the third ground they attained a special pliancy generated from their higher training in concentration, which they use on the fourth ground to totally eliminate all forms of laziness. These bodhisattvas are delighted to create virtue and are not impeded by laziness. Since discouragement, self-criticism, and low self-esteem—which are all forms of laziness—create big hindrances for us, it is important to note that these wrong consciousnesses can be abandoned and replaced by joyous effort and strong self-confidence.

The view of a personal identity grasps the I and mine to be an inherently existent person, and based on this, afflictions arise; its source is self-grasping ignorance. On the second through seventh grounds, progressive levels of ignorance, view of a personal identity, and the afflictions associated with them are gradually abandoned. At the beginning of the eighth ground, they are completely overcome. Here on the fourth ground, the level of ignorance that is the source for its corresponding level of view of a personal identity and afflictions is abandoned.

The ripening result is to choose to take birth as the ruler of the Suyāma Heaven, the third of six desire-realm heavens.

Regarding the qualities of fourth-ground bodhisattvas, the *Ten Grounds Sūtra* discusses the mental and personal qualities bodhisattvas gain by cultivating the path (DBS 108–9):

> [To leave behind wrong views, attachment, and actions], the bodhisattva mahāsattvas dwelling on the Radiant Ground confront all of the attachments related to the view imputing the existence of a true self in association with the body. These include the attachment to the existence of self, attachment to the existence of a being, and attachments to the existence of a person, an entity possessed of a lifespan, a knower, a perceiver in association with clinging to the five aggregates, the twelve sense sources, or the eighteen constituents. They observe that whatever arises in this connection, including whatsoever is contracted or extended, is withdrawn or set forth, or is caused to emerge or sink away is all carried forth by discursive thought's perception of something deemed to be a refuge or an individual territory worthy of affectionate attachment, or something worthy of being valued as precious. Consequently they completely sever all of these attachments.
>
> [To gain mental and personal qualities by cultivating the path] this bodhisattva then redoubles his vigor in the factors constituting requisites for the path that are developed through wisdom and skillful means. In accordance with what he cultivates, his mind becomes ever more gentle, harmonious, tractable to use, mentally inexhaustible, inclined to seek increasingly superior qualities, possessed of increased wisdom, devoted to rescuing all beings in the world, compliant with teachers, respectful in receiving teachings, and compliant in practice with what has been taught.
>
> At this time, this bodhisattva is cognizant of kindnesses received, knows to repay kindnesses, has a mind that becomes ever more inclined to congeniality and goodness, dwells happily together with others, is possessed of a straight mind, is possessed

of a pliant mind, is free of any form of deviousness, implements the practice of right meditative concentration, is free of arrogance and is consequently easy to engage in discussion, complies with teaching instructions, and realizes the intent of those who speak to him. It is in just such a manner that he becomes completely equipped with the good mind, the pliant mind, the quiescent mind, and the patient mind.

Fifth Ground, the Indomitable

The fifth is [called] the Indomitable,
since one cannot be subdued by any demons,
and one gains expertise in knowing
the subtle meaning of the āryas' truths and such.

Through the maturation of that [ground]
they become the celestial ruler of Tuṣita
and refute all the tīrthikas' (non-Buddhists') beliefs
concerning the efficacy of austerities.

The fifth ground is called "the Indomitable" (*sudurjayā*) because these bodhisattvas cannot be overcome by māras—worldly demons and ill-intentioned gods. They attain the surpassing practice of meditative stability that enables them to enter and emerge from the dhyānas and formless-realm absorptions. Doing this requires great mental skill and flexibility, for these meditative states are much more refined than our ordinary state of mind. These bodhisattvas can enter the first dhyāna and after a while emerge from it and immediately enter a higher meditative absorption, remain there for a time, and then emerge quickly and easily enter into a lower level of meditative absorption. This increase in ability from the fourth ground results from their having eliminated more grades of afflictions, created more merit, and strengthened their concentration.

Their wisdom that realizes the four truths has increased, and this brings greater ability to refute non-Buddhist assertions that claim the practice of extreme asceticism is necessary to overcome desire. These bodhisattvas can also easily overcome the wrong views of non-Buddhists regarding duḥkha, its origin, its cessation, and the path to that cessation. In this way they greatly benefit the holders of wrong views by directing them to the correct and efficacious path to liberation.

All phenomena are included in the two truths: veiled (conventional) and ultimate. Of the four truths of the āryas, true duḥkha, true origins, and true paths are conventional truths, and true cessations are ultimate truths, emptinesses. The four truths are set forth in order to show that true duḥkha and true origins are thoroughly afflictive phenomena to be abandoned, and true cessations and true paths are pure phenomena to be assumed. Unlike the essentialists who say that reliable cognizers directly realize only impermanent phenomena, Mādhyamikas assert that permanent phenomena, such as emptiness and true cessation, can be directly realized by reliable cognizers. Both emptiness of inherent existence and true cessations are directly realized in meditative equipoise, and the attainment of nirvāṇa involves directly realizing emptiness and selflessness. This is a stark difference between the essentialists—Yogācārins and below—and Mādhyamikas. Think about it—one says the ultimate nature of all phenomena can be seen directly by a reliable cognizer, the other says it cannot.

The object of negation—the inherent existence of all phenomena—does not exist at all; its negation is an ultimate truth. Nāgārjuna says in *Praise of the Dharmadhātu* (*Dharmadhātustava* 1–2):

> Homage and obeisance to the dharmadhātu.
> When it is not thoroughly understood,
> one wanders in the three existences,
> although it does in fact abide in all sentient beings.
>
> Just this is the truth body
> and the nirvāṇa that is the purity
> from having purified that which serves
> as the cause of saṃsāra.

Here "dharmadhātu" means emptiness. The empty nature of all phenomena is covered by defilements, the chief of which is the ignorance grasping inherent existence. When we don't understand the emptiness of inherent existence, we take rebirth again and again in the three realms of saṃsāra. The emptiness of the mind is purified when the mind, which is the base of that emptiness, is purified. That is, when all obscurations are eradicated from the mind, the emptiness of the mind becomes a nirvāṇa and a truth body—specifically the nature truth body, the emptiness and true cessation of a buddha's mind.

There are two objects of negation: objects negated by reasoning and objects negated by the path. Inherent existence, which has never existed and will never exist, is an *object negated by reasoning*; inherent existence can be disproven by reasoning. The defilements that obscure the mind and are the cause of saṃsāra are *objects negated by the path*; that is, the path removes these obscurations from the mind such that they can never reappear. These defilements are knowable phenomena, existents. Since they have not entered the nature of the mind, they are adventitious and can be eliminated. If these objects of negation could not be overcome, practicing the path would be useless.

In summary, the Buddha's mind has dual purity. From beginningless time it has been empty of inherent existence. In addition, when the adventitious defilements are eradicated by the path realizing emptiness, the mind is purified of adventitious defilements too. The purification of each grade of defilement of the mind is a true cessation. The complete purification of both objects of negation from the mind is nonabiding nirvāṇa and the truth body.

The compassion of fifth-grounders becomes indomitable as well. The *Ten Grounds Sūtra* (DBS 119–20) says:

> At this time, the bodhisattva's great compassion for beings becomes ever more supreme and directly manifest, and he is then able to bring forth the light of great kindness. Having acquired the power of wisdom such as this, he never forsakes any being and always strives to acquire the Buddha's wisdom. He contemplates all past and future conditioned phenomena in accordance with reality...
>
> He then thinks: "Common people and other beings are all so very strange. Because of their ignorance and afflictions, they take on a countless and unbounded number of bodies that have

> been destroyed, are now being destroyed, and will be destroyed in the future. In this way, they are forever subject to births and deaths. They are unable to bring forth thoughts of renunciation for the body, but rather ever increase the mechanisms for producing bodies subject to suffering. They are always swept along in the waters of the stream of cyclic births and deaths wherein they are unable to go against its current. They take refuge in the abode of the five aggregates and are unable to abandon it. They do not fear the poisonous snakes of the four great elements and are unable to extricate the arrows of their own pride and views. They are unable to extinguish the blazing fire of their attachment, animosity, and confusion, are unable to destroy the darkness of ignorance and afflictions, and are unable to dry up the great sea of their cravings and attachments.
>
> "They do not seek to encounter the great ārya and guide who possesses the ten powers. They always follow along with resolute intentions influenced by māras and, within the city of cyclic births and deaths, they are for the most part diverted by bad ideation and mental discursion. Such suffering, solitary, and poverty-stricken beings have no one to rescue them, no one to shelter them, and no one possessed of the ultimate path. There is only myself, this one person, who, with no comparable companions, will proceed to cultivate and accumulate merit and wisdom.
>
> "I will then use these provisions to cause all these beings to dwell in a state of utmost purity and then continue on in this until they are caused to acquire the Buddha's unimpeded power of wisdom with respect to all phenomena."

The strength of fifth-grounders' compassion propels them to increase their wisdom in order to fulfill their resolve to liberate all sentient beings. The ripening result of a fifth-grounder is having the choice to be born as the ruler of Tuṣita, the fourth heaven of the desire realm. This is not the Tuṣita where Maitreya Buddha abides.

Sixth Ground, the Approaching

> The sixth is called "the Approaching"
> because they approach the qualities of a buddha
> and are enhanced by the attainment of cessation
> through uniting insight and serenity.
>
> Through the maturation of that [ground],
> they become lord of the Celestials Who Delight in Emanations.
> Unsurpassable by the śrāvakas,
> they eliminate arrogant pride.

The sixth ground is called "the Approaching" (*abhimukhī*) because these bodhisattvas are approaching awakening. They attain a surpassing practice of the perfection of wisdom, as well as superior wisdom knowing the twelve links of dependent origination. Combining this wisdom with the surpassing practice of meditative stability on the fifth ground, they attain a powerful union of serenity and insight focused on emptiness that enables them to eradicate afflictions and their seeds.

People who attain serenity before entering a path practice worldly insight, which sees the disadvantages of lower levels of meditative absorption and the advantages of higher levels. By meditating in this way, they can attain higher levels of absorption. Such practice is also done by non-Buddhists. Buddhists who have realized emptiness by means of an inferential cognizer before entering a path have the wisdom arising from reflection on emptiness but not the wisdom arising from meditation on emptiness. They do not have a union of serenity and insight on emptiness. It is only after they enter a path and attain the union of serenity and insight on emptiness that marks entry into the path of preparation that they gain the wisdom arising from meditation on emptiness. At the sixth ground their union of serenity and insight and their wisdom arising from meditation on emptiness are much stronger and clearer than on the path of preparation. Now they have direct perception of emptiness, greater merit, and their concentration and wisdom are more refined.

The first six grounds correlate with development in the three higher trainings. On the first ground they excelled in generosity, which is the foundation for the three higher trainings. On the second ground, they gained surpassing ethical conduct, which includes the higher training in ethical conduct. On the third ground, their dexterity in concentration increases, advancing the higher training in concentration. On the fourth, fifth, and sixth grounds, bodhisattvas develop the higher training in wisdom: on the fourth ground, they become skilled in the wisdom of the coarse and subtle aspects of the thirty-seven aids to awakening; on the fifth ground they increase their competence in the wisdom of coarse and subtle aspects of the four truths of āryas; and on the sixth ground they cultivate great knowledge in the wisdom of the forward and reverse orders of the twelve links of dependent origination.

From the first ground onward, ārya bodhisattvas have attained the absorption on cessation (*nirodha-samāpatti*), a very refined state in an ārya's continuum in which coarse feelings and discriminations associated with the subtle mental primary consciousness have ceased. Upon attaining the sixth ground they directly see the emptiness of dependent arising and attain the uncommon absorption on cessation due to gaining a surpassing perfection of wisdom. They can remain for a long time in deep absorption on emptiness in a way that they could not on previous grounds. Here "cessation" means emptiness, and it is a pure emptiness in which all objects of negation—from self-sufficient substantial existence up to inherent existence—have been ceased in that they do not appear to a mind of meditative equipoise on emptiness. This absorption in cessation is unique because it is supported by a superior union of serenity and insight and the surpassing perfection of wisdom.

By the power of their perfection of wisdom, sixth-grounders directly perceive the equality of saṃsāra and nirvāṇa. That is, they directly perceive that the impure world of saṃsāra and pure nirvāṇa are equal in that they are both empty of inherent existence. They move toward the end of all pollutions, yet the motivation "I will bring all other beings to awakening with me" remains vivid in their minds. Although the "end of pollutions" (the perfect end) usually refers to the ability to place the mind on suchness for as long as one wishes, here it indicates the uncommon absorption of cessation, which is deep meditation on emptiness.

Although it may be tempting for them to remain in that meditative absorption and not emerge for a long time, their great compassion and bodhicitta will not allow them to do that. Wishing to protect sentient beings who are drowning in the ocean of saṃsāra, they instead deliberately take birth in the desire realms. They have total mastery in appearing as ordinary beings in many different forms in order to work for the welfare of sentient beings.

When they emerge, in post-meditation times true-grasping may arise, but only rarely and weakly. Everything they encounter appears to them to be like a reflection in a mirror—it appears truly existent but they know that appearance is totally false.

These bodhisattvas also acquire the three doors to liberation, and understanding these three correctly, their compassion does not flag as they continue to create the causes for supreme awakening. While doing that, they consciously "take rebirth in saṃsāra"—that is, they generate manifestations that benefit sentient beings who circle in saṃsāra. This illustrates that these bodhisattvas know that although all phenomena lack inherent existence, they exist conventionally as dependent arisings (DBS 140–42).

> At this time, pursuant to his reflections on the twelve links of causes and conditions, the bodhisattva contemplates and observes the nonexistence of self, nonexistence of beings, nonexistence of any entity possessed of a life, nonexistence of any person, the absence of any inherently existent nature, and the transcendence of any agent of actions, any director of actions, or any subjective entity. He observes that, because they belong to a multiplicity of subsidiary causes and conditions, they are devoid of anything at all that exists. When he contemplates in this manner, he then acquires the direct manifestation of *the emptiness door to liberation* (*śūnyatāvimokṣamukha*). Due to perceiving the cessation of these phenomena so that they no longer demonstrate any continuity of existence, he acquires what is known as the direct manifestation of *the signlessness door to liberation* (*ānimittavimokṣamukha*). Having realized both of these things, he then no longer feels any pleasure in taking on rebirths with the sole exception of doing so to implement the mind of great compassion in the transformative teaching of beings. He then acquires the direct manifestation of *the wishlessness door to liberation* (*apraṇihitavimokṣamukha*). When the bodhisattva cultivates

> these three doors to liberation, he abandons any mark of others or a self, abandons any mark of any agent of actions or anyone who undergoes experiences, and abandons any mark of either existence or nonexistence.
>
> His mind of compassion thus progressively increases. As a result of his emphasis on the importance of the mind of compassion, he becomes diligent in the practice of joyous effort. Thus, whichever factor facilitating awakening he has not yet brought to complete fulfillment, he then wishes to bring to complete fulfillment...
>
> Children of the Buddha, so it is that the bodhisattva realizes the manifold faults of conditioned dharmas and realizes that they are devoid of any inherently existent nature, that they exist apart from any characteristic of solidly established durability, and that they are neither produced nor destroyed. Even so, he becomes conjoined with the great kindness and great compassion, refrains from forsaking beings, and then immediately acquires the direct manifestation of the light of unimpeded perfection of wisdom.
>
> Having acquired just such wisdom, he proceeds to completely perfect the cultivation and gathering together of the causes and conditions for acquiring the unsurpassed, complete, and perfect awakening (*anuttarasamyaksaṃbodhi*), and yet, even in doing so, refrains from abiding in the midst of conditioned phenomena. He contemplates the nature of conditioned phenomena as characterized by quiescent cessation and yet refrains from abiding in this either. This is because he wishes to completely perfect the factors leading to the unsurpassable awakening.

Sixth-grounders cannot be surpassed by Fundamental Vehicle arhats in terms of intelligence, and from the seventh ground onward bodhisattvas outshine these arhats through the power of their wisdom. Due to the excellent qualities of sixth-ground bodhisattvas—their surpassing practice of the perfection of wisdom, their inability to be surpassed by Fundamental Vehicle arhats in terms of intelligence, and their proximity to the seventh ground when they will outshine Fundamental Vehicle arhats through their wisdom—these bodhisattvas overpower the arhats' "arrogance." Of course arhats have already abandoned arrogance, so this points to the differences between arhats' self-oriented complacency with having attained liberation and ārya bodhisattvas' continued enthusiasm that will lead them to buddhahood.

The ripening result is having the choice to take birth in the Heaven of the Celestials Who Delight in Emanations, the fifth desire-realm heaven.

REFLECTION

The first six grounds correlate with development in the three higher trainings.

1. Bodhisattvas excel in generosity, which is the foundation for the three higher trainings.
2. They gain surpassing ethical conduct, which includes the higher training in ethical conduct.
3. Their dexterity in concentration increases, advancing the higher training in concentration.
4. They become skilled in the wisdom of the coarse and subtle aspects of the thirty-seven aids to awakening.
5. They increase their competence in the wisdom of coarse and subtle aspects of the four truths of āryas.
6. They cultivate great knowledge in the wisdom of the forward and reverse orders of the twelve links of dependent origination. Grounds 4–6 pertain to the higher training in wisdom.

Seventh Ground, the Far Advanced

> The seventh is [called] the Far Advanced
> because the number [of excellent qualities] has advanced far,
> since on this [ground] they enter moment by moment
> into the equipoise of cessation.

Through the maturation of that [ground],
they become the powerful ruler of the celestials.
They become a great leader of knowledgeable teachers,
knowing the realizations of the āryas' [four] truths.

The seventh ground is called "the Far Advanced" (*dūraṅgamā*) because these bodhisattvas' surpassing perfection of skillful means in meditation and their intelligence has advanced far from the previous ground. In each instant they are adept at absorbing into and arising from the equipoise of cessation in which all elaborations of true existence have ceased. While in meditative equipoise on emptiness, the minds of seventh-grounders are nondually fused with emptiness, and a moment later they are able to emerge from that meditation in which only emptiness, the ultimate truth, appears, and immediately perceive conventionalities in all their numerous varieties. Then in another instant, they are able to reimmerse their minds in nonduality. Although Fundamental Vehicle arhats realize the same emptiness as bodhisattvas, they are not able to do this.

On the first ground bodhisattvas outshine śrāvakas in terms of lineage because their wisdom is supported by bodhicitta and the method aspect of the bodhisattva path. Although first-grounders are not equal to Fundamental Vehicle arhats in terms of afflictions that have been overcome, they later attain full awakening, whereas arhats remain in the personal peace of nirvāṇa. On the seventh ground, bodhisattvas outshine Fundamental Vehicle arhats through the power of their wisdom due to their unique ability to enter into and arise from meditative equipoise on emptiness in each moment. While first-grounders are like the monarch's young children, seventh-grounders resemble educated and competent youths who will soon ascend the throne. The *Ten Grounds Sūtra* says (DBS 285): "On this seventh ground, it is because of the power of their actual practice that these bodhisattvas cannot be overcome by any śrāvaka or solitary realizer learner," and, "Now, on this ground, the bodhisattva achieves superiority [over Fundamental Vehicle arhats] due to the power of his own knowledge."

When these bodhisattvas become buddhas, they will actualize the perfect cessation in which they will remain in meditative equipoise on emptiness forever and simultaneously engage in multifarious activities to benefit sentient beings. This is a remarkable and unique quality of buddhas, for whom meditative equipoise on emptiness and subsequent attainment are not contradictory and occur simultaneously in one consciousness. Seventh-ground bodhisattvas have advanced far on the path that will culminate in their ability to do this (DBS 159–60, 162).

> The bodhisattva abiding on this seventh ground has for the most part gone beyond the multitudes beset by desire and the other afflictions. One who resides on the seventh ground is not designated as possessed of afflictions nor is he designated as entirely free of the afflictions. Why is this so? It is because he does not generate any of the afflictions that he is not designated as possessed of afflictions. However, because he desires to acquire the Tathāgata's knowledge and he has not yet fulfilled his aspirations, he is not yet designated as entirely free of afflictions, either...
>
> As he abides on the Far-Advanced Ground, he becomes able to enter: the bodhisattva's samādhi of skillful investigative contemplation, the skillful consideration of meanings samādhi, the mind-augmenting samādhi, the distinguishing of the treasury of meanings samādhi, the selection of phenomena in accordance with reality samādhi, the secure abiding in solidly established roots samādhi, the gateway to knowledge and spiritual superknowledges samādhi, the Dharma realm samādhi, the Tathāgata's benefit samādhi, the treasury of many different meanings samādhi, and the samādhi leading neither toward saṃsāra nor toward nirvāṇa. In this way, he completely acquires hundreds of myriads of bodhisattva samādhis whereby he is able to carry out the purifying cultivation of this ground.
>
> Having acquired these samādhis, due to thoroughly purifying wisdom and skillful means and due to deep realization of the great compassion's power, this bodhisattva then becomes one who has passed beyond the grounds of śrāvaka and solitary realizer learners and progressed toward the ground of the Buddha's wisdom...
>
> It is beginning with the sixth ground that the bodhisattva mahāsattva has the ability to enter quiescent cessation. Now, even as he abides on this ground, he is able, even in each

> successive thought, to enter into quiescent cessation while nonetheless still refraining from entering final realization of quiescent cessation. This is what is known as the bodhisattva's perfection of the inconceivable karma of body, speech, and mind wherein he courses in the sphere of ultimate reality and yet still refrains from entering the final realization of ultimate reality [nirvāṇa].

Although these bodhisattvas could enter their own personal quiescent cessation of nirvāṇa, due to compassion for sentient beings, they do not.

Their ripening result is having the choice to become leaders of the gods in the Heaven Controlling Others' Emanations, the sixth and highest of the desire-realm heavens. Due to their powerful wisdom of the four truths and their surpassing perfection of skillful means, seventh-grounders become great leaders and knowledgeable teachers. The *Ten Grounds Sūtra* (DBS 289) says, "Although he has deep fondness for nirvāṇa, he still manifests bodies in saṃsāra."

REFLECTION

1. First-ground bodhisattvas outshine śrāvaka and solitary realizer arhats by way of lineage, just as a royal child outshines a senior government minister. The minister may be wise and powerful now but the child will become the monarch one day. Unlike arhats, bodhisattvas have great compassion, great resolve, bodhicitta, and a huge accumulation of merit.
2. On the seventh ground, bodhisattvas also outshine Fundamental Vehicle arhats in terms of their wisdom. They have overpowered the arhats' "arrogance" in that, unlike arhats who seek self-complacent nirvāṇa, ārya bodhisattvas seek buddhahood. Also, the quality of their concentration and ultimate bodhicitta exceeds those of arhats.

10 | Three Pure Bodhisattva Grounds

Eighth Ground, the Immovable

> The eighth is the youth's ground, the Immovable,
> because, free of conceptions, they are unshakable.
> The range of their physical, verbal,
> and mental activities is inconceivable.
>
> Through the maturation of this [ground],
> they become a Brahmā who rules a thousand worlds;
> they are unsurpassed by the śravakas and solitary realizers
> in determining the meaning of the Dharma.

The eighth ground is called "the Immovable" (*acalā*) because these bodhisattvas are not moved by self-grasping ignorance or the self-centered attitude. Their minds are completely purified of afflictive obscurations and all grasping true existence has been extinguished. Eighth-grounders have completely abandoned all acquired and innate afflictions and their seeds; saṃsāra is forever finished for them. They have a mental body that has similitudes of a buddha's signs and marks and is the nature of mind. They are now intent on completing the two collections of merit and wisdom to attain buddhahood and commence eradicating cognitive obscurations. At the eighth ground, even bodhisattvas with modest faculties have abandoned the latencies of self-centeredness that seeks only their own liberation. Since their minds are no longer moved by self-centeredness or by afflictions, the eighth ground is called "the Immovable," and the bodhisattvas on it have the ultimate fortitude with respect to suchness.

Although eighth-grounders overcome all afflictive obscurations, sentient beings are still drowning in saṃsāra. To draw these bodhisattvas out of their peaceful meditative equipoise on emptiness, buddhas radiate light rays and remind them of their previous aspirations and the importance of actualizing their spiritual goal of full awakening. They counsel these bodhisattvas to bring forth the qualities of buddhas such as buddhas' pure physical signs, and measureless wisdom, skillful means, pure lands, and speech. The buddhas then bestow on eighth-ground bodhisattvas "many doors into the generation of the causes and conditions associated with the development of wisdom."

As a result these bodhisattvas can manifest countless bodies with which they cultivate the bodhisattva path, and with countless voices they express wisdom in limitless places of rebirth and in immeasurable pure lands where they teach countless sentient beings and make offerings and serve innumerable buddhas. They manifest or emanate bodies in various saṃsāric realms motivated by their fervent aspirations and great compassion. In this way, eighth-grounders collect merit and wisdom in order to attain buddhahood and gain the buddhas' unsurpassable wisdom, compassion, and ability to benefit sentient beings.

The eighth, ninth, and tenth grounds are called "the pure grounds" because all afflictive obscurations have been forever abandoned. On the eighth ground, they have attained the yoga of the equality of saṃsāra and nirvāṇa. Now all true-grasping and all afflictions and their seeds have been eradicated forever from their mindstreams, and there is no true-grasping during the time of subsequent attainment either. Before this, their wisdom directly realizing the emptiness of true existence of both saṃsāra and nirvāṇa was manifest during meditative equipoise, but coarse exertion was necessary to prevent true-grasping from arising during subsequent attainment. Although coarse exertion for bodhisattvas is subtle compared with the exertion of ordinary beings, they still must exert effort to bring emptiness to mind to prevent manifest self-grasping from arising.

Having mastery over nonconceptual wisdom, they abide in the meditative concentration and absorption of the total pacification of all duḥkha and striving. This means they are free from coarse striving, so very little effort is needed to enter meditative equipoise on emptiness, and in post-meditation all their activities are supported by the realization of suchness. Although they could enter personal nirvāṇa, all self-centered thought has been erased from their mindstreams, so there is no inclination to abide in liberation for their own welfare alone.

With the dawning of the eighth ground, all true-grasping and its seeds have been cut from the root and can never manifest again. On the three pure grounds, during subsequent attainment everything automatically appears as empty of true existence and like an illusion. The two truths appear simultaneously to their minds during post-meditation time, but not directly. Only buddhas can directly perceive the two truths at the same time. At the eighth ground, coarse exertion is no longer required to see things as illusion-like. For this reason, there is a big difference in the experience of illusion-like appearances for bodhisattvas on the impure grounds and those on the pure grounds.

On the first ground, bodhisattvas began making special unshakable resolves or vows. Now, due to the breadth and depth of their physical, verbal, and mental activities, these unshakable resolves are extremely potent. We can get an inkling of the vastness of these bodhisattvas' aspirations to benefit sentient beings and their activities to actualize these aspirations by reading the "King of Prayers: The Extraordinary Aspiration of the Practice of Samantabhadra." If we begin to make such aspirations now as ordinary beings, later as bodhisattvas we will be able to actualize them.

As explained in the *Ten Grounds Sūtra*, eighth-grounders attain the ten masteries (*vaśitā*) through which they manifest in various bodies to benefit sentient beings.[102] (1) With mastery over lifespan, they live as long as they wish. (2) With mastery over the mind, they remain in concentration for as long as they wish and enter and emerge from meditative absorptions as they wish. (3) With mastery over necessities, they acquire the requisites for life without effort, can materialize physical objects, and can adorn entire world systems with ornaments. (4) With mastery over karma, they experience the ripening of their karma as they wish. (5) With mastery over rebirth, they are reborn wherever they wish. (6) With mastery over unshakable resolve, they show awakening wherever and whenever they wish and display a universe filled with buddhas. (7) With mastery over aspirations, they fill worlds with buddhas and fulfill the aspirations of all beings. (8) With mastery over emanations, they manifest emanations in all buddha lands and can manifest whatever sentient beings need. (9) With mastery over pristine wisdom, they show the Tathāgata's powers, fearlessness, unshared qualities, signs and marks, and complete awakening. (10) With mastery over the Dharma, they illuminate all Dharma doors devoid of extremes and give all necessary teachings without obstacle.

By means of the ten masteries and the mental body, these bodhisattvas emanate and display various bodies to sentient beings, and by working for their welfare, eighth-grounders advance in the two collections. The ten masteries are correlated with the six perfections; the first three are the result of generosity, the fourth and fifth are the result of ethical conduct, the sixth is the result of fortitude, the seventh is the result of effort, the eighth is the result of meditative stability, and the ninth and tenth are the result of wisdom. The ten masteries are also included in the twenty-one types of pristine wisdom mentioned in the *Ornament of Clear Realizations.*

Eighth-ground bodhisattvas are well established in ten types of power (STG 331): (1) the power of the pure mind through abandoning all afflictions, (2) the power of the resolute intentions through the mind's training in the pristine wisdoms of the bodhisattva grounds and its never departing from the path, (3) the power of the great compassion through never forsaking beings, (4) the power of the great kindness through rescuing the inhabitants of all worlds, (5) the power of the *dhāraṇīs* through never forgetting Dharma they have heard, (6) the power of eloquence through distinguishing and selectively choosing from among all abilities of the Buddha, (7) the power of the superknowledges through coursing in innumerable different worlds, (8) the power of unshakable resolve through never abandoning any bodhisattva practice, (9) the power of the perfections through cultivating and accumulating all qualities of the Buddha, and (10) the sustaining power of the Tathāgata through skillful development of the knowledge of all modes. Because these bodhisattvas have acquired powers of knowledge such as these, they remain free of fault in any of their endeavors.

Śrāvaka and solitary realizer arhats cannot surpass eighth-ground bodhisattvas in terms of their understanding the meaning of the Dharma and ability to explain it to sentient beings. Both arhats and eighth-grounders are similar in having eradicated the afflictive obscurations. However, the bodhisattvas are far advanced in that they have the special method side of the path that excels in bodhicitta and the ten perfections.

This enables them to fulfill the collections of merit and wisdom and attain buddhahood, something arhats cannot do. However, if the arhats overcome the subtle self-centered attitude that seeks only their own liberation, they can generate bodhicitta through either the seven cause-and-effect instructions or equalizing and exchanging self and others. They then enter the bodhisattva path of accumulation, and by accomplishing the bodhisattva paths and grounds, they will attain buddhahood.

Eighth-ground bodhisattvas have the choice to take birth as Brahmā who rules a thousand worlds. This gives them tremendous ability to influence a vast number of sentient beings and lead them on the path.

REFLECTION

1. Think of the abilities of the bodhisattva saṅgha refuge by reviewing the ten sovereign masteries and the ten types of power. In doing so, let your faith in the Saṅgha Jewel soar.
2. Reviewing these same qualities, think that you have the ability to develop them and imagine the good you will be able to do for sentient beings when you have these.
3. As you learn of the excellent qualities of the ninth- and tenth-ground bodhisattvas, stop and reflect on them as you did with the two points above: by increasing your confidence and trust in the Saṅgha Jewel and by increasing your confidence that you too can attain these qualities and benefit sentient beings as these great bodhisattvas do.

Ninth Ground, Excellent Intelligence

> The ninth, like a regency,
> is called "Excellent Intelligence,"
> since by attaining true awareness,
> [these bodhisattvas] have excellent understanding on this [ground].

> Through the maturation of this [ground],
> they become the lord of a million worlds;
> they are unsurpassed by arhats and such
> regarding qualms in the minds of beings.

The ninth ground, Excellent Intelligence (*sādhumatī*), is so called because these bodhisattvas have exceptional ability to explain the Dharma and eliminate the doubts and misconceptions of sentient beings. They possess a special practice of four perfect knowledges: the individual perfect knowledge of phenomena that knows the specific characteristics of each phenomenon, the meanings to be expressed, the words that are terms, and the self-confidence that comes from knowing the concordant causes of things. Although ninth-grounders' ability is not the same as that of the buddhas, they are extremely skilled in teaching sentient beings according to their dispositions and can easily resolve others' qualms and inspire them on the path. Fundamental Vehicle arhats cannot surpass them in this regard. Their unimpeded knowledge of the Dharma and eloquence in speaking make them inspiring and skilled teachers. For example, to enable disciples in a great assembly to understand the Dharma, they may employ a single utterance, use many different sorts of voices, remain silent and only emanate radiant light, cause all their hair pores to express the sound of the Dharma, make things in the universe resound with the Dharma, or cause a single sound to suffuse everywhere in the world. In this way they can perform the work of the Dharma for the benefit of sentient beings.

These bodhisattvas have exceptional knowledge that is in accord with reality concerning karma and karmic actions; the characteristics of afflictions and entangling difficulties; and sentient beings' realms, minds, faculties, beliefs, resolute intentions, latent tendencies, characteristics associated with births, habitual karmic propensities, and so on.

The ninth-ground bodhisattvas are extremely astute in guiding sentient beings and will adapt the teachings and their style of teaching in order to best communicate the Dharma to sentient beings (DBS 205).

> The bodhisattva dwelling on this ground knows all such characteristics in beings' different practices and, adapting to what will cause them to gain liberation, then provides them with the cor-

> responding causes and conditions. This bodhisattva knows those factors appropriate to the teaching of beings, knows those factors conducive to the liberation of beings, and, knowing these in accordance with reality, he then teaches the Dharma for their sakes.
>
> He knows in accordance with reality the characteristics of those with affinity for the Śrāvaka Vehicle, the characteristics of those with affinity for the Solitary Realizer Vehicle, the characteristics of those with affinity for the Bodhisattva Vehicle, and the characteristics of those with affinity for the ground of the Tathāgata. He then adapts to the causes and conditions of these beings and teaches the Dharma for their sakes.
>
> He adapts to the differences in their minds, adapts to the differences in their faculties, and adapts to the differences in their predilections, and then teaches the Dharma for their sakes. So too, he adapts to their bases in practice and their bases in wisdom and then explains the Dharma for their sakes. He knows the bases for all courses of action and, adapting specifically to those, he teaches the Dharma accordingly.
>
> He adapts to beings' realms and the particular entangling difficulties they have deeply entered and teaches the Dharma for them accordingly. He adapts to their rebirth destinies, adapts to the births they have taken on, adapts to their afflictions, and adapts to the permutations in their habitual karmic propensities and therefore teaches Dharma accordingly. He adapts to whichever vehicle would conduce to liberation and therefore teaches Dharma accordingly.

The eagerness and joy with which a ninth-ground bodhisattva seeks the Dharma and then shares it with others is truly amazing. For example (DBS 211):

> He redoubles the intensity of his vigor in acquisition of the light of knowledge such as this even to this degree: Suppose that on the tip of a single hair there existed great assemblies as numerous as the atoms in an ineffable number of ineffably many world systems wherein buddhas residing in the midst of each of those assemblies

> were expounding Dharma for beings' sakes. Suppose as well that each buddha therein adapted his discourse on Dharma to the minds of however many beings were present therein, thereby causing each and every one of those beings to acquire in his own mind however countlessly many dharmas he was setting forth.
>
> Suppose also that, just as this circumstance held for any one of those buddhas, so too did it also hold for all the buddhas residing in all of those great assemblies discoursing on Dharma. And suppose too that, just as this circumstance obtained on this one single hair point, so too did it also hold for all such places throughout the worlds of all the ten directions. Even in a circumstance such as this, he is accordingly able to bring forth just such a commensurately immense power of recall that, in but a single mind-moment, he is able to absorb all of the Dharma light received from all those buddhas and still not forget even a single sentence.

A ninth-ground bodhisattva also serves all buddhas and sentient beings with such enthusiasm and delight.

The ripening result is the choice to take birth as a Brahmā lord of a million worlds.

Tenth Ground, the Cloud of Dharma

> The tenth is the Cloud of Dharma
> because [bodhisattvas] rain down the holy Dharma,
> and these bodhisattvas are anointed
> with rays of light by the buddhas.
>
> Through the maturation of that [ground],
> they become the celestial ruler of the pure land,
> masters of inconceivable objects of wisdom,
> supreme among great lords.

The tenth ground, the Cloud of Dharma (*dharmameghā*), receives its name from an analogy: from clouds rain falls and causes crops to grow. Likewise, from the billowing clouds of the tenth-ground bodhisattvas' pure mind, the rain of Dharma teachings falls on sentient beings and the crops of virtue grow in their minds. The *Ten Grounds Sūtra* (DBS 235) tells us:

> He is able, simultaneously and in but a single mind-moment, to reach everywhere without exception throughout all those worlds as numerous as or even greater than the above-described number of atoms and, in accordance with beings' dispositions, he rains down the sweet-dew Dharma rain of the good Dharma, extinguishing the smoke and flames of beings' ignorance-generated afflictions. It is for this reason that this is known as the Dharma Cloud Ground.

The remaining defilements obscuring the minds of tenth-ground bodhisattvas are very thin; they are almost buddhas. These bodhisattvas enter many samādhis at the same time, experiencing each one distinctly and knowing the differences in their functions. These bodhisattvas have knowledge of the tathāgatas' secrets and the interpenetration of eons and have gained countless liberations. They have measureless samādhis, dhāraṇīs, and superknowledges as well as unlimited memory.

Tenth-ground bodhisattvas in their last lives before attaining buddhahood require no manifest effort to motivate them to teach the Dharma or to work for the welfare of sentient beings. This is a result of having "previously planted intentions" in the past when they engaged in bodhisattvas' activities with effort while repeatedly setting the intention to be able to effortlessly and spontaneously work to benefit sentient beings. As a result, now these bodhisattvas perfectly, spontaneously, and with minimal effort continually work for the benefit of sentient beings throughout all space. Fatigue and self-centeredness do not interfere with their vast activities. They teach sentient beings in accordance with their interests, capacities, and dispositions and emanate bodies with which they can benefit others. Through conduct suitable to the mentality of each sentient being, they engage in innumerable activities to subdue sentient beings' minds and lead them on the path.

In terms of the numbers of sentient beings they teach and in terms of their awakened activities, these tenth-ground bodhisattvas are equal to the Tathāgata. However, they are still impeded from seeing both ultimate and conventional truths simultaneously, so they are unable to remain in meditative equipoise on emptiness and simultaneously teach sentient beings. They continue their practice until they break through the last of the cognitive obscurations so that they can, at the same time, see phenomena as they actually are (their ultimate nature) and work for sentient beings (by relating to them on the conventional level).

On the pure grounds—the eighth, ninth, and tenth grounds—bodhisattvas counteract the residual latencies of the afflictions and the subtle dualistic appearance they cause as well as the taints that prevent them from seeing both the ultimate and conventional truths simultaneously with one consciousness. The last cognitive obscurations are removed by the vajra-like concentration at the end of the tenth bodhisattva ground. At that time, the buddhas confer an empowerment, and in an elaborate rite of initiation, a tenth-ground bodhisattva ascends a huge lotus throne. Magnificent sparkling offerings grace the entire space, and he or she is surrounded by all buddhas and ārya bodhisattvas. The buddhas emanate splendid and awe-inspiring radiant beams of light from the hair curls on their foreheads. The light beams circle around the worlds, display the spiritual powers of the buddhas, and extinguish all suffering in the unfortunate realms, and then gather together and enter the crown of the tenth-ground bodhisattva.[103] Thereupon he receives the great wisdom empowerment and enters the realm of the buddhas where he has completely developed the buddhas' ten powers and joins the ranks of the buddhas. All remaining defilements on his mind and all cognitive obscurations have been completely eradicated and he becomes a fully awakened buddha on the Mahāyāna path of no-more-learning. Now with one consciousness he can directly perceive all conventional and ultimate truths simultaneously.

At this time, the empty nature of his mind becomes the nature truth body of a buddha; his mind becomes the omniscient wisdom truth body. He no longer has mental bodies produced by the base of latencies of ignorance and unpolluted karma; instead he has a buddha's form body that manifests spontaneously and effortlessly wherever, whenever, and in whatever form is necessary to work for the welfare of sentient beings. The extremely subtle wind, which is one undifferentiable entity with that mind, manifests as the form bodies of a buddha—an enjoyment body that teaches ārya bodhisattvas in the pure lands and emanation bodies, such as Śākyamuni Buddha, that ordinary sentient beings perceive.

The ripening result is birth in the Akaniṣṭha pure land, where these bodhisattvas will experience the empowerment described above and attain full awakening. Tenth-ground bodhisattvas may also create their own pure land in which they attain full awakening. They do this because awakening cannot be attained in the desire realm according to the Perfection Vehicle, although it can according to the Tantra Vehicle.

Whereas the Perfection Vehicle describes ten bodhisattva grounds, scriptures in the Tantra Vehicle set forth varying numbers of grounds—thirteen, fourteen, sixteen, and so forth—although there is not a big difference in meaning between these ways of counting. The demarcations of the paths in Tantrayāna differ due to its practices and special meditative techniques.

Summary of the Ten Grounds

> These ten are renowned
> as the ten bodhisattva grounds.
> The buddhas' ground is different—
> in all ways immeasurably vast.

Although the qualities of the bodhisattvas of the ten grounds are countless, the *Ten Grounds Sūtra* (DBS 248–49) summarizes them by comparing the ten grounds to:

> a large and precious *maṇi* jewel that by virtue of possessing ten characteristic aspects is able to bestow all manner of precious things on beings. What then are those ten? They are:
>
> > First, it comes forth from the great sea;
> > second, it is enhanced by the refinements of a skillful artisan;
> > third, it is made ever more refined;
> > fourth, it is rid of defilements;
> > fifth, fire is used in its refinement;

sixth, it is adorned with a multitude of precious jewels;
seventh, it is strung with precious thread;
eighth, it is placed atop a tall pillar composed of lapis lazuli;
ninth, its light rays radiate in the four directions;
tenth, it rains down the many sorts of precious things in response to the king's wishes.

In his bringing forth the precious jewel of the resolve to realize bodhi (bodhicitta), the bodhisattva mahāsattva is also possessed of ten characteristic aspects. What then are those ten? They are:

First, from the point of bringing forth that resolve, he pursues the practice of giving and abandons miserliness;
second, he cultivates the observance of the moral precepts and practices the *dhūta* austerities;
third, through the dhyāna absorptions, liberations, and samādhis, he is caused to become increasingly refined in his marvelousness;
fourth, he brings forth purity in his path practices;
fifth, he trains himself in skillful means and spiritual superknowledges;
sixth, he creates adornments based on the profound dharma of causes and conditions;
seventh, whatever he does is strung together with all the different sorts of profound skillful means and wisdom;
eighth, he is placed high atop the pillar of the spiritual superknowledges and masteries;
ninth, he contemplates the actions of beings and then emanates the light of extensive learning and wisdom;
tenth, all buddhas bestow on him their consecration of his knowledge, at which time he becomes able to carry out for all beings the works of a buddha and then falls in among those counted as possessed of omniscience.

Do Bodhisattvas Take Birth in Cyclic Existence?

Bodhisattvas on the first two paths—the paths of accumulation and preparation—are reborn under the influence of afflictions and polluted karma. However, ārya bodhisattvas, who have the direct perception of emptiness on the path of seeing and above, do not take birth in saṃsāra under the control of afflictions and karma. Afflictions are mental factors that disturb the mind. Ārya bodhisattvas have afflictions and their seeds in their mindstream until the beginning of the eighth ground. However, their afflictions are weak and don't fulfill the meaning of the term "afflictions." Thus the craving and clinging that arise so easily in the minds of ordinary beings at the time of death do not arise in their minds, and any karmic seeds that could bring rebirth in saṃsāra are unable to ripen. It is said that ārya bodhisattvas intentionally "take birth in saṃsāra" by the power of fervent aspirations and compassion. The *Sūtra Requested by Sāgaramati* claims:

> Although the [ārya] bodhisattvas are completely free from being reborn through the power of karma and afflictions, their birth in cyclic existence is due to great compassion.

An ordinary bodhisattva on the phase of supreme dharma on the path of preparation attains the uninterrupted path of the path of seeing and becomes an ārya. The continuum of the person is the same from one path to another, but the physical base—the body—of an ārya bodhisattva isn't considered a product of afflictions and karma; it is a mental body. What enables the polluted body of a bodhisattva on the path of preparation to transform into the mental body of an ārya bodhisattva? It is ultimate bodhicitta and the bodhicitta that is the purity of the extraordinary great resolve. Śāntideva tells us (BCA 1.10):

> It is like the supreme gold-making elixir,
> for it transforms the unclean body we have taken
> into the priceless jewel of a buddha-form.
> Therefore firmly seize the bodhicitta.

When sharp-faculty bodhisattvas attain the path of seeing, due to the force of their great resolve and bodhicitta, their bodhicitta transforms into the bodhicitta that is the purity of the extraordinary great resolve. These ārya bodhisattvas definitely obtain a mental body, which arises from unpolluted karma—the intention to assume such a body—and the subtle latencies of ignorance. This body is not one entity with the mind, even though it is said to be in the nature of mind in that it is not made of atoms and lacks physical impediment. The mental body of sharp-faculty bodhisattvas on the first seven grounds is free of physical pain, although it is not free from the pervasive duḥkha of conditioning. Their bodies look similar to ours, and they show the aspect of sickness, aging, death, and so forth. If these bodhisattvas manifest in the animal, hungry ghost, or hell realm to benefit sentient beings there, they are merely assuming that appearance and are not beings of that realm.

Bodhisattvas with modest faculties definitely attain a mental body at the eighth ground, but if they exert effort, they can attain one on the first through seventh grounds. Only Fundamental Vehicle arhats and pure ground bodhisattvas effortlessly obtain a mental body.

For ārya bodhisattvas, "birth in cyclic existence" refers to taking a mental body in a process analogous to the way ordinary beings take rebirth in saṃsāra. In the case of ordinary beings, spurred by the links of craving and clinging that arise while actively dying, karmic seeds ripen and beings take rebirth with the polluted aggregates of a saṃsāric realm as a result of self-grasping ignorance and polluted karma. ("Polluted" means under the influence of ignorance.) In an analogous fashion, spurred by fervent aspirations and great compassion, pure ground bodhisattvas take rebirth in mental bodies as a result of the base of latencies of ignorance and unpolluted karma. The base of latencies of ignorance refers to latencies of ignorance, which are cognitive obscurations that give rise to the subtle dualistic view. Together with unpolluted karma, they are the cause for arhats and pure ground bodhisattvas to take a mental body.

To explain this analogy: Latencies of ignorance are cognitive obscurations. In general, they cause subtle dualistic appearances—the false appearance of true or inherent existence. All sentient beings who are not in meditative equipoise on emptiness have the mistaken appearance of true existence. In ordinary beings, it arises from true-grasping and its latencies, but for śrāvaka and solitary realizer arhats and pure ground bodhisattvas (known as the three kinds of persons), the mistaken appearance of true existence arises solely from the latencies of ignorance. The base of latencies of ignorance specifically refers to manifest cognitive obscurations in the form of subtle dualistic appearances. It is called a "ground" because it has provided the basis for the continuity of afflictions since beginningless time. The base of latencies of ignorance is distinguished from latencies of afflictions because, together with unpolluted karma, it is a cause or basis for the three kinds of beings to take a mental body.

In the above analogy, the base of latencies of ignorance involved in the rebirth of the three kinds of persons is like the first link of ignorance that causes the second link of karmic formations. Analogous to these polluted karmic formations is unpolluted karma, which is karma unpolluted by ignorance and afflictions and formed by the circumstances of the latencies of ignorance. Unpolluted karma is the karma created by Fundamental Vehicle arhats and pure ground bodhisattvas when they engage in various activities in post-meditation time—for example, when they practice generosity, ethical conduct, and fortitude. This karma is never nonvirtuous and leads out of saṃsāra. It is mental action and is the substantial cause of the mental body; it is also the subtle intentional force that creates the mental body and the speech of the three kinds of persons. When engaging in activities in post-meditation time, unpolluted karma is the subtle intention that the three kinds of beings generate for their physical, verbal, and mental actions because they have cognitive obscurations.

The mental body that arises and is caused by unpolluted karma as the substantial cause and the base of latencies of ignorance as a cooperative cause is analogous to the polluted body taken by ordinary beings. The mental body is not obstructed by physical objects and cannot be seen or known by beings on levels lower than the three kinds of persons. The ceasing of a mental body is analogous to old age and death under the power of afflictions and polluted karma. It is important for ārya bodhisattvas to take a mental body, because without it there's no way for them to benefit sentient beings directly.

Although they have the appearance of ordinary beings who are born, fall ill, age, and die, ārya bodhisattvas are not under the influence of afflictions and karma. To the eyes of us ordinary beings, the mental bodies of these bodhisattvas look like those of other beings born in our realm. In fact, we may know ārya bodhisattvas but not recognize them as such. To benefit ordinary beings, they may act like us, but their motivations are always altruistic. Whether or not we benefit from these ārya bodhisattvas appearing among us is up to us. We must create the causes to meet them and to be receptive to their guidance by making ourselves suitable vessels to receive their help. Any resistance we may have—which is a product of self-centered thoughts and afflictions—hinders this, so we must do our best to apply the antidotes to these.

Although ārya bodhisattvas remain in the world owing to their great compassion for sentient beings, they are not tainted by the world's chaos and negativity. As a result of their vast collection of merit, ārya bodhisattvas do not experience physical suffering, and as a result of their profound wisdom they do not experience mental pain. At the time of death, they do not have fear, craving, and clinging as ordinary beings do; their minds remain peaceful and undisturbed. Similar to lotuses that are born in the mud but are untainted by it, ārya bodhisattvas are born in the world but are not sullied by its afflictions and suffering. They are not under the control of afflictions and can choose the type of rebirth they take. They befriend sentient beings, and possessing the method and skill to benefit us, they lead us on the path to supreme awakening.

The *Sūtra Requested by Sāgaramati* speaks of eight causes that motivate ārya bodhisattvas to take birth in our world. They aspire to (1) continue to collect merit and wisdom, (2) happily care for other sentient beings who are suffering, (3) meet the Buddha in another life, (4) without discouragement, cause sentient beings to mature in their understanding of the Dharma, (5) enthusiastically preserve the Buddha's holy Dharma by becoming holders of the transmitted and realized Dharma, (6) joyfully work for the welfare of others in any way possible, (7) not separate from a mental state that is close to the Dharma, and (8) not discard any activity associated with the ten perfections motivated by bodhicitta.

Taking birth with these motivations, ārya bodhisattvas are born only in the desire and form realms. Beings born in the formless realm do not have physical bodies and are submerged in their captivating states of concentration, making it impossible for bodhisattvas to directly benefit them. Just as polluted afflictions bind sentient beings to rebirth in saṃsāra, these eight motivations are sometimes called "afflictions" in that they bind ārya bodhisattvas to take rebirth in saṃsāra in order to benefit sentient beings.

In short, although it is sometimes said that bodhisattvas relinquish their own awakening in order to benefit others, this means that if it were most beneficial for bodhisattvas not to become awakened, they would do so out of great compassion for others. However, clearly they can benefit others much more when all obscurations have been eradicated from their mental continuums and all good qualities have been developed completely. Thus they work diligently to attain the full awakening of a buddha.

How Bodhisattvas Practice

How do ārya bodhisattvas practice? Chapter 40 of the *Flower Ornament Sūtra* entitled "On Entering the Inconceivable State of Liberation through the Practices and Unshakable Resolves of the Bodhisattva Samantabhadra" gives us a glimpse of ten unshakable resolves that form the basis of the bodhisattva Samantabhadra's practice. As mentioned earlier, these are: pay homage and respect to all buddhas, praise the tathāgatas, make abundant offerings, repent misdeeds and destructive actions, rejoice at one's own and others' merits and virtues, request the buddhas to turn the Dharma wheel, request the buddhas to remain in the world, follow the teachings of the buddhas at all times, accommodate and benefit all living beings, and dedicate all merit and virtues to the full awakening of all beings.

In particular, with his ninth unshakable resolve Samantabhadra tells how to dedicate our lives to benefiting sentient beings. Here he speaks to the youth Sudhana, who is searching for the teachings leading to supreme awakening:

> Sudhana, to accommodate and benefit all living beings is explained like this: throughout the oceans of worlds in the ten directions exhausting the Dharma Realm and the realm of empty space, there are many different kinds of living beings. That is to say, there are those born from eggs, the womb-born, those born by transformation, as well as those who live and rely on earth, water, fire, and air for their existence. There are beings dwelling in space, and those who are born in and live in plants and trees. This

includes all the many species and races with their diverse bodies, shapes, appearances, lifespans, families, names, and natures. This includes their many varieties of knowledge and views, their various desires and pleasures, their thoughts and deeds, and their many different deportments, clothing, and diets.

It includes beings who dwell in different villages, towns, cities, and palaces, as well as gods, dragons, and others of the eight divisions, humans and nonhumans alike. Also there are footless beings, beings with two feet, four feet, and many feet, with form and without form, with thought and without thought, and not entirely with thought and not entirely without thought. I will accord with and take care of all these many kinds of beings, providing all manner of services and offerings for them. I will treat them with the same respect I show my own parents, teachers, elders, arhats, and even the tathāgatas. I will serve them all equally without difference.

I will be a good doctor for the sick and suffering. I will lead those who have lost their way to the right road. I will be a bright light for those in the dark night, and cause the poor and destitute to uncover hidden treasures. The bodhisattva impartially benefits all living beings in this manner.

Why is this? If a bodhisattva accords with living beings, then he accords with and makes offerings to all buddhas. If he can honor and serve living beings, then he honors and serves the tathāgatas. If he makes living beings happy, he is making all tathāgatas happy. Why is this? It is because all buddhas, tathāgatas, take the mind of great compassion as their substance. Because of living beings, they develop great compassion. From great compassion bodhicitta is born; and because of bodhicitta they accomplish supreme, perfect awakening.

It is like a great regal tree growing in the rocks and sand of barren wilderness. When the roots get water, the branches, leaves, flowers, and fruits will all flourish. The regal bodhi-tree growing in the wilderness of birth and death is the same. All living beings are its roots; all buddhas and bodhisattvas are its flowers and fruits. By benefitting all beings with the water of great compassion, one can realize the flowers and fruits of the buddhas' and bodhisattvas' wisdom.

Why is this? It is because by benefitting living beings with the water of great compassion, the bodhisattvas can attain supreme, perfect awakening. Therefore, bodhi belongs to living beings. Without living beings, no bodhisattva could achieve supreme, perfect awakening.

Good person, you should understand these principles in this way: When the mind is impartial toward all living beings, one can accomplish full and perfect great compassion. By using the mind of great compassion to accord with living beings, one perfects the making of offerings to the tathāgatas. In this way the bodhisattva constantly accords with living beings.

Even when the realm of empty space is exhausted, the realms of living beings are exhausted, the karma of living beings is exhausted, and the afflictions of living beings are exhausted, I will still accord endlessly, continuously in thought after thought without cease. My body, speech, and mind never weary of these deeds.

Essential Points

I would now like to draw together and review some of the essential points concerning the paths and grounds of the three vehicles. Śrāvaka, solitary realizer, and bodhisattva āryas all directly perceive the emptiness of both persons and phenomena. Nevertheless, due to certain factors, their respective awakenings and the results attained on their respective paths of no-more-learning differ. The differences between the final attainment of bodhisattvas and the final attainment of śrāvaka and solitary realizer arhats depend on special factors bodhisattvas cultivate on the path.

- *Motivation of bodhicitta.* Before entering the path of any of the vehicles, a person must train in the proper motivation and aspiration. Those who enter the Śrāvaka and Solitary Realizer Vehicles have firm renunciation of saṃsāra and strong aspiration for liberation. In addition to firm renunciation and aspiring for the liberation of all sentient beings, those who enter the Bodhisattva Vehicle have stable and spontaneous bodhicitta, seeking full awakening for the benefit of all sentient beings.

- The *vast collection of merit* they create by following the method side of the bodhisattva path and their trainings in the ten perfections. For bodhisattvas, the method side of the path includes the bodhicitta motivation and the perfections of generosity, ethical conduct, and fortitude. These three perfections are not direct antidotes to cyclic existence and cultivating them alone will not overcome self-grasping ignorance, the root of cyclic existence. However, through them, bodhisattvas accumulate merit that supports the direct realization of emptiness and makes that wisdom strong enough to counteract cognitive obscurations.
- Their use of *elaborate, multifaceted reasonings to realize emptiness*. Bodhisattvas approach the refutation of inherent existence from many angles, whereas śrāvakas and solitary realizers use compact reasonings. Whenever we have detailed reasons for something, our understanding is more powerful. For example, we cultivate elaborate reasons for being angry, "This person harmed me; he harmed my friends; he helped my enemies; he harmed me in the past, in the present, and he will harm me in the future too." Due to all these (erroneous) reasons, our anger becomes very forceful and not easily waylaid. Similarly, bodhisattvas refute inherent existence by meditating with many detailed reasonings—dependent arising, the seven-point analysis, the four extremes of arising, and so forth. They examine the emptiness of causes and effects, parts and wholes; agent, action, and object; and past, present, and future. Such investigation contributes to the strength of their wisdom, enabling it to cleanse the cognitive obscurations from their minds.
- Their *abandoning cognitive obscurations as well as afflictive obscurations*. Those on the śrāvaka and solitary realizer paths meditate on the selflessness of persons and phenomena to eliminate the afflictive obscurations from their mindstream. When they have completely removed these, those śrāvaka and solitary realizer arhats abide in nirvāṇa. However, the cognitive obscurations remain. Those on the bodhisattva path abandon both afflictive and cognitive obscurations in order to attain full awakening.

- Their *cultivation of the path for three countless great eons.* Because bodhisattvas seek to abandon both obscurations, they must accumulate merit for a long time—three countless great eons if they follow the Perfection Vehicle (Pāramitāyāna). Those following the Śrāvaka Vehicle accumulate merit for three lifetimes, and solitary realizers accumulate merit for one hundred great eons. Skilled and diligent bodhisattvas who follow the Vajrayāna may attain full awakening in this very lifetime due to its skillful method for accumulating vast merit and its techniques for accessing the subtlest mind. To enter the Vajrayāna with its sophisticated meditation techniques requires powerful bodhicitta that motivates them to attain awakening quickly as well as the willingness to exert strong effort in practice.

All of these factors play a role in bodhisattvas' attainment of full awakening or nonabiding nirvāṇa, where they abide neither in saṃsāra nor in the personal peace of their own nirvāṇa. From this description, two conclusions can be drawn. First, to free ourselves from saṃsāra and to attain the awakening of any of the three vehicles, realization of the emptiness of inherent existence is essential. Second, bodhisattvas' great deeds and their collection of merit, accumulated over eons, distinguish them from śrāvakas and solitary realizers and enable them to attain full awakening.

Here it is useful to recap the ways in which bodhisattvas outshine śrāvakas and solitary realizers. A first-ground bodhisattva is said to outshine śrāvaka and solitary realizer arhats by way of lineage. The analogy is given of a royal child and a senior government minister. Although still young, the child is of royal lineage and will one day ascend the throne and become the monarch. In the same way, although a first-ground bodhisattva is not yet free from saṃsāra, she will definitely become a buddha. While she does not outshine arhats by way of her wisdom at this point, she does outshine them by way of lineage due to her great compassion, great resolve, bodhicitta, and huge accumulation of merit. Doing all actions with a special type of bodhicitta called "the purity of the extraordinary great resolve," she accumulates great merit.

Seventh-ground bodhisattvas' skill in meditation is tremendous: while in meditative equipoise on emptiness, their mind is nondually fused with emptiness, and a moment later they are able to come out of that state and perceive conventionalities. Then in another instant, they are able to again immerse their mind in nonduality. Due to this ability, they outshine śrāvakas and solitary realizers not only by way of lineage but also by way of wisdom, due to the quality of their concentration and ultimate bodhicitta.

Although the differences in the resultant state of an arhat attained by those following the Fundamental Vehicle and the state of a buddha attained by those following the Mahāyāna are noticeable, as Buddhist practitioners we respect all āryas, arhats, and buddhas. Certainly all of them are much more spiritually advanced than we are at present. Although all sentient beings will eventually enter the Mahāyāna and attain full awakening, depending on our proclivities and the teachers we encounter we may initially enter different vehicles.

Emphasizing the bodhisattva path and result is not done to disparage those who seek arhatship. Their practice and goal are indeed admirable. However, since I accept one final vehicle and that all sentient beings have the buddha nature and will eventually become buddhas, I encourage people, if they are so inclined, to enter the Bodhisattva Vehicle directly.

The wisdom realizing emptiness serves as the condition for attaining all three types of awakening—that of a śrāvaka arhat, solitary realizer arhat, and buddha. But to attain the omniscient mind of a buddha, in addition to the direct realization of emptiness, the skillful means of a bodhisattva are required.

The moment someone generates genuine spontaneous bodhicitta, she becomes a bodhisattva. In contrast, even śrāvaka and solitary realizer āryas who have directly realized emptiness and arhats who are free from cyclic existence are not bodhisattvas, because they lack bodhicitta.

To generate bodhicitta, not just ordinary compassion is needed but a powerful compassion in which we ourselves are committed to bring all sentient beings out of saṃsāric duḥkha. To generate such potent compassion that has taken the responsibility of liberating all sentient beings, two factors are necessary. We first need to see sentient beings as endearing and feel close or connected to them. Without this sense of closeness, the great compassion that wishes them to be free of all duḥkha can't arise. Second, since great compassion focuses on suffering sentient beings and wishes them to be free, we also need to understand duḥkha deeply. To develop insight into others' duḥkha, we must first focus on our own, understanding and confronting our experiences of the duḥkha of pain, the duḥkha of change, and the pervasive duḥkha of conditioning. This brings us back to understanding the four truths, the framework for all the Buddha's teachings.

I make a point of bringing us back to the four truths so that we understand the path to awakening in its entirety. In this way, we will see all the teachings are interrelated and want to practice all of them. We will not simply verbally admire the paths and grounds of a bodhisattva, but will relate them to our daily practice. To do this, it is essential to apply the teachings to our own lives. Therefore, after we learn and practice the teachings of the initial capacity disciple, we must delve deeply into the four facts seen as true by āryas—duḥkha, its origins, its cessation, and the path to that state of true freedom.

Tantric Paths and Grounds

Bodhisattvas with especially strong bodhicitta, who feel the duḥkha of sentient beings is totally unbearable, want to attain buddhahood as quickly as possible. With this motivation they seek a fully qualified tantric spiritual master, receive empowerment, and keep the ethical restraints and commitments they have taken during the empowerment. They may begin by receiving empowerment into and doing the practices of action tantra, and then proceed to performance tantra, yoga tantra, and highest yoga tantra. In highest yoga tantra they first practice the generation stage, followed by the completion stage. Due to lacking the motivation of bodhicitta, śrāvakas and solitary realizers do not enter the tantric path. However, after attaining arhatship, generating bodhicitta, and following the bodhisattva path, they may later enter the Vajrayāna.

Pāramitāyāna and Vajrayāna bodhisattvas meditate on the same emptiness—there is no difference in subtlety with respect to their object of meditation. However, the mind realizing emptiness is more subtle in Tantra—it is the fundamental innate clear-light mind.

While authors writing from the Pāramitāyāna viewpoint describe that vehicle as a full path to awakening, according to the tantric teachings at some point bodhisattvas must enter the Tantrayāna in order to make manifest the fundamental innate clear-light mind and use it to realize subtle emptiness. Having done that, they will attain the vajra-like concentration in the Tantric Vehicle, which is the final uninterrupted path prior to the attainment of buddhahood.

On the Pāramitāyāna path, bodhisattvas are said to accumulate merit for three countless great eons. We may think that this is far too long—we just don't have the energy or the will to practice for such an extended period of time. Hearing that in Vajrayāna it is possible to attain awakening in this lifetime, we may think, "That's much better. I'll do that." But to succeed, we need to have full renunciation, uncontrived bodhicitta, and a realization of emptiness. Taking that into consideration, we see that there's no shortcut to investing time and energy in practice. Bodhisattvas will do whatever is necessary to benefit sentient beings, and thus if it takes eons to attain awakening, they are willing to do that. Considering that we have wasted much more time in cyclic existence, three countless great eons isn't such a long time to practice to end cyclic existence. It is such inner strength and determination that makes bodhisattvas exceptionally suitable vessels for highest yoga tantra and enables them to succeed on that path.

It is not very practical to think about time as we study and practice the Dharma; that only makes us anxious and discontent. In fact, attaining our noble spiritual goals is done more quickly if we focus on studying and practicing the path than if we are preoccupied with how long it takes to attain the resultant buddhahood. Pushing ourselves to hurry and take shortcuts makes the path slower, like the story of the tortoise and the hare. The Tibetans have their version of this story too.

A man from eastern Tibet was going to Lhasa on horseback. On the way he met an old lady and asked her how long it takes to get to Lhasa. She replied, "If you go slowly, it takes one week. If you go very fast and run there, it takes twenty-five days." Thinking that she didn't know what she was talking about, the man galloped ahead, getting his horse to run as fast as it could. Of course the horse got exhausted, as did the man, and they had to stop for long rests. In the end, it took him twenty-five days to arrive in Lhasa. After he got there, he asked Lhasa residents how long it takes to get from that place to Lhasa, and they confirmed, "If you go slowly, it takes a week." Let's practice steadily, without pressure or anxiety and attain awakening quickly.

Gradual Path versus Sudden Awakening

Do we train gradually or is awakening attained suddenly? This topic has intrigued scholars and practitioners in all Buddhist traditions.

The Nālandā tradition that heralds from the great monastic university in ancient India, and is now followed largely in Tibetan Buddhism, in general favors the gradual approach, although as noted below there are those advocating a sudden approach. The Pāli tradition, too, in general favors gradual and systematic training. In the *Kīṭāgiri Sutta*, the Buddha says (MN 70:23):

> How does there come to be gradual training, gradual practice, gradual progress? Here one who has faith (in a teacher) visits him. When he visits him, he pays respect to him. When he pays respect to him, he gives ear. One who gives ear hears the Dhamma. Having heard the Dhamma, he memorizes it. He examines the meaning of the teachings he has memorized. When he examines their meaning, he gains a reflective acceptance of those teachings. When he has gained a reflective acceptance of those teachings, zeal springs up in him. When zeal has sprung up, he applies effort. Having applied effort, he scrutinizes. Having scrutinized, he strives. Resolutely striving, he realizes with the [mind-]body the ultimate truth (nibbāna) and sees it by penetrating it with wisdom [of the supramundane path].

This succinct passage has great meaning, for it instructs us exactly how to proceed in order to accomplish our goal of liberation. Counteracting our ignorant ways that are entrenched in misconceptions, craving, and clinging is not a quick or easy process. It requires proper external conditions, such as a qualified spiritual mentor, and proper internal conditions, such as our own sincerity, faith, diligence, and effort.

As with both the Pāramitāyāna and Vajrayāna, the Pāli training begins with forming a relationship with a teacher who is capable of instructing and guiding us. We must not take the teacher or teachings for granted and expect them to come to us. Rather, we exert energy to visit our teacher. When we visit, we empty ourselves of arrogance and the desire to prove ourselves or impress someone else, and pay respect to our teacher. Then we listen to the Dharma teachings, not once but many times. Remembering what we have heard and read is important so that we can contemplate its meaning and gain the right understanding. Examining the meaning of the teachings takes time because we do not necessarily grasp the Buddha's intention at first. In addition, there are many teachings and we need to reflect on all of them and see how they fit together and complement one another to form a complete path.

By means of this process, we gain a reflective or conceptual acceptance of the teachings. The Pāli word *khanti* (S. *kṣānti*) may be translated as acceptance, patience, fortitude, tolerance, or forbearance. It connotes being willing and able to accept what is difficult to accept for the sake of a worthwhile purpose. This is similar to the practice of the perfection of fortitude for practicing the Dharma, which necessitates accepting the doctrine of emptiness that the ignorant mind resists.

Having gained intellectual acceptance, with zeal and enthusiasm we apply effort to investigate and analyze not only the meaning of the teachings but also the nature of phenomena. That scrutiny produces its own momentum as we begin to experience for ourselves the truth of the Dharma. Striving is needed to continue with investigation and analysis, because the defilements are stubborn. But when all the factors of the path come together, by means of refined wisdom that was cultivated diligently and with care, we will realize experientially ("with the body") the supreme or ultimate truth—nirvāṇa.

Master Sheng-yen (1930–2009),[104] a wise and respected Chan (Zen) master from Taiwan, and I have discussed the notion of gradual versus sudden awakening from the viewpoint of our respective traditions. It seems that in Chan Buddhism, "awakening" refers to having direct perception of emptiness. Although we may occasionally use "awakening" in that way in the Tibetan tradition, more often than not we use the term to refer to the end point of the path, for example the awakening of a śrāvaka or a solitary realizer, or the full awakening of a buddha.

When we understand the descriptions of the path in both the Nālandā tradition and Chan tradition in light of this difference in usage, there does not seem to be a big gap. To paraphrase what Master Sheng-yen told me: "As we read in the sūtras, at the time of the Buddha, many people attained awakening suddenly, after the Buddha had spoken only a few words or gave a short teaching to them. However, Zen stories of people suddenly realizing emptiness after being hit or scolded by their teacher apply only to highly accomplished and exceptional students. Not everyone is capable of sudden awakening, and those who are not must begin with the basics of Dharma practice.

"Although those with sharp faculties and good karma may attain awakening quickly or suddenly, they still have to practice after their first experience of awakening because they are not yet free from all afflictions. Only at buddhahood is one free from all defilements.

"Aside from those exceptional disciples with sharp faculties, everyone else practices a gradual path to amass the necessary factors, such as virtue and all the abilities of great bodhisattvas, before their awakening. Although sudden awakening is possible, it is not easy; it is not like getting something for nothing. People must still keep pure precepts and cultivate bodhicitta, concentration, and wisdom. Concentration and wisdom are said to be attained simultaneously. Chan requires great effort although it doesn't follow any fixed sequential method of practice."

In Tibetan Buddhism, some texts mention a sudden or instantaneous approach that isn't limited to the structure of gradual practice. I read one Kagyü text that explicitly explained Mahāmudrā as a sudden path, stating that those who understand it in a gradual way are afflicted. In Sakya writings we find mention of the "simultaneity of realization and liberation," and the Dzogchen practice found in Nyingma also speaks of this. But even in these paths, practitioners engage in preliminary practices (T. *sngon 'gro*) to purify their mind and create merit. They also engage in a preliminary practice called "seeking the true face of mind," which is similar to the four-point analysis to realize emptiness. And needless to say, they must study and practice the fundamental Buddhist teachings.

In the Gelug tradition, Tsongkhapa accepts the notions of simultaneity and instantaneous liberation. However, he points out that what appears to be sudden realization is actually the culmination of many causes accumulated over time finally coming together and resulting in liberation. For example, in ancient times one king saw a painting of the Wheel of Life and instantly understood its meaning and gained high realizations. The final, momentary event of seeing the painting was a catalyst for this to happen. However, the actual causes for his realization had been accumulated for a long time. Similarly, one of the Buddha's first five disciples realized emptiness immediately after listening to one teaching on the four truths. He had already renounced cyclic existence, accumulated great merit, and developed single-pointed concentration.

Similarly, although we say Milarepa attained awakening in that very lifetime, that was not his first exposure to the Dharma. He had engaged in serious Dharma practice for many previous lifetimes. As a result of his strong effort, determination, proper reliance on his spiritual mentor, and correct practice of Vajrayāna, he completed the collections of merit and wisdom and attained awakening in that very life.

Some highest yoga tantra literature contains statements about "spontaneous" or "instantaneous" attainment of awakening. These statements must be understood in relation to cases of exceptional people who have a great collection of merit and uncommon mental acuity due to having attained advanced levels of realization in their previous lives. But for people like us, there is not much hope for this, and in the long run practicing a gradual path will bring quicker results.

When a spaceship is launched, it appears to be moving upward very easily, but actually this is dependent on the hard work and effort of many generations of scientists. Over a long period of time, these people have analyzed and investigated every aspect and part of the spaceship. So many causes and conditions have to assemble for the spaceship to be launched.

Similarly, gradual accumulation of causes and conditions is needed for internal mental and spiritual development. Although the entire meaning and power of the path is brought together in the highest yoga tantra, we must begin at the elementary level and gradually master many methods in order to build up our merit and wisdom.

While numerous people work together to produce a spaceship, internal spiritual development requires our own effort. It is in our hands. We cannot hire anyone to practice the path for us, nor can we take a vacation and expect the work to continue without our participation. But isn't that good news? By putting forth effort ourselves, we can and will gain realizations; we don't need to wait for someone else to do it for us and we needn't please an external being to receive boons. Having found this precious human life, we should make use of it to learn, reflect, and meditate on the Buddha's teachings so that we can gain the same clear realizations that he did. Whether or not we attain awakening in this life, consistently familiarizing ourselves with the practices will make our lives meaningful.

11 Buddhahood: The Path of No-More-Learning

THROUGHOUT the *Library of Wisdom and Compassion* series, we have spoken about the aspiration to attain the full awakening of a buddha. What are the special qualities of a buddha? What do buddhas do to fulfill their determination to benefit sentient beings effectively? These are difficult questions to answer precisely because we are not buddhas and do not know with direct perception what a buddha experiences. However, by studying, reflecting, and meditating on the path and the content of the sūtras, we can infer the excellent qualities of buddhahood.

Although the qualities of tenth-ground bodhisattvas are expansive and unimaginable, they are not able to benefit sentient beings in the same way as buddhas. Huge differences still remain between tenth-ground bodhisattvas and buddhas. For example, the former require some effort to motivate their activities of body, speech, and mind in service of others. They are not able to see the two truths simultaneously with one consciousness, which prevents them from being in meditative equipoise on emptiness and at the same time teaching and benefitting sentient beings.

Normal conventions do not necessarily apply to awakened beings. Our usual ideas about time and space do not hold in buddhahood. An eon can be condensed into just a single moment, and a single moment can be expanded into an eon. As written in Milarepa's biography, he could fit into a yak's horn without the horn becoming larger or him becoming smaller.

Reviewing the chapters on refuge,[105] where the qualities of the Buddha, Dharma, and Saṅgha are described in detail, will give us an idea of the awakened state that we seek to actualize. In this chapter, we will look at more specific aspects of buddhahood, including the buddha bodies, the relationship among buddhas, what buddhas perceive, their awakening activities, and the inseparability of a buddha's body, speech, and mind.

The Buddha Bodies

The buddha bodies were explained in *Following in the Buddha's Footsteps* in the context of the Three Jewels that are our objects of refuge. Now we will go into more depth about them, seeing them as the result of the Bodhisattva Vehicle. Buddhahood is the state of having removed all defilements from the mind and having developed all excellent qualities. Each buddha has four buddha bodies—"body" meaning collections of qualities. We may speak of two, three, four, or five buddha bodies, depending on how many subdivisions of the basic two bodies—the truth and form bodies—are listed. To review, here is the overall layout of the buddha bodies:

(1) The *truth body* (*dharmakāya*) has the nature of the perfect abandonment of all defilements and the perfect realization of all excellent qualities. It is of two types:

1. The *wisdom truth body* (*jñāna dharmakāya*) is the omniscient mind of a buddha, which has three principal qualities. With *knowledge* (*jñāna*) buddhas know all phenomena; with *compassion* (*anukampā*) they seek to benefit sentient beings without hesitation; and with *power* or *ability* (T. *nus pa*) from their own side they lack all impediments to exercising their skillful means.
2. The *nature truth body* (*svabhāvika dharmakāya*) is of two types:

    - The *naturally pure nature truth body* is the emptiness of inherent existence of a buddha's mind.

    - The *adventitiously pure nature truth body* is a buddha's true cessations of afflictive obscurations (*kleśāvaraṇa*) that bind us to saṃsāra, and cognitive obscurations (*jñeyāvaraṇa*) that prevent us from knowing ultimate and veiled truths simultaneously with one consciousness.

(2) The *form bodies* (*rūpakāya*) are forms in which a buddha appears in order to enact the welfare of sentient beings. These are of two types:

1. An *enjoyment body* (*saṃbhogakāya*) is the form that a buddha manifests in his or her Akaniṣṭha pure land to teach ārya bodhisattvas.
2. *Emanation bodies* (*nirmāṇakāya*) are the forms a buddha manifests that are perceivable by ordinary beings. These are of three types:

   - A *supreme emanation body*—for example, Śākyamuni Buddha—turns the Dharma wheel.
   - An *ordinary emanation body* manifests in diverse appearances of various people or things.
   - An *artisan emanation body* subdues sentient beings' minds through showing certain worldly skills.

The dharmakāya is the fulfillment of a buddha's own purpose, in the sense that it is the complete perfection of the mind. Form bodies are the fulfillment of others' purpose because a buddha manifests these in order to benefit others.

There is another way to look at the aims or purposes of bodhisattvas: They aspire to actualize both the truth bodies and form bodies that purport to serve their own purpose. But now serving their own purpose becomes a means to fulfilling the purpose of others. This is likened to a thirsty traveler seeking water. The final purpose is to procure water to quench their thirst; the cup to drink it in is a means to fulfill that final purpose. For bodhisattvas, the water they seek is the buddhahood of all other sentient beings. Their own buddhahood is incidental. Stop and think about that for a moment. What would it be like to have such a motivation yourself? It would be completely transformative, wouldn't it? For this reason, Śāntideva marvels (BCA 1.10, 13, 26):

> Bodhicitta is like the supreme gold-making elixir,
> for it transforms the unclean body we have taken

into the priceless jewel of a buddha-form.
Therefore firmly seize this bodhicitta.

All other virtues are like plantain trees;
for after bearing fruit, they simply perish.
Yet the perennial tree of bodhicitta
unceasingly bears fruit and thereby flourishes without end.

This intention to benefit all beings,
which does not arise in others even for their own sake,
is an extraordinary jewel of the mind,
and its birth is an unprecedented wonder.

Together the wisdom dharmakāya and the nature dharmakāya are the last two of the four truths in their complete or final aspect: the wisdom dharmakāya being the final true path and the nature truth body being the final true cessation. These are one nature and different isolates—that is, one cannot exist without the other, yet they are nominally different. Candrakīrti says (MMA 11.17):

Through having burned completely the dry firewood of knowable objects,
that pacification is the truth body of the conquerors.
It is without arising and without cessation
and [thus] the mind has stopped, whereby [the dharmakāya] is actualized by the [enjoyment] body.

At the beginning of the eighth ground all afflictive obscurations—the afflictions and their seeds—have been eradicated by the pristine wisdom of meditative equipoise that directly and nonconceptually realizes emptiness. The cognitive obscurations—the latencies of the afflictions and the subtle dualistic view—still cover the mind; they are the "dry firewood of knowable objects" that are burned by the vajra-like concentration (*vajropamasamādhi*) at the end of the tenth ground. Here "knowable objects" refers to the cognitive obscurations, because cognitive obscurations cause all knowable objects to appear to the mind dualistically, as inherently existent.

When these obscurations have been pacified by this wisdom of meditative equipoise the final true cessation is actualized. This wisdom is free from inherently existent arising and ceasing and it has destroyed all latencies of grasping inherently existent arising and ceasing. This pacification—the cessation of cognitive obscurations—is the nature dharmakāya, and the wisdom realizing it is the wisdom dharmakāya. "The mind has stopped" doesn't mean the mind has become nonexistent. Rather, "mind" refers to all conceptual minds and conceptual mental factors. Since they have been completely pacified, there is no dualistic appearance of inherent existence, and the nonconceptual pristine wisdom and suchness are experienced undifferentiably, like water poured into water. Ultimate reality—suchness—is not known in the manner of dualistic appearance. Thus, on the conventional level, it is said that the truth body is actualized or attained by the enjoyment body of that buddha. Candrakīrti says (MMA 11.18):

> This body of peace arises like a wish-granting tree;
> and like a wish-fulfilling jewel it does not engage in
> conceptualization.
> Until [all] beings are free it remains eternal as a resource for the
> world;
> it appears to those [bodhisattvas] who are free of conceptual
> elaborations.

Buddhas newly attain supreme awakening in the aspect of the enjoyment body in the pure land of Akaniṣṭha. The enjoyment body is a body of peace in that it is free from the turbulence of conceptual minds. It appears only to ārya bodhisattvas and remains eternally for the benefit of sentient beings until saṃsāra ends. Although buddhas do not engage in conceptualization, thinking "I shall benefit this sentient being," like a wish-granting tree and a wish-fulfilling jewel, they effortlessly work for the welfare of sentient beings.

Candrakīrti says (MMA 11.44):

> Again you, who possess the unmoving [truth] body, descend to
> the three realms of existence.
> Your emanations come [from Akaniṣṭha], are born, and teach the
> wheel of peace and awakening.

> In this way you compassionately guide to nirvāṇa all beings of the world
> who are ridden with deceitful conducts and are bound by numerous snares of expectations.

The unmoving body is the dharmakāya that does not move from meditative equipoise on emptiness. Simultaneous with the attainment of awakening, a person attains the dharmakāya, the enjoyment body that appears in Akaniṣṭha, and the emanation body. When buddhas manifest as a supreme emanation body, such as Śākyamuni Buddha in the desire realm, they display the twelve deeds.

Emanation bodies do not get tired, frustrated, or discouraged by sentient beings' ignoring their help or even denouncing it. Rather, they continue to benefit each sentient being in accord with that sentient being's disposition and temperament. When we think about it, this is truly remarkable, isn't it? We may try to help someone in a small way, but if that person criticizes us, we become angry, fed up with their lack of appreciation for our effort, and quit.

Having this brief introduction to the buddha bodies, we'll now look at them in more depth.

Wisdom Dharmakāya

The wisdom dharmakāya is the ultimate true path, the omniscient mind of a buddha, the final pristine wisdom that directly and nonconceptually realizes all existents. Eternal, it never discontinues or relapses to a state of defilement. As a mind that apprehends different objects each moment, a buddha's mind is impermanent.

Buddhas possess all true cessations and all wisdom—the wisdom knowing ultimate truths, which knows phenomena's actual mode of being, suchness, and the wisdom knowing conventional truths, which knows the varieties of phenomena. Their wisdom knowing ultimate truths also knows conventional truths, and their wisdom knowing the varieties of phenomena also knows their actual mode of being. Buddhas' wisdom dharmakāya includes both wisdoms, which are inseparable and one nature with their abandonment of both obscurations. All their consciousnesses are omniscient and cross-functional. For example, their visual consciousness can perceive sounds, smells, tastes, as well as tactile and mental objects.

The *Ornament of Clear Realizations* speaks of twenty-one kinds of dharmakāya wisdom possessed by buddhas. Some of these wisdoms are practiced by bodhisattvas and those who haven't entered the path and are brought to fruition at buddhahood. Most of the practices to gain these wisdoms have been described in previous volumes; this is a good opportunity to review your understanding of them.

1. Thirty-seven harmonies with awakening (see chapters 11–14 in *Following in the Buddha's Footsteps*).
2. Four immeasurables (see chapter 1 in *In Praise of Great Compassion*).
3. Eight liberations (see chapter 8 in *Footsteps*).
4. Nine serial absorptions (see chapter 8 in *Footsteps*).
5. Ten totalities (*kasiṇa*): by single-pointed meditation on one or another of the ten kasiṇas (earth, water, fire, air, blue, yellow, red, white, space, and consciousness), its specific characteristic can be transferred to other phenomena. For example, the hardness of earth can be transferred to water so the meditator can walk on it, or the quality of space can be given to earth so a buddha can walk through a mountain.
6. Eight dominants. Four of these dominate or control shape: (1) perceiving themselves as embodied, buddhas have control over large forms; (2) perceiving themselves as physically embodied, they have control over small physical forms; (3) perceiving themselves as being disembodied, they have control over large forms; and (4) perceiving themselves as disembodied, they have control over small forms. Here "perceiving themselves as embodied or disembodied" means they are visible or invisible to others. Four dominate or have power over color: Perceiving themselves as disembodied, buddhas can control the four colors of external phenomena—blue, yellow, white, and red. By perceiving themselves as disembodied or having an indestructible form, they perceive material objects without the solid reality that we believe them to have. They can change big into small and small into big, performing many miraculous feats.
7. Concentration without defilement is the ability to not act as an object provoking others' afflictions. Before śrāvakas enter a village for alms,

they examine with their superknowledge if their presence will provoke others' attachment or anger. If so, they do not enter the village. Buddhas, to the contrary, go everywhere and benefit others by teaching the Dharma and employ all means to prevent afflictions from arising in the minds of others.

8. Exalted knower of aspirations. Śrāvakas must enter the fourth dhyāna when they wish to know something. Buddhas' exalted knowers are much vaster and have five unique qualities: (1) they know things effortlessly and spontaneously; (2) free from afflictive obscurations, they know phenomena without attachment; (3) free from cognitive obscurations, they know phenomena without any impediment; (4) they know all phenomena all the time without interruption; and (5) they can simultaneously answer all questions of each sentient being even if they are asked at the same time in different languages.
9. Six superknowledges (see chapter 8 in *Footsteps*).
10. Four individual perfect knowledges: (1) with perfect knowledge of the doctrine, they know all words of all aspects of the Dharma without confusion; (2) with perfect knowledge of the meaning, they know all the meanings expressed by those words; (3) they have perfect knowledge of how to teach, including all languages of sentient beings; and (4) they have perfect knowledge that is limitless intelligence and ability.
11. Four complete purities. Buddhas have: (1) purity of bodily existence, with mastery of assuming, abiding, and relinquishing a body; (2) purity of objects in that they emanate and transform the five sense objects; (3) purity of the mind that is the ability to enter and leave countless concentrations in each moment; and (4) purity of knowledge that is mastery over emptiness.
12. Ten masteries (*vaśitā*). These are listed in the explanation of the eighth ground.
13. Ten powers of a tathāgata (*tathāgatabala*, T. *de bzhin gshegs pa'i stobs*); see chapter 2 in *Footsteps*.
14. Four fearlessnesses or self-confidences (see chapter 2 in *Footsteps*).
15. Three behaviors without concealment: buddhas have no need to conceal their actions because all their physical, verbal, and mental activities are virtuous.
16. Three establishments of mindfulness: buddhas have equanimity

toward (1) those who want to listen and do so respectfully, (2) those who do not want to listen, and (3) those with a mixture of both attitudes.

17. Absence of forgetfulness and negligence: buddhas never forget or neglect the well-being of sentient beings, nor do they ever forget anything, no matter how long ago it occurred.
18. Complete destruction of latencies: unlike arhats, buddhas have abandoned all latencies of afflictions and all dysfunctional behavior.
19. Great compassion for all sentient beings that knows the situation of each sentient being, their disposition, who is receptive to the Dharma, and so forth, and helps accordingly (see *In Praise of Great Compassion*).
20. Eighteen unique qualities of a buddha (see chapter 2 in *Footsteps*).
21. Three exalted knowers: the exalted knowers of all aspects (omniscience), the knower of paths (of bodhisattvas), and the knower of bases (practices for śrāvakas and solitary realizers). An alternative explanation is that buddhas know all phenomena; they know the cause, nature, and result of the paths of śrāvakas, solitary realizers, and bodhisattvas (this knowledge is shared by bodhisattvas); they know that all phenomena of the base—the aggregates, sources, constituents, and so forth—are empty (this knowledge is shared by śrāvakas).

Of the twenty-one kinds of dharmakāya wisdom, the ten powers, four fearlessnesses, eighteen unique qualities, three behaviors without concealment, three establishments of mindfulness, complete destruction of latencies, and great compassion are qualities possessed only by buddhas. The ten strengths and four individual perfect knowledges are shared by bodhisattvas. All the others are shared by buddhas, bodhisattvas, solitary realizers, and śrāvakas.

Another way of classifying the wisdoms of the wisdom dharmakāya is into the five pristine wisdoms. In tantra, each of these is correlated with a specific dhyāna buddha, aggregate, wisdom, affliction, color, direction, symbol, empowerment, lineage, and element.[106]

A more concise way of speaking of the wisdom dharmakāya is in terms of (1) the omniscient knower that realizes suchness—emptiness, the ultimate truth—and (2) the omniscient knower that realizes the varieties of phenomena—conventionalities. Although both of these wisdoms perceive all existents, they are classified in terms of their primary object.

Clearly knowing all sentient beings' previous actions as well as their present dispositions and interests, buddhas know how to best benefit each being. Due to their great compassion and bodhicitta motivation, without having to think about what to do they naturally act to benefit sentient beings according to their receptivity. They do this through manifesting form bodies that effortlessly perform awakened activities.

REFLECTION

1. Contemplate the twenty-one kinds of the pristine wisdom of buddhas, knowing that they use these to guide you to full awakening. Know that the bodhisattvas are developing these wisdoms and are also using them to help you. With this knowledge, take refuge in the Three Jewels.
2. Contemplate the twenty-one kinds of the Buddha's pristine wisdom and think that these are the qualities you will have upon attaining buddhahood. Feel uplifted knowing that you have the potential to cultivate and perfect these.
3. Make a strong resolve to engage in the practices to develop these wisdoms.

Nature Dharmakāya

The nature dharmakāya is so called because it is emptiness, the ultimate nature of the mind. It is the natural state of the mind because it is permanent and unaltered by causes and conditions. Although the nature of ordinary sentient beings' minds is undefiled and pure by nature, it is still covered by adventitious defilements. When sentient beings attain buddhahood, these defilements have been forever eliminated. This indicates a double purity: the natural purity, which is the emptiness of the mind, and the purity of adventitious defilements, which is the true cessation that came about by cultivating the path and removing defilements. The naturally pure nature dharmakāya is the emptiness of a buddha's mind that has been empty of inherent existence from beginningless time. The adventitiously pure nature dharmakāya is the emptiness of a buddha's mind that has newly eliminated all adventitious obscurations. The *Sublime Continuum* speaks of four attributes of the nature dharmakāya (RGV 85):

> Because [the purified buddha nature] is the *truth body* [of all
> buddhas and it is] the *tathāgata*,
> it is [also] the *[ultimate] truth of āryas* as well as the ultimate nirvāṇa.
> Thus [since those are just variants in name], just as the sun and [its] rays [are
> indivisible, the truth body that is the *final nirvāṇa* and its] qualities are
> indivisible [in nature].
> Hence there is no [fully qualified] nirvāṇa aside from buddhahood.

1. The nature dharmakāya is the *truth body* because this ultimate purity exists indivisible from the potential for the arising of a buddha's qualities in the continuums of sentient beings. That is, in the naturally pure buddha nature in the continuum of sentient beings—the mind's emptiness, its suchness—there exists the potential to transform into a buddha's dharmakāya. This "dharmakāya" is present in the buddha essence (*tathāgatagarbha*) of each sentient being. Although the naturally abiding buddha nature in the continuums of sentient beings may be called the "dharmakāya," it is not the actual dharmakāya. However, when it is purified by applying antidotes—the collections of merit and wisdom—the defilements are totally eradicated and it becomes the ultimate dharmakāya of a buddha, the actual nature dharmakāya of a buddha.
2. It is the *tathāgata* because it is the emptiness of a buddha's mind that directly perceives its own ultimate nature. This ultimate nature is the naturally pure buddha nature that is now free from all defilements.
3. The nature dharmakāya is the *āryas' ultimate truth* because it is the ultimate nature of all phenomena. Unlike veiled truths, it is not false or deceptive and exists in the way it appears. It is empty and it appears empty to the mind directly perceiving it.
4. It is *nonabiding nirvāṇa* because it is an abandonment brought about by applying the antidotes to the defilements. Even though the naturally abiding buddha nature has been quiescent by nature

> since beginningless time—the defilements have never penetrated its nature—the defilements must still be removed. Nonabiding nirvāṇa is free from the extremes of saṃsāra and self-complacent nirvāṇa. The special meditative concentration that is the union of serenity and insight serves to stop saṃsāra by eliminating the defilements, and great compassion prevents self-complacent nirvāṇa by leading the yogī to full awakening.

With the attainment of buddhahood, our naturally abiding buddha nature—the suchness of our mind with defilements—becomes the nature dharmakāya, and our transforming buddha nature—all conditioned phenomena that have the capacity to transform into a buddha's wisdom truth body—sheds all defilements and completes all excellent qualities to become the wisdom dharmakāya. The totally pure state, the nature dharmakāya of a tathāgata, is immutable. The *Sublime Continuum* describes the nature dharmakāya in terms of four characteristics—permanent, stable, peaceful, and unalterable—that make it free from four characteristics of saṃsāra—birth, death, sickness, and aging, respectively.

The nature dharmakāya is *permanent*. While ordinary beings are born in saṃsāra due to ignorance and polluted karma, and ārya bodhisattvas take birth in saṃsāra due to the base of latencies of ignorance and unpolluted karma, the dharmakāya of a tathāgata does not take *birth* in either of these ways. A tathāgata's dharmakāya is unending—this is the meaning of "permanent" in this context. With its double purity, it is free from both (1) the twelve links of dependent origination fueled primarily by the afflictive obscurations, and (2) the twelve links of unafflicted dependent origination fueled by the base of latencies of ignorance and unpolluted karma, and supported by cognitive obscurations. There is no birth or death in the dharmakāya; it is permanent.

Being permanent, the nature dharmakāya of a buddha is not produced by causes and conditions, but it is attained by effort and fulfilling the two collections. The principal purifying factor that transforms the natural buddha nature into a buddha's nature body is the wisdom directly perceiving emptiness complemented by the method aspect of the path—bodhicitta and the other perfections. While the unconditioned qualities of a buddha are not produced, they do come into existence in dependence on other factors. The conditioned qualities of a buddha are produced by causes and conditions and are impermanent phenomena.

The Tathāgata's dharmakāya is *stable* because it is the final, unfailing refuge for sentient beings. Because it possesses natural purity and purity of all adventitious defilements, it abides continuously, without end, and is thus a stable refuge for beings lost in saṃsāra. In the dharmakāya, there is no *death* due to afflictions, and there is no death by the "inconceivable transformation" of the ceasing of a mental body. Therefore it is stable.

The dharmakāya is *peaceful* because it is naturally free from the two extremes of superimposition and deprecation, and in this sense it is nondual. Dwelling in suchness without conceptuality, it is naturally peaceful and also pacified of all adventitious defilements. It is not harmed by the *sickness* of afflictions and karma or by the nonafflictive latencies of ignorance. For this reason, too, it is peaceful.

The dharmakāya is *unalterable* because it is not affected by either afflictive or nonafflictive phenomena—such as polluted and unpolluted karma—and therefore doesn't undergo *aging*. Being unconditioned, it isn't subject to change and destruction due to the ripening of either polluted or unpolluted karma.

Buddhas are totally free from the extremes of saṃsāra and nirvāṇa. In an *ultimate sense*, this means that they do not grasp at either saṃsāra or nirvāṇa as inherently existent, nor do these appear inherently existent to buddhas.

In a *conventional sense*, freedom from the extreme of saṃsāra means that buddhas and ārya bodhisattvas do not see birth in saṃsāra as something to be totally abandoned in the same way that śrāvakas and solitary realizers do. While ārya bodhisattvas eradicate the causes of rebirth in saṃsāra from their own minds, they appear in saṃsāric worlds in order to benefit sentient beings and lead them to liberation and full awakening. Freedom from the extreme of nirvāṇa means they do not view personal nirvāṇa as the complete attainment, as do śrāvakas and solitary realizers. This is because buddhas and ārya bodhisattvas seek full awakening, nonabiding nirvāṇa. Buddhas have the means to stop these two extremes: through wisdom they have destroyed afflictions and polluted karma and do not fall to the extreme of saṃsāra, and through great compassion and bodhicitta they have overcome the wish to abide in the personal peace of nirvāṇa and do not fall to the extreme of personal nirvāṇa.

To be considered the nonabiding nirvāṇa—the unique state of a buddha that is beyond both saṃsāra and personal nirvāṇa, all the countless and inconceivable excellent qualities must be purified and complete in every aspect.

While śrāvakas and solitary realizers have also attained nirvāṇa, theirs is not the nonabiding nirvāṇa of buddhas, because it has yet to abandon every single adventitious defilement by the application of counterforces. In addition, śrāvaka and solitary realizer arhats do not have the limitless wisdom and pristine wisdom of buddhas. Nor have they developed their transforming buddha nature to its fullest by generating all the inconceivable qualities of fully awakened ones. Absorbed in meditative equipoise on emptiness, they are not inclined and do not have the ability to manifest the two form bodies to benefit sentient beings.

REFLECTION

1. Review and contemplate the four attributes of a nature dharmakāya: truth body, tathāgata, āryas' ultimate truth, and nonabiding nirvāṇa.
2. Review and contemplate the four characteristics of the nature dharmakāya: permanent, stable, peaceful, and unalterable.

Form Bodies

The pristine wisdom of the dharmakāya appears as the two form bodies—the enjoyment body and emanation bodies. Some people say that form bodies are mere other-appearances to sentient beings—that is, they exist in the continuums of sentient beings who see them but do not exist in the buddhas' continuums. They think that when someone becomes fully awakened, he or she is free from all elaborations, whereas form bodies, because they appear to sentient beings, are involved with elaborations. They assert that since form bodies cannot be included in buddhas' completely purified continuums, they must be in sentient beings' continuums, which are not free from elaborations. It is like the reflection of the moon in water: the moon is not in the water but the reflection is. Similarly, form bodies are within the sentient beings who see them.

Others refute this idea, saying that an awakened buddha can't be in the minds of sentient beings. If a buddha were, it would mean that bodhisattvas created the cause to attain buddhas' form bodies, but the buddhas' form bodies that are the final results of their practice were in the continuums of sentient beings. That contradicts the law of karma and its effects, in which the person who creates the cause is the one who experiences the effect.

Furthermore, saying the form bodies are in sentient beings' continuums would mean that we were once undefiled buddhas and later became defiled sentient beings. This is impossible because once the defilements have been completely eradicated, there is nothing that can cause a pure mind to become impure. The other alternative is that we are already buddhas, but if that were the case, ignorant buddhas would exist, and that is also not possible.

The Sakya tradition says that the resultant qualities of a buddha are in the clear-light mind of sentient beings as potential. We are not yet awakened, but we have the potential to become so.

When realized beings have actually seen their meditational deities, what are they seeing? Having a vision of a form body of a buddha is very mysterious and not easily explained.

A buddha's two form bodies are not made of material such as atoms and molecules. They are not appearances in the minds of disciples but exist as part of a buddha's continuum. Buddhas appear in forms that can skillfully relate to the various sentient beings, according to their differing levels of mental purity, dispositions, and interests.

The Enjoyment Body

An *enjoyment body* (*saṃbhogakāya*) is defined as "a final form body possessing the five certainties." It is the form a buddha takes in order to teach ārya bodhisattvas in the pure land. An enjoyment body is so called because with it a buddha brings enjoyment of the Dharma to the assembly of āryas; there is communal enjoyment of the Dharma. Each buddha has an enjoyment body that appears to ārya bodhisattvas in a pure land to teach them the Mahāyāna doctrine. In this way the enjoyment body of a buddha directly accomplishes the benefit of ārya bodhisattvas and indirectly accomplishes the benefit of ordinary beings by radiating emanation bodies. Amitābha Buddha in the Sukhāvatī pure land is an example of an enjoyment body. Mañjuśrī, Tārā, Avalokiteśvara, and other deities are also enjoyment bodies.

The body of the person who is an enjoyment body is a nonmaterial vajra body that has the nature of pristine wisdom. It lacks flesh, blood, empty spaces, and so forth, and is not born from an embryo. In each pore a buddha displays countless bodies of buddhas surrounded by bodhisattvas, gods, demi-gods, and humans.

Enjoyment bodies have five certainties, qualities that an enjoyment body is certain to have: (1) the certainty of *abode* is that it resides only in Akaniṣṭha;[107] (2) the certainty of *body* is that it is adorned with the clear and complete thirty-two signs and eighty marks of a buddha; (3) the certainty of *retinue* is that an enjoyment body is surrounded only by ārya bodhisattvas; no other sentient beings have the purity of mind or karma to receive teachings directly from an enjoyment body; (4) the certainty of *Dharma* means that enjoyment bodies teach only the Mahāyāna Dharma; and (5) the certainty of *time* shows that enjoyment bodies remain eternally, as long as cyclic existence is not emptied of sentient beings.

In ancient Indian culture, these thirty-two physical signs indicate a great person. In the Pāli sūtras, they are also mentioned as signs of a buddha. From a Mahāyāna perspective, they are found in both enjoyment bodies and supreme emanation bodies. In the context of supreme emanation bodies, they are part of the conventional appearance of a buddha as a human. Buddhas appear in this way to disciples in order to guide them on the path to higher rebirth and highest goodness. The thirty-two signs and eighty marks are ripenings, but they are not ripened results, because ripened results are neutral (unspecified), whereas the thirty-two signs are virtuous.

The thirty-two signs are presented from the perspective of their causes and indicate a great person. The eighty marks are presented from the perspective of being results and reveal the person's inner qualities. The list below is from the *Ornament of Clear Realizations* and was taken from the Prajñāpāramitā Sūtras. Another list is from the *Sūtra Requested by the Precious Daughter* (*Ratnadārikā Sūtra*) and is also found in the *Sublime Continuum*. The causes for each sign give us an idea of virtuous activities to engage in.

1. On the sole of each foot and palm of each hand is the impression of a thousand-spoke wheel. Although a buddha's feet do not touch the ground, and thus do not harm sentient beings that may be underneath, they leave the imprint of a wheel when he walks. The cause for this sign is greeting and escorting our spiritual mentors and selflessly offering service to others.
2. The soles of the feet are as smooth and level as the underside of a tortoise's shell, so they are always firmly planted. The causes for this are firmly living in accord with the transmitted and realized Dharma and safeguarding the three types of ethical restraints: the prātimokṣa precepts that restrain physical and verbal negativities; the samādhi restraints arising from single-pointed concentration that keep the mind from wandering, restlessness, and laxity; and the unpolluted restraint that arises from realizing emptiness and restrains the mind from afflictions.
3. A web of white light connects the fingers and toes. Rings can pass through the web, and the fingers retain their individual movement. This arises from practicing the four ways of gathering disciples.
4. The skin is unwrinkled and smooth like a baby's skin. This comes from generously providing others with nourishing food and drink, not just giving them what we don't like or don't want ourselves.
5. Seven parts of the body are rounded and slightly raised—the tops of each hand, foot, shoulder, and the back of the neck. This derives from giving others not only physical nourishment but also other pleasing and usable objects, such as shelter and clothes.
6. The root of the fingernails and toenails are extremely long. This comes from saving the lives of animals about to be slaughtered.
7. The heels of the feet are broad. The cause for this is compassionately going out of our way to help others, save their lives, or make them comfortable.
8. The body is very straight and is seven cubits tall (usually people's height is about four cubits). This arises from totally abandoning killing any sentient being.
9. The elbows and kneecaps don't protrude. This is from intensely engaging in the six perfections.

10. The bodily hairs grow up. This arises due to engaging in constructive practices and inspiring others to do the same.
11. The calves are well-rounded, like the legs of an antelope. This sign derives from admiring and mastering medicine, other sciences, arts, and crafts, and using these skills to benefit others.
12. The arms are extremely long. This is a result of never sending beggars away empty-handed.
13. The private organ is recessed and remains concealed. This is caused by strictly keeping the pledges of secrecy and safeguarding the confidential words of others.
14. The skin is luminous and golden. This comes from offering soft and comfortable seats to others.
15. The skin is fine and unblemished, like purified gold. The cause for this is accommodating those needing lodging and always providing excellent housing.
16. The body hair curls clockwise with never more than one hair growing from each pore. This is a result of completely abandoning mental wandering, busy work, and bustling confusion.
17. The white treasure-like strand of hair on the mid-brow curls very tightly clockwise. When pulled, it extends a huge distance, and when released, it tightly recoils. This arises from respectfully serving all superiors—parents, teachers, elders, abbots, and so forth—venerating them as a crown jewel. It also arises from helping others achieve upper rebirths.
18. The upper torso becomes progressively broader, like that of a lion. This arises from never humiliating or looking down on others regardless of their power, status, wealth, and so forth. It also comes from not scolding others privately or publicly and not belittling others' beliefs or religious traditions.
19. The tops of the shoulders are round and well-connected to the neck, and the network of veins isn't visible. This comes from freely giving praise and encouragement to all others, not just to friends.
20. The area between the collarbone and the shoulder is round, fleshy, and full, without any hollow depression. This derives from giving others medicine and healthy food.
21. No matter what is eaten, it always tastes delicious. This comes from

nursing the sick, old, and infirm, and especially caring for those who others find repulsive.

22. The body is stately and well-proportioned, like a full-grown peepul (bodhi) tree. The cause is building public gardens and parks for others' enjoyment and encouraging others to do the same.
23. The crown protrusion is made of radiant flesh; it is round and circles clockwise. At a distance, it seems to be four finger-widths high, but upon close scrutiny, its height cannot be measured. This is a result of visualizing our spiritual master on the crown of our head, visiting temples and monasteries, and practicing in them.
24. The tongue is extremely long and is able to extend to the top of the head, ears, and chest. This arises from speaking kindly to others, encouraging them, and treating them as gently as an animal licking her young.
25. The voice is melodious like that of an ancient song-sparrow, flowing without effort. It also resembles Brahmā's voice and temporarily relieves the suffering of those who hear it. This derives from communicating the Dharma in the individual language of each sentient being.
26. The cheeks are round and full like those of a lion. This comes from completely abandoning idle talk.
27. The eyeteeth are more brilliantly white than other teeth. The cause is offering special praise to the buddhas and bodhisattvas and showing them great respect.
28. The teeth are all of equal length. This arises from abandoning the five wrong livelihoods and always earning our living honestly.
29. The teeth are perfectly straight and properly aligned with no gaps between them. This comes from speaking the straight truth for three zillion eons, being honest, and not being devious or crooked with others.
30. There are forty teeth, with an equal number in upper and lower jaws. The cause is abandoning divisive language and working for unity and harmony among all.
31. The black and white portions of the eyes are clear and distinct, with no red or yellow discoloration. This comes from looking at others with compassionate eyes, working for their welfare, and generating equal concern for all whether their suffering is great or small.

32. The eyelashes are beautiful and long, like those of a bull, with each hair distinct. This arises from regarding others without attachment, anger, or confusion, and striving to gain full wisdom to be able to discriminate between virtue and nonvirtue.

Emanation Bodies

Emanation bodies (*nirmāṇakāya*) are the forms buddhas compassionately assume to benefit ordinary beings whose mindstreams are more polluted and whose karma does not allow them to engage directly with an enjoyment body. Seeing sentient beings drowning in saṃsāra's duḥkha, a buddha's enjoyment body manifests various emanation bodies in saṃsāra's impure realms without moving from the dharmakāya's meditative equipoise on emptiness. Emanation bodies do not have the five certainties and manifest in the realms of saṃsāra in order to guide sentient beings by assuming a form similar to the beings in that realm. They then teach disciples who have not yet entered the path of any of the three vehicles whatever will benefit, be it topics from the Fundamental Vehicle or topics from the Mahāyāna or Vajrayāna.

Both the enjoyment body and emanation bodies of a buddha are impermanent phenomena that change moment by moment. Among the different types of impermanent phenomena, they are considered persons, which are abstract composites. An enjoyment body is eternal and remains forever. Emanation bodies appear and are withdrawn according to their opportunity to benefit sentient beings. They manifest spontaneously and effortlessly according to the dispositions, interests, and receptivity of sentient beings. Emanation bodies appear in sentient beings' realms for as long as they can benefit those particular sentient beings. A buddha may radiate many emanation bodies in various parts of the universe simultaneously. They may even appear as inanimate objects. After serving their purpose, or when sentient beings' have consumed the karma to benefit from them, they absorb back into the enjoyment body.

There are three types of emanation bodies: supreme emanation bodies, ordinary emanation bodies, and artisan emanation bodies. Śākyamuni Buddha is an example of a *supreme emanation body*, so called because in that form the Buddha first turned the wheel of Dharma in our world, where previously the Buddhadharma was not in existence. Supreme emanation bodies perform the twelve deeds of a buddha and have the thirty-two signs and eighty marks of a great person.

The twelve deeds of supreme emanation bodies occur in the desire realm among human beings. In other realms and worlds, beings are either subject to such overwhelming suffering or experience such grand and stable pleasure that it is difficult for them to turn their minds to the Dharma. In our world, great disparity among sentient beings exists: some are rich, others poor; some live long, others do not. Due to this combination of suffering and happiness and the instability of both, it is easier for us to generate renunciation. For this reason, Śākyamuni Buddha enacted the twelve deeds here. The list of twelve deeds differs slightly in various texts; the following is from the *Sublime Continuum*. Although Śākyamuni Buddha was already fully awakened before performing the twelve deeds, he appeared in ordinary form so that his life would be an inspiring example for us to contemplate and follow.

1. He reigned in the blissful realm of Tuṣita, Maitreya Buddha's pure land, which is located in the outskirts of the Tuṣita celestial realm. Descending from the blissful land of Tuṣita is the first deed.
2. He enters his mother's womb.
3. He is born.
4. He masters the sciences and arts and is skilled in various sports.
5. He marries and enjoys sensual pleasures, family, and royal life. Although it is not mentioned here, he enters the city on four occasions, seeing a sick person, an old person, and a corpse, which brings him face to face with the tragedy of saṃsāric existence. Upon seeing a wandering mendicant during the fourth excursion, he has the idea that there is a way out of saṃsāra and wants to pursue it.
6. Longing for release from the tormenting cycle of birth and death, he leaves the palace and renounces his princely life, clothes, and appearance to live as a wandering renunciant.
7. Together with a small group of other renunciants, he engages in severe ascetic practices for six years.
8. Seeing that torturing the body does not purify the mind, he leaves behind the ascetic lifestyle, meditates under the bodhi tree, and makes a strong resolve to attain full awakening there.

9. Facing the demons of ignorance, anger, and attachment in his own mind, he overcomes the hosts of Māra—that is, all external and internal impediments to full awakening.
10. At dawn, he attains perfect supreme awakening.
11. He turns the Dharma wheel, teaching sentient beings the paths to higher rebirth, liberation, and full awakening.
12. He passes away, entering parinirvāṇa.

The twelve deeds occur in the time of subsequent attainment, but without moving from the dharmakāya. In bodhisattvas, subsequent attainment and meditative equipoise do not occur at the same time, but in buddhahood they do without any impediment, just as the sun and the sunshine occur simultaneously.

Rebirth or ordinary emanation bodies appear in various forms to guide us, for example appearing as wise and compassionate spiritual mentors who guide us on the path by giving teachings, ordination, and so forth. By appearing in the aspect of an ordinary being in any of the three realms, emanation bodies can communicate easily with ordinary beings. A buddha's manifestations as a bridge, blanket, or other material object are included in this category. *Artisan emanation bodies* are, for example, the appearance the Buddha assumed as a musician in order to subdue the conceit of a violinist and turn him toward the Dharma path. Ordinary emanation bodies and artisan emanation bodies do not necessarily have the clear and complete signs and marks and their physical appearance is usually indistinguishable from that of ordinary sentient beings of that realm.

However we count a buddha's bodies, the motivation for actualizing them is to benefit all sentient beings, and the path to actualize them is a complete path of method and wisdom. Reflecting on the qualities of fully awakened buddhas will inspire us to practice the path leading to buddhahood. It will also deepen our refuge and trust in our Teacher, Śākyamuni Buddha, and in all the buddhas who guide and inspire us along the path.

Buddha, Ārya Buddha, and Sentient Being

The eighth chapter of Maitreya's *Ornament of Clear Realizations* distinguishes between buddha and ārya buddha. *Buddha* is an excellent quality arisen from the fulfillment of the collections of merit and wisdom that are its causes. Buddha is synonymous with "resultant dharmakāya" and has four divisions—nature dharmakāya, wisdom dharmakāya, enjoyment body, and emanation body. Each of these is buddha. Since one of these—the nature dharmakāya—is permanent, that makes buddha permanent. (In philosophy, if one member of a category is permanent, even though other instances of that category are impermanent, the category itself is considered permanent.) Buddha is not a person. In general, a buddha's thirty-two signs, hands, feet, and so forth are buddha, because they are a buddha's physical qualities. The twenty-one unpolluted wisdoms in the continuum of an ārya buddha are also buddha.

Ārya buddha, on the other hand, refers to a person who is fully awakened—for example, an enjoyment body or emanation body. An ārya buddha is necessarily a buddha, but buddha is not necessarily an ārya buddha. Understanding the relationship between buddha and ārya buddha through four points is helpful.

- There is something that is buddha, but not an ārya buddha—for example, the nature truth body.
- There is something that is both an ārya buddha and buddha—for example, Śākyamuni Buddha.
- There is nothing that is an ārya buddha but not buddha.
- There is something that is neither—for example, a sentient being.

An ārya buddha is not a sentient being, although all other āryas—stream-enterers, once-returners, nonreturners, arhats, and bodhisattvas—are sentient beings. "Sentient being" literally means "having mind." Here "mind" refers to a mind with defilements, so "sentient being" refers to a person with defilements. All persons except ārya buddhas fall into this category.

When we speak more casually, "the Buddha" refers to Śākyamuni Buddha, and "a buddha" refers to an ārya buddha. The naturally pure nature dharmakāya is directly perceived only by āryas. The adventitiously pure nature dharmakāya and the wisdom dharmakāya are directly perceived only by ārya buddhas. The enjoyment body is directly perceived by ārya bodhisattvas. The supreme emanation body is directly perceived by sentient beings with pure karma. The other emanation bodies are directly perceived by all sentient beings.

A buddha is said to be an omniscient one, whose mind is omniscient (*sarvajñatā*). "Omniscient mind" refers only to the mental consciousnesses of a buddha, not to his or her sense consciousnesses or any other aspect of a buddha. However, buddhas' sense consciousnesses and all parts of their physical bodies are said to be omniscient in that they know all phenomena directly.

What Buddhas Perceive

Unlike buddhas, ārya bodhisattvas are unable to simultaneously nonconceptually and directly cognize the two truths. They must alternate knowing one and then the other, perceiving emptiness directly during meditative equipoise on emptiness and knowing conventionalities in the time of subsequent attainment. However, they are able to cognize the two truths simultaneously, but with different consciousnesses. During the time of subsequent attainment after arising from meditative equipoise on emptiness, ārya bodhisattvas engage in their daily life activities and teach emptiness to their students. At that time, they apprehend veilings—the students, books, the room, and so forth—with their sense consciousnesses, and simultaneously cognize emptiness conceptually with their mental consciousness. Although veilings appear truly existent to them, because their minds are informed by their prior direct realization of emptiness, they see these things as like illusions—as falsities because they appear truly existent although they are not. Ārya bodhisattvas' minds are relaxed; they do not get embroiled in reactive emotional responses to inherently existent things.

Ārya bodhisattvas have obscurations to perceiving all knowable objects simultaneously. In contrast, buddhas directly perceive all ultimate truths and veiled truths simultaneously with one consciousness. Buddhas never emerge from meditative equipoise, and for them meditative equipoise and subsequent realization become one entity; they no longer need to alternate between the two to know all phenomena. This ability is unique to a buddha.

All awakening activities of a buddha—the chief of which is their speech that teaches the Dharma to sentient beings—proceed effortlessly.

Buddhas have removed all impediments to knowing all existents. An omniscient mind explicitly knows all phenomena; all phenomena appear clearly and without confusion to a buddha's mind.

Free of all cognitive obscurations, buddhas do not have mistaken appearances. How then do they know veilings, which are falsities? What an omniscient mind knows from its own perspective differs from what it knows from others' perspectives. When unpolluted phenomena such as buddhas' signs and marks appear to sentient beings, they appear truly existent although they are not. This is not due to the signs and marks having arisen because of the latencies of ignorance, but due to sentient beings' minds being polluted by the latencies of ignorance. In other words, the mistaken appearances are due to the subject, the perceiving consciousness, not the object being perceived. From buddhas' perspective, these pure phenomena do not appear as false; buddhas have no mistaken appearances from their own perspective.

In contrast, the appearance of things such as the table and book that appear truly existent in the perspective of sentient beings is an appearance to buddhas only from the perspective of their appearing to sentient beings. While truly existent tables do not exist, the appearance of them to sentient beings does exist. For example, someone with vitreous floaters has the appearance of falling hairs. While the falling hairs do not exist, the appearance of them to that person does.

Since these mistaken appearances are existent phenomena, they must appear and be known by buddhas. They appear to buddhas' pristine wisdom of varieties not because buddhas have mistaken appearances from their own perspective. Rather, they perceive what sentient beings perceive, which are mistaken appearances. There is a big difference between sentient beings having the appearance of true existence because their minds are under the influence of ignorance and/or its latencies and buddhas having the appearance of true existence because these appearances are existent phenomena, and being omniscient, buddhas perceive them. From their own side, buddhas experience only purity. From the perspective of the pristine wisdom of varieties all phenomena appear as empty and selfless; they do not appear as truths, but as falsities.

Buddhas have two types of pristine wisdoms (*jñāna*): the exalted knower that cognizes things as they are that perceives emptiness, and the exalted knower that cognizes the varieties of phenomena that perceives all conventionalities. These two pristine wisdoms are inseparably one nature; both are omniscient and both know all ultimate and veiled truths directly. They are differentiated with respect to their objects. The pristine wisdom that cognizes things as they are knows emptiness—the ultimate truth—nondually. The pristine wisdom knowing varieties knows the diversity of phenomena—veiled truths—dualistically by means of their appearance to sentient beings.

A buddha's exalted knower that cognizes things as they are also perceives veilings, but *to the perspective of that exalted knower* veilings do not appear and are not seen. Similarly, the Buddha's exalted knower that cognizes the varieties also perceives emptiness, but *to the perspective of that exalted knower* emptiness does not appear and is not perceived. The exalted knower of things as they are is the fruition of meditative equipoise on emptiness, and the exalted knower of varieties is the result of meditation on illusion-like appearances in the subsequent realization time.

We may wonder: "If veiled truths are true for a mind influenced by ignorance, how can they exist for a buddha, whose mind is not influenced by ignorance in the least? Do conventional truths—the world, sentient beings, houses, and so forth—cease to exist at buddhahood because a buddha does not see them as true?" Veiled truths exist at buddhahood. A buddha perceives what we sentient beings perceive—veiled truths—but does not perceive them in the same way that we do. A buddha perceives them as false.

People who say that knowledge of the varieties of phenomena exists only in the continuums of sentient beings and that buddhas perceive only emptiness and not veilings disparage the buddhas' omniscience and their pristine wisdom of varieties. Similarly, saying that buddhas don't perceive conventionalities because the multifarious phenomena are nonexistent deprecates the buddhas' omniscience and their pristine wisdom of varieties. In addition, some hold the erroneous notion that pristine wisdom realizing the ultimate mode of existence, emptiness, does not exist in a buddha's continuum because meditative equipoise on emptiness abides just on a non-finding (of inherent existence), and if you find the non-finding, then the non-finding must be truly existent. These people disparage both pristine wisdoms.

In summary, in the insight section in his *Middle-Length Stages of the Path*, Tsongkhapa explains that in addition to perceiving ultimate truths, buddhas perceive impure and pure conventionalities, which appear to the exalted knower of varieties. Pure conventionalities are those that are not polluted by ignorance and its latencies. These include a buddha's speech, the qualities of a buddha's mind, and the thirty-two signs and eighty marks of a buddha's body, all of which are produced by a buddha's virtue, not by ignorance or its latencies. Impure veiled truths are those that are polluted by ignorance and the latencies of ignorance, for example all true duḥkha such as the aggregates of sentient beings in saṃsāra and the environments we live in.

When pure phenomena such as a buddha's signs and marks appear to sentient beings, they appear to exist from their own side, even though they do not exist in that way. This is due to the latencies of ignorance obscuring sentient beings' minds that make everything appear inherently existent. When these pure phenomena appear to a buddha's mind, they appear purely, without the appearance of inherent existence.

Buddhas experience only purity. If they experienced what is an impure thing to sentient beings, such as a foul smell, they would still experience it as pure. It's not that impure things don't appear to buddhas at all. They appear to them because buddhas perceive what appears to sentient beings. Although both pure and impure phenomena appear to buddhas, they experience only purity.

Impure phenomena appear to a buddha's exalted knower of varieties, but only from the viewpoint of their being appearances that exist for sentient beings. Nevertheless, a buddha's mind is nonmistaken, even though it perceives the mistaken appearance of inherently existent phenomena in the minds of sentient beings. From their own perspective, buddhas do not experience the impure phenomena that are true duḥkha and true origins of duḥkha.

Dual appearance or dual perception is of three types: (1) the appearance of veilings, (2) the appearance of subject and object as separate, and (3) the appearance of inherent or true existence. Buddhas have the appearance of veiled phenomena and the appearance of subject and object, so we can say they have dual appearance. However, they do not have *mistaken* dual appearances because they lack the aspect of the mind that mistakenly perceives or apprehends phenomena as truly existent.

Saying that the Buddha has pure appearance does not mean that he perceives impure things as pure or that his having pure appearances makes impure things pure. The Buddha still perceives sentient beings and our duḥkha. Sentient beings and their duḥkha don't cease to exist at buddhahood, but how they are perceived changes.

How we perceive and experience things depends on the state of our mind—from their side phenomena do not inherently exist as this or that. During a famine in India during the Buddha's time, the saṅgha had nothing to eat. A horse trainer offered to the monastics the only thing he had—grain husks. To the monastics it tasted terrible. Ānanda, the Buddha's attendant, started weeping thinking that he had failed to serve the Buddha well because the Buddha was eating such dreadful fare. However, the Buddha quelled Ānanda's sorrow by pulling out a piece of the husk that was stuck in his teeth and giving it to Ānanda to eat. When Ānanda put it in his mouth, he was amazed because it tasted delicious, unlike anything he had ever experienced before. He realized that due to the purity of the Buddha's mind, how the Buddha experienced things encountered in daily life was totally unlike the experience of ordinary beings.

When buddhas teach, although they use words to communicate with their audience, they do not have conceptions. Conceptual consciousnesses involve obscuration; they are mistaken consciousnesses that do not know their objects directly but get at them only by means of a conceptual appearance. Buddhas, however, have abandoned both afflictive and cognitive obscurations and thus have neither mistaken minds nor obscurations; thus they have no conceptions whatsoever. They also do not impute any objects, so when we say that things exist by being merely designated by term and concept, it is sentient beings' minds that are doing the designating, not buddhas.

I once asked the late Gen Nyima-la, "How does a buddha see an object without that object appearing truly existent?" He responded that we cannot explain this, because here we are talking about the uncommon field of experience (T. *spyod yul las 'das pa*) of a buddha that only a buddha can know. Of course we can talk about what buddhas perceive and how they perceive it, but it is not easy to gain a clear mental picture of what this means. We can say that buddhas see things as merely designated, but if we really think about this, it is very difficult to imagine what seeing something as merely designated would be. This is similar to the difference between talking about and directly perceiving emptiness. We ordinary beings can talk about emptiness as the mere absence of the object of negation, but unless our mind is intimate with emptiness, we don't really have an idea of what emptiness is. We may talk a lot about nonduality, but do we even have a correct assumption, let alone an actual experience, of nonduality?

We have many discussions about what the Buddha perceives and how. Does he perceive veiled truths—phenomena that appear true to the mind of ignorance? Or does he perceive nominal truths—phenomena that exist by being merely designated? How do the buddhas see their own omniscient minds? To answer these, the only alternative is to become a buddha ourselves, and then through our own experience we will know how a buddha perceives things. Otherwise, we are just poking our nose here and there and talking about things that are not within our own reach!

12 | Buddhahood: The Buddhas' Awakening Activities

The *Sublime Continuum* describes the buddhas' awakening activity (*samudācāra*) by which all buddhas work to benefit each sentient being spontaneously, continuously, and without partiality.

A buddha's awakening activity is spontaneous in that it requires no effort on the part of the buddhas. Because their minds are free from all obstructions, they know each sentient being's dispositions, aspirations, thoughts, and tendencies. They know which of the three vehicles each sentient being aspires to as well as the teachings and trainings of each vehicle so that they are able to instruct and guide that sentient being to upper rebirth, liberation, and full awakening. In addition, the buddhas effortlessly and intuitively know the suitable place, time, and manner to teach and train each sentient being, and manifest accordingly. All this is done without error and without having to ponder what to do. Without thought or intention, the reflection of the moon appears on dewdrops, ponds, and in countless containers that hold calm and clear water. Similarly, when sentient beings are ready to be led on the path, the Buddha's awakening activities spontaneously manifest. The *Sublime Continuum* says (RGV 4:3–4):

> For whom? How? By which training?
> Where? And when? Since conceptual thought
> regarding such [questions] does not occur,
> the *Muni* (Buddha) always [acts] spontaneously.
>
> The temperaments of the disciples,
> which of the many means for each,

which training at what place and time:
[the buddhas are not mistaken as to any of] these.

Awakening activity is also continuous and flows forth uninterruptedly. Having excellent qualities unmatched by others, buddhas have perfected the three higher trainings and the six perfections and possess profound wisdom. Having completed the two collections of merit and wisdom, they are able to ripen the minds of all sentient beings and have mastered all vehicles and paths to arhatship and buddhahood. As a result of these immaculate and extensive causes, they have attained complete and perfect awakening and can see that each and every sentient being possesses the treasure-like potential to become a buddha that is shrouded by clouds of afflictions and defilements. To overcome these adventitious defilements, the buddhas' awakening activity continuously flows.

Nine Similes for Awakening Activity

The *Adornment with the Light of Pristine Wisdom Entering the Domain of the Buddha Sūtra* (*Sarvabuddhaviṣayāvatārajñānālokālaṃkāra Sūtra*) speaks of nine similes that help us understand how the buddhas' awakened activities function. Elaborated on in the fourth chapter of the *Sublime Continuum*, the similes reveal the awakening activities of the Buddha's body, speech, mind, body and speech together, pristine wisdom, secrets of the Tathāgata's mind, secrets of his speech, secrets of his bodies, and compassion. Although we speak of the Buddha below, what is said applies to all buddhas.

(1) *The form of the god Indra illustrates the display of the illusory manifestations of the Tathāgata's body.* If the surface of the earth were to transform into polished and immaculate lapis lazuli, the reflection of Indra, his palace, and his entourage would appear on it. People who saw this would aspire to become like Indra, and to actualize that wish they would create virtue and abandon nonvirtue. As a result they would be born as Indra.

Although these people do not understand that they are perceiving only the reflection of Indra, not Indra himself, still the reflection, which is without intention, has a positive effect on them and aids them in attaining a higher rebirth. Similarly, due to the firm powers of faith, effort, mindfulness, samādhi, and wisdom, ārya bodhisattvas, whose minds are pure and polished like lapis lazuli, can see in their minds the appearance of the Buddha with thirty-two signs and eighty marks. Although the Buddha didn't think "I'm going to benefit sentient beings in this world," and although the Buddha did not move from the stillness of the dharmakāya, he emanates countless illusion-like forms that appear to the minds of those who have created the cause to perceive them.

When the supreme emanation body of the Buddha appears in the world, people are not aware that this is an appearance of his pristine wisdom. They may even cling to his body, mistakenly thinking it is made of atoms. These appearances of the Buddha are the Buddha; it would be a mistake to say they are not. It would also be mistaken to think they are made of coarse material. Nevertheless, all those who see them receive enormous benefit. Relying on beholding his form, all Mahāyāna followers are inspired to practice well and will come to generate bodhicitta and see their inner dharmakāya with their own pristine wisdom.

Although we do not think that this is the appearance of our own mind, it is a dependent arising relying on both the Buddha and our merit. Like the appearance of Indra reflected in the lapis lazuli ground, these appearances of the Buddha reflected in the ground of our virtuous mind should not be viewed as either existent or nonexistent—that is, they are neither truly existent nor totally nonexistent. Nevertheless, these appearances function to inspire us to become buddhas, and as a result, bodhicitta grows in our mind. We then engage in studying, thinking, and meditating on the Dharma and in practicing the bodhisattvas' compassionate deeds. Following the Mahāyāna path, we will realize the clear light—the true nature of the mind—and through this we will attain the ultimate result we long for, the truth body of a fully awakened buddha.

The Buddha does not leave the state of dharmakāya to radiate out this appearance. It happens naturally when all the causes and conditions come together. From the Buddha's side, his completion of all the abandonments and realizations of a buddha give him the ability to benefit others effortlessly. From our side, our faith, merit, bodhicitta, meditation, and practice of the six perfections make us receptive vessels. When ārya bodhisattvas, who have created all these causes, see the enjoyment body in their pure minds, it becomes a cause contributing to their attainment of full awakening.

(2) *The celestial drum illustrates the Tathāgata's speech expressing the holy Dharma.* In the God Realm of the Thirty-Three, a celestial drum is suspended in the sky. A product of the gods' past virtuous karma, without effort (it is not beaten by anyone), without origin (such as being produced by the vocal cords, tongue, and lips), without thought (of a thinking mind), without vibration (of any physical basis), and without intention (to make a sound), the drum produces the meaningful sound of the four seals: all conditioned things are impermanent; all polluted things are in the nature of duḥkha, all phenomena are selfless, and nirvāṇa is peace.[108] This sound awakens the gods from their indulgence in sense pleasures and alerts them to the impending attacks of the jealous demi-gods, and in this way enables them to maintain peace.

In the same way, the Buddha effortlessly teaches all sentient beings who have sufficient virtue, without generating the motivation or energy to do so and without thinking about who to teach and what to teach them. The Buddha's speech expresses the Dharma in accordance with sentient beings' various levels of aspirations and capacities, without effort, origin, thought, physical basis, or intention. In this way, the Buddha answers sentient beings' spiritual questions, dispels their doubt, and instructs them in what to practice and abandon. By hearing the teachings and putting them into practice, sentient beings are able to overcome their afflictions, subdue their suffering, and attain the peace of nonabiding nirvāṇa. In the meantime, hearing the Buddha's speech enables them to have favorable rebirths in order to continue their Dharma practice.[109]

Just as someone who lacks good hearing cannot hear the subtle sounds of a drum, sentient beings whose merit and wisdom are minimal are oblivious to the subtle meaning of the Dharma teachings. Those with good hearing who listen attentively can hear the sound of the drum clearly. What we are able to take in and benefit from depends on our merit and wisdom as well as the effortless speech of the Buddha. While the Buddha's teachings are always available, we must study and put them into practice, thereby purifying our minds and creating the conditions to be able to hear and understand the teachings in the future.

It is said that all virtue of any sentient being anywhere depends on the Buddha's awakened activity of giving teachings and guidance. Of all the various types of awakening activities of the buddhas, their speech is principal, for teaching us the Dharma is the primary way that they lead us to liberation and awakening. As that is the case, we should rely on the Buddha's speech. Doing so will enable those who have not attained a path to attain one and those who have entered the path to deepen their understanding and progress through the paths and grounds to full awakening (RGV 4:43).

> Any cause of happiness for worldly beings and gods,
> in whichever sphere of the world without exception,
> briefly spoken, fully depends upon this melody [of the Buddha's teachings]
> that pervades all the worlds, not forsaking one.

(3) *Clouds illustrate the all-pervading nature of the Tathāgata's mind of compassion and wisdom.* In hot Indian summers, monsoon clouds continuously and effortlessly pour down rain that nourishes the rice paddies and produces abundant crops. In a similar way, in the unpolluted space of emptiness from the clouds of the dharmakāya, stirred by the wind of love and compassion, effortless and uninterruptedly the Buddha rains down the impeccable Dharma, bringing about a harvest of virtue in the minds of sentient beings.

Just as the rain water is pure but acquires different tastes and qualities depending on the type of land it falls on, the Dharma will take on the taste of the Śrāvaka, Solitary Realizer, or Bodhisattva Vehicle depending on the mind, dispositions, and aspirations of those to be tamed. While the nectar of the Dharma is of a single taste—nirvāṇa—it assumes a different flavor depending on the vessel into which it is poured.

When the monsoon rain falls, human beings are delighted because it will nourish their fields; peacocks are indifferent because rain neither helps nor hinders their activities; and hungry ghosts are unhappy because it appears as hail to them. Similarly, the three dispositions of sentient beings respond in different ways to the Dharma rain. Those who have cultivated conviction and confidence in the Mahāyāna are nourished by the rain, those who are uninterested are neither happy nor unhappy, and those who have wrong views and are hostile to the Mahāyāna doctrine are unhappy.

The clouds do not think "I will cause benefit or harm," they simply allow the rain to fall. Some people take shelter and enjoy the rainfall, mindful of the crops that will flourish, but insects may dislike the downpour. Similarly, the cloud of the Buddha's compassion lets fall the rain of the Dharma without the notion "I will purify the negativities and afflictions of those with faith in the Mahāyāna" or "I will ripen the seeds of wrong views in those who are antagonistic to it." Whether sentient beings benefit or not from the buddhas' activities in the short term depends on their situation, but the buddhas' awakening activities are always conducted with compassion to benefit sentient beings in the long term.

Buddhas fully understand the implications of being born in cyclic existence with its three types of duḥkha. Because they realize the danger of sentient beings remaining apathetic toward the dire situation they are in, from the cloud of compassion they shower the Dharma upon us continuously and in accordance with our dispositions and karma. Sentient beings who have some discriminating wisdom see the nature of saṃsāra and nirvāṇa and leave behind all hankering for the former and seek the latter. Having cultivated faith based on understanding the path in previous lives, in this life they again follow the Buddhist path and understand that duḥkha is to be known, its origin is to be abandoned, and its true cessation is to be actualized. With that in mind, they gladly practice the path that leads to the fruit they desire. This is what we too must do. With that in mind, in the *Guru Pūjā*, we request teachings with this verse:

> Please let fall a rain of vast and profound Dharma from a hundred thousand billowing clouds of wisdom and compassion, to nurture, sustain, and propagate a garden of kunda flowers for the benefit and bliss of all limitless beings.

(4) *The god Brahmā illustrates the illusory emanations of the Tathāgata's body and speech.* Without departing from the Brahmā Heaven, the Great Brahmā effortlessly sends out illusory manifestations of himself to the desire-realm gods. Seeing these manifestations, they want to emulate Brahmā and forsake their attachment to the delights of the desire realm to create the causes to be born as a Brahmā god.

In the same way, without departing from the dharmakāya—the omniscient mind that dwells in emptiness yet knows all conventionalities at the same time with one consciousness—the Tathāgata effortlessly emanates a multitude of illusion-like forms in all realms of saṃsāra to benefit the beings who have the karmic fortune to encounter them. By meeting a supreme emanation body that performs the twelve deeds, sentient beings are inspired to emulate him and so observe the law of karma and its effects and practice renunciation, bodhicitta, and the correct view.

Brahmā's ability to emanate these manifestations is due to aspirational prayers he made in previous lives to benefit the gods. In addition, in previous lives, the gods aspired to see Brahmā and created the merit for this to happen. In this way the situation of their seeing his illusory emanations now occurs. Similarly, by the power of aspirational prayers made by the Buddha when he was a bodhisattva and the power of the virtue created by sentient beings who want to meet and practice the teachings, now these sentient beings are able to see the illusion-like emanation body of the Buddha. These emanations effortlessly flow forth from the Buddha's truth body when the causes and conditions assemble for sentient beings to benefit from them. Thus Śākyamuni Buddha appeared in our world, and like all supreme emanation bodies, he performed the twelve deeds.

(5) *The sun illustrates the Tathāgata's mind radiating the light of pristine wisdom.* When the sun shines, lotuses blossom and display their beauty, while kumuta flowers close. Yet the sun does not praise one or criticize the other, nor is the sun encouraged by the former and discouraged by the latter. In the same way, the sun of the Tathāgata sheds its rays of the sacred Dharma on the beings to be trained, without any thought or judgment, just with the wish to be of benefit. The lotus of wisdom unfolds in those with merit who are receptive to the Dharma, while the kumuta-flower minds of those who are obscured close.

The radiant sun will be reflected in whatever upturned vessels are filled with water. The acuity and brilliance of the reflections depend on the clarity of the water. In the same way, numberless form bodies are reflected in the vessels of various disciples. Depending on the degree to which their minds have been purified of defilements, the clarity of the reflection will differ. Like vessels that are upside down, those whose minds are disinterested in or even hostile to the Buddhadharma are temporarily immune to the reflections of the Buddha's wisdom.

In the clear, open sky, the sun rises and shines its rays first on the highest mountain peaks, then on the medium-sized mountains, and finally on the hills. Likewise, in the space of the nature truth body, the sun-like omniscient mind of the Buddha arises and with its wisdom illuminates the minds of sentient beings: first those with great merit, then those with medium merit, followed by those of least merit. In this way the Buddha leads sentient beings who are subject to great suffering in unfortunate births to take a human birth. He illuminates with wisdom the minds of human beings immersed in wrong views, enabling them to attain freedom from saṃsāra. And his brilliant sun of wisdom propels arhats and bodhisattvas to full awakening. Just as the sun dispels darkness and stimulates growth, so too does the awakening activity of the Buddha's wisdom spontaneously dispel the darkness of ignorance and stimulate the growth of realizations within sentient beings' minds.

(6) *A wish-fulfilling gem illustrates the secret aspect of the Tathāgata's mind.* Just as a wish-fulfilling jewel is continuously present and without exertion grants riches to those beings in its field of activity according to their wishes, the Buddha continuously shares the teachings, fulfilling the spiritual aspirations of all those who rely on him. A wish-fulfilling jewel lies deep underground or in the ocean and is very hard to find. It has no intention or thought to give one thing to one person and another thing to another, but when people are near this jewel and pray to it, it fulfills each and every one of their wishes—whatever it may be—spontaneously and fully. In the same way, sentient beings with different dispositions seek teachings and practices according to their aspirations and interests, and the Buddha fulfills their spiritual needs completely.

From its side, a wish-fulfilling jewel doesn't discriminate whose wishes it grants and whose it doesn't; that depends on whether a person is near the jewel and prays to it or not. Similarly, from the Buddha's side, he guides all sentient beings equally, whether those people have faith in his teachings or not. Whether people receive his guidance or not depends on their receptivity, sincerity, merit, and eagerness to learn.

Once a person finds a wish-fulfilling jewel, he or she cares for it meticulously, never being careless or taking it for granted. Similarly, the pure Dharma teachings are difficult to encounter during our countless saṃsāric rebirths and in the vastness of our universe. This is especially the case for those with little merit and strong mental poisons. Once finding the precious teachings, we must treasure them as being more valuable than a wish-fulfilling jewel, for they can end the suffering that a jewel can never touch (RGV 4:73).

> As a precious gem, which is free from thought, fully bestows
> the desired riches on others, doing so without effort,
> the Buddha always stays for others' sake, as merited by each,
> and as long as existence lasts, doing so without any effort.

(7) *An echo illustrates the secret aspect of the Tathāgata's speech.* The cave that reflects a sound has no intention of making an echo and exerts no energy to do so. The echo abides nowhere; it isn't like the sound of a conch that exists externally, and it's not like a thought that exists internally. Nevertheless, while appearing as various sounds, an echo communicates a meaning according to the perception of those who hear it. Likewise, the sound of the buddhas' speech appears in various tones but it takes meaning in the minds of disciples in accordance with their perceptions—their individual perspectives and dispositions. The Buddha is free from effort or thought to teach a specific topic to a specific individual. Like the echo, the source of the Buddha's speech cannot be located, even though it arises due to causes and conditions.

(8) *Space illustrates the secret aspect of the Tathāgata's bodies.* Uncreated space is not a material thing. As the absence of obstructing contact, it does not appear, it has no form, and it is not an object of our senses. There is no way for us to hold on to it or point out where it is. And yet appearances of beings and their environments arise in space and these appearances are high and low and consist of a variety of colors. While space appears in these ways, this is not its actual nature. Similarly, the infinite illusory appearances, emanations, and manifestations of the Buddha appear but cannot be pinpointed anywhere. All the illusion-like appearances of the Buddha, such as his twelve deeds, appear because of the aspirations and temperaments of disciples. While manifesting in forms that arise and cease, the ultimate Buddha is not subject to arising and disintegration. Nevertheless it pervades everywhere, endures forever, and allows all excellent qualities to exist until all beings are freed from cyclic existence.

(9) *The earth illustrates the awakening activity of the Buddha's compassion.* All flowers and fruit, as well as everything that sustains us, grow from or

exist within the earth. Although the earth has no intention to grow plants or yield minerals, it does so without any exertion. Without thought, seeds germinate, plants take root, and trees and bushes grow, providing nourishment for the earth's denizens. In the same way, the fully awakened Buddha does not think "I must benefit these sentient beings," but when sentient beings rely on him, the seeds of our good qualities sprout and soon the flowers and fruits of realizations and the two collections flourish. In this way, due to great compassion, the Buddha is the source and support of sentient beings' spiritual growth.

Maitreya explained the Buddha's awakening activity through these nine similes because it is hard for us to conceptualize how the Buddha's awakening activity functions. We are so habituated to every activity requiring thought, planning, effort, and evaluation that we find it puzzling to consider that the Buddha's awakening activities can occur without these. His being able to do so is a result of the innumerable causes he created as a bodhisattva before attaining awakening. These causes include the vastness of his spiritual realizations and the magnitude of his dedication prayers. The depth of his compassion and the urgency with which he cultivates the wisdom that will abolish all defilements and perfect all good qualities are of such an intensity that the Buddha's ability to benefit sentient beings never dissipates and continues spontaneously and without interruption until the end of saṃsāra.

As seen through these similes, the benefit we receive from the Buddha's awakened activities also depends on the causes we have created. Our karma and the Buddha's awakening activities are of equal strength in bringing results. If we have strong virtuous karma, we can receive the Buddha's awakening influence and make great progress in our spiritual practice. If our virtue is weak and our nonvirtuous karma strong, the Buddha's awakening activity cannot override the force of our negativities. However, as we direct our energy away from destructive thoughts and actions and toward constructive ones, we create the space in which the Buddha's awakening activity can reach and touch us. Our wish to change our ways and make ourselves into a receptive vessel is often fueled by the weariness of constantly experiencing dissatisfaction or misery. It may also be sparked by seeking meaning in our lives. A strong impetus for making changes in our lives may be meeting a qualified spiritual mentor.

The nine similes are presented in a particular order. Although each simile resembles the Buddha's awakened activities in a certain aspect, it does not resemble them in another aspect. Each subsequent simile eliminates the way in which the previous simile does not correspond to the Buddha's awakened activities.

1. The Buddha's body is similar to the reflection of Indra in the smooth lapis lazuli surface in that countless illusory physical manifestations of the Buddha are displayed in sentient beings' minds. It is dissimilar in that Indra's reflection is voiceless and cannot turn the Dharma wheel, whereas the Buddha can.
2. The Buddha's speech is similar to the great celestial drum teaching the four seals in that the Buddha's speech turns the Dharma wheel and gives teachings to sentient beings. However, the great drum doesn't benefit everyone in all directions and is not able to fulfill the welfare of sentient beings for all time, whereas the Buddha's benefit pervades all worlds for all time.
3. The Buddha's awakened mind is similar to a vast cloud whose rain ripens crops in all directions in that the Buddha's mind matures disciples by means of its compassion and wisdom. Nevertheless, the cloud does not eliminate harmful or worthless factors, whereas the rain of Buddha's compassion and wisdom eliminates the sufferings of sentient beings and the afflictions and karma that cause them.
4. The Buddha's awakened body and speech are similar to Brahmā in that just as Brahmā eliminates the worthless factors of attachment to sense gratifications, so does the endless display of the Buddha's body and speech. However, Brahmā doesn't benefit sentient beings extensively or continuously, nor does he enable sentient beings to experience ultimate happiness. In contrast, the Buddha's physical and verbal activities continuously lead sentient beings to final, complete fulfillment and joy.
5. The Buddha's radiant light of pristine wisdom is similar to the radiating light of the sun that ripens all crops in that the radiating light of the Buddha's pristine wisdom continuously ripens the crops of

realizations in disciples. However, the sun shines on crops only during the daytime, not continuously, and it does not overcome darkness everywhere. The radiating light of the Buddha's pristine wisdom shines on all sentient beings everywhere without interruption and overcomes the darkness of ignorance.

6. The secrets of the Buddha's mind are similar to a wish-granting jewel that, by means of its brilliance, continuously eliminates darkness at all times. Similarly the mysterious aspect of the Buddha's mind radiates the light of nonconceptual pristine wisdom forever, without end. Nevertheless, compared to the mysteries of the Buddha's mind, a wish-granting jewel is more readily present. It can be found with the nāgas and in the sea. However, it is hard and rare to find the Buddha, for the Awakened One cannot appear to sentient beings who lack the karmic fortune to encounter him. In addition, to accomplish the mysteries of the Buddha's mind necessitates collecting merit and wisdom for three countless great eons.
7. The secrets of the Buddha's speech are similar to an echo, which is difficult to pinpoint because it cannot be found. Likewise, the mysteries of the Buddha's speech that give the excellent teachings are also hard to find. Nevertheless, an echo occurs due to causes and conditions, whereas the Buddha's nature body is self-arising, uncreated, and does not appear due to causes and conditions.
8. The secrets of the Buddha's body are similar to space, which does not arise from causes and conditions and is uncreated, but which appears as a variety of things. Similarly, the mysteries of his body display countless illusion-like manifestations. However, space is not a basis for virtue, whereas the Buddha is the basis of all purified virtuous qualities.
9. The Buddha's awakened activities are like the earth that is the basis supporting everything in that his awakened activities are the basis for all goodness and virtue and for whatever is best for ordinary beings and āryas. The awakening activities of all buddhas is the basis on which the sacred Dharma arises. The Dharma is the three vehicles, the paths that lead us beyond saṃsāra to personal nirvāṇa and nonabiding nirvāṇa; the śrāvakas, solitary realizers, and bodhisattvas all depend on it. Based on the Buddha's awakening, the path of the ten

virtues, which are the cause of happiness in the desire realm, arises; the four dhyānas and four immeasurables, which constitute the happiness in the form realm, arise; and the four formless absorptions also arise. Thus all worldly happiness of the three saṃsāric realms depends on the awakening of the Buddha and the Dharma he taught.

Twenty-Seven Awakening Activities

The awakening activities of all the buddhas are classified into twenty-seven types. They are pure qualities of the wisdom dharmakāya, meaning that they arise depending on the wisdom dharmakāya. The wisdom truth body appears to sentient beings as the enjoyment body and emanation bodies in order to work for their welfare. These awakening activities operate spontaneously and without interruption to set sentient beings in the realizations of the path. "Setting" does not mean a buddha physically or mentally places realizations in sentient beings; that is impossible because each of us must train our own mind. Rather, "setting" indicates that the buddha's wisdom dharmakāya knows our dispositions and interests, and the two form bodies display the awakening activities by explaining the Dharma in a way that each of us can understand at our present level. Through hearing and practicing the teachings, we gain understandings that set us on the next level.

Although these twenty-seven awakening activities are delineated in terms of bodhisattvas who have entered the path, each buddha works for the welfare of all sentient beings in all realms of saṃsāra. Initially buddhas instruct us in the preciousness of a human life with its freedoms and fortunes, as well as in impermanence and death, to set us in understanding the importance of engaging in Dharma practice.

In each line below, "them" indicates the specific disciples on the various paths and grounds that a buddha is setting on this level. The buddhas give similar instructions to others who are at lower as well as higher levels.

Gyaltsab's *Ornament of the Essence* (*Rnam bshad snying po rgyan*), a subcommentary on *Ornament of Clear Realizations*, explains the twenty-seven awakening activities in two ways: according to Vimuktisena (sixth century) and Haribhadra (eighth century). The following is according to Vimuktisena:

	SETTING TRAINEES ON THE PATH OF ACCUMULATION
1	Setting them in the excellent attitude, the intention to attain liberation rather than seeking higher rebirths in saṃsāra.
2	Setting them in the maturing of others' continuums by teaching them the four ways to gather disciples so that they will gather and benefit their own disciples.
3	Setting them in the wisdom that realizes the four truths so they realize that true duḥkha and true origins are afflictive factors to be abandoned and true cessations and true paths are pure factors to be adopted, and that none of these exist inherently.
	SETTING TRAINEES ON THE PATH OF PREPARATION
4	Setting them in the intention of others' welfare, the realization of the exact meaning of the mode of abidance.
5	Setting them in the method to complete the qualities of a buddha in their own continuums by completing the practice of the six perfections.
6	Setting them in the basis of accomplishing the welfare of self and others by practicing the paths of the ten virtues, which forms a good foundation for accomplishing the two welfares.
7	Setting them in the pure view, the realization of the emptiness of inherent existence with a mundane wisdom arisen from meditation.
	SETTING TRAINEES ON THE PATH OF SEEING
8	Setting them in new and direct realization of the emptiness in which the elaborations of inherent existence have been extinguished.
	SETTING TRAINEES ON THE PATH OF MEDITATION
9	Setting them on the second and third grounds through the perfections of ethical conduct and fortitude and understanding that all phenomena in these grounds are mere imputations.
10	Setting them in the fourth, fifth, and sixth grounds through the wisdoms knowing the thirty-seven harmonies with awakening, the four truths, and dependent origination conjoined with the realization of emptiness.
11	Setting them in the seventh ground through the perfection of skillful means so they will ripen other sentient beings' minds.
	SETTING TRAINEES ON THE EIGHTH GROUND
12	Setting them in the knower of paths that directly knows the śrāvaka, solitary realizer, and bodhisattva paths.
13	Setting them in the extinction of manifest grasping at true existence.
14	Setting them in the attainment of awakening that is imputed "Buddha Jewel," which is so called because eighth-grounders, like buddhas, do not need coarse effort to work for the benefit of sentient beings.

15	Setting them in the application of the pure land so they purify their own buddha field in which they will attain full awakening.
	SETTING TRAINEES ON THE NINTH GROUND
16	Setting them in the definite attainment of buddhahood so they will have the ability to set others in definitely attaining buddhahood without falling to the Śrāvaka or Solitary Realizer Vehicles.
17	Setting them in accomplishing the immeasurable welfare of sentient beings in a huge number of world systems.
	SETTING TRAINEES ON THE TENTH GROUND
18	Setting them on the about-to-be-attained tenth ground by their accomplishing the special excellent qualities of relying on the buddhas, hearing the excellent Dharma, making offerings, and so forth in a huge number of world systems.
	Setting them in increasing realization.[110]
19	Setting them in completing all virtues, which are the branches of awakening.
20	Setting them in directly seeing that coarse and subtle actions do not go to waste.
21	Setting them in seeing the complete four truths.
22	Setting them in abandoning the four errors of seeing the impermanent as permanent, the impure as pure, and so forth.
23	Setting them in the realization of the mode—the absence of grasping true existence—which is the basis for generating the four errors.
24	Setting them in the completion of the completely pure that realizes the equality of all phenomena in being empty of true existence.
25	Setting them in the completion of the two collections that are the causes of awakening.
26	Setting them in the realization of the equality of conditioned saṃsāra and unconditioned nirvāṇa in being empty of true existence.
	SETTING TRAINEES IN THE RESULT OF THE PATH—THE PATH OF NO-MORE-LEARNING
27	Setting them in the nonabiding nirvāṇa of a tathāgata.

REFLECTION

1. Contemplate that at this moment there are buddhas who are trying to set you in Dharma understandings. You are not alone on the path; the more you make yourself a receptive vessel, the more the buddhas' awakening activities can affect you.

2. What can you do now to make yourself more receptive to the Buddha's awakening activities?

3. Think that when you attain buddhahood, you will spontaneously and effortlessly be able to work for the benefit of sentient beings through enacting the twenty-seven awakening activities. How would it feel to be able to do this for sentient beings?

4. How can you begin to benefit others right now?

Ānanda Settles His Doubts

Despite knowing the Buddha's marvelous awakening activities, if you nevertheless wonder if the Buddha possesses the capability to liberate all beings, this story from Nāgārjuna's *Exegesis on the Great Perfection of Wisdom Sūtra* will assuage your doubts.[111]

> Ānanda once thought to himself, "In the past, at the time of Burning Lamp Buddha, the world was a fine one, the lifespan of the people was long, and they were easy to teach and bring across to liberation. Now, in the time of Śākyamuni Buddha, the world is an evil one, the lifespan of the people is short, and they are difficult to teach. Will the Buddha nonetheless go ahead and enter nirvāṇa even though the Buddha's work will not have been completed?"
>
> It was early in the morning when [Ānanda] expressed this concern to the Buddha. The sun had already risen. At that very time the Buddha then entered into the sunrise samādhi. Just as when the sun rises, its light illuminates all of Jambudvīpa, so, too, it was with the body of the Buddha. His hair pores all sent forth light that universally illuminated worlds throughout the ten directions as numerous as the grains of sand of the Ganges.
>
> Each of the rays of light put forth a seven-jeweled thousand-petalled lotus blossom. Atop each blossom, a buddha was seated. Each one of those buddhas sent forth an incalculable number of

light beams. On each ray of light was a seven-jeweled, thousand-petalled lotus blossom. Atop each blossom a buddha was seated.

All these buddhas universally filled up worlds throughout the ten directions as numerous as the grains of sand of the Ganges, and each of them carried forth with the teaching and transforming of beings. In some cases they spoke Dharma. In some situations they remained silent. In some cases they were walking along. In some circumstances they engaged in displays of the superknowledges wherein they transformed their bodies and made water or fire pour forth from them. In manners such as these they employed all sorts of skillful means whereby they crossed over to liberation beings throughout the ten directions who were immersed in the five realms of rebirth.

Due to receiving assistance from the awesome spiritual power of the Buddha, Ānanda was able for a time to completely observe these phenomena. The Buddha then withdrew his manifestation of the fulfillment of spiritual power and then arose from samādhi, asking of Ānanda whether or not he had seen these phenomena and whether or not he had heard these phenomena.

Ānanda replied, "Having received the assistance of the Buddha's awesome spiritual power, I have indeed seen and I have indeed heard."

The Buddha asked, "Given that the Buddha possesses powers such as these, is he able to bring the Buddha's work to ultimate completion or is he not?"

Ānanda replied, "Bhagavān, even in a case where beings filled up worlds throughout the ten directions as numerous as the grains of sand of the Ganges, if the Buddha were to employ powers such as these for just a single day of his life, he would still certainly be able to completely implement the work of the Buddha."

Ānanda exclaimed, "This is a matter such as I have never experienced before. Bhagavān, the Dharma of the buddhas is immeasurable, inconceivable, and ineffable."

Individuals Acting in Unison

In the *Ornament of the Mahāyāna Sūtras* (*Mahāyānasūtrālaṃkāra*), Maitreya speaks of individual sentient beings becoming awakened using the similes of the suns' rays illuminating the world and rivers flowing into a great ocean. These similes help us understand what happens to the individual at the time of full awakening and the relationship of the individual buddhas to each other. Maitreya says (10:3–4):

> Just as the immeasurable rays of the sun all intermingle (mix together, merge)
> in the sun's corona,
> always engaged in the same activity,
> that of illuminating the world,
> likewise in the stainless dhātu,
> innumerable buddhas intermingle, engaged in the same deeds,
> illuminating pristine wisdom.

Later in the same chapter he says (10:84–87):

> As long as rivers have not merged in the ocean,
> they have different locations and separate waters,
> are small and have different activities,
> providing only slight support for aquatic life.
>
> Once they merge into the ocean, their location is one,
> and their water has become one great body.
> They act as one and provide support
> for great quantities of aquatic life.
>
> As long as they have not become buddhas,
> they have separate bases[112] and intellects,
> little realization, and do separate deeds,
> able to provide for the welfare of only a few sentient beings.

When they enter buddhahood their forms
and realizations are not different;
all of their deeds converge into one and they provide forever
for the welfare of great hosts of beings.

These verses illustrate the great advantage of attaining buddhahood. As sentient beings, we have different bodies and minds that are all under the control of afflictions and polluted karma, our understanding of the Dharma is small, and each of us acts separately. In sum, we are able to benefit only a few others.

However, when sentient beings attain buddhahood, each of them has an omniscient mind. These omniscient minds are not different in the sense of one having higher realizations and another lower. Each of them perceives all phenomena without impediment, and in that way they are the same. Similarly, there is no difference in the capacity of each buddha to perform awakened deeds to benefit sentient beings. When any buddha acts to benefit a sentient being—for example, when Mañjuśrī radiates awakening deeds—it is all the buddhas acting in unison. There is no difference in the awakened deeds of all the buddhas. What Mañjuśrī does to help sentient beings is the same as what Tārā, Chenrezig, Yamāntaka, and all other buddhas do. We can't say this is the awakened deed of Mañjuśrī but it's not the awakened deed of the other buddhas.

When water from many rivers flows into the ocean, although all the molecules of water have the same qualities, they do not become one molecule. They remain distinct molecules, and a buddha is able to differentiate them, "This molecule is from the Ganges; that molecule is from the Brahmaputra." Nevertheless, they function in union to support aquatic life, and in this sense they cannot be differentiated. Water from both the Ganges and the Brahmaputra contribute to the Indian Ocean, but once they intermingle with other water molecules in the ocean, we can't tell which water molecule is from which river and all of them perform the same function.

Since there are already countless buddhas benefiting sentient beings, why is it important for us to become buddhas? Before becoming buddhas, each of us had different relationships with various sentient beings. Because of these different karmic links formed when we were sentient beings, it may be easier for us after we attain buddhahood to guide a specific sentient being to awakening. This indicates that each buddha has his or her own mental continuum, although their awakened activities flow forth in unison with other buddhas.

Another indication that buddhas have individual mindstreams is that when they were bodhisattvas on the path they expressed different unshakable resolves that they would accomplish as buddhas. For example, due to the strong unshakable resolve that Amitābha Buddha made while he was a bodhisattva, he was able to establish Sukhāvatī pure land as a buddha. As a result of the strong unshakable resolves made by each of the thirty-five buddhas, they are able to aid sentient beings with purifying specific destructive karma.

In the *Treasury of Knowledge*, Vasubandhu says that all buddhas are the same in three aspects: (1) their attainment of the dharmakāya, the state of full awakening; (2) their completion of the two collections of merit and wisdom; and (3) their activities directed toward the benefit of sentient beings. However, to benefit sentient beings in the most suitable and extensive way, they appear differently in the world in three ways: (1) they have different form bodies, (2) the lifespan of their supreme emanation bodies differ, and (3) the size and appearance of the bodies that they emanate are different.

The mindstreams of sentient beings do not become one at the time of attaining full awakening. According to the Vajrayāna, the combination of the subtlest wind, which becomes the enjoyment body of that buddha, and the subtlest mind, which becomes the dharmakāya of that buddha, is the basis of designation of that particular buddha. A buddha, like all sentient beings, has five aggregates; however, a buddha's aggregates are pure, whereas those of sentient beings are not. A buddha's five aggregates act as the basis of designation of that buddha. Nevertheless the buddhas who are merely designated in dependence on a set of aggregates do not have a reified sense of I and mine and instead relate to I and mine as mere designations that fulfill a purpose conventionally.

Questions about the Buddha

As we learned in the chapters about refuge and the Three Jewels in *Following in the Buddha's Footsteps*, buddhas have many unique features that are not shared with ordinary beings or even with other āryas. Here we'll look at some questions that arise about the qualities and abilities of buddhas.

Does a buddha create karma? A buddha's awakening activity is action (*carya*), but it is beyond polluted and unpolluted karma. Polluted karma is created by those who have not directly realized emptiness, and unpolluted karma is created by āryas who still have latencies of ignorance and other cognitive obscurations. The āryas who are arhats and pure-ground bodhisattvas take a mental body that arises due to the base of latencies of ignorance and unpolluted actions, all of which a buddha has abandoned. Because of having this mental body, bodhisattvas of the pure grounds cannot act in completely spontaneous ways, whereas all of a buddha's activity is spontaneous and effortless. For this reason, the mental body is called "the subtle māra of the aggregates," a negative force that buddhas have overcome. In contrast, a buddha's body is not a mental body like that. The purified subtlest winds have become an enjoyment body that is the nature of that buddha's wisdom mind.

Buddhas have no conceptual consciousnesses and perceive all phenomena directly and nonconceptually. How do they identify objects without conception? Identifying objects occurs due to the mental factor of discrimination, which is one of the five omnipresent mental factors that accompany all consciousnesses. Buddhas also have this mental factor. In sentient beings, discrimination accompanies nonconceptual minds such as visual direct perceivers, where it discerns one color from another, for example. It also accompanies conceptual mental consciousnesses. In higher-level mental functions, discrimination plays an important role in determining the attributes of an object and in discerning the value of one idea over another. Although buddhas no longer have such conceptual consciousnesses, discrimination functions in their mental consciousnesses—which are all nonconceptual—to identify objects.

Discrimination performs a similar function in other nonconceptual consciousnesses of āryas as well. For example, the uninterrupted path of the path of seeing is a nonconceptual mental consciousness that realizes emptiness directly. It does not think, "This is emptiness," because the mind and emptiness are nondual, like water mixed in water. Nevertheless the mental factor of discrimination in this mind identifies emptiness correctly.

In the state of full awakening, there is no conceptual thought, so there is no sense of I and mine. That doesn't mean there are no designations of I and mine, because the Buddha himself said "I'm walking" and "in my past life, I was so-and-so." Prāsaṅgikas say that buddhas use names and labels to accord with conventional reality so that they can communicate with sentient beings, not because they have conceptual thoughts.

The Buddhas' Three Mysteries

Candrakīrti says the qualities of a tenth-ground bodhisattva are beyond the cognition and comprehension of ordinary beings and are inexpressible in language. If the qualities of a tenth-grounder are like this, needless to say the resultant stage of buddhahood is beyond our ability to express in language or to know through our limited conceptual mind.

The inexhaustibility of the Buddha's three mysteries—the awakened body, speech, and mind—is spoken of primarily from the tantric perspective. These three mysteries of the Buddha are inseparable; they are one nature, and the ultimate source for attaining them is the subtlest wind-mind that we have at present. Because our current subtlest mind and subtlest wind are one nature, they can be transformed into the inseparable body, speech, and mind of a buddha. The subtlest wind is the mount that consciousness rides on. The subtle wind manifests as our voice, which is an expression of or the tone of that wind. At the time of attaining buddhahood, the subtlest wind becomes a buddha's speech as well as a buddha's form bodies; the subtlest mind becomes the wisdom truth body, and its emptiness becomes the natural stainless purity of a buddha's nature truth body. A buddha's body, speech, and mind are one nature but nominally different.

To effect a buddha's activities, body, speech, and mind must be unified, and to bring that about, the complete unmistaken path as shown in highest yoga tantra must be practiced. How does a buddha's inseparability of body, speech, and mind come about? The coarse bodies and minds of ordinary beings are different natures. Although the continuity of the mental consciousness continues after death, the coarse body ceases. The sense consciousnesses, such as the visual consciousness, that depend on the brain, also cease. At the time of death, the coarse consciousnesses—the sense consciousnesses and coarse mental consciousness—absorb into the subtlest clear light. This extremely subtle mind is without beginning or end and is inseparable from the subtlest wind. This subtlest wind-mind is inexhaustible in that it continues on forever. When its continuity is purified by means of tantric practices, it transforms into the body, speech, and mind of a buddha.

When advanced practitioners of highest yoga tantra emerge from meditation on the actual clear light and spontaneously generate a pure illusory body on the completion stage, that pure illusory body and the actual clear-light mind are one nature; they are now free of all afflictive obscurations. As these advanced yogīs continue to practice, they eliminate the cognitive obscurations and become buddhas. At that time, their truth bodies and form bodies are inseparable and are one nature. The subtlest wind that became the pure illusory body is the substantial cause for a buddha's body. The radiance of the subtlest wind becomes a buddha's speech. The subtlest clear light, which became the actual clear light, is the substantial cause for a buddha's mind. A buddha's body, speech, and mind are the inexhaustible source of benefit for all sentient beings, because through them a buddha manifests, teaches, and leads us to full awakening.

These three are called "mysteries" or "secrets" because the inseparability of a buddha's body, speech, and mind is very different from the obvious and coarse body, speech, and mind of ordinary beings, which are not one nature and separate after death. They are also called "mysteries" because they are difficult to understand with our conceptual minds. Only buddhas fully understand and experience them.

Seeing the Buddha

People may speak of "seeing the Buddha," but what does that really mean? The *Flower Ornament Sūtra* says:[113]

> Even if, across the course of a hundred thousand eons,
> one constantly gazed at the Tathāgata,
> he would still not be relying on the genuine meaning
> in his contemplation of the World's Protector.
>
> This person, so seizing on appearances,
> simply increases the scope of his net of foolishness and delusion
> and ties himself up in the prison of births and deaths
> wherein, entirely blind, he fails to see the Buddha at all.

If, in deeply contemplating all phenomena,
one sees that they are devoid of any inherent existence,
sees that as befits their characteristic arising and ceasing,
they are mere utterances of false names,
sees that all phenomena undergo no production at all,
and sees that all phenomena undergo no destruction at all—
if one is able to comprehend them in these ways,
then all buddhas will always appear directly before him.

The nature of phenomena is fundamentally empty and peaceful,
and as such, has nothing one can grasp and nothing one can see.
The emptiness of any inherent nature is just the Buddha
and is such as one cannot assess through thought.

If one realizes that all phenomena
are in their essential nature just thus,
this person then will not become
defiled by and attached to the afflictions.

When the common person observes any phenomenon,
he simply follows the permutations in its characteristic signs,
fails to completely comprehend that phenomena are utterly signless,
and on account of this, then fails to perceive the Buddha.

The *Muni* has gone beyond the three periods of time,
has completely perfected all of the characteristic signs,
abides in nonabiding,
is universally present everywhere and yet unmoving.

In this volume we have learned about the six and ten perfections as well as how śrāvakas, solitary realizers, and bodhisattvas progress along the paths of their respective vehicles. In addition, since all sentient beings will become fully awakened buddhas, the qualities, realizations, and awakening activities of the buddhas have been explained. But don't think that just because buddhahood has been described that the *Library of Wisdom and Compassion* is nearing its end. In this volume the perfection of wisdom was briefly introduced, but there is a lot more to learn about selflessness, emptiness, the two truths, and the mind that realizes these. In addition, the tantric path must be explained, since it is also a major branch of the Mahāyāna. So there are several more volumes of the *Library of Wisdom and Compassion* to come!

Notes

1. The *Mahāprajñāpāramitā Upadeśa* is Nāgārjuna's extensive commentary on the *Twenty-Five-Thousand-Line Perfection of Wisdom Sūtra*. Translated into Chinese by Kumārajīva in 402–5, this text has been popular and influential in China throughout the centuries and is the central text of the Sanlun (Madhyamaka) school in China. Étienne Lamotte does not attribute this exegesis to Nāgārjuna but thinks it was written by a monk of the Sarvāstivāda or Mūlasarvāstivāda school from northwest India. Unfortunately, the text was not translated into Tibetan.
2. The root text says:

   Then there are its twenty-two aspects:
   Similar to the earth, gold, the moon, and fire,
   a treasure, jewel mine, and the ocean,
   a vajra, mountain, medicine, and guide,

   a wish-fulfilling jewel, the sun, and a song,
   a king, a treasury, and a great highway,
   an excellent horse, and a spring of water,
   sweet-sounding music, a river, and a cloud.

   See *In Praise of Great Compassion*, 56, 157, and 163–69 for details on the twenty-two types of bodhicitta, each of which is correlated with a level of the bodhicitta path and has an accompanying feature that enhances it.
3. Of the ten nonvirtues, three are done physically: killing, stealing, and unwise sexual behavior; four are verbal: lying, creating disharmony with our speech, harsh speech, and idle talk; and three are mental: coveting, ill will or maliciousness, and wrong views.
4. The meaning is the virtue created by generosity is ours; the merit will ripen in good conditions in future lives. But whatever we do not give because of our miserliness, we must leave behind at death. Neither it nor the virtue from giving it away is ours.
5. See chapters 10–12 in *The Foundation of Buddhist Practice* for more about karma and its effects.

6. See chapter 7 in *Approaching the Buddhist Path* for the text of the "Eight Verses of Thought Transformation" and His Holiness's commentary on it.
7. Monastics may not take lower levels of prātimokṣa precepts such as the eight one-day prātimokṣa precepts, but they can take the eight Mahāyāna precepts.
8. Twelve ascetic practices taught by the Buddha, as laid out in the Dharmaguptaka Vinaya, which concern *shelter* (staying in a forest, beneath trees, in a charnel ground, or in an open area without a roof); *sleeping* (sleeping sitting up cross-legged, using grass as a mattress); *food* (going on alms, eating only one meal a day, not taking a second helping, not omitting any house when on alms round); and *clothes* (wear robes made from discarded material, have only one set of the three robes).
9. Depending on their faculties and aptitude, at different points on the path bodhisattvas will receive signs that they will definitely not relapse to lower levels. For those with high faculties, this occurs on the path of preparation, for those of middle faculties on the path of seeing, and for those of lesser faculties on the eighth ground. One of the signs they receive is either meeting a buddha or having a vision of a buddha who prophesies the circumstances of that bodhisattva's awakening.
10. See chapter 2 in *The Foundation of Buddhist Practice* for more about syllogisms and reliable cognizers.
11. Access concentration in the Pāli tradition is equivalent to the capable preparation in the Sanskrit tradition. See chapters 8 and 9 in *Following in the Buddha's Footsteps* for more about access concentration and the capable preparation.
12. Found in the "King of Prayers: The Extraordinary Aspiration of the Practice of Samantabhadra," in the *Array of Stalks Sūtra* (*Gaṇḍavyūha Sūtra*), which is included in the *Flower Ornament Sūtra.*
13. Found in the "Pure Conduct" chapter of the *Flower Ornament Sūtra.*
14. For example, in the paths and grounds texts, they are generally synonymous, while in Tantrayāna they are not.
15. Asaṅga's explanation does not divide the perfection of wisdom and the perfection of pristine wisdom into fixed categories. As mentioned above, the last four perfections are branches of the perfection of wisdom, and as noted in the description of the perfection of wisdom, one type of the perfection of wisdom knows conventional truths such as the five fields of knowledge.
16. The fundamental innate clear-light mind that is focused on emptiness is the ultimate meaning of "ultimate bodhicitta" in Tantra. The secret meaning of "bodhicitta" is the subtle drops of the male and female, which are neither conventional nor ultimate bodhicitta.
17. Does the subtle innate clear-light mind of sentient beings transform at the time of awakening or not? There are two positions: Some say that it does not transform when awakening is attained. They give the analogy of ice and water. Although ice melts and changes into water, the nature of water and ice is the same. Similarly, in terms of the nature of their subtle innate clear-light minds, there is no difference between sentient beings and buddhas. Others say that the subtle innate clear-light mind of sentient beings transforms when they become buddhas. This is because

the subtle innate clear-light mind of sentient beings is not yet free from cognitive obscurations and does not yet possess all the qualities of a buddha.

18. The Tzu Chi Foundation, founded by the Chinese nun Dharma Master Cheng Yen, is an international organization that reaches out to refugees, victims of natural disasters, and many others. Buddhist Global Relief, founded by the American monk Bhikkhu Bodhi, directs its efforts toward resolving hunger across the globe. The Bodhicitta Foundation, begun by the Australian nun Ayya Yeshe, serves the Dalits in India and women and children in developing countries.
19. "The vast" refers to the method aspect of the path, especially the bodhisattva deeds that collect merit. "The profound" refers to the wisdom aspect of the path, especially the wisdom realizing emptiness and the collection of wisdom.
20. These sūtras most likely existed in other schools among the early eighteen schools in India. For example, a version of the *Ratana Sutta* is found in the *Mahāvastu*, a text in the Lokottaravāda school. A comparative study of the Pāli and Sanskrit versions can be found at https://www.ancient-buddhist-texts.net/Buddhist-Texts/C1-Ratanasutta/Ratanasutta.htm.
21. Some verses from the *Jewel Sutta* were explained in chapter 1 of *Following in the Buddha's Footsteps.*
22. http://www.lotsawahouse.org/powerful_words_of_truth.html.
23. http://www.tibet.com/DL/truth.html.
24. *Mind-Seal of the Buddhas: Patriarch Ou-i's Commentary on the Amitābha Sūtra*, trans. J. C. Cleary (San Francisco: Sūtra Translation Committee of the United States and Canada, 1997), 103–4. Chih-hsu Ou-i (1599–1655) was a distinguished Pure Land master.
25. The recollections of the Buddha, Dharma, and Saṅgha are described in chapter 2 of *Following in the Buddha's Footsteps.*
26. This text is from the Khuddaka Nikāya in the Pāli canon. Together with the *Buddhavaṃsa* and *Apadāna*, it is considered a later text.
27. Found in the Khuddaka Nikāya and also in the Chinese and Tibetan canon, this is a collection of stories of Śākyamuni Buddha's previous lives as both a human being and animal. Popular in traditional societies, these stories illustrate valued qualities such as generosity and ethical conduct.
28. The *Bodhisattvabhūmi* is the fifteenth chapter of the *Yogācārabhūmi*. The Tibetans attribute it to Asaṅga, whereas the Chinese attribute it to Asaṅga's teacher, Maitreya.
29. Bhikkhu Bodhi said the sections from the *Bodhisattvabhūmi* that Dhammapāla included were those on the practice of the perfections, the four shackles to giving, and the special accomplishments resulting from the practice of the perfections. However, nothing from Mahāyāna philosophy—for example, the three buddha bodies, the emptiness of inherent existence, one final vehicle—was included.
30. *Adhiṭṭhāna* originally meant "foundation" or "basis" in Pāli but later came to mean "determination." The Sanskrit equivalent, *adhiṣṭhāna*, acquired yet another meaning—"blessing" or "transformation into magnificence" (T. *byin rlab*), referring to the Buddha's spiritual power that inspires and transforms the minds of

practitioners so they will gain Dharma realizations. Perhaps this meaning of *adhiṣṭhāna* derives from it being seen as a foundation or support that sustains bodhisattva practitioners. In its usage in Vinaya, *adhiṣṭhāna* refers to determining, mentally resolving, or designating that these robes are one's monastic robes. Sometimes it has been mistranslated in English as "blessing the robes," and people mistakenly think that some special power of the Buddha is absorbed into the robes. However, the action is more prosaic: we are determining that these particular robes are our set of robes.

31. *Mettā* is sometimes translated as "loving-kindness."
32. These four are keeping the prātimokṣa precepts, controlling our senses so they don't wander, procuring our daily requisites or livelihood in a completely pure way, and relying only on the requisites permitted for a monastic to use in daily life.
33. Osadhi is a "bright star"—it is actually the planet Venus—that is balanced in the sense that it does not deviate from its course. This is analogous to the chief disciples not deviating from the truth.
34. The translator, Bhikkhu Ñāṇamoli, gives as an endnote to this passage, "For 10 powers and 4 fearlessnesses, see MN 12. For 6 knowledges see *Paṭisambhidāmagga* i, 12lf. For 18 states of awakened one, see *Cariyāpiṭaka* Commentary."
35. In general, "renunciation" in the Pāli tradition refers to relinquishing attachment to sense pleasures, which usually leads someone to leave the household life and take up the homeless life of a monastic.
36. According to Mingun Sayādaw (http://homepage.ntlworld.com/pesala/Nibbana/html/fruit.html), these are (1) having no hindrance with regard to knowledge of the past, (2) having no hindrance with regard to knowledge of the present, (3) having no hindrance with regard to knowledge of the future, (4) being preceded by wisdom in all physical actions, (5) being preceded by wisdom in all verbal actions, (6) being preceded by wisdom in all mental actions, (7) having no falling off in intention, (8) having no falling off in energy, (9) having no falling off in concentration, (10) having no falling off in wisdom, (11) having no falling off in teaching the Dhamma, (12) having no falling off in emancipation, (13) not indulging in joking and laughter, (14) not making blunders, (15) having nothing that cannot be gauged by wisdom, (16) having nothing that needs to be attended in a hurry, (17) never being negligent, and (18) not undertaking anything without due reflection. These are the same in the Sanskrit tradition.
37. The thirteen ascetic practices (*dhutaṅga*) are the practices of the (1) refuse-rag wearer who wears robes made from discarded or torn cloth and does not accept ready-made robes offered by lay followers; (2) triple-robe wearer who possesses and wears only three robes without having any additional allowable robes; (3) alms-food eater who consumes only food collected on alms round and does not accept food brought to the monastery or offered at lunch dāna by a lay follower; (4) house-to-house seeker who goes to all houses on alms round and not only to wealthy households or those chosen for special reasons; (5) one-sessioner who eats one meal a day and does not take food offered before midday; (6) bowl-food eater in whose bowl all the food is mixed together; (7) later-food refuser who does not

accept any more food after he has shown that he is satisfied, although lay followers want to offer more; (8) forest dweller who does not live in a town or village but in a secluded place; (9) tree-root dweller who lives under a tree without the protection of a roof; (10) open-air dweller who dwells in the open with only a tent made of his robes; (11) charnel-ground dweller who lives in or near a charnel ground, graveyard, or cremation ground; (12) any-bed user who is content with any place he is given to sleep; and (13) sitter who stays only in the postures of walking, standing, and sitting without ever lying down.

38. These are the ten kasiṇas, the ten impurities, the ten recollections, the four immeasurables, the four formless states, the one perception, and the one analysis.
39. The twelve sources are a way of classifying phenomena according to the type of object and the faculty facilitating its perception. The eighteen constituents are a way of categorizing phenomena according to the object, faculty, and perceiving consciousness. See chapter 3 of *The Foundation of Buddhist Practice*.
40. See chapter 8 in *Following in the Buddha's Footsteps* for more on the superknowledges.
41. See Vism chapters 18–22 for more on the five purifications.
42. The antidotes to anger that Dhammapāla proposes are very similar to the ones Śāntideva teaches in chapter 6 of *Engaging in the Bodhisattvas' Deeds*.
43. A declaration of truth is a statement of fact spoken with a strong virtuous intention motivated by love and compassion. The truth of this fact assures the occurrence of an event. In this case, the chick's mind was transformed into virtue by reflecting on the marvelous qualities of the Three Jewels. The power of that virtuous mind was expressed in the declaration of truth and resulted in the chick escaping the fire.
44. The four foundations are also found in the *Sutta on the Exposition of the Elements* (*Dhātuvibhanga Sutta*, MN 140.11).
45. According to the Pāli tradition, bodhisattvas only become āryas when they take their seat under the bodhi tree and attain the four paths and fruitions in immediate succession. According to the Sanskrit tradition, they become āryas at the path of seeing and at that time they are free from manifest malice, jealousy, competitiveness, hypocrisy, miserliness, stubbornness, and arrogance.
46. These physical signs of a buddha are spoken of in the Pāli canon. The Pāli tradition says the thirty-two signs are found in the treatises of the brahmins, although strangely, they are not found in the Vedas and their ancillary texts that have come down to us in the present day. In any case, the presence of these signs were the way that many brahmins determined that the Buddha was a great man (P. *mahāpurisa*). See the *Brahmāyu Sutta*, MN 91:9. In another sūtra (SN 47.11), the Buddha says a great man is one who has a liberated mind gained through practicing the four establishments of mindfulness.
47. Here the truth body refers to all the magnificent qualities of the fully awakened ones. It does not refer to the Buddha's subtle form body as explained in the Mahāyāna.
48. According to the Prajñāpāramitā Sūtras, these are six unique behaviors: a

buddha has no mistaken physical actions, verbal actions, lack of mindfulness, unequipoised mind, discordant appearances, or indifference of not investigating individual characteristics of phenomena; six unique realizations: a buddha has undeclining aspiration, joyous effort, mindfulness, concentration, wisdom, and complete liberation; three unique awakening activities of body, speech, and mind; and three unique pristine wisdoms that know everything in the past, present, and future. See chapter 2 of *Following in the Buddha's Footsteps*.

49. According to several Pāli commentaries and narrative texts, solitary realizers teach others ethical conduct and concentration meditation practices. They ordain and take disciples. But they don't convey the essence of their realization—that is, they don't lead others to final liberation. See the commentary to the *Suttanipāta* (Sn), the chapter on the *Rhino Horn Sutta*.
50. Those called bodhisattvas in any of the three vehicles are not yet āryas. They become āryas only with the attainment of stream-entry. For fully awakened buddhas and solitary realizers, the passage through the four ārya levels occurs in one session. Once śrāvakas become stream-enterers, they are no longer considered bodhisattvas. Bodhisattva status pertains only to the period prior to actual attainment.
51. According to the Sarvāstivādins and Vaibhāṣikas, this is a sequential process of sixteen moments, while in the Pāli tradition, it occurs in one single moment.
52. The person who questioned the Buddha spoke from the perspective of standard Buddhist doctrine that says lay practitioners do not attain arhatship and continue to lead the household life. Although it is possible for lay practitioners to attain arhatship—the merchant's son Yasa and the courtesan Khemā did so—they do not remain as lay practitioners afterward. Immediately after becoming arhats, they either pass away (like the Buddha's father) or they seek monastic ordination (like Yasa and Khemā). There are no accounts in the Pāli canon of a layperson attaining arhatship and continuing to live the lay life.
53. The *Greater Series of Questions and Answers* (*Mahāvedalla Sutta*, MN 43) describes several kinds of liberation of mind: the neither-painful-nor-pleasant liberation of mind is the fourth dhyāna; the immeasurable liberation of mind is the meditative attainment of the four immeasurables; the liberation of mind through nothingness is abiding in the meditative absorption on nothingness; the liberation of mind through emptiness is insight into the emptiness of self in persons and things; and the signless liberation of mind is the attainment of fruition (nirvāṇa is the signless element in which all signs of conditioned phenomena are absent). The liberations of mind of the four immeasurables, nothingness, and emptiness are considered mundane. However, the commentary also explains that there are different types of these three liberations, some that are the four paths and four fruits. In a monastic whose defilements have been destroyed, the liberations of mind of the four immeasurables, nothingness, emptiness, and the signless liberation refer to the fruition attainment of arhatship, which is also called the "unshakable liberation of mind" (P. *akuppa cetovimutti*). Here immeasurable,

nothingness, emptiness, and the signless are all names for nirvāṇa, the object of that fruition attainment.

54. According to the Prāsaṅgika system, the view of a personal identity is a form of self-grasping ignorance. Prāsaṅgikas assert that ignorance actively grasps at inherent existence, the opposite of reality, and since the view of a personal identity grasps the inherent existence of I and mine, it is a form of ignorance. Thus they say that both ignorance and view of a personal identity, in both their acquired and innate forms, are totally eradicated at arhatship or upon a bodhisattva attaining the eighth ground.

According to the Pāli tradition, the view of a personal identity holds that one or another of the aggregates is a self, whereas ignorance is obscuration that does not clearly know the four truths. Eradicating the view of a personal identity when attaining the fruit of stream-enterer does not remove all deluded notions of I and mine; the conceit "I am" remains and is eliminated only with the attainment of arhatship. The conceit "I am" and the spontaneous notion of I remain in the stream-enterers, once-returners, and non-returners. These graspings of I may still arise in them, threatening to give rise to pride or conceited self-love, but these āryas are able to recognize them as afflictive and dispel them. While such thoughts may arise, they cannot crystallize into a view of a substantial, findable self as held by the view of a personal identity. In the *Khemaka Sutta* (SN 22:89), Bhikkhu Khemaka states that he does not regard anything among the five aggregates as self or as belonging to self. Nor does he regard anything among the aggregates as "This I am." However, he admits he is not an arhat because the residual conceit "I am," the desire "I am," and the underlying tendency "I am" in relation to the aggregates have not yet been uprooted. By repeatedly contemplating the rising and ceasing of the five aggregates, these deeper layers of grasping at self are totally eradicated. The *Khemaka Sutta* says:

> Suppose there was a cloth that had become soiled and dirty, and the owners gave it to a laundryman. With various kinds of lye and soap he washes out the dirt, yet there is still a remainder of smell. By mixing it with various kinds of fragrance he makes that disappear. In the same way, although rightly contemplating these five aggregates of clinging as not-self and not belonging to a self, still the learned ariya disciple has not yet abandoned the conceit "I am" in relation to these five aggregates of clinging, the desire [related to the notion] "I am," and the underlying tendency toward "I am"; he has not yet fully understood it, not yet become separated from it, not yet vomited it out.

55. Svātantrikas say these stream-enterers will be reborn in the desire realm no more than three more times; Prāsaṅgikas say no more than one time.

56. Although only nonreturners are reborn in the pure abodes, there is no pervasion that all nonreturners are reborn there.

57. A qualm is raised here. Nonreturners have eliminated the fetters of sensual

desire and malice, which are two of the five hindrances that impede attaining the dhyānas. It would seem that someone who has eliminated those two fetters would therefore have also attained at least the first dhyāna. Also, since nonreturners may be born in the pure lands in the fourth form realm, it would seem that they should have attained dhyāna. According to certain sutras, dhyāna is a condition to become a nonreturner.

58. See chapter 8 in *Following in the Buddha's Footsteps* for more about this meditative state.
59. In the Chinese āgama counterparts to SN 12:70, the monks who become arhats explicitly deny having attained any of the dhyānas when they say they are liberated by wisdom. The *Mahāvibhāṣā* commentary to that sūtra explains that arhats liberated by wisdom have not necessarily attained full dhyāna, although they have access concentration (*sāmantaka*, *upacāra samādhi*).
60. For more on Dhamma followers and faith followers see SN 25:1.
61. The seven purifications are also mentioned in the *Relay Chariots Sutta* (*Rathavinīta Sutta*, MN 24). They are included in the list of nine factors of the effort for perfect purity (P. *pārisuddhi-padhāniyangāni*) in the *Expanding Decades Sutta* (*Dasuttara Sutta*, DN 34.2.2), where the purities of wisdom and liberation are added to make nine factors.
62. See Vism chapters 14–17.
63. See Vism chapters 1 and 2.
64. See Vism chapters 3–13.
65. See Vism chapters 18–22 for more on the following five purifications.
66. A proximate cause of a mental state is the immediately preceding mental state that gave rise to it without any intervening mental state. It is a cause whose result arises in immediate succession to it.
67. A path consciousness resembles an uninterrupted path in the Nālandā tradition, and a fruition consciousness is comparable to a liberated path.
68. For more about nirvāṇa from the viewpoints of both the Pāli and Sanskrit traditions, see chapter 11 of *Saṃsāra, Nirvāṇa, and Buddha Nature*.
69. For the etymology of a few of the other synonyms for nirvāṇa, see Vism 8:247.
70. Looked at from another perspective, could these perhaps intimate that nirvāṇa is free from the conception of "inherent existence"?
71. Included in the Khuddaka Nikāya is the *Chronicle of Buddhas* (*Buddhavaṃsa*), which most scholars believe was written during the first and second centuries BCE and is a late addition to the Pāli canon. Here Śāriputra asks the Buddha how he attained buddhahood, and the Buddha relates the story of his encounter as the ascetic Sumedha with the past Buddha Dīpaṅkara.
72. See *Saṃsāra, Nirvāṇa, and Buddha Nature* for a detailed description of the four truths.
73. The exception to this is that Yogācāra-Svātantrikas say that the principal meditation object for solitary realizers is the nonexistence of subjects and objects as different substantial entities.

74. From the *Sūtra on the Miserliness of One in Trance* (*Dhyāyitamuṣṭi Sūtra*), as cited in the twenty-fourth chapter of Candrakīrti's *Clear Words*.
75. See *Following in the Buddha's Footsteps*, 449, for a brief explanation of the five paths.
76. According to Bhikkhu Bodhi, the etymology for the Pāli word *abhisamaya* is *abhi* = superior; *sam* = together, but also functions as a simple intensifier; *aya* = going, but sometimes has the sense of "to know." The etymology according to the Sanskrit tradition is *abhi* = toward, over; *sam* = together with; *i* = to understand. In general, it means a coming together of a knower and an object to be known. The Tibetan *mngon* = clear; *rtogs* = realization and could refer to liberation, so a clear realization is a path that leads to liberation.
77. See EOM, *A Brief Presentation of the Grounds and Paths of the Perfection Vehicle, Essence of the Ocean of Profound Meaning* (*Phar phyin theg pa'i lugs kyi theg pa gsum gyi sa dang lam gyi rnam par bzhag pa mdo tsam du brjod pa zab don rgya mtsho'i snying po*) by Losang Tayang (Rje btsun Blo bzang rta dbyangs), trans. Jules Levinson.
78. You may want to review chapter 8, especially 226–27, in *Following in the Buddha's Footsteps*, which speaks about the various grades of ignorance and afflictions.
79. The mental basis of a practitioner refers to the sphere of consciousness he or she possesses in meditation. See *Following in the Buddha's Footsteps*, 212, for more about this topic. The mental basis of approachers to stream-enterer and approachers to once-returners is a preparation of the first concentration and not an actual dhyāna. This is because these practitioners have not yet eliminated the five hindrances to concentration and thus have not attained an actual dhyāna.
80. Also see chapter 8 of *Following in the Buddha's Footsteps*.
81. Nevertheless, śrāvaka and solitary realizer arhats will experience aging, sickness, and death under the influence of karma because their body is true duḥkha.
82. See chapter 8 of *Following in the Buddha's Footsteps* for more about these four.
83. Although in English these practitioners are referred to by one term, "solitary realizers," in Sanskrit and Tibetan they may be referred to as *pratyekabuddha* (self-buddha, T. *rang sangs rgyas*) or *pratyekajina* (self-victor, T. *rang rgyal*).
84. The manuals of individual monasteries may have different explanations of when this transference can occur.
85. See chapter 5 of *In Praise of Great Compassion*.
86. In his introduction to the text Losang Tayang (aka Losang Dadrin) says, "Within the Mahāyāna there are two [vehicles], the causal Perfection Vehicle and the effect Vajra Vehicle. I will express briefly a presentation of the grounds and paths of the three vehicles in the system of the first [of those], the Perfection Vehicle, in accordance with the uncommon mode of assertion of the glorious Prāsaṅgikas, the great thoroughly nonabiding Mādhyamikas." See EOM.
87. Some people say these bodhisattvas have attained serenity before entering the path of accumulation; others say that if they have not already attained it, they do so during the path of accumulation.

88. For more on analogies for the twenty-two types of bodhicitta, see chapter 4 of *In Praise of Great Compassion*.
89. See chapter 8 for more on the concentration of the stream of Dharma and how to attain it.
90. Human beings born in the Northern Continent (according to ancient Indian cosmology), hermaphrodites, and neuters are not able to enter the bodhisattva path of being in that lifetime.
91. Śrāvakas and solitary realizers can attain their path of seeing with access concentration—a preparation for an actual dhyāna. Bodhisattvas, on the other hand, have definitely attained the fourth dhyāna by meditating on aspects of peace and grossness on the path of preparation.
92. This is according to the Prāsaṅgikas. Vaibhāṣikas assert that each fortitude is followed by its own knowledge. That is followed by the next fortitude and its knowledge, and so on.
93. See Karl Brunnhölzl, *Groundless Paths: The Prajñāpāramitā Sūtras, The Ornament of Clear Realization, and Its Commentaries in the Tibetan Nyingma Tradition* (Boston: Snow Lion Publications, 2012).
94. For a sharp-faculty bodhisattva, twenty of the forty-four signs of irreversibility occur on the path of preparation: eleven on the heat stage, six on the peak stage, two on the fortitude stage, and one on the supreme mundane dharma stage.
95. Some texts limit the realization of the fortitude of nonarising of dharmas to the bodhisattva path of seeing or the eighth bodhisattva ground. However, as a realization of the truth of emptiness, it can also be applied to the Fundamental Vehicle path of seeing.
96. Although the Pāli tradition does not differentiate between acquired and innate levels of afflictions, it says that these same three afflictions are abandoned by stream-enterers.
97. This is the view of Tsongkhapa and Kedrup Gelek Palzang. Gyaltsab Darma Rinchen says that bodhisattvas on the first through seventh grounds can attain a mental body if they exert effort, but only śrāvaka arhats and pure-ground bodhisattvas effortlessly obtain a mental body.
98. In this context "unpolluted karma" refers to the mental factor of intention free from the influence of afflictive obscurations.
99. Base (ground) of latencies of ignorance has the same meaning as latencies of ignorance. When speaking of latencies of ignorance, we are also speaking of the latencies of all afflictions.
100. The Buddha prescribed the twelve austere practices—which concern shelter, bedding, food, and clothing—for disciples with great attachment. There are various versions of these twelve, and some texts say there are thirteen practices. They are to stay in the forest, beneath trees, in a charnel ground, or in the open air; to sleep sitting cross-legged, not lying down, using grass as a mattress; to eat by going for alms, having one meal a day without going for another helping, and eating from one's alms bowl; and to wear robes made from discarded material, having only one set of three robes (five for nuns).

101. Another doubt may arise: At the path of seeing, some bodhisattvas make strong effort and attain a mental body that is not produced by afflictions and polluted karma but through prayers and virtue. How is it possible to cut the body of these bodhisattvas when they no longer have gross physical bodies like ours? To the perspective of ordinary beings, an ārya bodhisattva's mental body appears to be an ordinary body that can be cut into pieces.
102. Some scholar-adepts say that eighth-grounders are nearing the ten masteries and completely attain them at buddhahood, because the set of ten masteries is one of the twenty-one kinds of dharmakāya wisdom possessed by buddhas.
103. Some people may wonder if descriptions of such elaborate ceremonies are to be taken literally considering that the transition from the last uninterrupted path as a sentient being to the liberated path of buddhahood occurs in meditative equipoise on emptiness. I (Chodron) think that the point is for us to pause and contemplate what attaining full awakening means, rejoice that bodhisattvas in the past, present, and future will attained it, and be energized to do the same ourselves.
104. Master Sheng-yen established Dharma Drum Mountain as well as several other associated institutions for the propagation of the Dharma. He invited His Holiness to give several days of teachings in New York City in 1998. At the conclusion of this, the two had a public dialogue during which the following topics about Chan Buddhism and the Nālandā tradition were discussed. See H. H. the 14th Dalai Lama and Venerable Chan Master Sheng-yen, *Meeting of Minds: A Dialogue on Tibetan and Chinese Buddhism* (Taiwan: Dharma Drum Publications, 1999).
105. See *Following in the Buddha's Footsteps*, chapters 1 and 2.
106. The place of each buddha in a maṇḍala may differ according to the maṇḍala. Vairocana's and Akṣobhya's elements are exchanged in some versions.
107. Various places are called Akaniṣṭha. This particular one is a pure land outside of saṃsāra that is not made of coarse matter. Each buddha establishes their own Akaniṣṭha pure land that has arisen due to their great collections of merit and wisdom.
108. See chapter 1 in *The Foundation of Buddhist Practice* for more about the four seals that make a teaching Buddhist.
109. In Chinese temples and monasteries, when the Dharma drum is sounded in the early morning to arouse the monastics, they imagine that all sentient beings from the hell realms to the god realms hear the Dharma that alleviates their suffering.
110. This is a branch of setting trainees on the tenth ground although it is not listed as one of the twenty-seven awakening activities. It has eight branches itself (19–26) that count among the twenty-seven.
111. Nāgārjuna, *Exegesis on the Great Perfection of Wisdom Sūtra*, in *Nāgārjuna on the Six Perfections*, trans. Bhikṣu Dharmamitra (Seattle: Kalavinka Press, 2009), 523–25.
112. "Basis" most likely refers to the body in this context. However, one geshé suggested that it could refer to the emptiness of the mind. In the Perfection of Wis-

dom sūtras and the *Ornament of Clear Realizations* "basis" often refers to the emptiness that is the basis for accomplishing the path.

113. From chapter 14, "The Praise Verses on Sumeru's Summit," in the *Mahāvaipulya Buddhāvataṃsaka Sūtra* as translated into Chinese in 699 by Śikṣānanda in T10n0279_p0081c07–22. From unpublished manuscript provided by courtesy of the translator, Bhikṣu Dharmamitra.

Glossary

Abhidharma. A field of study and its texts that contain detailed reworkings of material in the Buddhist sūtras according to schematic classifications.

absolutism (eternalism, permanence, *śāśvatānta*). The belief that phenomena inherently exist.

access. *See* preparatory stages for a dhyāna.

access concentration (P. *upacāra samādhi*). Pāli tradition: a level of concentration that prepares the mind to enter the next actual dhyāna. It is comparable to a preparation (*sāmantaka*) in the Sanskrit tradition.

actual dhyāna (T. *bsam gtan gyi dngos gzhi*). A more refined dhyānic concentration attained upon completing its preparatory stages.

afflictions (*kleśa*). Mental factors that disturb the tranquility of the mind. These include disturbing emotions and wrong views.

afflictive obscurations (*kleśāvaraṇa*). Obscurations that mainly prevent liberation; afflictions and their seeds.

aggregates (*skandha*). The four or five components that make up a living being: form (except for beings born in the formless realm), feelings, discriminations, miscellaneous factors, and consciousnesses.

analytical meditation (*vicārabhāvanā*, T. *dpyad sgom*). Meditation done to understand an object.

arhat (P. *arahant*, T. *dgra bcom pa*). Someone who has eliminated all afflictive obscurations and attained liberation.

ārya (P. *ariya*). Someone who has directly and nonconceptually realized the emptiness of inherent existence; someone who is on the path of seeing, meditation, or no-more-learning.

ārya buddha. A person who is fully awakened, such as an enjoyment body or emanation body.

awakening activity (*samudācāra*, T. *'phrin las*). A buddha's spontaneous, continuous, and impartial activity that helps bring all sentient beings to higher rebirth, liberation, and full awakening.

basis of designation. The collection of parts or factors in dependence on which an object is designated.

base of latencies of ignorance. Cognitive obscurations that give rise to the subtle dualistic view. Together with unpolluted karma, they are the cause for arhats and pure-ground bodhisattvas to take a mental body; latencies of ignorance.

bhavaṅga. A deep, underlying consciousness that accounts for the continuity of mind.

bodhicitta. A main mental consciousness induced by an aspiration to bring about others' welfare and accompanied by an aspiration to attain full awakening oneself. Its arising in an uncontrived manner marks entry into the Mahāyāna.

bodhisattva. Someone who has genuine, uncontrived bodhicitta.

bodhisattva ground. A consciousness in the continuum of an ārya bodhisattva characterized by wisdom and compassion. It is the basis for the development of good qualities and for the eradication of obscurations to full awakening.

Bön. An indigenous spiritual tradition in Tibet.

buddha. All aspects of a buddha. It includes the four buddha bodies.

Buddhadharma. The teachings of the Buddha.

clear realization / clear realizer (breakthrough, *abhisamaya*, T. *mngon rtogs*). A path, an exalted knower. According to the Pāli tradition, it is a supramundane path.

cognitive obscurations (*jñeyāvaraṇa*). Obscurations that mainly prevent full awakening; the latencies of ignorance and the subtle dualistic view that they give rise to.

collections (requisites, *sambhāra*, T. *tshogs*). A bodhisattva's practice of method and wisdom that lead to full awakening. Śrāvakas and solitary realizers create the two collections, but they are not fully qualified ones.

collection of merit (*puṇyasaṃbhāra*). A bodhisattva's practice of the method aspect of the path that accumulates merit and is the main cause for a buddha's form body.

collection of wisdom (*jñānasaṃbhāra*). A bodhisattva's practice of the wisdom aspect of the path—a Mahāyāna exalted knower that focuses on the ultimate truth, emptiness, and is the main cause for a buddha's truth body.

concentration (*samādhi*). A mental factor that dwells single-pointedly for a sustained period of time on one object; a state of deep meditative absorption; single-pointed concentration that is free from discursive thought.

concomitant (T. *mtshungs ldan*). Accompanying or occurring together in the same mental state.

consciousness (*jñāna*). That which is clear and cognizant.

conventional existence (*saṃvṛtisat*). Existence.

conventional truth (veiled truth, *saṃvṛtisatya*). All phenomena except ultimate truths.

counterpart sign (P. *paṭbhāga-nimitta*). The meditation object of a dhyāna consciousness; a conceptual object that arises on the basis of an object that is form.

cyclic existence (*saṃsāra*). The cycle of rebirth that occurs under the control of afflictions and karma.

death (*maraṇabhava*). The last moment of a lifetime when the subtlest clear-light mind manifests.

defilement (*mala*, T. *dri ma*). Either an afflictive obscuration or a cognitive obscuration.

deity (*iṣṭadevatā*, T. *yi dam*). A manifestation of the awakened mind that is meditated on in Tantra.

dependent arising (*pratītyasamutpāda*). This is of three types: (1) causal dependence—things arising due to causes and conditions, (2) mutual dependence—phenomena existing in relation to other phenomena, and (3) dependent designation—phenomena existing by being merely designated by terms and concepts.

desire realm (*kāmadhātu*). One of the three realms of cyclic existence; the realm where sentient beings are overwhelmed by attraction to and desire for sense objects.

deva. A being born as a heavenly being in the desire realm or a being born in the form or formless realms.

dhyāna (P. *jhāna*). A meditative absorption in the form realm.

dualistic appearance. The appearance of subject and object as separate, the appearance of inherent existence, the appearance of conventional phenomena.

duḥkha (P. *dukkha*). Unsatisfactory experiences of cyclic existence.

duḥkha of change. Mundane happiness and pleasure that are unstable and change into pain or discomfort.

duḥkha of pain. Evident physical and mental pain.

Dzogchen. A tantric practice emphasizing meditation on the nature of mind, practiced primarily in the Nyingma tradition.

eight liberations (*vimokṣa*, *vimokkha*, T. *rnam thar*). Eight concentrations that are the mind's temporary release from defilements. They are brought about by mastering certain meditative skills.

eight worldly concerns (*aṣṭalokadharma*). Attachment or aversion regarding material gain and loss, fame and disrepute, praise and blame, pleasure and pain.

eighteen constituents. A way of categorizing phenomena according to the object, faculty, and perceiving consciousness. See chapter 3 in *The Foundation of Buddhist Practice*.

eighteen unique qualities of a buddha. Eighteen distinctive qualities of a buddha that are not shared by arhats.

emanation body (*nirmāṇakāya*, T. *sprul sku*). The buddha body that appears as an ordinary sentient being or as an inanimate object to benefit others.

emptiness (*śūnyatā*). The ultimate nature of persons and phenomena; the lack of inherent existence, true existence, and so forth.

enjoyment body (*saṃbhogakāya*, T. *longs sku*). The buddha body that appears in the highest pure lands to teach ārya bodhisattvas.

establishments of mindfulness (*smṛtyupasthāna*, *satipaṭṭhāna*, T. *dran pa nyer bzhag*). One of the seven sets of practices comprising the thirty-seven harmonies with awakening. It focuses mindfulness on the body, feelings, mind, and phenomena.

exalted knower (*jñāna*, T. *mkhyen pa*). A realization of someone who has entered a path. It exists from the path of accumulation to the buddha ground.

fetters (*saṃyojana*). Factors that keep us bound to cyclic existence and impede the attainment of liberation. The five lower fetters—view of a personal identity, deluded doubt, view of bad rules and practices, sensual desire, and malice—bind us to rebirth in the desire realm. The five higher fetters—desire for existence in the form realm, desire for existence in the formless realm, arrogance, restlessness, and afflicted ignorance—prevent a nonreturner from becoming an arhat.

five dhyānic factors. Investigation (*vitarka*, *vitakka*), analysis (*vicāra*, *vicāra*), joy (*prīti*, *pīti*), bliss (*sukha*), and one-pointedness of mind (*ekāgratā*, *ekaggatā*).

five hindrances (*āvaraṇa*, T. *sgrib pa*). Hindrances that interfere with attaining serenity: sensual desire (*kāmacchanda*), malice (*vyāpāda*, *byāpāda*), lethargy and sleepiness (*styāna-middha*, *thīna-middha*), restlessness and regret (*auddhatya-kaukṛtya*, *uddhacca-kukkucca*), and deluded doubt (*vicikitsā*, *vicikicchā*).

form body (*rūpakāya*). The buddha body in which a buddha appears to sentient beings; it includes the emanation and enjoyment bodies.

form realm (*rūpadhātu*). A realm in saṃsāra in which the beings have subtle bodies; they are born there by having attained various states of concentration.

formless realm (*ārūpyadhātu*). The realm in saṃsāra in which sentient beings do not have a material body and abide in deep states of concentration.

fortitude of the nonarising of dharmas (*anutpattika dharmakṣānti*, T. *mi skye ba'i chos la bzod pa*). A special realization of emptiness and nonduality by bodhisattvas that makes them irreversible on the path to full awakening.

four buddha bodies. These are the nature dharmakāya, wisdom dharmakāya, enjoyment body, and emanation body.

four fearlessnesses. The Tathāgata is completely confident and lacks all fear in declaring that (1) he is fully awakened regarding all phenomena, (2) he has destroyed all pollutants, (3) he has correctly identified all obstructions to be eliminated on the path, and (4) when practiced, his teachings lead to the complete destruction of duḥkha.

four seals (*caturmudrā*). Four views that make a philosophy Buddhist: all conditioned phenomena are transient, all polluted phenomena are duḥkha, all phenomena are empty and selfless, nirvāṇa alone is true peace.

four truths of the āryas (*catvāry āryasatyāni*). The truths of duḥkha, its origin, its cessation, and the path to that cessation.

four ways of gathering or assembling (*saṃgrahavastu*, *saṅgahavatthu*, T. *bsdu ba'i dngos po*). This is (1) being generous and giving material aid, (2) explaining the Dharma according to the listeners' disposition, (3) encouraging them to practice, and (4) acting congruently and living the teachings through example.

full awakening (*samyaksaṃbodhi*). Buddhahood; the state where all obscurations have been abandoned and all good qualities developed limitlessly.

fundamental innate mind of clear light (T. *gnyug ma lhan cig skyes pa'i 'od gsal gyi sems*). The subtlest level of mind.

Fundamental Vehicle. The vehicle leading to the liberation of śrāvakas and solitary realizers.

god. *See* deva.

grasping inherent existence (*svabhāvagraha*). For Prāsaṅgikas: grasping persons and phenomena to exist by its own entity without being posited through the force of an internal mind; grasping persons and phenomena to exist from their own side, independent of all other phenomena.

grasping true existence (true-grasping, *satyagrāha*). For Prāsaṅgikas: grasping persons and phenomena to exist objectively through their own entity without being posited by thought.

ground (*bhūmi*). A path. Ten bodhisattva grounds span the bodhisattva paths of seeing and meditation.

guru yoga. Joining the qualities of our body, speech, and mind with those of a spiritually advanced spiritual mentor.

harmonies with awakening (*bodhipākṣya-dharma*, *bodhipakkhiya-dhamma*). Thirty-seven practices condensed into seven sets that lead to liberation and awakening.

hell being (*nāraka*). A being born in an unfortunate realm of intense physical pain due to strong destructive karma.

highest yoga tantra (*anuttarayogatantra*). The most advanced of the four classes of tantra.

hungry ghost (*preta*). A being born in one of the unfortunate realms who suffers from intense hunger and thirst.

ignorance (*avidyā*). A mental factor that is obscured and grasps the opposite of what exists. There are two types: ignorance regarding ultimate truth and ignorance regarding karma and its effects.

impermanent (*anitya*, *anicca*). Momentary; not remaining in the next moment.

inferential cognizer (*anumāna*). A mind that ascertains its object by means of a correct reason.

inferential realization. An infallible conceptual cognizer that arises in direct dependence on a correct reason or a consequence as its basis. This mind is a reliable cognizer.

inherent existence (*svabhāva*). For Prāsaṅgikas, it means existence without depending on any other factors; independent existence. Such existence does not exist.

insight (*vipaśyanā*, *vipassanā*, T. *lhag mthong*). A wisdom of thorough discrimination of phenomena conjoined with special pliancy induced by the power of analysis.

insight knowledge (P. *vipassanā-ñāṇa*). Mundane (P. *lokiya*) knowledge of the three characteristics gained through insight. It leads to supramundane (P. *lokuttara*) path knowledge that realizes the four truths and nirvāṇa.

insight wisdom (P. *vipassanā-paññā*). Wisdom of the three characteristics gained through insight.

introspective awareness (*saṃprajanya*, *sampajañña*). An intelligence that causes one to engage in activities of body, speech, or mind heedfully.

karma. Intentional (volitional) action; it includes intention karma (mental action) and intended karma (physical and verbal actions motivated by intention).

karmic seeds. The potencies from previously created actions that will bring their results.

knowable objects (*jñeya*, T. *shes bya*). Existents, phenomena.

latencies (*vāsanā*). Predispositions, imprints, or tendencies.

liberated path (*vimuktimārga*, T. *rnam grol lam*). A wisdom that directly follows an uninterrupted path and has definitely abandoned and is completely free from the objects of abandonment of that path.

liberation (*mokṣa*, T. *thar pa*). A true cessation that is the abandonment of afflictive obscurations; nirvāṇa, the state of freedom from cyclic existence.

liberation of mind by love (P. *mettā cetovimutti*). A mind genuinely wishing all beings to be happy that has temporarily abandoned the five hindrances, especially anger and malice, through the force of concentration.

Madhyamaka. A Buddhist tenet system that asserts there are no truly existent phenomena.

Mahāmudrā. A type of meditation that focuses on the conventional and ultimate natures of the mind.

maṇḍala offering. A spiritual practice in which we offer the universe and all the beautiful objects in it, imagined in their pure form, to the holy beings.

meditative equipoise on emptiness. The mind of someone on a path who is focusing single-pointedly on the emptiness of inherent existence. On the paths of accumulation and preparation, it is conceptual; on the ārya paths, it is nonconceptual.

mental body. The body taken by arhats and pure-ground bodhisattvas caused by the base of latencies of ignorance and unpolluted karma.

mental consciousness (*mano-vijñāna*). A primary consciousness that knows mental phenomena in contradistinction to sense primary consciousnesses that know physical objects.

mental factor (*caitta*). An aspect of mind that accompanies a primary consciousness and fills out the cognition, apprehending particular attributes of the object or performing a specific function.

mind (*citta*). That which is clear and aware; the part of living beings that cognizes, experiences, thinks, feels, and so on. In some contexts it is equivalent to primary consciousness.

mindfulness (*smṛti, sati*). A mental factor that brings to mind a phenomenon of previous acquaintance without forgetting it and prevents distraction to other objects.

mindstream (*cittasaṃtāna*). The continuity of mind.

momentary (*kṣaṇika*). Not enduring to the next moment.

monastic. Someone who has received monastic ordination; a monk or nun.

nature truth body (*svabhāvika dharmakāya*). The buddha body that is the emptiness of a buddha's mind and the true cessations in the mindstream of that buddha.

nihilism (*ucchedānta*). The belief that our actions have no ethical dimension; the belief that nothing exists.

nimitta. The sign or mental image that is the object for cultivating serenity. It is of three types: the preliminary, learning, and counterpart nimittas.

nine stages of sustained attention (*navākārā cittasthiti*, T. *sems gnas dgu*). Stages of concentration on the way to attaining serenity.

nirvāṇa. The state of liberation of an arhat; the purified aspect of a mind that is free from afflictions.

nirvāṇa with remainder (*sopadhiśeṣa-nirvāṇa*, *sopādisesa-nibbāna*). (1) The state of liberation when an arhat is still alive and possesses the remainder of the polluted aggregates, (2) an arhat's nirvāṇa in which things appear to be truly existent in post-meditation time.

nirvāṇa without remainder (*anupadhiśeṣa-nirvāṇa*, *anupādisesa-nibbāna*). (1) The state of liberation when an arhat has passed away and no longer has the remainder of the polluted aggregates, (2) an arhat's meditative equipoise on emptiness where there is no appearance of true existence whatsoever.

nonabiding nirvāṇa (*apratiṣṭha-nirvāṇa*). The nirvāṇa of a buddha that does not abide in either saṃsāra or the personal peace of a śrāvaka's or solitary realizers's nirvāṇa.

nonexistent (*asat*). That which is not perceivable by mind.

nonreturner (*anāgāmin*, *anāgāmi*, T. *phyir mi 'ong pa*). A Fundamental Vehicle ārya who has eliminated the five lower fetters.

object (*viṣaya*, T. *yul*). That which is known by an awareness.

object of negation (*pratiṣedhya*, T. *dgag bya*). A nonexistent that sentient beings erroneously grasp as existent. It is negated or refuted by reasoning.

observed object (*ālambana*, *ārammaṇa*, T. *dmigs pa*). The basic object that the mind refers to or focuses on while apprehending certain aspects of that object.

once-returner (*sakṛdāgāmin*, *sakadāgāmi*, T. *lan gcig phyir 'ong pa*). A Fundamental Vehicle ārya who has abandoned three of the lower fetters and significantly reduced sensual desire and malice and who will be born in the desire realm at maximum only one time before attaining nirvāṇa.

one final vehicle. The belief that all beings—even śrāvakas who have become arhats—will eventually enter the Mahāyāna and become buddhas.

ordinary being (*pṛthagjana*, *puthujjana*, T. *so so skye bo*). Someone who is not an ārya.

path (*mārga*, *magga*, T. *lam*). Sanskrit tradition: an exalted knower that is conjoined with uncontrived renunciation. Pāli tradition: a consciousness of an ārya that realizes the four truths.

path knowledge (P. *magga-ñāṇa*). A supramundane path that knows nirvāṇa.

path of accumulation (*sambhāramārga*, T. *tshogs lam*). First of the five paths. It begins when one aspires for liberation day and night for a śrāvaka path or when one has spontaneous bodhicitta for the Mahāyāna path.

path of meditation (*bhāvanāmārga*, T. *sgom lam*). The fourth of the five paths. This begins when a meditator begins to eradicate innate afflictions from the root.

path of no-more-learning (*aśaikṣamārga*, T. *mi slob lam*). The last of the five paths where a trainee attains the final goal of their vehicle: arhatship or buddhahood.

path of preparation (*prayogamārga*, T. *sbyor lam*). The second of the five paths. It begins when a meditator attains the union of serenity and insight on emptiness.

path of seeing (*darśanamārga*, T. *mthong lam*). The third of the five paths. It begins when a meditator first has direct, nonconceptual realization of the emptiness of inherent existence.

permanent (*nitya*, *nicca*, T. *rtag pa*). Unchanging, static. It does not mean eternal.

permanent, unitary, independent self. A soul or self (*ātman*) asserted by non-Buddhists.

permissory ritual (T. *rjes snang*). A meditative ceremony in which the recipient receives the inspiration of an awakened deity's body, speech, and mind and is qualified to do the practice of that deity.

person (*pudgala*). A being designated in dependence on the four or five aggregates.

pervasive duḥkha of conditioning. Taking the five aggregates under the influence of afflictions and polluted karma. This is the basis of the duḥkha of pain and the duḥkha of change.

pliancy (tranquility, *praśrabdhi*, *passaddhi*). A mental factor that enables the mind to apply itself to a constructive object in whatever manner it wishes and dissipates mental or physical rigidity.

polluted (*āsrava*, *āsava*). Under the influence of ignorance or its latencies.

Prāsaṅgika. The Buddhist philosophical tenet system that asserts that all phenomena lack inherent existence both conventionally and ultimately.

prātimokṣa. The various sets of ethical precepts for monastics and lay followers to uphold in their pursuit of liberation.

preliminary practices. (1) Meditating on important initial stages of the path, such as preciousness of a human life with freedom and fortune, death and impermanence, karma and its effects, and the defects of saṃsāra. (2) In the context of tantra, practices that purify negativities and collect merit, such as taking refuge, reciting the names of the buddhas and prostrating to them, making offerings, reciting the mantra of Vajrasattva, guru yoga, and so on.

preparatory stages for a dhyāna (access, preparations, *sāmantaka*, T. *bsam gtan po'i nyer bsdogs*). Stages of meditation that prepare the mind to enter an actual dhyāna.

primary consciousness (*vijñāna*). A consciousness that apprehends the presence or basic entity of an object. There are six types of primary consciousness: visual, auditory, olfactory, gustatory, tactile, and mental.

pristine wisdom of meditative equipoise (*samāhitajñāna*, T. *mnyam bzhag ye shes*). A clear realization that perceives emptiness directly and nonconceptually with a concentration that is the union of serenity and insight.

pristine wisdom of subsequent attainment (*pṛṣṭhalabdha-jñāna*, T. *rjes thob ye shes*). A subsequent clear realization of someone who has arisen from a liberated path.

proliferations (*prapañca*, *papañca*, T. *spros pa*). Mental fabrications ranging from anxious thoughts to grasping true existence.

pure lands. Places created by the unshakable resolve and merit of buddhas where all external conditions are conducive for Dharma practice.

realization (T. *rtogs pa*). An awareness that eliminates superimpositions on an object and is able to induce ascertainment of it. It may be inferential (conceptual) or direct (nonconceptual).

realized Dharma. The realizations in a person's mindstream.

sādhana. The means of achievement expressed in a tantric text or manual that details the steps of visualization and meditation in the practice of a deity.

samādhi. *See* concentration.

saṃsāra. (1) Constantly recurring rebirth under the control of afflictions and polluted karma. (2) The five aggregates of a person who has taken rebirth in this way.

Sautrāntika. A Fundamental Vehicle tenet system that asserts that functional things are ultimate truths and phenomena that are imputed by thought are conventional truths.

self (*ātman*). A person or inherent existence.

self-grasping (*ātmagrāha*). Grasping inherent existence.

self-sufficient substantially-existent person (T. *gang zag rang rkya thub pa'i rdzas yod*). A self that can be identified independent of the aggregates. Such a self does not exist.

sentient being (*sattva*). Any being that has a mind and is not a buddha.

serenity (*śamatha, samatha*). Sanskrit tradition: concentration arisen from meditation that is accompanied by the bliss of mental and physical pliancy in which the mind abides effortlessly without fluctuation for as long as we wish on whatever virtuous object it has been placed. Pāli tradition: one-pointedness of mind; the eight attainments (meditative absorptions) that are the basis for insight.

six perfections (*ṣaḍpāramitā*). The practices of generosity, ethical conduct, fortitude, joyous effort, meditative stability, and wisdom that are motivated by bodhicitta.

solitary realizer (*pratyekabuddha*). A person following the Fundamental Vehicle who seeks liberation and emphasizes understanding the twelve links of dependent arising and who aspires to spend their last lifetime in saṃsāra without depending on a teacher.

sphere of three. The agent, object, and action.

śrāvaka (hearer, disciple, P. *sāvaka*). Someone practicing the Fundamental Vehicle path leading to arhatship who emphasizes meditation on the four truths.

stabilizing meditation (*sthāpyabhāvanā*, T. *'jog sgom*). Meditation to focus and concentrate the mind on an object.

stages of the path to awakening (T. *lamrim*). A systematic presentation of the path to awakening found in Tibetan Buddhism.

stream-enterer (*srotāpanna*, *sotāpanna*, T. *rgyun zhugs*). A Fundamental Vehicle practitioner who has eliminated the first three fetters of the five lower fetters: view of a personal identity, deluded doubt, view of bad rules and practices.

substantial cause (*upādāna-kāraṇa*). The cause that becomes the result, as opposed to cooperative causes that aid the substantial cause in becoming the result.

subtle latencies. Latencies of ignorance and other afflictions that are cognitive obscurations that prevent simultaneous nonconceptual cognition of the two truths.

subsequent attainment (*pṛṣṭha-labdha*). Post-meditation time when āryas do practices to create merit and meditate on other topics aside from meditative equipoise on emptiness.

superknowledge (*abhijñā*, *abhiññā*, T. *mngon shes*). Direct, experiential knowledge, of six types: (1) supernormal powers, (2) divine ear, (3) knowledge of others' minds, (4) recollection of past lives, (5) divine eye (includes knowledge of the passing away and rearising of beings and knowledge of the future), and (6) the destruction of the pollutants. The sixth is attained only by liberated beings.

supernormal powers (*ṛddhi, iddhi*). The first of the six superknowledges, gained in deep samādhi: to replicate one's body, appear and disappear, pass through solid objects, go under the earth, walk on water, fly, touch the sun and moon with one's hand, go to the Brahmā world, and so forth.

supramundane (transcendental, *lokottara*, P. *lokuttara*). Pertaining to the elimination of fetters and afflictions; pertaining to āryas.

tathāgata. A buddha.

ten powers. The ten powers are knowing (1) what is worthwhile and worthless, (2) the ripening result of all actions, (3) the path leading to various rebirths, (4) the temperaments and (5) aspirations of sentient beings, (6) their faculties, (7) meditative stability, and (8) past lives, (9) sentient beings passing away and being reborn, and (10) liberation and full awakening.

tenets (*siddhānta*). A philosophical principle, belief, or system.

thought (*kalpanā*). Conceptual consciousness.

three characteristics. Impermanence, duḥkha, and no-self.

three kinds of persons. Śrāvaka and solitary realizer arhats and pure ground bodhisattvas. They are grouped together because all have eradicated the afflictive obscurations.

three realms (*tridhātuka, tedhātuka*). Desire, form, and formless realms.

transmitted (*scriptural*) *Dharma*. The words and meanings of the Buddha's teachings in the form of speech and scriptures.

true cessation (*nirodhasatya*). The cessation of a portion of afflictions or a portion of cognitive obscurations. It can also refer to the cessation of all afflictive obscurations, cognitive obscurations, or both obscurations.

true existence (*satyasat*). The objective existence of phenomena through their own entity without being posited by thought. True existence does not exist.

truth body (*dharmakāya*). The buddha body that includes the nature truth body and the wisdom truth body. Sometimes it refers only to a buddha's omniscient mind.

twelve links of dependent origination (*dvādaśāṅga-pratītyasamutpāda*). A system of twelve factors that explains how we take rebirth in saṃsāra and how we can be liberated from it.

twelve sources. A way of classifying phenomena according to the type of object and the faculty facilitating its perception. See chapter 3 of *The Foundation of Buddhist Practice.*

twenty-two faculties (*indriya*). Six are sense faculties: sight (*cakṣus*), hearing (*śrotra*), smell (*ghrāna*), taste (*jihvā*), touch (*kāya*), mind (*manas*). Three are physical faculties: male organ (*puruṣendriya*), female organ (*strīndriya*), vital organ (*jīvitendriya*). Five are feeling faculties: sensation of pleasure (*sukha*), pain (*duḥkha*), mental happiness (*saumanasya*), mental suffering (*daurmanasya*), equanimity (*upekṣā*). Five are spiritual faculties: faith (*śraddhā*), energy (*vīrya*), mindfulness (*smṛti*), concentration (*samādhi*), wisdom (*prajñā*). Three are faculties of understanding the truths: thinking "I shall know the unknown" (*anaññāta-ñassāmīt-indriya*), gnosis (*aññ-indriya*), one who knows (*aññātā-vindriya*).

two truths (*satyadvaya*). Ultimate truths and veiled (conventional) truths.

ultimate nature. The ultimate or deepest mode of existence of persons and phenomena.

ultimate truth (*paramārthasatya*). The ultimate mode of existence of all persons and phenomena; emptiness.

unfortunate realms (*apāya*). Unfortunate states of rebirth as a hell being, hungry ghost, or animal.

uninterrupted path (*ānantaryamārga*, T. *bar ched med lam*). A wisdom that abandons the objects of abandonment of that path.

union of serenity and insight. Absorption in which the bliss of mental and physical pliancy has been induced by analysis.

unpolluted (*anāsrava*). Not under the influence of ignorance.

unpolluted karma. The mental factor of intention that is the subtle effort supporting arhats' and pure-ground bodhisattvas' motivation to assume a mental body.

Vajrasattva. A meditation deity whose practice is associated with purification of destructive karmic seeds and other defilements.

veiled truths (conventional truths, *saṃvṛtisatya*). Objects that appear true to ignorance, which is a veiling consciousness; objects that appear to exist inherently to their main cognizer although they do not exist that way.

veilings. Conventionalities.

view of a personal identity (view of the transitory collection, *satkāyadṛṣṭi*, *sakkāyadiṭṭhi*). Grasping an inherently existent I or mine (according to the Prāsaṅgika system).

Vinaya. Monastic discipline; a body of texts about monastic life, discipline, and conduct.

wind (*prāṇa*, T. *rlung*). One of the four elements; energy in the body that influences bodily functions; subtle energy on which levels of consciousness ride.

wisdom truth body (*jñāna dharmakāya*). The buddha body that is a buddha's omniscient mind.

Yogācāra (*Cittamātra*). A philosophical tenet system asserting that objects and the consciousnesses perceiving them arise from the same substantial cause, a seed on the foundation consciousness, and that the mind is truly existent.

Recommended Reading

Apple, James B. *Stairway to Nirvāṇa: A Study of the Twenty Saṃghas Based on the Works of Tsong Kha Pa*. Albany: State University of New York Press, 2009.

Aronson, Harvey B. *Love and Sympathy in Theravāda Buddhism*. Delhi: Motilal Banarsidass Publishers, 1996.

Chodron, Thubten. *Don't Believe Everything You Think: Living with Wisdom and Compassion*. Boston: Snow Lion Publications, 2012.

______. *Good Karma: How to Create the Causes for Happiness and Avoid the Causes of Suffering*. Boston: Shambhala Publications, 2016.

______. *Working with Anger*. Ithaca, NY: Snow Lion Publications, 2001.

Dharmamitra, Bhikshu, trans. *On Generating the Resolve to Become a Buddha*. Seattle: Kalavinka Press, 2009.

Goodman, Charles. *The Training Anthology of Śāntideva: A Translation of the Śikṣā-samuccaya*. New York: Oxford University Press, 2016.

Gyaltsen, Sakya Drakpa. *Chandragomin's Twenty Verses on the Bodhisattva Vow and Its Commentary*. Translated by Mark Tatz. Dharamsala: Library of Tibetan Works and Archives, 2002.

Gyatso, Tenzin, the Fourteenth Dalai Lama. *An Open Heart: Practicing Compassion in Everyday Life*. Edited by Nicholas Vreeland. New York: Little, Brown and Company, 2001.

______. *Beyond Religion: Ethics for a Whole World*. Boston: Houghton Mifflin Harcourt, 2011.

______. *Healing Anger: The Power of Patience from a Buddhist Perspective*. Ithaca, NY: Snow Lion Publications, 1997.

______. *How to Expand Love: Widening the Circle of Loving Relationships*. Translated and edited by Jeffrey Hopkins. New York: Atria Books, 2005.

______. *How to See Yourself as You Really Are*. Translated and edited by Jeffrey Hopkins, PhD. New York: Atria Books, 2007.

_____. *The Four Noble Truths*. Translated by Thupten Jinpa. Edited by Dominique Side. London: Thorsons, 1997.

_____. *The Good Heart: A Buddhist Perspective on the Teachings of Jesus*. Introduction and Christian context by Laurence Freeman, OSB. Translated from the Tibetan by Geshe Thupten Jinpa. Edited by Robert Kiely. Boston: Wisdom Publication, 1996.

_____. *Transforming the Mind: Teachings on Generating Compassion*. Translated by Thupten Jinpa. Edited by Dominique Side. London: Thorsons, 2000.

His Holiness the Dalai Lama, and Howard C. Cutler, MD. *The Art of Happiness: A Handbook for Living*. New York: Riverhead Books, 1998.

His Holiness the Fourteenth Dalai Lama, and Venerable Chan Master Sheng-yen. *Meeting of Minds: A Dialogue on Tibetan and Chinese Buddhism*. Taiwan. Dharma Drum Publications, 1999.

Hopkins, Jeffrey, trans. and ed. *Compassion in Tibetan Buddhism by Tsong-ka-pa*. Ithaca, NY: Snow Lion Publications, 1980.

_____. *Cultivating Compassion: A Buddhist Perspective*. New York: Broadway Books, 2001.

_____. *Meditation on Emptiness*. Boston: Wisdom Publications, 1996.

Horner, I. B., trans. *Chronicle of Buddhas* (*Buddhavaṃsa*) and *Basket of Conduct* (*Cariyāpiṭaka*), in *The Minor Anthologies of the Pāli Canon*, vol. 3. London: The Pāli Text Society, 2007.

Jinpa, Thupten, trans. *Essential Mind Training*. Tibetan Classics 1. Boston: Wisdom Publications, 2011.

_____, trans. *Mind Training: The Great Collection*. Library of Tibetan Classics 1. Boston: Wisdom Publications, in association with the Institute of Tibetan Classics, 2005.

Kolts, Russell, and Chodron, Thubten. *An Open-Hearted Life: Transformative Methods for Compassionate Living from a Clinical Psychologist and a Buddhist Nun*. Boston: Shambhala Publications, 2015.

Levinson, Jules. *The Metaphors of Liberation: A Study of Grounds and Paths according to the Middle Way School*. Charlottesville: University of Virginia Press, 1994.

Makransky, John. *Buddhahood Embodied: Sources of Controversy in India and Tibet*. Albany: State University of New York Press, 1997.

Napper, Elizabeth. *Traversing the Spiritual Path: Kön-chog-jig-may-wang-po's Presentation of the Grounds and Paths with Dan-ma-lo-chö's Oral*

Commentary. Edited by Jeffrey Hopkins. UMA Institute for Tibetan Studies, 2016. https://uma-tibet.org/pdf/greatbooks/NapperPaths.pdf.

Rinchen, Geshe Sonam. Translated and edited by Ruth Sonam. *Eight Verses for Training the Mind*. Ithaca, NY: Snow Lion Publications, 2001.

Rinpoche, Venerable Dagpo Lama. *The Bodhisattva Vows: A Practice Guide to the Sublime Ethics of the Mahāyāna*. Seri Kembangan, Malaysia: E Publication Sdn Bhd, 2007.

Sonam, Ruth, trans. and ed. *The Yogic Deeds of Bodhisattvas: Gyel-tsap on Āryadeva's Four Hundred*. Commentary by Geshe Sonam Rinchen. Ithaca, NY: Snow Lion Publications, 1994. [A translation of the root text from the Tibetan edition with Gyaltsap Je's commentary.]

Sopa, Geshe Lhundub, with Michael Sweet and Leonard Zwilling. *Peacock in the Poison Grove: Two Buddhist Texts on Training the Mind*. Boston: Wisdom Publications, 1996.

Tegchok, Geshe Jampa. *Transforming Adversity into Joy and Courage*. Ithaca, NY: Snow Lion Publications, 2005.

Yeshe, Lama. *Life, Death, and After Death*. Edited by Nicholas Ribush. Boston: Lama Yeshe Wisdom Archive, 2011.

Index

H

I

J

Q

R

S

Śāntideva, 55, 138. See also *Engaging in the Bodhisattvas' Deeds*
Śāriputra, 123, 146, 179, 208, 227–28, 231, 236–37, 262, 408n71
Sarvāstivāda school, 198, 199, 406n51
Sautrāntika school, 241, 258
Sautrāntika-Svātantrika, 283
science, 3, 85–86
self-centered attitude
  attachment to, 41
  discouragement as, 74
  on eighth ground, 317
  freedom from, 34, 301
  karma and, 64
  love and, 185
  overcoming/releasing, 2, 5, 42, 101–2, 285, 321, 919
self-confidence, 44, 75–76, 102, 239, 293, 303
self-grasping, 50, 67
  acquired, 254, 257, 273, 274
  four manifest forms of, 271
  innate, 255, 256, 276, 277
self-grasping ignorance, 88–89, 90, 306–7
  abandonment, complete, 257
  on bodhisattva grounds, 303, 317
  eighty-one grades of, 247–48
  temporary suppression of, 97, 98
  two obscurations and, 283
selflessness, 294
  anger and, 56
  in cultivating serenity and insight, 93
  direct realization of, 306–7
  of persons, 67, 68, 87, 88–89
  of phenomena, 67, 68, 87, 89–90, 231
  on third ground, 301
  variant views on, 92, 240–42
sense consciousnesses, 107, 180, 288, 368, 396
sense pleasures, 172–73, 230
sensual desire. *See under* desire
sentient beings, 367
  buddha nature of, 355–56
  and buddhas, lack of difference between, 402n17
  cherishing, 5, 186, 301, 338
  as children or relatives, contemplating, 191
  differences in, 333–34, 393
  eleven groups of, 48–49, 73, 84
  equanimity toward, 186, 191
serenity (*śamatha, samatha*), 79, 81, 94–95, 97, 270, 409n87. *See also* union of serenity and insight
seven awakening factors, 228–29, 237
seven treasures, 298, 299
seven-limb prayer, 100
Sheng-yen, 342–43, 411n104
signlessness, 311, 398, 406n53
sincerity, 122–23, 145, 152
Singapore, 157
Sivi, King, 145, 159
six perfections, xv, 112, 361, 376, 377
  in accomplishing welfare of others, 16–17
  as antidotes, 22–23
  difficulty of, 25
  distinguishing factors of, 70
  in ensuring human rebirth, 18–19
  in generosity, three types, 21
  method and wisdom in, 11–12
  nature of, 15
  order of cultivating, 20
  perfection, meaning of term, 12
  relationship between, 23–24
  results of, 18–19
  state of mind and, 13
  suitability for, 14
  ten masteries and, 320
  two aims and, 17–18, 21
  two collections and, 8, 9
  See also under bodhicitta
Sixty Stanzas (Nāgārjuna), 8
skillful means, 338
  in all ten perfections, 164–65
  of buddhas, 346, 391
  collection of merit and, 8
  perfection of, 98–99, 105, 314, 328
  and wisdom, balancing, 175
  See also method

About the Authors

The Dalai Lama is the spiritual leader of the Tibetan people, a Nobel Peace Prize recipient, and an advocate for compassion and peace throughout the world. He promotes harmony among the world's religions and engages in dialogue with leading scientists. Ordained as a Buddhist monk when he was a child, he completed the traditional monastic studies and earned his geshe degree (equivalent to a PhD). Renowned for his erudite and open-minded scholarship, his meditative attainments, and his humility, Bhikṣu Tenzin Gyatso says, "I am a simple Buddhist monk."

Peter Aronson

Bhikṣuṇī Thubten Chodron has been a Buddhist nun since 1977. Growing up in Los Angeles, she graduated with honors in history from the University of California at Los Angeles and did graduate work in education at the University of Southern California. After years studying and teaching Buddhism in Asia, Europe, and the United States, she became the founder and abbess of Sravasti Abbey in Washington State. A popular speaker for her practical explanations of how to apply Buddhist teachings in daily life, she is the author of several books on Buddhism, including *Buddhism for Beginners*. She is the editor of Khensur Jampa Tegchok's *Insight into Emptiness*. For more information, visit sravastiabbey.org and thubtenchodron.org.

Also Available from the Dalai Lama and Wisdom Publications

Buddhism
One Teacher, Many Traditions

The Compassionate Life

Ecology, Ethics, and Interdependence
The Dalai Lama in Conversation with Leading Thinkers on Climate Change

Essence of the Heart Sutra
The Dalai Lama's Heart of Wisdom Teachings

The Essence of Tsongkhapa's Teachings
The Dalai Lama on the Three Principal Aspects of the Path

The Good Heart
A Buddhist Perspective on the Teachings of Jesus

Imagine All the People
A Conversation with the Dalai Lama on Money, Politics, and Life as It Could Be

Kalachakra Tantra
Rite of Initiation

The Life of My Teacher
A Biography of Kyabjé Ling Rinpoche

Meditation on the Nature of Mind

The Middle Way
Faith Grounded in Reason

Mind in Comfort and Ease
The Vision of Enlightenment in the Great Perfection

MindScience
An East-West Dialogue

Opening the Eye of New Awareness

Practicing Wisdom
The Perfection of Shantideva's Bodhisattva Way

Science and Philosophy in the Indian Buddhist Classics, vol. 1
The Physical World

Science and Philosophy in the Indian Buddhist Classics, vol. 2
The Mind

Sleeping, Dreaming, and Dying
An Exploration of Consciousness

The Wheel of Life
Buddhist Perspectives on Cause and Effect

The World of Tibetan Buddhism
An Overview of Its Philosophy and Practice

Also Available from Thubten Chodron

Insight into Emptiness
Khensur Jampa Tegchok
Edited and introduced by Thubten Chodron

"One of the best introductions to the philosophy of emptiness I have ever read."—José Ignacio Cabezón

Practical Ethics and Profound Emptiness
A Commentary on Nagarjuna's Precious Garland
Khensur Jampa Tegchok
Edited by Thubten Chodron

"A beautifully clear translation and systematic explanation of Nagarjuna's most accessible and wide-ranging work. Dharma students everywhere will benefit from careful attention to its pages."
—Guy Newland, author of *Introduction to Emptiness*

Awakening Every Day
365 Buddhist Reflections to Invite Mindfulness and Joy

Buddhism for Beginners

The Compassionate Kitchen

Cultivating a Compassionate Heart
The Yoga Method of Chenrezig

Don't Believe Everything You Think
Living with Wisdom and Compassion

Guided Meditations on the Stages of the Path

How to Free Your Mind
Tara the Liberator

Living with an Open Heart
How to Cultivate Compassion in Daily Life

Open Heart, Clear Mind

Taming the Mind

Working with Anger

About Wisdom Publications

Wisdom Publications is the leading publisher of classic and contemporary Buddhist books and practical works on mindfulness. To learn more about us or to explore our other books, please visit our website at wisdomexperience.org or contact us at the address below.

Wisdom Publications
199 Elm Street
Somerville, MA 02144 USA

We are a 501(c)(3) organization, and donations in support of our mission are tax deductible.

Wisdom Publications is affiliated with the Foundation for the Preservation of the Mahayana Tradition (FPMT).